In the name of God, the Compassionate, the Merciful

Sayyid Quṭb

IN THE SHADE OF
THE QUR'ĀN

Fī Ẓilāl al-Qur'ān

VOLUME VIII

SŪRAH 9

Al-Tawbah

Translated and Edited by
Adil Salahi

THE ISLAMIC FOUNDATION
AND
ISLAMONLINE.NET

Published by

THE ISLAMIC FOUNDATION,

Markfield Conference Centre,
Ratby Lane, Markfield, Leicestershire LE67 9SY, United Kingdom
Tel: (01530) 244944, Fax: (01530) 244946
E-mail: i.foundation@islamic-foundation.org.uk
Website: www.islamic-foundation.org.uk

Quran House, PO Box 30611, Nairobi, Kenya

PMB 3193, Kano, Nigeria

ISLAMONLINE.NET,
PO Box 22212, Doha, Qatar
E-mail: webmaster@islam-online.net
Website: www.islamonline.net

British Library Cataloguing-in-Publication Data
Qutb, Sayyid, 1903–1966
   In the shade of the Qur'an: Fi zilal al-Qur'an,
   Vol. 8: Surah 9: Al-Tawbah
   1. Koran – Commentaries
   I. Title II. Salahi, Adil III. Islamic Foundation
   IV. Fi zilal al-Qur'an
   297.1'227

ISBN 0 86037 363 0
ISBN 0 86037 368 1 pbk

Typeset by: N.A.Qaddoura
Cover design by: Imtiaze A. Manjra

Printed and bound in Great Britain by
Antony Rowe Ltd., Chippenham, Wiltshire

Contents

Transliteration Table

Consonants. Arabic

initial: unexpressed medial and final:

ء	'	د	d	ض	ḍ	ك	k
ب	b	ذ	dh	ط	ṭ	ل	l
ت	t	ر	r	ظ	ẓ	م	m
ث	th	ز	z	ع	'	ن	n
ج	j	س	s	غ	gh	ـه	h
ح	ḥ	ش	sh	ف	f	و	w
خ	kh	ص	ṣ	ق	q	ي	y

Vowels, diphthongs, etc.

Short: ـَ a   ـِ i   ـُ u

long: ـَا a   ـِي ī   ـُو ū

diphthongs: ـَوْ aw

ـَىْ ay

Jihād and Justice

Introduction by Adil Salahi

During the last few years, Islamophobia has been pushed to even new heights among wider groups of the world population, particularly in Western societies. Ever since the tragic events of September 11, 2001, the association of Islam with terrorism has been strengthened in the Western mind, particularly because, in their rush for scoops and on-the-spot coverage of events, the media can afford little time for reflection. Accuracy and objectivity cannot compete with the need to be at the scene as news breaks out.

In today's world, it is normal media practice that whenever a terrorist attack takes place anywhere in the world, Islam is the first to be blamed for it. The presumption of guilt is always against Islam. It is as though Islam is 'guilty until proven otherwise.' This has caused many Muslims to ask how and why this state of affairs has come about. There may be no ready answer, and people do arrive at different explanations. Whatever we may feel to be the cause, we are unlikely to be able to change the situation in the present global climate. There is simply no political or religious authority in the Muslim world or outside it, which commands sufficient influence to bring the sort of change that objective hearing of the case of Islam requires. Hence, Muslims need to use any means available to them to present Islam in its true colours: a religion that enshrines the concepts of justice and freedom for all mankind.

Islam treats every human being as one who belongs to a species of creation honoured by God, who has given man the faculties of reasoning, perception and freedom of choice. Furthermore, everyone is responsible for the choices they make both in belief and in action. All human beings, across all generations, will stand before God on Judgement Day when they will have to account for their deeds. Each one stands in his or her own private capacity. They are answerable to God whose essential attributes include absolute justice and unlimited mercy and forgiveness.

One of the most important elements in the Islamic faith is the fact that we all have a personal relationship with God Almighty. This relationship starts with what Islam advocates of man's freedom of choice. Every human being is born with the ability to choose what to believe in. Choice of beliefs is based on conviction only. No one can force another to accept a certain faith. If coercion is used in order to ensure that a particular person complies with what is required, such coercion is rejected, and its effects are rendered invalid. And the end is also personal. No one is asked about anyone else's actions or beliefs. Each is accountable for their own choices. While freedom and personal responsibility is granted by God at the beginning and end, what lies in between is the result of man's own choice.

This personal relation with God, enshrined at the individual level, helps a Muslim to always look beyond this life. Everything in this life is important, no doubt. After all, man's task is to build a happy human life on earth. Islam provides a code of living which should be implemented in human life in order to ensure happiness and justice for all. But life in this world is not to be considered the be all and end all. What we miss here we are certain to find in the hereafter. This provides Muslims with a life perspective which is different from that of all other groups and communities. To Muslims, our life in this world is merely a stage in a continuous process that aims to achieve happiness in the life to come. This does not mean that we do not wish to be happy in this world. We indeed achieve such happiness, regardless of the particular circumstances in which we find ourselves in this life. Our happiness is generated by our belief in God, and our sense of the personal relation we have with Him. We look at life in this world as a test that may vary in the questions it sets for each one of us, but passing the test is easy when we look at life and all that it offers through an Islamic perspective. Each one of us has this test to contend with: some are tested with adversity, while others are tested with ease; some encounter hardship that seems to have no end, while others enjoy comforts and riches. It is how we respond to our circumstances that determines our results. God will reward each one of us on the basis of His absolute justice, and unlimited mercy.

But we have a task to fulfil in this present life. Islam is the final message God has given to mankind. Muslims are the trustees of this message, and they must make it known to mankind, pointing out to them the fact that God wants them to believe in it and implement it in life. Muslims, however, may not impose this message on any individual or community. God defined the role of Muḥammad, His last Messenger, telling him: "You are not bound to do more than to deliver [God's message]" (42: 48).

God's message gives man a complete code of living which ensures man's happiness both in this world and in the world beyond. It fits with human nature, answers its needs, elevates its concerns, fulfils its expectations and establishes a bond of brotherhood that is open to all mankind. Justice in this world is a primary concern of the Islamic message. Yet justice in our world is in short supply. This is primarily due to the fact that God's message is neglected and banished from human life. When people implement the code God has laid down for their life, injustice will disappear from their world. When we look at history, we find that justice has been consistently associated with the implementation of God's message. This applied before Islam in the case of all divine messages, and it applied after the revelation of God's final message, which is Islam.

We need to distinguish here between two things: Islam as God revealed it, and the behaviour of Muslims during different historical periods. While Islam upholds justice in all situations, with friend and foe alike, Muslims may fall short of what Islam requires of them. In history, there were periods, situations and regimes when Muslims did not live up to the standards Islam required of them. Some rulers did not uphold Islamic standards despite claiming to derive their authority from their aim to implement Islamic rule. Such a gulf between claims and practices is common to all nations and communities. What is most important is that we do not confuse practice with an ideal. Islam must not be blamed for actions taken in its name, if these are at variance with its principles and values.

Human history is full of examples where rulers attain power under a particular system, pledging to honour commitments and duties specified in a constitution, code of law, social tradition or some other methods specifically set up to ensure justice, people's rights and freedom. Yet once such a ruler manages to consolidate his position, he begins to abuse his power. The blame should be laid fairly and squarely at the door of the one who abuses the system, not the system itself.

Democracy is the best man-made system that provides a good balance between the rights of the individual and those of the community. Yet many a ruler reverted to dictatorship after attaining power through democratic means. We cannot blame democracy for such events. The blame is primarily on those who abused their democratic powers in order to change the system to a dictatorial one.

Long established democracies have learnt to establish checks and balances to ensure that their systems do not degenerate into dictatorship. Yet even these are sometimes bypassed in order to give the government of the day some dictatorial powers. The early years of this twenty-first century have seen some of the well established democracies of the West taking measures that are characteristic of despotic regimes only. The justification is that they are needed for 'national security.' This is indeed the very reason advanced by tyrannical governments to justify their suppression of all opposition. Needless to say, when democracies adopt dictatorial measures, this bodes ill for all humanity.

Islam uses a much more effective method to ensure that rulers and governments do not step over the line in exercising their authority. Muslims are individually and collectively responsible for ensuring that justice is upheld in all situations. Injustice must be stamped out, using all legitimate means. An individual who stands up to a tyrannical ruler, advocating justice and freedom, and loses his life at the hands of that ruler as a result attains the highest position with God, among the most honoured martyrs. The Prophet says: "The masters of all martyrs are Ḥamzah ibn 'Abd al-Muṭṭalib[1] and a person who stands up to a tyrannical ruler, speaking out for what is fair and against what is wrong, but that ruler kills him." Needless to say, a martyr attains a very high position in heaven because he sacrifices his life for the cause of Islam.

Moreover, Islam makes *jihād* a duty of both the individual and the Muslim community. *Jihād* has become a highly maligned word, particularly in Western media where it is often translated as holy war. The very concept of a holy war is alien to Islam. Islam does not rule out the possibility of war, but it accepts it only as a last resort, in defence of justice, right and freedom. No other purpose or objective justifies war from the Islamic point of view. When war is fought by Muslims for such objectives, it is a form of *jihād*. But *jihād* is a much

---

1. Ḥamzah was the Prophet's uncle and a heroic fighter for the cause of Islam. He fell a martyr in the Battle of Uḥud after having served Islam well over a period of ten years.

wider concept than war. It means the exertion of effort, striving, or struggle for God's cause. This is normally done by word of mouth and by peaceful action, but when physical impediments are put in the way of such noble aims, suitable action must be taken to remove them, even if this means going to war. The aim of *jihād* is to establish what is right and beneficial to the community, and to ensure freedom and justice. All Muslims are required to do what they can to serve these purposes. When they do, Muslims are engaged in *jihād*.

It is not surprising that *jihād* is a very dear concept to Muslims everywhere. They even use it and its derivatives as names which they give to their children. Scholars give particular attention to it because it has a central role in Islam on the one hand, and because they are keen to ensure that it remains free of abuse on the other. The Qur'an illustrates this Islamic concept in different ways in order to instil its right picture in the minds of its followers. Hence, it is perfectly natural that a commentary like *In the Shade of the Qur'ān* should speak at length about the concept of *jihād* and its application in the life of the Muslim community and its individual members. The Prologue to *Sūrah* 8, (Volume 7), which comments on the Battle of Badr, the first major military encounter the Prophet had to fight, is a treatise explaining this concept and the different stages it took during the Prophet's lifetime. In the present volume, the author gives a further explanation of the final stage of this concept, because *Sūrah* 9, which this volume discusses, comments on the last military effort the Prophet had to undertake.

In both volumes, the author shows that *jihād* is a proactive movement that uses all means possible in order to establish justice, and defend man against all tyranny that seeks to deprive people of their freedom. It is a call for the liberation of all mankind, so that they may live free from all oppression, religious, political, ethnic or racial. He defends the right of Islam, God's final message to mankind, to take action in order to remove any such oppression, even though it may happen to be outside the Muslim world. He uses all his literary talent to comment on Qur'ānic verses that most powerfully emphasize the concept of *jihād* and its proactive approach. This renders his writing most appealing in our world which is undeniably rife with all forms of oppression. Those of us who dream of an ideal world, where people are genuinely free, find him expressing their very hopes with the maturity of a scholar who thoroughly knows his subject.

Yet it is easy to misread what any author says. Indeed under the Nasser regime, false accusations were concocted against the author and his group, putting them to summary trials before military courts. The result was that the author paid for his writings with his life. Many were those who spent several years in prison, accused of nothing more than reading one or two of his books. The prosecution made a very heavy meal of his writings, accusing him of encouraging sedition and the overthrow of government. Yet his approach was totally opposed to such action. His aim was only to elaborate on what God says in the Qur'an. Hence, he dwells at length on the importance of ensuring freedom of thought, expression and belief for all. Such freedom was an anathema to a brutal regime like that of Egypt under Nasser. Hence, the mass arrests, physical torture, summary trials and executions. Had his writings been objectively studied, in an atmosphere of freedom, nothing of this would have taken place. Had the regime been more amenable to human rights, or even less brutal in its grasp of power, it would not have found in them anything that threatened its existence. But tyranny does not know that no one should be condemned for having an opinion that differs with that of the ruling authorities. Hence, to human perception, the author's death falls under the one mentioned in the *hadīth* already quoted: "The masters of all martyrs are Ḥamzah ibn ʿAbd al-Muṭṭalib and a person who stands up to a tyrannical ruler, speaking out for what is fair and against what is wrong, but that ruler kills him."

Enthusiastic advocates of Islamic revival are also given to misreading the author. Faced with oppression, which takes several forms and comes from different quarters, young advocates of Islam go a bit too far in their understanding of Qur'ānic verses and the author's explanation of these verses. They become eager to take action, here and now, even though it may be unwise. In their haste, they can overstep the line, thinking that their action serves Islam when it actually undermines its cause. Certain Islamic groups have perpetrated some actions which, in modern political jargon, may be described as terrorist. There is no doubt that Islam does not condone any terrorist action against civilians and non-combatants, even though they may belong to a hostile society. It must also be noted that not all these groups justify their actions on the basis of what the author has said. Indeed some of them may not even recommend their followers to read him.

Both types of misreading of the author may be understandable. Dictatorial regimes are averse to any call for freedom and justice, but they are much more so when such a call is based on Islam which has a very powerful appeal. Enthusiasts may admire the call for jihad and see it as the means to achieve their ideals. But what is not understandable is the hostile attitude to the author that some Western media have adopted after the terrible events of September 11, 2001. As early as November of that year, *The Guardian* of London sought to establish a link between our author and Bin Laden. The fact is that the latter was only a young child when the author died. There is nothing in what the author wrote in any of his books that may be construed as justifying or condoning actions like the attack on the World Trade Centre in New York. The paper plainly refused to publish a reply by the present writer. On 23 March 2003, the *New York Times* carried a very long article with the emotive headline, "The Philosopher of Islamic Terror." Full of half-quotations and half-truths, the article names the author as providing the philosophical basis for all terrorist actions for which fringe groups calling themselves 'Islamic' are blamed. Again, when approached, the paper was unwilling to publish a reply.

Such a reading of the author's ideas is grossly mistaken and devoid of justification. Yet such misreading bodes ill for our world because it plays into the hands of those who are trying to fuel what has come to be known as a clash of civilizations. There will be calls for a whole range of ideas to be drummed up in order to counter this terror philosophy. The Western media will oblige, because it will fill space and provide material for chat shows, phone-ins and heated debates. Yet all will be in vain. A similar case in point is that of a man who dropped his gold ring at night in a dark street, and he went to look for it half a mile away. When asked why he was looking for it so far away, he pointed to the lamp post next to him and said that there was no light at the spot where he dropped the ring. By focusing their attack on Sayyid Quṭb, Western media choose the wrong target because terrorism was as hateful to him as it is to any fair-minded person who values justice and freedom as basic human rights. He always felt a strong bond of love with all humanity, because this comes naturally to advocates of Islam. In his much maligned book, *Milestones*, he writes: "We are not inviting people to Islam to obtain some reward from them; we do not desire anything at all for ourselves, nor is the reckoning of our actions or our reward given to us by human beings. We invite people to Islam because we love them and we wish them well, no matter how much harm they inflict on us. Such are the motives and the nature of Islamic advocacy."[2]

In all his writings, the author is keen to drive home to the advocates of Islam the need to purge from their minds any thoughts of material gain, or any reward in this world. He even makes it clear that they must not seek any reward in this world, not even the triumph of Islam at their hands. Their objective is to follow the Prophet's guidance and seek God's pleasure. This is not done through gaining political power, but through Islamic advocacy by intellectual argument when they have the freedom to do so, and by removing material impediments if they are put in their way. Otherwise, their actions and practices, in all situations, must be in line with Islamic principles and values. These methods are totally unlike what he is falsely accused of preaching.

Yet I will not be surprised if the present trend of focusing on the author will continue and Western media will carry more misrepresentation of his ideas. The West has shown that it continues to uphold its values only within its own communities, or when they suit its interests. These values of fair play, justice and freedom of expression are easily overlooked when that serves the interests of those who hold power. In its dealings with the Muslim world, from the nineteenth century onwards, the West has shown that the only justice it upholds is that of the victor; and democratic values are upheld only within its own societies. It is always ready to deal with dictators in what it terms as 'the third world' as long as these dictators guard its interests. Such examples are too numerous to mention.

On our part we will continue to do justice to the author by presenting his works as they are. Eventually, those who criticize him now will come to see him for what he is: a committed believer who is concerned only with advocating a profound faith that preaches justice and freedom for all mankind.

London   **Adil Salahi**
Rabī' II, 1424
June, 2003

---

2. Sayyid Quṭb, *Milestones*, IIFSO, Kuwait, p. 205. (The translation is slightly amended to bring it closer to the author's words. – Editor's note.)

SŪRAH 9

Al-Tawbah

(The Repentance)

Prologue

Revealed in Madinah, this *sūrah* is one of the last, if not actually the last[1] Qur'ānic revelation. Hence, it contains final rulings on relations between the Muslim community and other people. It also includes the classification of the Muslim community itself, establishing its values together with a full description and outline of the status of each of its groups or classes.[2]

As such, the *sūrah* has a particular importance in clarifying the nature of the Islamic method of action, its different steps and stages. However, we need to review its final rulings in the light of the provisional ones given in earlier *sūrahs*. Such a review will show this method of action to be at one and the same time both flexible and firm. Yet without such a holistic reading, rules, pictures and judgements become very confused. This is what happens whenever verses that outline provisional rulings are taken to be final, while the verses giving final rulings are

---

1. According to the weightier opinion, *Sūrah* 110, Victory, was the last to be revealed.
2. The classes we are referring to here are not the same as the narrow sense of the term 'social classes' suggests. These are classes based on purely Islamic values, as in the case of the very early Muslims among the *Muhājirīn* and the *Anṣār*, the People of Badr, and those who pledged their lives to the Prophet, those who fought and donated generously before the al-Ḥudaybiyah peace treaty or after it, and, by contrast, the people who did not join campaigns of *jihād*, the hypocrites, etc.

read in such a way as to match provisional ones, particularly in relation to *jihād* and the relations between the Muslim community and other groups. We pray to God to enable us to set the record straight and present a full and clear picture, both in this Prologue and in the discussion of the *sūrah* and its passages.

From an objective study of the text of the *sūrah* in the light of the reports giving the immediate circumstances leading to the revelation of its different parts, as well as the various events during the Prophet's lifetime, we can conclude that the *sūrah* as a whole was revealed in the ninth year of the Prophet's settlement in Madinah. However, we also have to say that it was not revealed in one single instance. Although we cannot give a conclusive judgement of the accurate timings of the revelation of the different passages of the *sūrah*, we can say that its revelation occurred over three time stages: the first was prior to the expedition to Tabūk, which took place in Rajab of year 9, while the second stage extended over the period of preparation for the expedition until it was actually in progress. The third stage occurred after the Muslims had returned home. However, the first passage, from verse 1 to verse 28, was the last of its passages to be revealed, towards the end of that year, shortly before the pilgrimage season, i.e. either in the month of Dhu'l-Qa'dah or even in Dhu'l-Ḥijjah. This is in short what we believe to be the case.

In its first section, verses 1–28, the *sūrah* defines the final shape of relations between the Muslim community and the idolaters in the Arabian Peninsula, highlighting the practical, historical and ideological bases of these relations. All this is given in the inimitable Qur'ānic style, with its strong rhythm and the powerful impressions it creates. (See in particular verses 1–16, 23–24, and 28.)

The style employed in these verses, and in the passage as a whole, and the strong emphasis laid on fighting the idolaters in Arabia and the encouragement to take part in such fighting make it clear that at least a section of the Muslim community was very reluctant to take such a decisive step. We will explain here, and in the subsequent commentary, the different factors that came into play to cause such reluctance.

The second section defines the final shape of relations between the Muslim community and the people of earlier revelations generally, also outlining their practical, historical and ideological bases. The passage also shows the independent nature of Islam, as well as the deviation of the people of earlier revelations from the divine faith, both in beliefs and behaviour. Hence, from the Islamic point of view, they are no longer following a divine faith. (Verses 29–35)

The Qur'ānic style in this passage shows very clearly that the Muslims were particularly reluctant to adopt the type of relations defined in the first verse of this passage towards the people of earlier revelations generally, or the great majority of them. The fact is that the confrontation was initially intended with the Byzantines and their allies, the Arab Christians in Syria and beyond. This is clearly intimidating, considering that the Byzantine Empire was the main superpower of the day. Yet the texts apply to all the people of earlier revelations who have the same qualities and characteristics given in this verse. More of this later.

The third section begins its denunciation of those who have been called upon to get ready for the expedition, but who hesitated or were too lazy to join. Not all of these were hypocrites, as will be seen. This fact explains how hard the whole affair was for the Muslims. When we discuss the passage, we will, God willing, explain the factors making it so hard. (Verses 38–41)

We note in this passage the repeated reproaches, coupled with threats and reminders to the believers that God had supported His Messenger when the idolaters drove him out of his home town. No human being had taken part in providing such support. We also note the uncompromising order to the believers to join the Prophet and march with him, no matter what their position might be. All this gives us a clear indication of the hardships involved, leading to much reluctance, fear and an inclination to stay behind. Hence, the repeated reminders, reproaches and clear orders to the community of believers.

The fourth section, the longest in the *sūrah*, is devoted to exposing the hypocrites and their methods in undermining the Muslim community. It describes their psychology, as well as their attitude at the time of the Tabūk Expedition, as well as their previous and later attitudes. It exposes their true intentions, scheming and devious methods, as well as their flimsy excuses with which they try to justify their staying behind and their attempts to weaken the believers' morale.

It also speaks about how they tried to hurt the Prophet and devoted believers. This exposure of the true nature of the hypocrites is further emphasized by a warning to the believers against the hypocrites' schemes. The *surah* defines the nature of the relations between the two camps, which must be set on a clear basis that distinguishes each group through its own actions. This section, taking up more than half of the *surah*, shows that hypocrisy was more widespread after the fall of Makkah to Islam, while it had almost disappeared prior to that. We will explain the reasons for this later. (Verses 42, 47–50, 56–59, 61–68, 73–77, 79–85)

This sustained attack reveals the extent of the hypocrites' scheming to undermine the Muslim community and to divert the attentions of the Muslims from pursuing their goals by means of false claims. It also shows that there were certain weaknesses within the ranks of the Muslim community during that period. This is indicated by the statement: "*There are among you some who would have lent them ear.*" (Verse 47) Another indication is seen in the emphatic order not to pray for the hypocrites or appeal to God for their forgiveness. This situation was a by-product of the fact that large groups declared their acceptance of Islam, when they were not yet committed to the new faith. They had not acquired the proper Islamic attitudes. All this will come in for detailed discussion when we look at the classification the *surah* provides of the groups living within the Muslim community at the time of the Prophet.

We find this classification in the fifth section of the *surah*. We learn in this section that in addition to the leading group of the *Muhājirīn* and the *Anṣār*, which constituted the solid base of the Muslim community, there were several other groups. There were, for example, the Bedouin Arabs among whom there were some good believers and others who were either hypocrites or unbelievers. There were also hypocrites among the people of Madinah. Others were those who mixed good and bad deeds and had not yet fully integrated into the Muslim community. Another group was of unknown status. This group is left to God to judge on the basis of His knowledge of their true nature. There were also some who conspired against the Muslim community under a religious guise. The *surah* speaks about all these groups in a brief but adequate way. It defines how they should be treated within the Muslim community, directing the Prophet and the believers to respond to them in the way so described. (Verses 97–103, 106–108)

That such a multiplicity of groups, classes and standards existed within the Muslim community at the time points to the extent of incoherence that existed after Makkah had fallen to Islam. Prior to the conquest of Makkah, the Muslim community in Madinah had almost rid itself of such weaknesses.

The sixth and final section of the *sūrah* provides a clear definition of the nature of the Islamic pledge the believers give to God to strive for His cause. It also defines the nature of this struggle, or *jihād*, and the duty of the people of Madinah and the Bedouins living close to them. It makes it clear that they cannot stay behind when the Prophet marches forth, seeking their own safety. They need to disassociate themselves from unbelievers and hypocrites. Within the context of this section a judgement is given on the cases of those who did not join the Muslim army, although they were good believers who entertained no hypocrisy. It also describes certain aspects of the attitude of the hypocrites towards Qur'ānic revelations. (Verses 111, 113–114, 117–118, 120–123, 127)

The *sūrah* then concludes with a description of God's Messenger (peace be upon him) and a directive to him to place His trust in God alone. (Verses 128–129)

We have cited here numerous verses to refer to before discussing them in detail. This is done deliberately because the *sūrah* paints a full picture of the Muslim society in Madinah in the days following the conquest of Makkah, describing its organic composition. It is clear from this picture that there was a lack of consistency in the way people approached faith, in addition to structural weaknesses. Certain phenomena are described, such as apathy, unwillingness to sacrifice, hypocritical attitudes, reluctance to do one's Islamic duties, confusion with regard to relations between the Muslim community and others. None of this, however, detracts from the fact that the *Muhājirīn* and the *Anṣār* constituted a solid base that showed no sign of weakness.

We have already mentioned that this state of affairs was due to the fact that after the conquest of Makkah large and divergent groups of people declared their acceptance of Islam, but did not receive the kind of education necessary for full integration within the Muslim community. But this general statement cannot be fully understood unless we review the historical situation before and after the conquest of Makkah, which we will now turn to.

A Historical View

The Islamic movement in Makkah encountered difficulties right from the time when it was born. *Jāhiliyyah*, represented in this instance by the Quraysh, soon sensed the danger it was facing from the message declaring that 'there is no deity other than God, and Muḥammad is God's Messenger.' It realized that this new message was an outright revolution against all authority not derived from God's own. It was a rebellion against all tyranny, seeking God's protection. *Jāhiliyyah* also sensed that the new message, led by God's Messenger, began to form a new organic grouping pledging sole and complete allegiance to God and His Messenger. Thus, it rebelled against the leadership of the Quraysh and the situation prevailing under *jāhiliyyah*. No sooner did the Quraysh sense this danger than it launched a determined attack on the new message, grouping and its leadership. It utilized in this attack all its power to inflict physical harm and to sow discord through intrigue and wicked designs.

In fact this *jāhiliyyah* society sought every means to defend itself against a danger it felt to threaten its very existence. This is the normal state of affairs whenever a movement begins to advocate God's Lordship in a community where Lordship is exercised by some people over others. Whenever such advocacy is undertaken by an organized movement that has its own leadership, it will be in direct confrontation with *jāhiliyyah* society, as the two cannot be accommodated within the same community.[3]

At this stage, every individual in the new Islamic grouping was subjected to oppression and persecution in every way, to the extent that many were killed. At the time, only a person who had dedicated himself and his life to God, and who was willing to endure persecution,

---

3. For a full discussion of this, refer to the commentary of Verses 8: 72–75, in Vol. 7, Chapter 4.

hunger and even a ghastly death would join the new group, declaring his belief that there is no deity other than God and that Muḥammad is God's Messenger.

In this way a solid foundation was established for Islam, comprising the most determined individuals in Arabian society. Others who could not endure the hardship succumbed to the pressure and reverted to unbelief. But there were very few of these because the issues were clear at the outset. It was only people of distinction that were willing to take the decisive step and join Islam, despite the great danger that such a move involved.

This is how God chose those rare elements to be the early supporters of His message and to form the solid foundation of Islam in Makkah, i.e. the *Muhājirīn*, then to join the early *Anṣār* to form its core group in Madinah. Although the *Anṣār* were not subjected to the same pressures and persecution as the *Muhājirīn*, the pledge they gave to the Prophet at ʿAqabah indicated that they were equal to the task required by Islam. On that night when the pledge was given, as Ibn Kathīr reports, ʿAbdullāh ibn Rawāḥah said to the Prophet: 'Stipulate whatever you wish for your Lord and yourself.' He said: 'As for my Lord, my condition is that you worship Him alone, associating no partners with Him. And as for myself, my condition is that you protect me as you would protect yourselves and your property.' They asked: 'What will be our reward in return?' He said: 'Paradise.' They said: 'It is a profitable deal. We accept no going back and we will not go back on it ourselves.'

Those who made this deal with God's Messenger, seeking no reward other than Paradise, and declaring that they would accept no going back, either by themselves or the Prophet, were aware that it was no easy option they were undertaking. In fact, they were certain that the Quraysh would fight them determinedly, supported by all the other Arabs. They realized that they would never again be able to live in peace with *jāhiliyyah* which had its roots deep in the whole of Arabia, including the areas adjoining Madinah.

Jābir ibn ʿAbdullāh, a Companion of the Prophet, reports: For ten years in Makkah, God's Messenger continued to approach people in their encampments at ʿUkāẓ, al-Majannah and in the pilgrimage season. He would ask: 'Who will give me shelter and support until I have delivered my Lord's message, and he will be in Paradise in return?' No one would extend to him a hand of support. Indeed, a man would be about to set out from the Yemen, or from his tribe of Muḍar, and his people and relatives would warn him, 'Beware lest the Qurayshi man tempt you.' He would go among them and they would point to the Prophet with their hand. This continued to be the case until God sent us to him from Yathrib, when we gathered to him and believed in him. A man from among us would go to him and declare his acceptance of his message. The Prophet would teach him the Qur'ān, and the man would come back to his people and they would follow his suit and embrace Islam. Indeed, every quarter of the *Anṣār* had a number of Muslims who declared their faith.

Then we all conferred and said: 'Until when are we going to leave the Prophet approaching different people, being chased around and in fear?' A group of 70 people from among us went out to meet him in the pilgrimage season.[4] We agreed to meet him at 'Aqabah. We went there individually or two men at a time, until we all gathered there. We asked him: 'Messenger of God! What pledge do we give you?' He said: 'You pledge to me to obey and comply in situations of ease and hardship, and to donate for God's cause in times of poverty and plenty, and to enjoin what is right and forbid what is evil, and to stand up for God's cause fearing no blame from anyone, and to support me and protect me when I come to you as you protect yourselves, your wives and children. Your reward will be Paradise.'

We stood up to give him our pledges, but As'ad ibn Zurārah, who was one of the youngest among them,[5] said: 'Cool it, people of Yathrib. We have not travelled all this distance to meet him without knowing that he is certainly God's Messenger. However, to take him from his people will be an act of confrontation with all the Arabs, which could mean that the best among you may be

---

4. The fact is that they were 72, but the Arabs often round their figures.
5. In al-Bayhaqī's version, 'He was the youngest of the 70 apart from me.'

killed and that swords will be put into you. If you accept to take all that patiently, you take him and seek your reward from God. On the other hand, if you fear that you may slacken, leave off now, and explain your reasons. This may be better for you in God's sight.' They said: 'Step aside, As'ad. By God, we will not turn away from our pledge, and we will not let anyone take it away from us.' We stood up and gave him our pledges. He stipulated his conditions, and promised us that we will be rewarded with Paradise.[6]

The *Anṣār*, then, were fully aware of the likely consequences of their pledge once they had given it. They were also aware that they were not promised anything in this world in return for their efforts. They were not even promised victory over their enemies. The only reward they were promised was admittance into heaven. Yet they were still keen to offer their pledges. Hence, they were definitely with the early *Muhājirīn* in taking the necessary preparations so that they would constitute the solid foundation of the first Islamic society in Madinah.

Early Indications of Weakness

But the Madinah society did not maintain this level of purity despite the spread of Islam. Many people, especially those who were in positions of influence, felt they had to take a similar stand to their people in order to maintain their positions. When the Battle of Badr took place, the leading figure among these, 'Abdullāh ibn Ubayy ibn Salūl, thought that Islam had established firm roots and could not be easily dislodged. Hence, he pretended to be a Muslim. It was perhaps inevitable that many accepted Islam in order to keep abreast of their people. They were not hypocrites, but they had not fully understood Islam or moulded themselves according to it. This meant that the community in Madinah had different levels of commitment to the new faith.

---

6. Reported by Ibn Kathīr in his book *Al-Bidāyah wa'l-Nihāyah*, Maktabah al-Ma'ārif, Beirut and Riyadh, 1996, Vol. 3, p. 159, as related by Imām Aḥmad. There are several versions of this *ḥadīth*, reported by *Ḥadīth* scholars.

At this point, the unique Islamic method of education began its work under the Prophet's supervision in order to mould these new elements. It aimed to achieve coherence within the Muslim community at the ideological, moral and behavioural levels.

When we read the *sūrahs* revealed in Madinah, in the approximate order of their revelation, we note the great effort that aimed to absorb and remould the new elements in the Muslim community, particularly because there were always newcomers. This was the case despite the determined opposition of the Quraysh and its attempts to win other Arabian tribes to its side, and despite the wicked designs of the Jews and their efforts to marshal hostile forces to the new faith and its advocates. Hence, the effort to bring newcomers to the same level as the elite, for this was needed if they were to continue with determination.

Nonetheless, weaknesses continued to surface, particularly in times of difficulty. There were indications of hypocrisy, reluctance, unwillingness to make physical or financial sacrifices, and a general turning away from danger. There were also signs of confusion concerning the relationship between a Muslim and his non-Muslim relatives. Qur'ānic texts in different *sūrahs* provide a clear idea of these phenomena and the method the Qur'ān employed to deal with them. Examples of these texts are given below:

> *Just as your Lord brought you forth from your home for the truth, even though some of the believers were averse to it. They would argue with you about the truth even after it had become manifest, just as if they were being driven to certain death and saw it with their very eyes. God promised you that one of the two hosts would fall to you. It was your wish that the one which was not powerful to be yours, but it was God's will to establish the truth in accordance with His words and to wipe out the unbelievers. Thus He would certainly establish the truth firmly and show falsehood to be false, however hateful this might be to the evildoers.* (8: 5–8)

> *He it is who has sent down to you the Book, containing verses which are clear and precise – and these are the essence of the Book – and others are allegorical. Those whose hearts have swerved from the truth pursue that part of it which is allegorical, seeking to create dissension and trying to give it an arbitrary meaning. None save*

God knows its final meaning. Those who are firmly grounded in knowledge say: 'We believe in it; it is all from our Lord.' But only those who are endowed with insight take heed. 'Our Lord, let not our hearts swerve from the truth after You have guided us; and bestow on us mercy from Yourself. You are indeed the great giver. Our Lord, You will indeed gather mankind together to witness the Day of which there is no doubt. Surely, God never fails to keep His promise.' (3: 7–9)

Are you not aware of how the hypocrites speak to their unbeliever brethren from among the people of earlier revelations: 'If you are driven away, we shall most certainly go forth with you, and shall never pay heed to anyone against you; and if war is waged against you, we shall most certainly come to your succour.' But God bears witness that they are most flagrantly lying. Indeed, if those are driven away, they will not go forth with them; and if war is waged against them, they will not come to their succour; and even if they succour them, they will most certainly turn their back in flight, and in the end will themselves find no succour. You strike more fear in their hearts than God. This, because they are people who fail to grasp the truth. (59: 11–13)

Believers! Remember the blessings which God bestowed on you when [enemy] hosts came down upon you, whereupon We let loose against them a stormwind and hosts that you could not see. Yet God saw all that you did. They came upon you from above you and from below you, and when your eyes became dim and your hearts came up to your throats, and when most conflicting thoughts about God passed through your minds. It was there and then that the believers were tried, and severely shaken. The hypocrites and those whose hearts are diseased said, 'God and His Messenger have promised us nothing but delusions.' A group of them said, 'People of Yathrib! You cannot withstand the enemy here. Therefore, go back.' A party among them asked leave of the Prophet, saying, 'Our houses are exposed!' The fact is that they were not really exposed. They simply wanted nothing but to flee. Now if their town had been stormed, and they had been asked to commit apostasy, they would have done so without much delay... (33: 9–14)

11

Believers, be fully prepared against danger, and go to war either in small groups or all together. There are indeed among you such as would lag behind, and then, if a calamity befalls you, say, 'God has bestowed His favours upon me in that I was not present with them!' But if good fortune comes to you from God, he is sure to say – just as if there had never been any question of love between you and him – 'Oh, would that I had been with them; I would surely have had a [share in a] mighty triumph.' (4: 71–73)

Are you not aware of those who have been told, 'Hold back your hands [from fighting], and attend regularly to prayer, and pay your zakāt [i.e. the purifying dues]'? When, at length, the order for fighting was issued to them, some of them stood in awe of men as one should stand in awe of God – or in even greater awe – and said, 'Our Lord! Why have you ordered us to fight? If only You had granted us a delay for a little while!' Say, 'Brief is the enjoyment of this world, whereas the life to come is the best for all who are God-fearing. None of you shall be wronged by as much as a hair's breadth. Wherever you may be death will overtake you, even though you be in towers built up strong and high.' Yet, when a good thing happens to them, some [people] say, 'This is from God,' whereas when evil befalls them, they say, 'This is from you!' Say, 'All is from God.' What is amiss with these people that they are in no wise near to grasping the truth of what they are told? (4: 77–78)

The life of this world is but a play and a passing delight. But if you believe and are God-fearing, He will grant you your deserts, and will not demand of you to sacrifice your property. If He were to demand it of you, and urge you, you would niggardly cling to it, and so He would bring out your moral failings. Now, you are called upon to spend freely in God's cause; but there are among you those who turn out to be niggardly! He who acts niggardly [in God's cause] is but niggardly towards his own self. For God is indeed self-sufficient, whereas you stand in need of Him. And if you turn away from Him, He will cause other people to take your place, and they will not be the likes of you. (47: 36–38)

Are you not aware of those who would be friends with people whom God has condemned? They are neither of you nor of those others.

They knowingly swear to a falsehood. God has readied for them severe suffering. Evil indeed is what they are wont to do. They have made their oaths a cover, and thus they turn others away from God's path. Hence, shameful suffering awaits them. Neither their worldly possessions nor their offspring will be of the least avail to them against God. It is they who are destined for the fire, therein to abide. On the Day when God will raise them all from the dead, they will swear before Him as they now swear before you, thinking that they are on firm ground. They are indeed the liars. Satan has gained mastery over them, and has caused them to remain oblivious of the remembrance of God. Such as these are Satan's partisans. Most certainly, the partisans of Satan will truly be the losers. Those who contend against God and His Messenger shall find themselves among the most abject. God has ordained: 'I shall most certainly prevail, I and My messengers.' God is indeed Powerful, Almighty. You cannot find people who believe in God and the Last Day and [at the same time] love anyone who contends against God and His Messenger, even though they be their fathers, sons, brothers or their kindred. It is they [the believers] in whose hearts He has inscribed faith, and whom He has strengthened with inspiration from Himself, and whom He will admit into gardens through which running waters flow, therein to abide. Well-pleased is God with them, and they with Him. They are God's partisans. Most certainly, God's partisans shall be the ones who are successful. (58: 14–22)

Believers, do not take the Jews and the Christians for your allies. They are allies of one another. Whoever of you allies himself with them is indeed one of them. God does not bestow His guidance on the wrongdoers. Yet you see those who are sick at heart rush to their defence, saying, 'We fear lest a change of fortune should befall us.' God may well bring about victory [for believers] or some other event of His own making, and those [waverers] will terribly regret the thought they had secretly harboured within themselves. The believers will say: 'Are these the self-same people who swore by God their most solemn oaths that they were with you?' All their works are in vain and they will lose all. (5: 51–53)

Believers, do not take My enemies, who are your enemies as well, for your allies, showing them affection even though they do not believe in the truth that has come to you. They have driven the Messenger and yourselves away, only because you believe in God, your Lord! If you have gone forth from your homes to strive in My cause, and out of a longing for My goodly acceptance, [do not] incline towards them in secret affection. I am fully aware of all that you may conceal and all that you do openly. Any of you who does this has already strayed from the right path. If they could but overcome you, they would remain your foes, and would stretch forth their hands and tongues against you with evil intent; for they desire that you should be unbelievers. Neither your kinsfolk nor your own children will be of any benefit to you on Resurrection Day when He will decide between you. God sees all that you do. Indeed, you have had a good example in Abraham and those who followed him, when they said to their people: 'We are quit of you and of all that you worship instead of God. We deny whatever you believe; and between us and you there has arisen enmity and hatred, to last until such a time as you come to believe in the One God.' The only exception was Abraham's saying to his father, 'I shall pray for God's forgiveness for you, although I do not have it in my power to obtain anything from God on your behalf. Our Lord! In You have we placed our trust, and to You do we return. To You is all journey's end.' (60: 1–4)

These ten quotations, each drawn from a different *sūrah* are sufficient to give us a fair idea of the weaknesses that might naturally and inevitably appear in the Muslim community as a result of the constant influx of new elements. For it takes time and effort before they are fully integrated with the solid base of the community.

The Process of Integration

However, the structure of the Muslim community in Madinah remained generally sound, because it essentially relied on its solid foundation, made up of the elite of the *Muhājirīn* and the *Anṣār*. This foundation gave the Muslim community its strong constitution that withstood all weakening elements and overcame all hazards that might have been brought in by newcomers who had not yet been integrated into it.

Gradually, these new elements were integrated into the solid core, and the numbers of the weak, the hypocrites, and those who lacked the ideological clarity that serves as the basis of all relations and ties dwindled. Shortly before the conquest of Makkah, the Muslim community in Madinah was very close to complete integration, providing the closest model of society Islamic education seeks to bring into existence.

There undoubtedly remained different levels of participation according to the various actions different individuals undertook for Islam. Some groups were distinguished by the dedication, work and sacrifice they made to serve God's cause. Examples of these were the earliest to believe in Islam among the *Muhājirīn* and the *Anṣār*, the people of Badr, those who were party to the pledge given to the Prophet at al-Ḥudaybiyah, and generally those who donated and fought before the conquest of Makkah. Qur'ānic and *ḥadīth* texts, as well as the practical situation in the Muslim community confirmed these distinctions that resulted from action taken for Islam.

- *"As for the first to lead the way, of the* Muhājirīn *and the* Anṣār, *as well as those who follow them in [the way of] righteousness, God is well-pleased with them, and well-pleased are they with Him. He has prepared for them gardens through which running waters flow, where they shall abide for ever. That is the supreme triumph."* (9: 100)

- "It may well be that God has looked at the people of Badr and said: 'Do as you like, for heaven is indeed your deserved reward.'" (This occurs in an authentic *ḥadīth* related by al-Bukhārī. It comes as the Prophet's reply to 'Umar when he requested the Prophet's permission to kill Ḥāṭib ibn Abī Balta'ah who, in a moment of weakness, sent word to the Quraysh telling them of the Prophet's intention to march to Makkah.)

- *"Well pleased indeed was God with the believers when they pledged their allegiance to you under that tree. He knew what was in their hearts; and so He bestowed inner peace upon them from on high, and rewarded them with the happy news of a victory soon to come and of many war-gains which they would achieve. God is indeed Almighty, Wise."* (48: 18–19)

- *"Not equal are those of you who spent and fought in God's cause before the victory. They are of a higher rank than those who would spend and fight after it, although God has promised the ultimate good to both. God is aware of all that you do."* (57: 10)

- "Take it easy, Khālid! Leave my Companions alone. By God, had you had Mount Uḥud in gold and you spent it all for God's cause, you could not match a single trip of any one among my Companions, nor a return trip." (This *ḥadīth* is mentioned by Ibn al-Qayyim in *Zād al-Maʿād*. It is the Prophet's reply to Khālid ibn al-Walīd when he fell out with ʿAbd al-Raḥmān ibn ʿAwf – may God be pleased with them both. There is no doubt that Khālid ibn al-Walīd is the man given the title *Sayf Allāh*, or God's Sword, for his great achievements as a commander of Muslim armies. ʿAbd al-Raḥmān, however, was one of the very first people to accept Islam. Hence, the Prophet's words in describing such a group of special distinction in the Muslim community of Madinah.)

That there were these different grades on the basis of strength of faith was no barrier to bridging the gap between them in the Madinah society before the conquest of Makkah. In fact, most of the apparent weaknesses within the ranks of the Muslim community were remedied, and their symptoms disappeared. Hence the whole of Madinah society could be considered as forming a solid Islamic basis.

However, when Makkah fell to Islam in year 8, followed by the surrender of the Hawāzin and the Thaqīf tribes, which were the last two large tribes to put up resistance to Islam, this ushered in a great influx of new Muslims. Needless to say, these were of different levels with regard to their outlook. Some among them were hypocrites, while others simply adopted Islam, the new overpowering force. Others still needed to be won over to Islam. Mostly, however, these were people who had not yet understood the fundamentals of Islam and their souls had not yet interacted with its values and principles.

The stubborn opposition of the Quraysh continued to act as a barrier preventing the advance of Islam into the rest of Arabia. The Quraysh tribe had the ultimate say in all religious matters in Arabia, and it exercised a very strong influence over economic, political and social matters. Hence its determined and uncompromising opposition to the new faith ensured that the rest of Arabia turned away from it, or at least adopted a wait and see attitude until the fight between the Quraysh and one of its children had produced a clear winner. When the Quraysh declared its submission, followed by the major tribes of Hawāzin and Thaqīf, and when the three main Jewish tribes in Madinah had previously been subdued, and those of Khaybar had been defeated, people embraced the new faith in flocks. The whole of Arabia submitted to Islam within one year.

Advances and Weaknesses

This rapid expansion in the geographical area of Islam heralded the resurgence, on an even more intensive scale, of all the symptoms experienced after the resounding victory the Muslims achieved in the Battle of Badr. The Muslim community had almost managed to rid itself of those, thanks to the seven-year-long education process it had enjoyed after that battle. The rapid geographical expansion of Islam in Arabia could have had some serious negative effects, had it not been for the fact that Madinah had become, in its entirety, the solid base of Islam. It was God Almighty who looked after the new faith and charted its course. He had prepared the first core of believers, the *Muhājirīn* and the *Anṣār*, to be the first solid base of Islam after the relatively important expansion that followed the victory at Badr. He also made the whole of Madinah the solid base which would withstand the great expansion brought about by the splendid triumph achieved when Makkah was won over to Islam. God certainly knows what forces to mobilize in support of His message.

The first symptom of the new dangers appeared on the day of the Battle of Ḥunayn, mentioned in this *sūrah*: "*God has granted you His support on many a battlefield, and also in the Battle of Ḥunayn, when you took pride in your numerical strength, but it availed you nothing. For all its vastness, the earth seemed too narrow for you, and you turned*

17

back in flight. God then bestowed from on high an air of inner peace on His Messenger and on the believers, and He sent down forces whom you could not see, and punished those who disbelieved. Such is the reward for the unbelievers." (Verses 25–26)

One of the apparent reasons for the defeat at the beginning of the battle was that 2,000 of those the Prophet had pardoned in Makkah, and who embraced Islam after the fall of that city, had joined the 10,000-strong army which originally travelled from Madinah to subdue the Quraysh in Makkah. The presence of those 2,000 men alongside the others who came from Madinah was a cause of imbalance in the Muslim ranks. There was also the fact that the Hawāzin took the Muslims by surprise. What that meant was that the army did not wholly belong to the solid, well-knit base which had been nurtured over the several years separating the Battle of Badr and the conquest of Makkah.

Similarly, the negative symptoms that appeared at the time of the Tabūk Expedition were a natural result of this rapid expansion and the great influx of new Muslims with varying standards of faith. These symptoms are discussed fully in this *sūrah* in a long exposition with varied styles and methods of treatment.

We now go on to review the historical events in the Muslim community within two years of the fall of Makkah. When the Prophet passed away, most parts of Arabia abandoned Islam. Only the Muslim society in Madinah, the solid base of Islam, remained steadfast. Now we can easily explain this phenomenon. Two years were not sufficient to allow the truth of Islam to settle in the hearts of the great multitude of people who declared their acceptance of Islam after the fall of Makkah. With different levels of faith, the Prophet's death sent a shock wave throughout Arabia, leading to uncertainty. The solid base, however, remained firmly committed. Pure, strong and united, it was able to reverse the tide of apostasy and return all Arabia back to Islam.

This fact gives us a clear idea that God allowed the campaign of persecution mounted against the Muslims in Makkah to continue for many years for a definite purpose. In His wisdom, God left the tyrants of idolatry to continue their persecution to the extent of bloodshed, killing some Muslims and torturing many others. God knew that this was part of the proper education of the first Muslim community to form the solid base for Islam. Without such a long trial, people do not grow sufficiently solid to withstand great pressures. It is such a degree of steadfastness, dedication and commitment – in the face of torture, hardship, and killings, with people turned away from their homes, suffering hunger and hardship, yet being small in number and without any human support – that is needed by the hard core of the new faith as it makes its first march.

This hard core of the early *Muhājirīn* was subsequently joined by the early *Anṣār*, and both groups formed the solid base in Madinah, before the Battle of Badr. They were the ones who remained strongly committed when elements of weakness appeared following the influx of newcomers who accepted Islam after the Badr victory, but who had not had time to integrate with the hard core or achieve its level of commitment.

The solid base itself grew in numbers so as to include, just before the fall of Makkah, the whole Madinah society. Again, this solid base was the one to protect Islam and spare it several pitfalls after the Makkan victory, and then again at the time of the Prophet's death, when most parts of Arabia rebelled against Islam.

While this fact explains the wisdom behind allowing the hard trial the Muslims endured in Makkah and the great dangers faced by the Muslim society in Madinah, up to the time of signing the al-Ḥudaybiyah peace treaty, it also gives us an insight into the method of action the Islamic message follows at all times and in all societies.

All efforts should be directed at first to establish the hard core of true believers, who withstand trials and cannot be shaken. They need further education in their faith so as to grow in strength and awareness. Extreme caution should be exercised in order to guard against horizontal expansion before this hard core comes into being: solidly committed and having profound insight. Indeed, shallow horizontal expansion represents grave dangers that threaten the very existence of any Islamic movement, because it would then be following a different way from that of the first Islamic community and adopting a different method of action.

Yet it is God who ensures that His message follows the right way. Whenever He wishes to allow a truly Islamic movement to emerge, He exposes its early advocates to a long trial. He lets victory be slow coming, and leaves them few in number, with other people taking a negative attitude towards them, until they show their steadfastness and firm commitment. Thus, they prove that they are able to form the hard, enlightened core who can be trusted with His message. He will then show them their way ahead. God is able to achieve His purpose, but most people do not know this.

Jihād and its Final Rulings

Now we will have a brief look at the main topics addressed in the surah, particularly the final rulings concerning relations between the Muslim community and other communities. Since the rulings given in this surah are the final ones, they represent the ultimate line of action.

We need to quote here what we stated in the Prologue to Sūrah 8 (Volume 7) about the nature of the Islamic method of action. We can only understand the present final rulings in the light of the earlier, provisional ones. Even though this may be repetitive in this book, a reminder of these is certainly both useful and important.

In his priceless book Zād al-Ma'ād, Imām Ibn al-Qayyim includes a chapter with the title, 'The Progress of the Prophet's Guidance on Dealing with the Unbelievers and the Hypocrites from the Start of His Mission to the End of His Life'. This is given below in a highly summarized form:

> The first revelation given to the Prophet by his Lord – limitless is He in His glory – was His order to him, "*Read in the name of your Lord who created man out of a germ-cell.*" (96: 1–2) This was the start of his prophethood. The instruction to him was to read within himself. At that point, He did not order him to convey anything to anyone. He subsequently revealed to him: "*You who are enfolded, arise and warn!*" (74: 1–2) This means that God made him a prophet by telling him to read, and He gave him his mission by saying, "*You who are enfolded, arise and warn!*" (74: 1–2) God then ordered him to warn his immediate clan. Subsequently, he gave the same warning to his own people, then to the surrounding Arabian tribes, then to all Arabs, then to mankind generally.

For more than a decade after the start of his prophethood, Muḥammad [peace be upon him] continued to advocate the faith without resorting to fighting or the imposition of any loyalty tax, i.e. *jizyah*. Throughout this period he was ordered to stay his hand, forbear patiently and overlook all opposition. Later, God gave him permission to migrate [from Makkah to Madinah] and permitted him to fight. He then instructed him to fight those who wage war against him and to maintain peace with those who refrain from fighting him. At a later stage, God ordered him to fight the idolaters until all submission is made to God alone.

After the order was given to the Prophet to strive and fight for God's cause [i.e. *jihād*], unbelievers were in three categories with regard to their relations with him: those with whom he was in peace and truce, combatants fighting him, and those under his protection [i.e. *ahl al-dhimmah*]. God ordered him to honour his treaties with those whom he had a peace treaty, as long as they honoured their commitments. If he feared treachery on their part, he was to revoke the treaty but would not fight them until he had informed them of the termination of their peace treaty. On the other hand, he was to fight those who violated their treaties with him.

When *Sūrah* 9, Repentance, was revealed, it outlined the policy towards all these three categories. The Prophet is ordered there to fight his enemies from among the people of earlier faiths until they submit to his authority, paying the loyalty tax, *jizyah*, or embrace Islam. He is also ordered in the same *sūrah* to strive hard against the unbelievers and the idolaters. He strove against the unbelievers with arms, and against the hypocrites with argument and proof.

A further order to the Prophet in *Sūrah* 9 was to terminate all treaties with unbelievers, classifying such people into three groups. The first group he was ordered to fight, because these were the ones who violated their treaties with him and who were untrue to their commitments. He fought them and was victorious. The second group consisted of those with whom he had a peace treaty which they had honoured fully, and the treaty was to run for a specific term. They had given no support to any person or group who opposed the Prophet. With these he was to honour the peace treaty until it had run its course. The third group included those with whom the Prophet had no treaty and no previous fighting engagements, as well as those who had an open-ended agreement. The Prophet was instructed to give these four months' notice, after which he was to fight them. The Prophet acted on these instructions, fought those who violated their treaties, and gave four-months' notice to those who had no treaty or had one without a specific term. Those who honoured their treaty were to have it honoured by the Prophet until the end of its term. All these embraced Islam before the end of their term. As for those who pledged loyalty to him, they were to pay the loyalty tax, *jizyah*.

Thus, after the revelation of *Sūrah* 9, the unbelievers were in three different categories with regard to the Prophet's relations with them: combatants, or bound by a specified-term treaty, or loyal. The second category embraced Islam shortly thereafter, leaving the other two groups: combatants who feared him, and those who were loyal. Thus, all mankind were divided into three classes: Muslims who believed in the Prophet's message; those at peace with him who enjoyed security; and those who were hostile and feared him.

As for the hypocrites, he was instructed to accept from them what they professed, leaving the final verdict on them to God. He was to strive against them with informed argument. He was further instructed to turn away from them and to be hard so that he would deliver his message to them in a way that they could not refute. He was forbidden to pray for them when they died, or to visit their graves. He was informed that if he were to pray for them to be forgiven, God would not forgive them.

Such was the Prophet's policy towards his opponents, both unbelievers and hypocrites.[7]

---

7. Ibn al-Qayyim, *Zād al-Ma'ād*, Mu'assasah al-Risālah, Beirut, 1994, Vol. 3, pp. 158–161.

This excellent summary of the different stages of the development of *jihād*, or striving for God's cause, reveals a number of profound features of the Islamic approach which merit discussion; but we can only present them here very briefly.

The first of these features is the serious realism of the Islamic approach. Islam is a movement confronting a human situation with appropriate means. What it confronts is a state of ignorance, or *jāhiliyyah*, which prevails over ideas and beliefs, giving rise to practical systems that are supported by political and material authority. Thus, the Islamic approach is to confront all this with vigorous means and suitable resources. It presents its arguments and proofs to correct concepts and beliefs; and it strives with power to remove the systems and authorities that prevent people from adopting the right beliefs, forcing them to follow their errant ways and worship deities other than God Almighty. The Islamic approach does not resort to the use of verbal argument when confronting material power. Nor does it ever resort to compulsion and coercion in order to force its beliefs on people. Both are equally alien to the Islamic approach as it seeks to liberate people from subjugation so that they may serve God alone.

Secondly, Islam is a practical movement that progresses from one stage to the next, utilizing for each stage practical, effective and competent means, while at the same time preparing the ground for the next stage. It does not confront practical realities with abstract theories, nor does it use the same old means to face changing realities. Some people ignore this essential feature of the Islamic approach and overlook the nature of the different stages of development it contains. They cite Qur'ānic statements stating that they represent the Islamic approach, without relating these statements to the stages they addressed. When they do so, they betray their utter confusion and give the Islamic approach a deceptive appearance. They assign to Qur'ānic verses insupportable rules and principles, treating each verse or statement as outlining final Islamic rules. Themselves a product of the sorry and desperate state of contemporary generations who have nothing of Islam other than its label, and defeated both rationally and spiritually, they claim that Islamic *jihād* is always defensive. They imagine that they are doing Islam a service when they cast away its objective of removing all tyrannical powers from the face of the earth, so that people are freed from serving anyone other than God. Islam does not force people to accept its beliefs; rather, it aims to provide an environment where people enjoy full freedom of belief. It abolishes oppressive political systems depriving people of this freedom, or forces them into submission so that they allow their peoples complete freedom to choose to believe in Islam if they so wish.

Thirdly, such continuous movement and progressive ways and means do not divert Islam from its definitive principles and well-defined objectives. Right from the very first day, when it made its initial address to the Prophet's immediate clan, then to the Quraysh, and then the Arabs and finally putting its message to all mankind, its basic theme remained the same, making the same requirement. It wants people to achieve the same objective of worshipping God alone, submitting themselves to none other than Him. There can be no compromise over this essential rule. It then moves towards this single goal according to a well-thought-out plan, with progressive stages, and fitting means.

Finally, we have a clear legal framework governing relations between the Muslim community and other societies, as is evident in the excellent summary quoted from *Zād al-Ma'ād*. This legal framework is based on the main principle that submission to God alone is a universal message which all mankind must either accept or be at peace with. It must not set up any impediment to this message, in the form of a political system or material power. Every individual must remain free to make his or her absolutely free choice to accept or reject it, feeling no pressure or compulsion. Anyone who puts such impediments in the face of the message of complete submission to God, must be resisted and fought by Islam.

The Final and Provisional Rulings

In the light of this excellent exposition we can understand the reasoning behind the final rulings outlined in this *sūrah*. These include the termination of treaties with idolaters, except for the ones with treaties specifying a term of expiry, provided that they had not violated their treaties or collaborated with others against Islam. Others who had open-ended treaties, or with no treaties, or who had violated the terms of their treaties are given a period of four months grace, during which they are safe. When this grace period was over, they were to be taken and killed wherever they happened to be found. They could not move in safety. We can also understand the rulings about fighting the people of earlier revelations who had deviated from the true divine religion until they are humbled and agreed to pay the submission tax. We understand the final rulings concerning *jihād* against the hypocrites, together with the unbelievers, and being harsh to them, unwilling to pray for their dead or stand over their graves. All these rulings amend earlier, provisional ones given before the revelation of the present *sūrah*. We believe that this amendment is now clear.

We cannot speak here in detail about these final rulings, or even about the provisional ones, or about other topics addressed in this *sūrah*. All this will come in for detailed discussion as we comment on the Qur'ānic text.

However, we need to clarify that those provisional rulings have not been abrogated in the sense that they can no longer be implemented in any situation the Muslim community finds itself in. The fact is that the practical situation faced by the Muslim community in different circumstances, places and times may determine, through absolute scholarly effort and discretion, which ruling is most suited to a particular situation, time and place. However, sight must not be lost of the final rulings to which the community should revert whenever it is able to implement them, as was the case at the time when this *sūrah* was revealed. These rulings were subsequently implemented during the Islamic conquests, in the treatment of both unbelievers and the people of earlier revelations.

Some defeatist elements are overwhelmed by the pressures resulting from the desperate situation of present-day Muslims, who have nothing of Islam other than its name, and from the wicked attack by the Orientalists on the concept of *jihād*. Hence they try to find excuses by relying on provisional rulings and ignoring the true basis of the Islamic approach that moves forward to liberate mankind from servitude to other human beings, so that they can worship God alone. Its aim is to destroy tyrannical forces and regimes which force people to submit to a rule different from that of God, and apply a law other than His own.

Such defeatists quote verses like: "*If they incline to peace, then incline you to it as well, and place your trust in God.*" (8: 61) "*As for such [of the unbelievers] who do not fight against you on account of your faith, and neither drive you forth from your homelands, God does not forbid you to show them kindness and to behave towards them with full equity.*" (60: 8) "*Fight for the cause of God those who wage war against you, but do not commit aggression. Indeed, God does not love aggressors.*" (2: 190) "*Say: 'People of earlier revelations! Let us come to an agreement which is equitable between you and us: that we shall worship none but God, that we shall associate no partners with Him, and that we shall not take one another for lords beside God.' And if they turn away, then say: 'Bear witness that we have surrendered ourselves to God.'*" (3: 64)

They go on to say that Islam, then, does not fight anyone other than those who fight against the people in the land of Islam, within its area, or those who threaten it from outside. They further cite the fact that the Prophet signed the peace treaty with the idolaters at al-Ḥudaybiyah, and prior to that he had a treaty with the Jews and idolaters in Madinah. This defeatist logic means that Islam has nothing to do with the rest of mankind. It does not, or should not, care what deities they worship, or if one group of people are made lords over others, as long as it is safe within its own territory. This smacks of disrespect for Islam and God Almighty, resulting from a feeling of utter defeat.

What is worse, when these people feel unable to change the miserable conditions of today's Muslims, or face up to international forces hostile to Islam, they do not see that their weakness is the result of their moving away from Islam. On the contrary, they persistently try to attribute their own weakness and defeat to Islam, the noble faith God has laid down for mankind.

The texts to which they resort are provisional ones, addressing a particular situation. The state of affairs they addressed may happen again. In such conditions, the provisional rulings may be applied because the Muslim community lives a similar situation to the one they addressed the first time. But this does not mean that these are the ultimate rulings, and the approach they follow is the final one Islam provides. What it means is that the Muslim community needs to persist in trying to improve its situation, removing any impediments standing in its way, until it can apply the final rulings given in this last *sūrah*. Needless to say, these addressed a situation entirely different from that addressed by the provisional ones.

In relation to the idolaters, the final statements say:

> *Disavowal by God and His Messenger [is hereby announced] to those of the idolaters with whom you have made a treaty. [Announce to them:] You may go freely in the land for four months, but you must realize that you can never escape God's judgement, and that God shall bring disgrace upon the unbelievers. And a proclamation from God and His Messenger is hereby made to all mankind on this day of the greater pilgrimage: God is free from obligation to the idolaters, and so is His Messenger. If you repent, it shall be for your own good; and if you turn away, then know that you can never escape God's judgement. Give the unbelievers the news of grievous suffering, except for those idolaters with whom you have made a treaty and who have honoured their obligations [under the treaty] in every detail, and have not aided anyone against you. To these fulfil your obligations until their treaties have run their term. God loves those who are righteous. When these months of grace are over, slay the idolaters wherever you find them, and take them captive, besiege them, and lie in wait for them at every conceivable place. Yet if they should repent, take to prayer and pay the* zakāt, *let them go their way. For God is Much-forgiving, Merciful. If any of the idolaters seeks asylum with you, grant him protection, so that he may hear the word of God, and then convey him to his place of safety. That is because the idolaters are people who lack knowledge.* (Verses 1–6)

And in relation to the people of earlier revelations, the final rulings are: "*Fight against those who – despite having been given scriptures – do not truly believe in God and the Last Day, and do not treat as forbidden that which God and His Messenger have forbidden, and do not follow the religion of truth, till they [agree to] pay the submission tax with a willing hand, after they have been humbled.*" (Verse 29)

If the Muslims today, in their present situation, cannot implement these final rulings, then they are not, now and for the time being, required to do so. For God does not charge anyone with more than he or she can do. They may resort to the provisional rulings, approaching them gradually, until such a time when they are able to implement these final rulings. But they may not twist the final texts in order to show them as consistent with the provisional ones. They may not impose their own weakness on the divine faith, which remains firm and strong. Let them fear God and not attempt to weaken God's faith under the pretext of showing it to be a religion of peace. It is certainly the religion of peace, but this must be based on saving all mankind from submission to anyone other than God. Islam is the code God has given to mankind so that they may elevate themselves to be worthy of it, and to enjoy its good fruits. It is not devised by any human being. Hence, its advocates must not be ashamed of declaring that their ultimate goal is to destroy all forces that stand in its way of liberating mankind from any shackle that prevents the free choice of adopting Islam.

When people follow human codes and apply man-made laws to regulate their lives, every doctrine and code has the right to live in peace within its own area, as long as it does not entail aggression against others. In this case, coexistence of different creeds, regimes and social orders should be the norm. But when there is a divine code requiring complete submission to God alone, and there are alongside it systems and conditions that are man-made, advocating submission to human beings, the matter is fundamentally different. In this case, it is right that the divine system should move across barriers to liberate people from enslavement by others. They will then be free to choose their faith in a situation where people surrender themselves to God alone.

Those defeatists twist texts in order to save themselves from their imagined embarrassment in trying to explain why Islam moves beyond its original borders to save mankind from submission to anyone other than God. They forget the great truth of a divine system based on submission to God alone facing man-made systems under which people submit to one another.

From the Islamic point of view, *jihād* has its own justification, derived from its own system. Defeatists will be well advised to examine this justification. Perhaps when they do so, God will give them added strength and a criterion which He has promised to His God-fearing servants.

Special to This *Sūrah*

Finally, unlike all other *sūrahs*, this one does not have the usual phrase we find at the beginning of each *sūrah* in the original master copies written at the time of ʿUthmān.

> Al-Tirmidhī reports that ʿAbdullāh ibn ʿAbbās, a close and learned Companion of the Prophet, said that he had asked ʿUthmān ibn ʿAffān, the third Caliph who is universally recognized as having authorized the compilation of the Qurʾānic text as we have it today, why *Sūrah 8*, al-Anfāl, consisting of less than 100 verses, was placed before *Sūrah 9*, al-Tawbah, which comprises over 100 verses, and which, unlike other *sūrahs*, does not contain the usual opening phrase of *"In the name of God, the Compassionate, the Merciful"*? He further enquired of him why *Sūrah 8* was grouped with the seven long *sūrahs* [that appear at the beginning of the Qurʾān]?

> ʿUthman answered, "The Prophet (peace be upon him) used to receive verses or passages from several *sūrahs* at the same time. He would call the scribes and instruct them to put specific verses at specified places in their respective *sūrahs*. Al-Anfāl was one of the earliest *sūrahs* revealed in Madinah while al-Tawbah was one of the latest, but their subject matter was very similar that I suspected they might be one *sūrah*. The Prophet passed away without clarifying this particular point. Therefore, I placed them one after the other without separation."

This report is the most acceptable explanation for the juxtaposition of the two *sūrahs* without separating them by the normal line of *In the name of God, the Compassionate, the Merciful*. It also gives us a clear statement that the position of each verse in all *sūrahs* and the order they were placed in the Qurʾān was made on the basis of instructions given by the Prophet himself. More than one *sūrah* might be in the process of revelation at the same time. Hence, when one or more verses were revealed to address a particular situation or to outline or prepare for a definitive ruling, according to Islam's practical approach and method of action, the Prophet would order that these verses be placed in their particular position in the *sūrah* in which they should be included. Thus, every verse was given its position, and every *sūrah* was given its proper order.

We have repeatedly said that each *sūrah* has its own character and features. Moreover, each has its own ambience, and employs particular phrases that bring out in full relief its character and distinctive features. Perhaps the preceding paragraph and the *ḥadīth* quoted before it explain this clear Qur'ānic phenomenon.

I

The Basis of Inter-Communal Relations

Al-Tawbah (The Repentance)

Disavowal by God and His Messenger [is hereby announced] to those of the idolaters with whom you have made a treaty. (1)

[Announce to them:] You may go freely in the land for four months, but you must realize that you can never escape God's judgement, and that God shall bring disgrace upon the unbelievers. (2)

And a proclamation from God and His Messenger is hereby made to all mankind on this day of the greater pilgrimage: God is free from obligation to the idolaters, and so is His Messenger. If you repent, it shall be for your own good; and if you turn away, then know that you can never escape God's judgement. Give the unbelievers the news of grievous suffering, (3)

بَرَآءَةٌ مِّنَ ٱللَّهِ وَرَسُولِهِۦٓ إِلَى ٱلَّذِينَ عَٰهَدتُّم مِّنَ ٱلْمُشْرِكِينَ ۝١

فَسِيحُوا۟ فِى ٱلْأَرْضِ أَرْبَعَةَ أَشْهُرٍ وَٱعْلَمُوٓا۟ أَنَّكُمْ غَيْرُ مُعْجِزِى ٱللَّهِ وَأَنَّ ٱللَّهَ مُخْزِى ٱلْكَٰفِرِينَ ۝٢

وَأَذَٰنٌ مِّنَ ٱللَّهِ وَرَسُولِهِۦٓ إِلَى ٱلنَّاسِ يَوْمَ ٱلْحَجِّ ٱلْأَكْبَرِ أَنَّ ٱللَّهَ بَرِىٓءٌ مِّنَ ٱلْمُشْرِكِينَ وَرَسُولُهُۥ فَإِن تُبْتُمْ فَهُوَ خَيْرٌ لَّكُمْ وَإِن تَوَلَّيْتُمْ فَٱعْلَمُوٓا۟ أَنَّكُمْ غَيْرُ مُعْجِزِى ٱللَّهِ وَبَشِّرِ ٱلَّذِينَ كَفَرُوا۟ بِعَذَابٍ أَلِيمٍ ۝٣

except for those idolaters with whom you have made a treaty and who have honoured their obligations [under the treaty] in every detail, and have not aided anyone against you. To these fulfil your obligations until their treaties have run their term. God loves those who are righteous. (4)

إِلَّا ٱلَّذِينَ عَٰهَدتُّم مِّنَ ٱلْمُشْرِكِينَ ثُمَّ لَمْ يَنقُصُوكُمْ شَيْـًٔا وَلَمْ يُظَٰهِرُوا۟ عَلَيْكُمْ أَحَدًا فَأَتِمُّوٓا۟ إِلَيْهِمْ عَهْدَهُمْ إِلَىٰ مُدَّتِهِمْ إِنَّ ٱللَّهَ يُحِبُّ ٱلْمُتَّقِينَ ٤

When these months of grace are over, slay the idolaters wherever you find them, and take them captive, besiege them, and lie in wait for them at every conceivable place. Yet if they should repent, take to prayer and pay the zakāt, let them go their way. For God is Much-forgiving, Merciful. (5)

فَإِذَا ٱنسَلَخَ ٱلْأَشْهُرُ ٱلْحُرُمُ فَٱقْتُلُوا۟ ٱلْمُشْرِكِينَ حَيْثُ وَجَدتُّمُوهُمْ وَخُذُوهُمْ وَٱحْصُرُوهُمْ وَٱقْعُدُوا۟ لَهُمْ كُلَّ مَرْصَدٍ فَإِن تَابُوا۟ وَأَقَامُوا۟ ٱلصَّلَوٰةَ وَءَاتَوُا۟ ٱلزَّكَوٰةَ فَخَلُّوا۟ سَبِيلَهُمْ إِنَّ ٱللَّهَ غَفُورٌ رَّحِيمٌ ٥

If any of the idolaters seeks asylum with you, grant him protection, so that he may hear the word of God, and then convey him to his place of safety. That is because the idolaters are people who lack knowledge. (6)

وَإِنْ أَحَدٌ مِّنَ ٱلْمُشْرِكِينَ ٱسْتَجَارَكَ فَأَجِرْهُ حَتَّىٰ يَسْمَعَ كَلَٰمَ ٱللَّهِ ثُمَّ أَبْلِغْهُ مَأْمَنَهُۥ ذَٰلِكَ بِأَنَّهُمْ قَوْمٌ لَّا يَعْلَمُونَ ٦

How can there be a treaty with God and His Messenger for the idolaters, unless it be those of them with whom you have made a treaty at the Sacred Mosque? So long as they are true to you, be true to them; for God loves those who are God-fearing. (7)

كَيْفَ يَكُونُ لِلْمُشْرِكِينَ عَهْدٌ عِندَ ٱللَّهِ وَعِندَ رَسُولِهِۦٓ إِلَّا ٱلَّذِينَ عَٰهَدتُّمْ عِندَ ٱلْمَسْجِدِ ٱلْحَرَامِ فَمَا ٱسْتَقَٰمُوا۟ لَكُمْ فَٱسْتَقِيمُوا۟ لَهُمْ إِنَّ ٱللَّهَ يُحِبُّ ٱلْمُتَّقِينَ ٧

How [else could it be] when, should they prevail over you, they will respect neither agreement made with you, nor obligation of honour towards you? They try to please you with what they say, while at heart they remain adamantly hostile. Most of them are transgressors. (8)

كَيْفَ وَإِن يَظْهَرُواْ عَلَيْكُمْ لَا يَرْقُبُواْ فِيكُمْ إِلَّا وَلَا ذِمَّةً يُرْضُونَكُم بِأَفْوَهِهِمْ وَتَأْبَى قُلُوبُهُمْ وَأَكْثَرُهُمْ فَسِقُونَ ﴿٨﴾

They barter away God's revelations for a paltry price and debar others from His path. Evil indeed is what they do. (9)

اشْتَرَوْاْ بِـَٔايَتِ ٱللَّهِ ثَمَنًا قَلِيلًا فَصَدُّواْ عَن سَبِيلِهِۦٓ إِنَّهُمْ سَآءَ مَا كَانُواْ يَعْمَلُونَ ﴿٩﴾

They respect neither agreement nor obligation of honour with regard to any believer. Those indeed are the aggressors. (10)

لَا يَرْقُبُونَ فِى مُؤْمِنٍ إِلًّا وَلَا ذِمَّةً وَأُوْلَٰٓئِكَ هُمُ ٱلْمُعْتَدُونَ ﴿١٠﴾

Yet, if they repent, take to prayers and pay the zakāt, they are your brethren in faith. Clear do We make Our revelations to people of knowledge. (11)

فَإِن تَابُواْ وَأَقَامُواْ ٱلصَّلَوٰةَ وَءَاتَوُاْ ٱلزَّكَوٰةَ فَإِخْوَٰنُكُمْ فِى ٱلدِّينِ وَنُفَصِّلُ ٱلْـَٔايَٰتِ لِقَوْمٍ يَعْلَمُونَ ﴿١١﴾

But if they break their pledges after having concluded a treaty with you, and revile your religion, then fight these archetypes of faithlessness who have no [respect for a] binding pledge, so that they may desist. (12)

وَإِن نَّكَثُوٓاْ أَيْمَٰنَهُم مِّنۢ بَعْدِ عَهْدِهِمْ وَطَعَنُواْ فِى دِينِكُمْ فَقَٰتِلُوٓاْ أَئِمَّةَ ٱلْكُفْرِ إِنَّهُمْ لَآ أَيْمَٰنَ لَهُمْ لَعَلَّهُمْ يَنتَهُونَ ﴿١٢﴾

Will you not fight against people who have broken their solemn pledges and set out to drive out the Messenger, and who were the first to attack you? Do you fear them? It is God alone whom you should fear, if you are true believers. (13)

أَلَا تُقَـٰتِلُونَ قَوْمًا نَّكَثُوٓا أَيْمَـٰنَهُمْ وَهَمُّوا بِإِخْرَاجِ ٱلرَّسُولِ وَهُم بَدَءُوكُمْ أَوَّلَ مَرَّةٍ أَتَخْشَوْنَهُمْ فَٱللَّهُ أَحَقُّ أَن تَخْشَوْهُ إِن كُنتُم مُّؤْمِنِينَ ۝

Fight them: God will punish them at your hands, and will bring disgrace upon them; and will grant you victory over them and will grant heart-felt satisfaction to those who are believers, (14)

قَـٰتِلُوهُمْ يُعَذِّبْهُمُ ٱللَّهُ بِأَيْدِيكُمْ وَيُخْزِهِمْ وَيَنصُرْكُمْ عَلَيْهِمْ وَيَشْفِ صُدُورَ قَوْمٍ مُّؤْمِنِينَ ۝

removing all angry feelings from their hearts. God will turn in His mercy to whom He wills. God is All-knowing and Wise. (15)

وَيُذْهِبْ غَيْظَ قُلُوبِهِمْ وَيَتُوبُ ٱللَّهُ عَلَىٰ مَن يَشَآءُ وَٱللَّهُ عَلِيمٌ حَكِيمٌ ۝

Do you think that you will be left alone, unless God takes cognizance of those of you who strive hard for His cause and establish close association with none other than God, His Messenger and the believers? God is well aware of what you do. (16)

أَمْ حَسِبْتُمْ أَن تُتْرَكُوا وَلَمَّا يَعْلَمِ ٱللَّهُ ٱلَّذِينَ جَـٰهَدُوا مِنكُمْ وَلَمْ يَتَّخِذُوا مِن دُونِ ٱللَّهِ وَلَا رَسُولِهِۦ وَلَا ٱلْمُؤْمِنِينَ وَلِيجَةً وَٱللَّهُ خَبِيرٌ بِمَا تَعْمَلُونَ ۝

It is not for the idolaters to visit or tend God's houses of worship; for they are self-confessed unbelievers. Vain shall be their actions and they shall abide in the fire. (17)

مَا كَانَ لِلْمُشْرِكِينَ أَن يَعْمُرُوا مَسَـٰجِدَ ٱللَّهِ شَـٰهِدِينَ عَلَىٰٓ أَنفُسِهِم بِٱلْكُفْرِ أُوْلَـٰٓئِكَ حَبِطَتْ أَعْمَـٰلُهُمْ وَفِي ٱلنَّارِ هُمْ خَـٰلِدُونَ ۝

God's houses of worship may be tended only by those who believe in God and the Last Day, are constant in prayers, pay *zakāt* (i.e. the obligatory charity) and fear none other than God. It is those who are likely to be rightly guided. (18)

إِنَّمَا يَعْمُرُ مَسَٰجِدَ ٱللَّهِ مَنْ ءَامَنَ بِٱللَّهِ وَٱلْيَوْمِ ٱلْأَخِرِ وَأَقَامَ ٱلصَّلَوٰةَ وَءَاتَى ٱلزَّكَوٰةَ وَلَمْ يَخْشَ إِلَّا ٱللَّهَ فَعَسَىٰ أُوْلَٰٓئِكَ أَن يَكُونُوا۟ مِنَ ٱلْمُهْتَدِينَ ۝

Do you, perchance, consider that the provision of drinking water to pilgrims and tending the Sacred Mosque are equal to believing in God and the Last Day and striving for God's cause? These are not equal in God's sight. God does not provide guidance for people who are wrongdoers. (19)

أَجَعَلْتُمْ سِقَايَةَ ٱلْحَاجِّ وَعِمَارَةَ ٱلْمَسْجِدِ ٱلْحَرَامِ كَمَنْ ءَامَنَ بِٱللَّهِ وَٱلْيَوْمِ ٱلْأَخِرِ وَجَٰهَدَ فِى سَبِيلِ ٱللَّهِ لَا يَسْتَوُۥنَ عِندَ ٱللَّهِ وَٱللَّهُ لَا يَهْدِى ٱلْقَوْمَ ٱلظَّٰلِمِينَ ۝

Those who believe, and leave their homes and strive hard for God's cause with their property and their lives stand higher in rank with God. It is they who shall triumph. (20)

ٱلَّذِينَ ءَامَنُوا۟ وَهَاجَرُوا۟ وَجَٰهَدُوا۟ فِى سَبِيلِ ٱللَّهِ بِأَمْوَٰلِهِمْ وَأَنفُسِهِمْ أَعْظَمُ دَرَجَةً عِندَ ٱللَّهِ وَأُوْلَٰٓئِكَ هُمُ ٱلْفَآئِزُونَ ۝

Their Lord gives them the happy news of bestowing on them His grace, and acceptance, and of the gardens of eternal bliss (21)

يُبَشِّرُهُمْ رَبُّهُم بِرَحْمَةٍ مِّنْهُ وَرِضْوَٰنٍ وَجَنَّٰتٍ لَّهُمْ فِيهَا نَعِيمٌ مُّقِيمٌ ۝

where they shall reside for ever. God's reward is great indeed. (22)

خَٰلِدِينَ فِيهَآ أَبَدًا إِنَّ ٱللَّهَ عِندَهُۥٓ أَجْرٌ عَظِيمٌ ۝

Believers, do not take your fathers and brothers for allies if they choose unbelief in preference to faith. Those of you who take them for allies are indeed wrong-doers. (23)

يَٰٓأَيُّهَا ٱلَّذِينَ ءَامَنُواْ لَا تَتَّخِذُوٓاْ ءَابَآءَكُمْ وَإِخْوَٰنَكُمْ أَوْلِيَآءَ إِنِ ٱسْتَحَبُّواْ ٱلْكُفْرَ عَلَى ٱلْإِيمَٰنِ وَمَن يَتَوَلَّهُم مِّنكُمْ فَأُوْلَٰٓئِكَ هُمُ ٱلظَّٰلِمُونَ ٢٣

Say: 'If your fathers, your sons, your brothers, your spouses, your clan, and the property you have acquired, and the business in which you fear a decline, and the dwellings in which you take pleasure, are dearer to you than God and His Messenger and the struggle in His cause, then wait until God shall make manifest His will. God does not provide guidance to the evildoers.' (24)

قُلْ إِن كَانَ ءَابَآؤُكُمْ وَأَبْنَآؤُكُمْ وَإِخْوَٰنُكُمْ وَأَزْوَٰجُكُمْ وَعَشِيرَتُكُمْ وَأَمْوَٰلٌ ٱقْتَرَفْتُمُوهَا وَتِجَٰرَةٌ تَخْشَوْنَ كَسَادَهَا وَمَسَٰكِنُ تَرْضَوْنَهَآ أَحَبَّ إِلَيْكُم مِّنَ ٱللَّهِ وَرَسُولِهِ وَجِهَادٍ فِى سَبِيلِهِ فَتَرَبَّصُواْ حَتَّىٰ يَأْتِىَ ٱللَّهُ بِأَمْرِهِ وَٱللَّهُ لَا يَهْدِى ٱلْقَوْمَ ٱلْفَٰسِقِينَ ٢٤

God has granted you His support on many a battlefield, and also in the Battle of Ḥunayn, when you took pride in your numerical strength, but it availed you nothing. For all its vastness, the earth seemed too narrow for you, and you turned back in flight. (25)

لَقَدْ نَصَرَكُمُ ٱللَّهُ فِى مَوَاطِنَ كَثِيرَةٍ وَيَوْمَ حُنَيْنٍ إِذْ أَعْجَبَتْكُمْ كَثْرَتُكُمْ فَلَمْ تُغْنِ عَنكُمْ شَيْئًا وَضَاقَتْ عَلَيْكُمُ ٱلْأَرْضُ بِمَا رَحُبَتْ ثُمَّ وَلَّيْتُم مُّدْبِرِينَ ٢٥

God then bestowed from on high an air of inner peace on His Messenger and on the believers, and He sent down forces whom you could not see, and punished those who disbelieved. Such is the reward for the unbelievers. (26)

ثُمَّ أَنزَلَ ٱللَّهُ سَكِينَتَهُۥ عَلَىٰ رَسُولِهِ وَعَلَى ٱلْمُؤْمِنِينَ وَأَنزَلَ جُنُودًا لَّمْ تَرَوْهَا وَعَذَّبَ ٱلَّذِينَ كَفَرُواْ وَذَٰلِكَ جَزَآءُ ٱلْكَٰفِرِينَ ٢٦

God will then turn in His mercy to whom He wills, for God is Much-forgiving, Merciful. (27)

ثُمَّ يَتُوبُ ٱللَّهُ مِنۢ بَعۡدِ ذَٰلِكَ عَلَىٰ مَن يَشَآءُۗ وَٱللَّهُ غَفُورٞ رَّحِيمٞ ٢٧

Believers, know that the idolaters are certainly impure. So, let them not come near to the Sacred Mosque after this year is ended. If you fear poverty, then in time God will enrich you with His own bounty, if He so wills. Truly, God is All-knowing, Wise. (28)

يَٰٓأَيُّهَا ٱلَّذِينَ ءَامَنُوٓاْ إِنَّمَا ٱلۡمُشۡرِكُونَ نَجَسٞ فَلَا يَقۡرَبُواْ ٱلۡمَسۡجِدَ ٱلۡحَرَامَ بَعۡدَ عَامِهِمۡ هَٰذَاۚ وَإِنۡ خِفۡتُمۡ عَيۡلَةٗ فَسَوۡفَ يُغۡنِيكُمُ ٱللَّهُ مِن فَضۡلِهِۦٓ إِن شَآءَۚ إِنَّ ٱللَّهَ عَلِيمٌ حَكِيمٞ ٢٨

Overview

This opening passage was revealed later than the rest of the *sūrah*. We have explained in earlier volumes that the final ordering of the verses in each *sūrah* followed instructions given by the Prophet himself. This means that such ordering is final and done on the basis of instructions received by the Prophet from on high.

This passage terminates treaties and agreements that were in force at the time between the Muslims and the unbelievers. A notice of four months is given to those who have treaties running indefinitely, or those who have violated their treaties. Others who have treaties running for a specified term and have honoured their obligations under those treaties, without ever backing or aiding anyone against the Muslims, are promised to have their treaties honoured by the Muslims to the end of their specified terms. Thus, the final outcome is the termination of all treaties with unbelievers in the Arabian Peninsula, and an end to the very concept of having a treaty with idolaters. This takes the form of a disavowal of all obligations towards idolaters and questioning the very idea of idolaters having a treaty or covenant with God and His Messenger.

The passage also includes a ban on idolaters from doing the *ṭawāf*, which is the ritual walk around the Ka'bah, or visiting it for worship in any way or form. This abrogates the earlier mutual pledges of security between the Prophet and the idolaters ensuring the safety of all people in the Ka'bah and during the sacred months.

When we review the events that took place during the Prophet's lifetime so as to draw an outline of the historical progress and nature of the proactive approach of Islam, its progressive stages and ultimate goals, we see very clearly that this decisive step was taken at its most appropriate time. It was now possible to reorganize relations between the Islamic community and other camps, whether idolaters or people of earlier revelations.

Stage after stage and event after event, it was practically demonstrated that it was impossible to achieve coexistence between two diametrically opposed ways of life with such deep-rooted and fundamental differences that affect every detail of concepts, beliefs, moral values, social behaviour, as well as social, economic and political structures. Such fundamental differences were bound to surface as a result of the differences in beliefs and concepts. We have one way of life based entirely on submission of all mankind to God alone who has no partners, and another that makes people submit to other human beings and false deities. The two are bound to be in conflict at every step and in every aspect of life.

It was not just a coincidence that the Quraysh should take such a permanently hostile attitude to the Islamic call which raised the banner that "there is no deity other than God, and Muḥammad is God's Messenger." Its hostility continued throughout the period when the Prophet was in Makkah and sought to crush it in open warfare after he migrated to Madinah. Nor was it by coincidence that the Jews in Madinah should stand up in opposition to the Islamic message or that they should join forces with the idolaters, in spite of the Scriptures in which they professed to believe. Both the Quraysh and the Jews tried to forge an alliance grouping all Arab tribes in an all-out effort to exterminate the whole Muslim community. They felt that the establishment of the Muslim state in Madinah on the basis of faith and its implementation of the divine way of life represented a danger that threatened them and which they felt they had to remove.

We will learn presently that the same can be said for the Christians' attitude towards the Islamic message despite the fact they also had divine Scriptures. This was the case in Yemen, Syria and beyond both these areas, and at all times. It is all in the nature of things.

Those who adopt other creeds and philosophies know that it is in the nature of the Islamic approach to insist on the establishment of a state based on belief in God. It aims to liberate all mankind from submission to other creatures so that they may submit to God alone, and to remove all physical and material impediments that prevent human beings from exercising their right to freedom of choice. It is also natural that those who follow other creeds try to crush the divine way of life in which they see a real threat to their very existence, their systems and social set-ups. Such a polarization is, then, inevitable.

Such hostility, inevitable as it certainly is, surfaced in a variety of forms, time after time, and served to emphasize the need for this final step announced in this *sūrah*. The immediate causes mentioned in some reports were only episodes in a long chain of events that had been going on ever since the early days of the Islamic message.

When we adopt such a broad perspective and try to delve into the root causes dictating attitudes and actions, we can properly understand the need for this final step. We must not overlook the immediate causes because these, in turn, were only episodes in a long series of events.

In his commentary on the Qur'ān, Imām al-Baghawī quotes earlier commentators as saying: "When the Prophet set out on his expedition to Tabūk, the hypocrites started to spread rumours while the idolaters began to violate the treaties they had with the Muslims. God then revealed this verse which is applicable to the latter group. He gave them four months' notice if their treaties were of shorter duration, and announced the termination of longer-lasting treaties after four months."

Reviewing the views of other commentators, Imām al-Ṭabarī says:

> As for the notice given by God permitting idolaters with a treaty to '*go freely in the land for four months*,' perhaps the more accurate view is to say that this notice is given by God to those idolaters who, despite having peace treaties, collaborated with others against the Prophet and the Muslim community violating their treaties before they ran out. As for those who fulfilled their obligations

under such treaties and refrained from collaborating with others, God – limitless is He in His glory – ordered His Messenger to honour his treaty with them until their term had been completed. This is clear in the Qur'ānic statement: "*Except for those idolaters with whom you have made a treaty and who have honoured their obligations [under the treaty] in every detail, and have not aided anyone against you. To these fulfil your obligations until their treaties have run their term. God loves those who are righteous.*" (Verse 4)[1]

Al-Ṭabarī also quotes Mujāhid as saying:

In the statement, '*Disavowal by God and His Messenger [is hereby announced] to those of the idolaters with whom you have made a treaty,*' the reference here is made to the tribe of Mudlij and the Arabs bound by a treaty with the Muslims and all other peoples with similar treaties. It is reported that when the Prophet returned from Tabūk, he wanted to go on pilgrimage. He then thought, 'the Ka'bah is visited by idolaters who do the *ṭawāf* naked. I would rather delay my pilgrimage until such a practice is stopped.' He sent Abū Bakr and 'Alī who went to see people at Dhu'l-Majāz and other markets, as well as their encampments in pilgrimage. They gave notice to all people who had treaties with the Prophet that they would have four months of peace. When those four consecutive months, beginning with the twenty days remaining of Dhu'l-Ḥijjah to the tenth day of Rabī' II, were over, the treaties would come to an end. All people in Arabia would then be in a state of war with the Muslims unless they believed in God and His Messenger. The whole Arab population of Arabia became Muslims and none continued with their old religion.[2]

A number of immediate causes were naturally a factor in taking this final and decisive step. Nevertheless they were only links in a long chain which arises from the basic conflict between the two ways of life

---

1. Muḥammad ibn Jarīr al-Ṭabarī, *Jāmi' al-Bayān*, Dār al-Fikr, Beirut, 1984, Vol. 10, pp. 62–63.
2. Al-Ṭabarī, ibid., pp. 61–62.

which cannot coexist except for short periods and which are bound to come to an end sooner or later.

Peace or No Peace

The late Shaikh Muḥammad Rashīd Riḍā', a leading scholar of the late nineteenth and early twentieth centuries, tries to identify these links in the chain right from the early days of the Islamic message. However, he does not try to outline the basic and permanent conflict which gives rise to the whole episode, leading eventually to the natural result outlined in this *sūrah*. In his commentary, *al-Manār*, he writes:

An indisputable fact known to all people is that God sent His Messenger, Muḥammad, the last of all prophets, with the message of Islam that provides a complete and final version of the divine faith. His greatest proof is the Qur'ān, which defies human beings with a multifaceted challenge that we have outlined in our commentary on verse 3 of *Sūrah* 2. The essence of advocacy of the divine message is based on irrefutable rational and scientific evidence.[3] He has also established clearly that compulsion could in no way be adopted as a means of spreading the faith. This has been outlined in our commentary on verse 256 of *Sūrah* 2.

The idolaters took an attitude of resistance, subjecting the believers to a campaign of persecution and torture to force them to turn away from Islam. They also tried to forcibly prevent the Prophet from conveying his message to people. No one who accepted the new faith and believed in the Prophet's message felt safe or secure from death and torture unless he enjoyed the protection of an ally or a relative. Hence they had to migrate time after time.

Then they escalated their campaign against the Prophet. They considered arresting him permanently, and they also thought of

---

3. It should be stated here that Shaikh Rashīd Riḍā' was a proponent of the same school of Imām Muḥammad 'Abduh, which is clearly influenced by Descartes and his philosophy, which is alien to Islam. This school places very strong emphasis on reason, allowing it great scope in matters of faith. Hence, it is important to add to rational and scientific proofs the simple, instinctive and natural evidence which appeals to the entire human make up, including mind and feeling.

banishing him, and they also considered killing him openly in their meeting place. They finally opted to murder him. God then ordered him to emigrate, as we have explained when commenting on verse 30 of *Sūrah* 8.[4] The Prophet emigrated with those of his Companions who were able to do so. They settled in Madinah where they found support by the *Ansār* who were believers in God and His Messenger, showing their love of those who migrated to settle in their land, and extended to them fine hospitality and a most generous treatment.

The conditions that prevailed between them and the idolaters of Makkah and other areas in Arabia were naturally war conditions, as would have been expected at the time. The Prophet entered into a peace treaty with the Jews in Madinah and the surrounding area. But they violated their treaty and forged an alliance with the idolaters, supporting them in their campaigns against the Prophet and Islam. We have outlined all this in commenting on *Sūrah* 8.

At al-Ḥudaybiyah, the Prophet entered into a peace treaty with the idolaters which provided for peace and security for ten years. He accepted conditions which were most favourable to the idolaters, but this was an act of magnanimity, not weakness. He wanted peace to prevail so that he could ensure the propagation of his faith through clear argument and irrefutable evidence.[5] The tribe of Khuzā'ah entered into a treaty with the Prophet, while the tribe of Bakr joined an alliance with the Quraysh. The latter launched an aggression against the former and they were helped in this by the Quraysh who supported them with arms, thus violating their treaty with the Prophet.

This was the cause for ending the peace and returning to a situation of war which resulted in the Prophet's campaign that ended with

---

4. *Sūrah* 8 is discussed in Volume 7. – Editor's note.
5. This is true if it means that the initial and basic standpoint is to try to spread the faith by argument and conviction. However, it goes too far if it means to argue that *jihād* is only a defensive strategy to protect the Muslims, and that peace is obligatory in any other situation as Shaikh Muḥammad Rashīd Riḍā' (may God shower His mercy on him) seems to have maintained.

Makkah falling peacefully to Islam. This was an event that considerably weakened and humiliated the idolaters. However, they continued to fight against the Prophet whenever they felt strong enough to do so. Experience had shown that they could never be relied upon to honour their pledges, whether their position was one of strength or weakness. We will presently see, in verse 7, the exclamation, *"How can there be a treaty with God and His Messenger..."* leading to the instruction in verse 12: *"Fight these archetypes of faithlessness who have no [respect for a] binding pledge, so that they may desist."* This means that they will never honour their pledges or fulfil their obligations. What the *sūrah* emphasizes here is that Muslims cannot coexist with them under the provisions of their treaties, in order to ensure peace and security, while they remain idolaters, observing no well-defined law which would have committed them to fulfil the conditions of their treaty. Indeed, the people of earlier Scriptures, who should have demonstrated a greater degree of integrity and honour, were even quicker to violate their covenants and breach their treaties.[6]

This is the basis of the provisions outlined in this *sūrah* which abrogated their open-ended treaties, and allowed other treaties to run their course, provided they remained faithful to such treaties. The reason for this was to remove idolatry from the Arabian Peninsula so that it became wholly and purely for the Muslims. All this is done while observing at the same time and as far as possible the earlier rules, such as *'Fight for the cause of God those who wage war against you, but do not commit aggression,'* (2: 190), and *'If they incline to peace, then incline you to it as well.'* (8: 61) Nevertheless, many scholars are of the view that this latter verse

---

6. Shaikh Riḍā' (may God bless his soul) touches here on the fundamental truth that it is impossible for the Muslims to coexist with idolaters and the people of earlier revelations on the basis of treaties, except for a certain period. Nevertheless, he is more inclined to argue that relations between the Muslim state and other camps should generally be based on peace agreements, unless the Muslims are victims of aggression in their own land. He feels that this is always possible while the lack of such peace treaties is the exception. He says that the whole question concerns the idolaters in Arabia at the time of the Prophet. While this is basically true, what applied to them applies to all idolaters everywhere.

has been abrogated by the verse instructing the Muslims to abrogate treaties with the idolaters and to fight them.[7]

It is clear from this presentation and the subsequent comments, as well as what follows in Shaikh Muḥammad Rashīd Riḍā''s commentary that he properly defines the real cause of this long series of treacherous actions by the idolaters who were always on the look-out for an opportunity to suppress Islam and overpower its advocates. Nevertheless, he does not dig deep enough to see how outstretched the roots behind this attitude were. Nor does he visualize the fundamental quality in the nature of this religion and its method of action, or the nature of radical differences between the divine way of life and those devised by God's creatures. Such differences make a meeting between the two practically impossible. Hence, there can be no permanent peaceful coexistence between a community implementing God's law and other communities.

Under Strong Pressure

By contrast, in his book, *al-Tafsīr al-Ḥadīth*, Muḥammad 'Izzat Darwazah goes far beyond the root causes on which the Islamic attitude to other communities is based. Like other contemporary authors writing under oppressive pressures of the miserable conditions of today's Muslims and the all-too-visible strength of contemporary idolaters, atheists and followers of other religions, he has a clear purpose in mind. Hence, he tries hard to prove that Islam is a religion of peace, aiming at nothing more than to live within its borders in peace. Wherever it is possible to make a peace treaty, Islam should be keen to put it in place, making it its clear objective.

Hence, Muḥammad 'Izzat Darwazah finds no reason for these new and final provisions, included in this present *sūrah*, other than the violation by some idolaters of their treaties. As for those who honoured their treaties, whether these were of limited or indefinite duration, the

---

7. Muḥammad Rashīd Riḍā', *Tafsīr al-Manār*, Dār al-Ma'rifah, Beirut, Vol. 10, pp.149–150.

sūrah gives instructions to the Muslims to honour them. Indeed, he claims that new treaties may be concluded with them after the expiry of their present ones. The same applies, in his view, to the violaters of their present treaties. He considers the verses giving provisional rulings to prevail over the principles given in the final verses.

In his discussion of the first passage of the *sūrah* he identifies the following verses: "*except for those idolaters with whom you have made a treaty and who have honoured their obligations [under the treaty] in every detail, and have not aided anyone against you. To these fulfil your obligations until their treaties have run their term. God loves those who are righteous. When these months of grace are over, slay the idolaters wherever you find them, and take them captive, besiege them, and lie in wait for them at every conceivable place. Yet if they should repent, take to prayer and pay the* zakāt, *let them go their way. For God is Much-forgiving, Merciful.*" (Verses 4–5) He then says:

> In these two verses and the ones preceding them we have scenes of life towards the end of the Madinah period at the time of the Prophet. We note from these verses that there were peace agreements between Muslims and unbelievers which were in force after the fall of Makkah to Islam, and perhaps were signed before that event. We note that some idolaters honoured their agreements while others violated them, or contemplated such violations.

> We stated earlier that commentators describe the second of these two verses as 'the verse of the sword', and treat it as abrogating every previous verse which gives instructions to adopt a reconciliatory attitude towards the idolaters and allowing them time to make their position clear, and to forbear and let matters take their course. They consider this verse to order fighting them as the proper attitude. Some commentators make an exception in the case of those who have a treaty allowing such treaties to run to the end of their terms. Others do not make such exceptions, saying that their only option after the revelation of this verse is that they must embrace Islam. We also made it clear that such an explanation is too extreme and contradicts a number of definitive rulings that prohibit fighting anyone other than enemies and orders fair and kindly treatment of those who adopt a peaceful attitude.

45

When discussing this verse, commentators repeatedly quote reports attributed to the earliest commentators on the Qur'ān. Ibn Kathīr, for example, quotes Ibn 'Abbās's view that the verse contains an order to the Prophet to take up arms against those with whom he had a treaty until they have embraced Islam. He is further ordered to terminate the conditions he approved when negotiating such treaties. The same commentator quotes a singular view attributed to Sulaymān ibn 'Uyaynah which groups these verses together with other verses in this and other *sūrahs* that do not refer to fighting and calls these verses, the swords. He claims that the Prophet sent his cousin 'Alī ibn Abī Ṭālib to convey these verses to people on the day of the greater pilgrimage. These included this verse which he describes as a sword on the Arab idolaters. Another sword was against the hypocrites, and it is included in the later verse: "*Fight against those who – despite having been given Scriptures – do not truly believe in God and the Last Day, and do not treat as forbidden that which God and His Messenger have forbidden, and do not follow the religion of truth, till they [agree to] pay the submission tax with a willing hand, after they have been humbled.*" (Verse 29) A third sword against the hypocrites is included in this verse: "*Prophet, strive hard against the unbelievers and the hypocrites, and press on them. Their ultimate abode is hell, and how vile a journey's end.*" (Verse 73) A fourth sword is levelled against rebels, which is included in *Sūrah* 49: "*If two groups of believers fall to fighting, make peace between them. But then, if one of the two goes on acting wrongfully towards the other, fight against the one that acts wrongfully until it reverts to God's commandment.*" (49: 9) What is most singular is that al-Ṭabarī expresses the view that this present verse (i.e. Verse 5) applies equally to those who are bound by a treaty and those with no treaty. Yet he himself takes a different view when commenting on the following verse: "*For such of the unbelievers as do not fight against you on account of your faith, and neither drive you forth from your homelands, God does not forbid you to show them kindness and to behave towards them with full equity. Surely God loves those who act equitably.*" (60: 8) He says that this last verse is definitive, making clear that God does not forbid extending kindly and fair treatment to those who adopt an attitude of peaceful coexistence and neutrality, whatever their faith may be. These may not even be bound by a treaty.

All this when it is clear that the verse refers, in context and import, to fighting only the idolaters who violate their treaties. It is reasonable to say that considering it a sword pointed at all idolaters, regardless of their position and attitude, is to impose on it an interpretation it cannot admit. The same may be said about the claim that it abrogates several earlier statements given in a form of definitive principles, such as the prohibition of compulsion in matters of religion and faith, the advocacy of the divine message with wisdom, kindly admonition and fair argument, the order to extend kindly and fair treatment to those who do not fight against the Muslims and not to drive them out of their homeland. A few verses on, the *sūrah* also includes a clear order to all Muslims to remain faithful to their commitments towards people with whom they have concluded treaties in the vicinity of the Sacred Mosque, as long as the latter continue to honour their obligations. This last verse gives clear support to our view.

Two points may be raised concerning the rulings included in the two verses quoted above. The first refers to the exception made in the first verse in respect of the completion of the term of a treaty. The question asked here is whether the idolaters who have such a treaty will be included in the disavowal declared by God and His Messenger, and in this case must they be fought? Commentators generally seem to answer this question in the affirmative. We for our part have not seen any authentic report attributed to the Prophet on this particular point. Hence, what commentators say may be questioned if they treat it as universally applicable. The whole matter requires clarification.

Those unbelievers who are party to a treaty with the Muslims could have been prior to the treaty either enemies who fought the Muslims in war and then negotiated a peace treaty with them, as was the case with the Quraysh when they signed the al-Ḥudaybiyah peace treaty, or else they might have wished to have such a peace treaty without ever having been at war against the Muslims. Consider this following verse: "*Except in the case of those of them who have ties with people to whom you yourselves are bound by a covenant, or those who come to you because their hearts shrink from the thought of fighting you or fighting their own people. Had God so willed, He would have given them power over you, and they would have fought you. Therefore, if they leave you alone, and do not make war on you, and offer you peace, God has given you no way against them.*" (4: 90) We believe that this verse speaks of a true situation.

In the Prophet's history we have several examples, such as the report by Ibn Saʿd to the effect that the Prophet made an agreement with the Ṣakhr clan of the Kinānah tribe that neither party would raid the other, and that they would never aid any party against the Prophet and his Companions. All this was put in a written agreement. There is nothing in this verse, or indeed in any other verse, to prevent the renewal of the treaty or extending its term, should the other party desire that, without having ever given any indication of violating their commitments. Muslims may not refuse such an extension because they are ordered to fight only those who wage war or launch an aggression against them. A later verse in the *sūrah* includes an express order to the Muslims to remain true to their treaties with idolaters as long as those idolaters continue to honour such treaties. This supports our view.

The second point concerns the last part of the second verse which makes releasing the idolaters and stopping the fight against them that resulted from their treaty violations conditional upon a fundamental change indicated by turning away from idolatry, attending regularly to prayer and paying the obligatory charity, i.e. *zakāt*.

What appears to me is that by violating their original treaties and fighting the Muslims, the idolaters actually forfeited their right to have a new treaty. It is right that the Muslims should now impose the condition that guarantees their safety and security, which is that they should accept Islam and fulfil its worship requirements, ritual and financial. This does not

AL-TAWBAH (The Repentance) 9

constitute any compulsion to force them to become Muslims. Suffice it to say that idolatry represents a very low ebb to which humanity may sink when it allows its reason to be subservient to ideas and forces that have no trace of truth or logic. Besides, idolatry is an ignorant system governed by oppressive tradition and bizarre habits. When they embrace Islam, they are certain to rid themselves of all that and rise to a position of respectability in thought, morality, faith, belief, worship and daily practices. Besides, we do not see any reason to prevent the renewal of treaties with those whom the Muslims have fought for violating their original treaties, should the interests of the Muslim community require such renewal.

These paragraphs and many similar ones in the author's commentary make it clear that he does not even consider that Islam has an inalienable and absolute right to move forward to liberate mankind from the evil of submission to other human beings so that people may submit themselves to God alone. Islam does so whenever it is feasible, regardless of whether the Muslim community is under attack or not. This concept, which is the basis of *jihād* in Islam, does not figure at all in this author's thinking. Without it Islam is denied its right to remove physical obstacles impeding its progress, and it loses its serious, practical approach which requires facing obstacles with suitable and adequate means. It will have to confront physical powers with verbal advocacy. This is far from satisfactory.[8]

It is also clear that this author does not pay sufficient attention to the method of action Islam adopts, which requires that any situation should be faced with adequate means. He attaches final rulings to provisional texts and rulings which were given earlier. In so doing, he does not take into consideration the fact that the earlier rulings dealt with practical situations different from the ones that prevailed at the time of the revelation of the final verses. It is true that the earlier rulings are not abrogated in the sense that makes them inapplicable to any situation. They remain in force but only to face new situations that are

---

8. Reference may be made to the Prologue of Vol. 7, pp. 1–64, where this is discussed at length.

largely similar to the ones they originally addressed. However, these earlier rulings do not restrict the Muslims should they face situations similar to the ones that prevailed at the time when the final rulings were revealed. The whole question requires broader knowledge, and a good understanding of the nature of Islam and its method of action.

The Nature of Islamic International Relations

At the beginning of our commentary we said: "When we review the events that took place during the Prophet's lifetime so as to draw an outline of the historical progress and nature of the proactive approach of Islam, its progressive stages and ultimate goals, we see very clearly that this decisive step was taken at its most appropriate time. It was now possible to reorganize relations between the Islamic community and other camps, whether idolaters or people of earlier revelations."

One experience after another had revealed the nature of the law that governs relations between Islamic society which attributes Godhead, Lordship, sovereignty and the authority to legislate to God alone, and ignorant or, to use the Islamic term, *jāhiliyyah* societies which assign all this to some beings other than God, or claim that God has partners sharing with Him all these attributes. This law is essentially one of conflict, which is expressed in God's statements in the Qur'ān: *"Were it not that God repels some people by means of others, monasteries, churches, synagogues and mosques – in all of which God's name is abundantly extolled – would have been destroyed."* (22: 40) *"Had it not been for the fact that God repels one group of people by another, the earth would have been utterly corrupted."* (2: 251)

The practical results of this essential law were manifested in two practical phenomena. The first was that Islam moved from one step, expedition and stage to the next following the divine approach and conveying God's message to one area and tribe after another. This was a necessary step towards conveying the message to all mankind and removing all material obstacles that prevented the divine message from reaching all people. This continued to be the case until Makkah fell to Islam and the Quraysh tribe, the major obstacle in the face of the Islamic march, was vanquished. The large tribes of Hawāzin and Thaqīf, which were akin to the Quraysh in strength, also surrendered to the

Muslim state. Islam had then enough power to strike fear in the hearts of its enemies. It was thus able to take the final and decisive step in the Arabian Peninsula, in preparation for taking the same step across the rest of the world, as and when circumstances allowed. The ultimate aim being that there should be no strife on earth and all submission be made to God alone.

The other phenomenon was the violation of treaties and covenants which were made with the Muslims in different circumstances, whenever a chance presented itself to violate such treaties with impunity. At the first suggestion that the Muslims were going through some difficulty which made the idolaters, and even the people of earlier revelations, feel they could safely violate their treaties, such violations were certain to come. The treaties were not made in the first place as a result of any keen desire to live in peace with the Muslims. The enemies of Islam were compelled, by force of circumstance, to go into such treaties to serve their own interests. *Jāhiliyyah*, which is the name Islam gives to any society that rejects God's law, does not like to see Islam establishing its solid presence when it contradicts the very basis of its existence and every detail of the programmes of such societies. *Jāhiliyyah* knows that by virtue of the active nature of Islam, and its instinctive desire to stamp out tyranny from human life, it will work hard to bring people back to the worship of God alone.

It is to emphasize this last phenomenon that God says with reference to the unbelievers: *"They shall not cease to fight you until they force you to renounce your faith, if they can."* (2: 217) He also says about the people of earlier revelations: *"Many among the people of earlier revelations would love to lead you back to unbelief, now that you have embraced the faith. This they do out of deep-seated envy, after the truth has become manifest to them."* (2: 109) Concerning them He also says: *"Never will the Jews nor yet the Christians be pleased with you unless you follow their faith."* (2: 120) In all these categorical statements God makes it clear that all those in the camp of *jāhiliyyah* have the same objectives when it comes to dealing with Islam and Muslims. They pursue their goals with clear persistence that never fades with the passage of time, nor does it change as a result of changing circumstances.

Unless we understand this essential law that is inherent in the nature of the relationship between the Muslim community and the camp of *jāhiliyyah*, we cannot understand the nature of Islamic *jihād*, or the motives for that long struggle between the two. Nor can we, without such understanding of this law, comprehend the motives of the early Muslims, or the secrets of Islamic conquests, or the war that has been waged against Islam by hostile forces over the 14 centuries of Islamic history. It continues to be waged against the children of Muslim communities, despite the fact that these have sadly abandoned true Islam, with its holistic approach to life, and are content to keep it in name only. The war continues to be waged against those latter-day Muslim communities, even those living in the midst of hostile creeds such as communism and idolatry of all forms, whether in Russia, China, Yugoslavia, Albania, India, Kashmir, Ethiopia, Zanzibar, Cyprus, Kenya, South Africa or the United States. All this comes on top of the brutal attempts to exterminate the advocates of Islamic revival in the Muslim World, or more accurately, the world which used to be Muslim. Communism, idolatry, and other world powers collaborate with, and give active support to, the regimes that undertake such extermination efforts against the advocates of Islamic revival. They pour their aid on these governments to the extent that they practically give them every type of help to ensure that they stay in power. Their support often takes the form of tacit or silent approval of what they are doing to those noble believers who seek to persuade people to believe in God and implement His law.

Such understanding of all these aspects can only be achieved when we understand the essential law we have talked about and the phenomena it brings into our life. This law demonstrated itself in the period leading to the conquest of Makkah, in the two phenomena we have outlined. At that time, it appeared clearly that a decisive step must be taken in the Arabian Peninsula, against the idolaters, which we will discuss presently, and against the people of earlier revelations which we will discuss in Chapters 2 and 3.

Crystallizing Attitudes

The need for such a decisive step might have been very clear for the Islamic leadership at the time, but that did not necessarily mean that it was similarly clear to all groups in the Muslim community, particularly the newcomers to Islam and those who were only on friendly terms with the Muslims.

Some people in the Muslim community, perhaps among the noblest and most dedicated Muslims, might have felt uneasy about the termination of all treaties with the unbelievers on the terms outlined in the *sūrah*: after four months for those who violated their treaties, and those with treaties that did not specify a term, and those whose treaties ended in less than four months and those who had no treaties and were not at war with the Muslims. Those who had treaties with specified terms and continued to honour their obligations would have their treaties respected and observed for the remainder of their terms. Such conscientious Muslims might have understood that the treaties with the violators and those from whom violation was expected should be terminated, as was clear in the provisional instructions given to the Prophet in the previous *sūrah*: *"if you fear treachery from any folk, cast [your treaty with them] back to them in a fair manner. God does not love the treacherous."* (8: 58) However, the termination of treaties after four months or after their term was over might have appeared to those people contrary to the familiar practice of maintaining peaceful relations with those who did not adopt any hostile attitude. God, on the other hand, had a far greater objective than maintaining what was familiar practice.

Other people in the Muslim community, perhaps also among the noblest and most dedicated Muslims, might have felt that there was no longer any need to fight the idolaters generally after Islam had attained supremacy in Arabia, leaving only scattered pockets of resistance which represented no threat whatsoever. On the contrary, they were expected to change their attitude to Islam gradually after peace would have been maintained for sometime in Arabia. Such Muslims might have felt particularly uneasy about fighting against relatives and friends as well as people with whom they might have had social and economic relations. After all there was still hope that such people would still see the light of Islam without resorting to such a drastic measure. But God wanted faith to be the basic bond that united people in a cohesive community. He also wanted the Arabian Peninsula to be a secure base for Islam, as He was aware of the plots the Byzantines were preparing against the Muslim state. This will be explained later.

Yet others in the Muslim community, some of whom might have been among the noblest and most dedicated Muslims, might have feared economic depression ensuing from the disruption to business transactions in Arabia as a result of declaring war against all Arabian idolaters. That was bound to affect the pilgrimage season, particularly after it had been announced that no idolater would be allowed to go on pilgrimage after that year, and that idolaters would not be allowed to enter into mosques and places of worship. Such people's fears were made even greater by the fact that such a step was not particularly necessary. Its outcome could have been reached in a slower but more peaceful way. But, as we have said, God wanted the basic bond to unite people in the Muslim community to be the bond of faith, so that faith should be felt to have far greater weight than blood relationships, friendships and economic interests. He also wanted the Muslims to realize that He alone gave them all the provisions they had and was their only provider. The means they might have had to earn their living were not the only ones He could have granted them.

There were others in the Muslim community who lacked strength of faith, or were hesitant, or who were hypocrites, or who might have been among the large numbers who embraced Islam but had not yet fully absorbed its truth. Most of these feared the possibility of open warfare with the idolaters, the economic depression that might result from war, the lack of security for trade and travel, the disruption of contacts and transport and worried about the likely costs of mounting a *jihād* campaign. Such people might have not reckoned with such a prospect of full-scale war. They might have been encouraged to embrace Islam by the fact that it appeared victorious, and that it would have enjoyed security and stability. To them, embracing Islam might have seemed the best alternative that allowed them to gain much for a little outlay. Newcomers to Islam as they were, they felt ill at ease with what was required of them. God, on the other hand, wanted to test people's intentions and their commitment and determination. He says to the believers: *"Do you think that you will be left alone, unless God takes cognizance of those of you who strive hard for His cause and establish close association with none other than God, His Messenger and the believers? God is well aware of what you do."* (Verse 16)

All these aspects made it necessary to give a detailed account which employs various modes of expression and produces varied effects which are calculated to remove the traces of weakness in people's hearts and remove whatever doubts they might be entertaining. Hence the *sūrah* opens with a general announcement of disavowal by God and His Messenger of all dealings with the idolaters. The same disavowal is repeated another time, with similar forcefulness and clarity after only one verse in the *sūrah* so that no believer will entertain any thought of maintaining relations with such people when God and His Messenger are acquitting themselves of any dealings with them. *"Disavowal by God and His Messenger (is hereby announced) to those of the idolaters with whom you have made a treaty."* (Verse 1) *"And a proclamation from God and His Messenger is hereby made to all mankind on this day of the greater pilgrimage: God is free from obligation to the idolaters, and so is His Messenger."* (Verse 3)

The believers are also reassured while the unbelievers are threatened with misery and humiliation. Those who turn away are warned that they cannot escape God's judgement: *"You may go freely in the land for four months, but you must realize that you can never escape God's judgement, and that God shall bring disgrace upon the unbelievers."* (Verse 2) *"If you repent, it shall be for your own good; and if you turn away, then know that you can never escape God's judgement. Give the unbelievers the news of grievous suffering."* (Verse 3)

The very idea that idolaters may have a treaty with God and His Messenger is questioned, except for those who had shown true commitment in observing their treaty with honesty. With these the existing treaties were to be honoured for the rest of their terms, as long as the unbelievers remained faithful to them. The believers are warned, however, that the idolaters would try to do them harm whenever they could as also feeling that they would escape punishment. *"How can there be a treaty with God and His Messenger for the idolaters, unless it be those of them with whom you have made a treaty at the Sacred Mosque? So long as they are true to you, be true to them; for God loves those who are God-fearing. How [else could it be] when, should they prevail over you, they will respect neither agreement made with you, nor obligation of honour towards you? They try to please you with what they say, while at heart they remain adamantly hostile. Most of them are transgressors. They barter away God's revelations for a paltry price and debar others from His path. Evil indeed is what they do. They respect neither agreement nor obligation of honour with regard to any believer. Those indeed are the aggressors.* (Verses 7–10)

The believers are further reminded of their own bitter experiences with them, and their feelings of happiness at the crushing of their enemy by God's might. *"Will you not fight against people who have broken their solemn pledges and set out to drive out the Messenger, and who were the first to attack you? Do you fear them? It is God alone whom you should fear, if you are true believers. Fight them: God will punish them at your hands, and will bring disgrace upon them; and will grant you victory over them and will grant heart-felt satisfaction to those who are believers, removing all angry feelings from their hearts. God will turn in His mercy to whom He wills. God is All-knowing and Wise."* (Verses 13–15)

They are told that they must cut themselves off, as far as family relations with the unbelievers were concerned. They are required to weaken the effects of their family ties with the unbelievers. They are told to choose between those ties of blood and friendship on the one hand and God and His Messenger on the other. *"Believers, do not take your fathers and brothers for allies if they choose unbelief in preference to faith. Those of you who take them for allies are indeed wrongdoers. Say: 'If your fathers, your sons, your brothers, your spouses, your clan, and the property you have acquired, and the business in which you fear a decline, and the dwellings in which you take pleasure, are dearer to you than God and His Messenger and the struggle in His cause, then wait until God shall make manifest His will. God does not provide guidance to the evildoers.'"* (Verses 23–24)

They are also reminded of the numerous victories they achieved with God's help, the most recent of which was the Battle of Ḥunayn. They were able to achieve victory only when God provided them with His help and gave reassurance to His Messenger who remained steadfast: *"God has granted you His support on many a battlefield, and also in the Battle of Ḥunayn, when you took pride in your numerical strength, but it availed you nothing. For all its vastness, the earth seemed too narrow for you, and you turned back in flight. God then bestowed from on high an air of inner peace on His Messenger and on the believers, and He sent down forces whom you could not see, and punished those who disbelieved. Such is the reward for the unbelievers."* (Verses 25–26)

They are also reassured about their provisions, and that they should not fear any loss of trade or lack of business. What they get is subject to God's will, not to the apparent causes people associate with profitable business: *"Believers, know that the idolaters are certainly impure. So, let them not come near to the Sacred Mosque after this year is ended. If you fear poverty, then in time God will enrich you with His own bounty, if He so wills. Truly, God is All-knowing, Wise."* (Verse 28)

All these concerns which required reassurance and clear judgement are indicative of the situation that prevailed in the Muslim state in Madinah. Had it not been for the fact that the Muslim community in Madinah was firm in its belief, stable and enlightened, these conditions might have represented a serious threat to it, and to the very existence of Islam itself.

Having given this detailed preview, we now begin to discuss the verses of this passage in more detail.

An Announcement is Made

Disavowal by God and His Messenger [is hereby announced] to those of the idolaters with whom you have made a treaty. (Announce to them:) You may go freely in the land for four months, but you must realize that you can never escape God's judgement, and that God shall bring disgrace upon the unbelievers. And a proclamation from God and His Messenger is hereby made to all mankind on this day of the greater pilgrimage: God is free from obligation to the idolaters, and so is His Messenger. If you repent, it shall be for your own good; and if you turn away, then know that you can never escape God's judgement. Give the unbelievers the news of grievous suffering, except for those idolaters with whom you have made a treaty and who have honoured their obligations [under the treaty] in every detail, and have not aided anyone against you. To these fulfil your obligations until their treaties have run their term. God loves those who are righteous. When these months of grace are over, slay the idolaters wherever you find them, and take them captive, besiege them, and lie in wait for them at

57

*every conceivable place. Yet if they should repent, take to prayer and
pay the* zakāt, *let them go their way. For God is Much-Forgiving,
Merciful. If any of the idolaters seeks asylum with you, grant him
protection, so that he may hear the word of God, and then convey
him to his place of safety. That is because the idolaters are people
who lack knowledge.* (Verses 1–6)

These verses and the following ones, up to verse 28, provide a
framework demarcating relations between the Muslim community,
now well established in Madinah and the Arabian Peninsula generally,
and the unbelievers in Arabia who chose not to accept Islam. Relations
were thus regulated with those Arabs who had violated their treaties
with the Prophet when they felt that the Muslims were about to meet
their match from the Byzantines at Tabūk. Relations were also put on
a proper footing with those Arabs without a treaty but who maintained
good relations with the Muslims, and those who had a treaty which
they continued to observe, entertaining no thoughts of treachery.

The style employed in these verses takes the form of a general
declaration coupled with high resonance to ensure perfect harmony
between the subject matter, the general atmosphere surrounding the
whole issue and the mode of expression.

Several reports speak of the general conditions prevailing at the time
when this declaration was made, as well as the method and the person
chosen for its announcement. Perhaps the most accurate and more
fitting with the prevailing situation of the Muslim community and
the nature of the Islamic approach is the one chosen by Ibn Jarīr al-
Ṭabarī, an early commentator on the Qur'ān. We will quote here some
of his comments on the various reports which support our view of the
event and how it took place. The following report he attributes to
Mujāhid:

> In the statement, *'Disavowal by God and His Messenger [is hereby
> announced] to those of the idolaters with whom you have made a
> treaty,'* the reference is made to the tribe of Mudlij and the Arabs
> bound by a treaty with the Muslims and all other peoples with
> similar treaties. It is reported that when the Prophet returned from
> Tabūk, he wanted to go on pilgrimage. He then thought, 'the

Ka'bah is visited by idolaters who do the *ṭawāf* naked. I would rather delay my pilgrimage until such a practice is stopped.' He sent Abū Bakr and 'Alī who went to see people at Dhu'l-Majāz and other markets, as well as their encampments in pilgrimage. They gave notice to all peoples who had treaties with the Prophet that they would have four months of peace. When those four consecutive months, beginning with the twenty days remaining of Dhu'l-Ḥijjah to the tenth day of Rabī' II, were over, the treaties would come to an end. All people in Arabia would then be in a state of war with the Muslims unless they believed in God and His Messenger. All the population of Arabia became Muslims and none continued with their old religion.[9]

Examining the views of other commentators, Imām al-Ṭabarī says:

As for the notice given by God permitting idolaters with a treaty to '*go freely in the land for four months,*' perhaps the more accurate view is to say that this notice is given by God to those idolaters who, despite having peace treaties, collaborated with others against the Prophet and the Muslim community violating their treaties before they ran out. As for those who fulfilled their obligations under such treaties and refrained from collaborating with others, God – limitless is He in His glory – ordered His Messenger to honour his treaty with them until their term had been completed. This is clear in the Qur'ānic statement: "*Except for those idolaters with whom you have made a treaty and who have honoured their obligations [under that treaty] in every detail, and have not aided anyone against you. To these fulfil your obligations until their treaties have run their term. God loves those who are righteous.*" (Verse 4)

Some people may feel differently, taking the order to mean that once the truce was over, the Muslims were meant to kill all unbelievers. They may quote in support of their view the next verse which states: '*When these months of grace are over, slay the*

---

9. Al-Ṭabarī, op.cit., p. 62.

idolaters wherever you find them.' (Verse 5) But this view is wrong. Verse 7 confirms our view and shows the opposite as wrong: *'How can there be a treaty with God and His Messenger for the idolaters, unless it be those of them with whom you have made a treaty at the Sacred Mosque? So long as they are true to you, be true to them; for God loves those who are God-fearing.'* Those people to whom this verse refers are idolaters, and God commands the Prophet and the believers to remain faithful to their treaty with them as long as they kept their part and fulfilled their obligations.

Numerous are the reports which confirm that when the Prophet sent 'Alī to declare the disavowal of treaties to people, he also commanded him to make it clear that "whoever had a treaty with the Prophet, that treaty continued until its specified expiration date." This provides the clearest support of our view. God did not order the Prophet to terminate a treaty with any group of people who remained faithful to it. He only put on four-month notice those who had violated their treaties and those whose treaties had no specified term. The treaties which ran for a specific term and were observed properly by the other side were to remain in force until their term was over. The Prophet sent his Companions to announce this during the pilgrimage, for this would ensure the announcement was well publicized.[10]

In another comment on the various reports concerning treaties, al-Ṭabarī says:

The four-month notice was made to those whom we have mentioned. As for those whose treaties specified a term of expiry, God did not allow the Prophet and the believers to terminate such treaty in any way. Hence, the Prophet fulfilled God's order and honoured his commitments under these treaties to their final dates. This is clearly stated in God's revelations, and confirmed by many reports attributed to the Prophet.[11]

---

10. Al-Ṭabarī, ibid., pp. 62–63.
11. Al-Ṭabarī, ibid., p. 66.

If we discard the reports which are doubtful and overlook those which might have been coloured by the political differences between the Shiah and the Sunnis, we may say with confidence that the Prophet sent Abū Bakr as the leader of pilgrimage that year. The reason for that was that the Prophet did not like to perform the pilgrimage when the idolaters continued with their abominable practice of doing the *tawāf*, or the ritual walk around the Ka'bah in the nude. After Abū Bakr had left for pilgrimage, the opening passage of this *sūrah*, Repentance, was revealed. The Prophet despatched 'Alī to join Abū Bakr and make the declaration. He did this outlining all its final provisions at the gathering which ensured that all people in Arabia would be aware of them. Among these provisions was the one which made it clear that no idolater would be allowed in Makkah to do the *tawāf* or the pilgrimage.

Al-Tirmidhī relates a report which quotes 'Alī as saying: "God's Messenger sent me after the revelation of the *sūrah* Repentance to announce four points: no one may do the *tawāf* naked, and no idolater may come near the Sacred Mosque after that year, and whoever had a treaty with God's Messenger, their treaty would be observed until it had expired, and that no one may enter heaven except one who submits totally to God." This report is the most authentic in this connection.

The Principles of International Relations

"Disavowal by God and His Messenger [is hereby announced] to those of the idolaters with whom you have made a treaty." (Verse 1) This is a general declaration, carrying a sharp rhythm, which outlines the basic principles that governed relations between the Muslims and the idolaters at the time, throughout the Arabian Peninsula. The treaties to which it refers were those that the Prophet had concluded with the idolaters in Arabia. The disavowal of these treaties by God and His Messenger defines the attitude of every Muslim. It generates a very strong impression on Muslim minds to leave no room whatsoever for hesitation or second thought.

This general statement is followed by qualifications and explanations: *"[Announce to them:] You may go freely in the land for four months, but you must realize that you can never escape God's judgement, and that God shall bring disgrace upon the unbelievers."* (Verse 2) This statement clarifies the terms now given to the unbelievers: they are given a period of four months during which they can move about freely to carry out business transactions, fulfil their commitments and modify their situations in peace. Those were four months when they would be sure that their treaties would be scrupulously honoured. That included even those idolaters who were quick to violate their treaties, when they felt that the Prophet and his followers would never return from their expedition to Tabūk, but would instead be taken captive by the Byzantines. That was also the eventuality expected by the hypocrites in Madinah.

It is pertinent to ask here: when was this notice outlining this period of truce and security given? It followed a long period of treaty violations by the unbelievers, whenever they felt that they could get away with it and remain immune from punishment. It came after a long series of events which showed clearly that the idolaters would continue to fight the Muslims until they had turned them away from their faith, if they could. At what period in history was it announced? It was at a time when humanity was governed by the law of the jungle. What dictated relations between communities was merely the ability to invade others: no notice was given, no hint was dropped, no commitment was considered binding. Once the opportunity was there, it was taken mercilessly.

Islam maintains the same position it adopted at the outset, when it was first revealed. Its constitution is outlined by God and its principles and foundations are not meant to be influenced or modified by the passage of time. Time allows human beings to develop and improve their conditions within the framework of Islamic principles. Islam deals with changing human conditions using appropriate methods.

With this four-month notice period, the idolaters are reminded of God's will which in turn sends fear into their hearts. They are meant to open their eyes to the fact that they can never escape God's judgement. They cannot seek refuge against what God has determined for them, which was certain disgrace and humiliation: *"You must realize that you can never escape God's judgement, and that God shall bring disgrace upon the unbelievers."* (Verse 2) How could they escape God's judgement and what refuge could they seek when they, and the whole world, were in His grasp? He has predetermined to inflict misery and disgrace on the unbelievers. No power can ever stop God's will.

This is followed by specifying the time when this disavowal was to be announced to the unbelievers, so that they would be fully aware of the time limits it included: *"And a proclamation from God and His Messenger is hereby made to all mankind on this day of the greater pilgrimage: God is free from obligation to the idolaters, and so is His Messenger. If you repent, it shall be for your own good; and if you turn away, then know that you can never escape God's judgement. Give the unbelievers the news of grievous suffering."* (Verse 3)

Reports vary on which is the day of the greater pilgrimage: the day of 'Arafāt or the day of sacrifice? It is perhaps more accurate to say that it is the day of sacrifice. The Arabic term used in this passage for 'proclamation' signifies an assurance that those to whom the proclamation is made have received it. This properly took place during the pilgrimage, when the disavowal by God and His Messenger of all treaties with all idolaters was made. An exception was then added in the next verse which allowed certain treaties to run their term. This is most appropriate. First the general principle is outlined because it is the one which constitutes the permanent situation. Then the exception is made because it applied to specific cases that would end once the term specified had been reached.

With the termination of all treaties and the proclamation of absolute disavowal, the unbelievers are encouraged once again to seek and follow divine guidance and warned against the consequences of remaining in error: *"If you repent, it shall be for your own good; and if you turn away, then know that you can never escape God's judgement. Give the unbelievers the news of grievous suffering."* (Verse 3)

This warning and encouragement to the unbelievers to mend their ways, coming as they do in this particular context of disavowal of treaties, are indicative of the Islamic approach. It is first and foremost an approach seeking to give guidance to people. The idolaters are given this four-month grace period not only because Islam does not like to take them by surprise but also because it does not want to inflict on them unnecessary humiliation. These have always been the essence of power relations, except under Islam. The truce also gives the idolaters a chance to reflect and reconsider their options. Hence they are encouraged to choose divine guidance and turn back to God in submission. They are warned against turning away and shown that it will inevitably lead them to a position of grievous suffering in the hereafter, which compounds their humiliation in this life.

At the same time it provides reassurance to the Muslims which removes any lingering worries or fears of what may happen. The whole matter has been determined by God Himself. The eventual outcome has been sealed.

Honouring Commitments

The exception is then made in the case of treaties specifying a term of validity. These were allowed to remain in force for the rest of their term: *"Except for those idolaters with whom you have made a treaty and who have honoured their obligations [under the treaty] in every detail, and have not aided anyone against you. To these fulfil your obligations until their treaties have run their term. God loves those who are righteous."* (Verse 4)

Perhaps the most accurate report concerning the identity of those people who benefited by this exception is that they were a clan of Bakr, named the Khuzaymah ibn 'Āmir clan of the Bakr ibn Kinānah tribe. They were party to the Treaty of al-Ḥudaybiyah which the Prophet had concluded with the Quraysh and their allies. This clan did not take part in the attack made by the Bakr against the Khuzā'ah tribe. That aggression, in which the Bakr were aided by the Quraysh, violated the al-Ḥudaybiyah peace treaty. Thus, that treaty which was to last for ten years, was treacherously breached after only two years. This Khuzaymah clan continued to observe the terms of their agreement while other unbelievers did not. The Prophet is here instructed to honour his obligations under the treaty to those people for the rest of the term agreed.

This report which we endorse is related by Muḥammad ibn 'Abbād ibn Ja'far, who quotes al-Suddī as saying: "These were two clans of Kinānah known as Ḍamrah and Mudlij." Mujāhid, an authoritative early scholar says: "The tribes of Mudlij and Khuzā'ah had entered into treaties and these were the ones meant in the instruction: *"To these fulfil your obligations until their treaties have run their term. God loves those who are righteous."* (Verse 4) It should be noted, however, that the Khuzāʻah tribe embraced Islam after the conquest of Makkah, but this statement of exception applied to the idolaters who did not accept Islam.

Our view is confirmed by a statement that follows: *"How can there be a treaty with God and His Messenger for the idolaters, unless it be those of them with whom you have made a treaty at the Sacred Mosque? So long as they are true to you, be true to them; for God loves those who are God-fearing."* (Verse 7) These two clans from Kinānah were among those who were party to the peace treaty at al-Ḥudaybiyah. They did not violate their treaty and were true to their obligations under it, aiding no party against the Muslims. It is to these, then, that the exception applies, as confirmed by early scholars and commentators on the Qur'ān, and by Shaikh Muḥammad Rashīd Riḍā.

Muḥammad ʻIzzat Darwazah, however, expresses his opinion that the phrase, *'with whom you have made a treaty at the Sacred Mosque,'* refers to a group of people other than those mentioned in the first exception. This is in line with his view which permits the negotiating and concluding of permanent treaties with idolaters. Relying on the instruction, *"so long as they are true to you, be true to them,"* he concludes that Islam does not object to the negotiation of treaties with unbelievers. This view seems extremely odd and does not fit with the nature of the Islamic method of operation and general attitudes.

Islam has honoured its obligations to those who were true to theirs. It did not give them notice of termination, as it did with all others. It allowed their treaties to run their term in recognition of their faithful observance of their obligations. This was the Islamic attitude, although Islam was in urgent need of eradicating all idolatry from the whole of Arabia, so that the Peninsula could become its safe base. The enemies of Islam in neighbouring countries were alerted to the danger to themselves that Islam represented. They began to make preparations for an eventual encounter with the Muslims, as we will explain in our discussion of the Tabūk Expedition. Indeed, the earlier Battle of Muʼtah served as a warning of the preparations the Byzantines had started for a battle with Islam. Moreover, they were in alliance with the Persians in Yemen, in southern Arabia.

Subsequent events, as mentioned by Ibn al-Qayyim, witnessed that all those in whose favour the exception was made and with whom treaties were to be observed embraced Islam before their treaties expired. Indeed the others who were keen to violate their treaties as well as the rest of those put on four-month notice also opted for acceptance of Islam. No one remained an idolater for the rest of the four-month notice.

As He determined the path of the Islamic message and the various steps it would take in practical matters, God was aware that it was time for this decisive step which represented a final attack at the roots of idolatry. Suitable preparations were made for such a decisive step, which took place in accordance with God's design for the progress of His message.

It is important to reflect on the comment which concludes the verse that requires the Muslims to remain true to their obligations: *"To these fulfil your obligations until their treaties have run their term. God loves those who are righteous."* (Verse 4) It relates the fulfilment of obligations to righteousness and to God's love of the righteous. Thus, God makes the fulfilment of obligations to people an act of worship addressed to Him and an aspect of the righteousness He loves. This is the basis of Islamic ethics. Islam does not act on the basis of gain and interest, or on the basis of constantly changing traditions. All Islamic ethics are based on worshipping God and fearing Him, which is the essence of righteousness. A Muslim brings his behaviour in line with that which he knows to please God. His aim is to win God's pleasure and to ensure that He is not displeased with him. This is the essence of the strong hold Islamic ethics have on Muslims. These ethics also serve people's interests and work for their benefit. They establish a society in which friction and contradiction are reduced as much as possible. They also help human beings in their continuous march to a higher standard of humanity.

When the Period of Grace is Over

Thus the opening verses of the *sūrah* make it clear that God and His Messenger would have no dealings whatsoever with the idolaters, whether or not they had a treaty with the Prophet. They were given a four-month period of grace in which they were safe. When this period was over, treaties would continue to be observed to the end of their terms, but only with those who were true to their obligations under those treaties, and did not collaborate with any enemy of the Muslims. Now the *sūrah* mentions what the Muslims were to do when the four-month grace period was over.

The Qur'ānic instruction is very clear. A state of all-out war was then to be declared: "*When these months of grace are over, slay the idolaters wherever you find them, and take them captive, besiege them, and lie in wait for them at every conceivable place. Yet if they should repent, take to prayer and pay the* zakāt, *let them go their way. For God is Much-forgiving, Merciful.*" (Verse 5)

The word which is used here to describe those four months in the Qur'ānic text is '*ḥurum*', which is the one that describes the four months when fighting is not allowed except to repel aggression. These form two periods every year when people can go freely, secure from any danger of war. Because of the same usage scholars have disagreed in their interpretations of this statement here, on whether the four months meant the same ones observed annually, i.e. Dhu'l-Qa'dah, Dhu'l-Ḥijjah, Muḥarram and Rajab. In that case, the remaining period of grace given after the declaration of the termination of treaties would only be the rest of Dhu'l-Ḥijjah and Muḥarram, i.e. 50 days. Or were these four months, when fighting was forbidden, to start on the day of sacrifice and to end on 10 Rabī' II? A third point of view suggests that the first interpretation applies in the case of those who had violated their treaties and the second applies to those who did not have any treaty and those who had treaties with an unspecified duration.

The correct interpretation, in our view, is that the four months meant here are different from the four sacred months observed annually. The same description is given to both because fighting during them is forbidden. This new period of grace also applied to all, except in the case of those who had treaties lasting for a specified length of time, in which case such treaties were to be honoured in full. Since God has said to them: "*You may go freely in the land for four months,*" then the four months must start from the day when the announcement was made to them. This fits with the nature of this announcement.

God's instructions to the Muslims were clear: when the four months were over, they were to kill any idolater wherever he was found, or they were to take him captive, or besiege him if he was in a fortified place, or lie in wait for him so that he could not escape without punishment, except for those to whom obligations were to be observed for as long as their treaties remained in force. Indeed the idolaters were given enough notice, which meant that they were not taken by surprise. Nor did they fall victim to any treachery. Their treaties were terminated publicly and they were made fully aware of what was to be done with them.

Moreover, this was not meant as a campaign of vengeance or extermination, but rather as a warning which provided a motive for them to accept Islam. *"If they should repent, take to prayer and pay the* zakāt, *let them go their way. For God is Much-Forgiving, Merciful."* (Verse 5) For 22 years they had been listening to the message of Islam put to them in the clearest possible way. For 22 years they were, nevertheless, trying to suppress the message of Islam by persecution, open warfare and forging alliances to destroy the Islamic state. This was a long history that contrasted with the never failing tolerance of Islam, as demonstrated by God's Messenger and his Companions. Nevertheless, Islam was now opening its arms to them. Instructions are here issued to the Prophet and the Muslims, the very victims of persecution who were driven out of their homeland and suffered a war of aggression, to extend a hand of welcome to those idolaters should they turn to God in repentance. Such repentance should be genuine, confirmed by their observance of the main duties of Islam. That is because God never rejects anyone who turns to Him in sincere repentance, no matter how great his sins are: *"For God is Much-forgiving, Merciful."* (Verse 5)

We do not here want to go into any of the arguments which are frequently found in books of commentary on the Qur'ān or Islamic jurisprudence, i.e. *fiqh*, concerning the proviso mentioned in this verse: *"If they should repent, take to prayer and pay the* zakāt, *let them go their way."* (Verse 5) These arguments discuss whether these are the essential conditions of being a Muslim, in the sense that a person who does not observe them is considered an unbeliever. They also discuss whether these are sufficient for the acceptance of anyone who declares repentance without going into the other basic duties of

Islam. We do not feel this verse is concerned with any such argument. Rather, it simply tackles a real situation involving the idolaters in Arabia at the time. None of these would have declared their repentance, prayed regularly and paid the *zakāt* without the full intention of submitting themselves to God and being Muslims in the full sense of the word. Hence the Qur'ānic verse specifies the declaration of repentance, regular prayers and *zakāt* payment as a mark of the acceptance of Islam in full with all its conditions and significance. The first of these is naturally the submission to God by declaring one's belief that there is no deity other than God and belief in the Prophet Muḥammad's message by declaring that Muḥammad is God's Messenger. This verse is not, then, about making any rulings on legal matters, but it outlines practical steps to deal with a particular situation where certain circumstances applied.

Asylum for the Enemy

Yet despite the declaration of war against all the idolaters after the four months are over, Islam continues to demonstrate its grace as well as its serious and realistic approach. It does not seek to exterminate all idolaters. On the contrary, it also declares a campaign of guidance whenever that is possible. Individual idolaters who are not part of a hostile and belligerent community are guaranteed safety in the land of Islam. God instructs His Messenger to give them asylum so that they may listen to God's word and become aware of the nature of the Islamic message before they are given safe conduct to their own domiciles. All this, even though they are still idolaters: *"If any of the idolaters seeks asylum with you, grant him protection, so that he may hear the word of God, and then convey him to his place of safety. That is because the idolaters are people who lack knowledge."* (Verse 6)

This shows how Islam was keen to reach out to every heart with its guidance. No single case was to be taken lightly. Whoever appeals for protection shall be granted it. Anyone who seeks such asylum cannot at the same time try to join a hostile force seeking to undermine the Muslim community. Hence granting protection to such a person provides him with the opportunity to listen to the Qur'ān and to get to know the true nature of the Islamic faith. When God's word is heard in such an atmosphere, hearts may well respond positively. Even if they do not, the Muslims are still required to ensure the safety of anyone who appeals for their help until he is returned to a place where he feels secure.

This is one of the sublime heights to which Islam raises its community. Protection is provided for an idolater, an enemy who might have participated in persecution of the Muslims themselves. Now they are required to give him safe conduct until he has reached a place where he feels secure outside the Muslim state. This is a mark of the Islamic method of action. It is a method of guidance, and guidance remains its ultimate goal even when its efforts are concentrated on the protection of the land of Islam.

Yet some people claim that the purpose of Islamic *jihād* was to compel people to accept Islam. There are others who try to defend Islam against such a charge by claiming that *jihād* was merely a war of self defence within national borders. Both need to look at this great instruction given to the Prophet and the Muslim community: *"If any of the idolaters seeks asylum with you, grant him protection, so that he may hear the word of God, and then convey him to his place of safety. That is because the idolaters are people who lack knowledge."* (Verse 6)

This religion seeks to provide knowledge to those who lack such knowledge, and to give protection to whoever appeals for protection, even though they may belong to the enemy camp and who might have fought to suppress the Islamic message. It resorts to the use of force only to destroy physical forces that prevent people from listening to God's word and stop them from knowing what He has revealed. Such forces deprive them of the chance to follow God's guidance and force them into submission to beings other than God. When such physical forces have been destroyed and impediments have been removed, individuals are given protection, despite choosing to remain unbelievers. Islam only informs them of God's word without subjecting them to fear or pressure, and grants them protection and security, the fact that they continue to reject God's message notwithstanding.

There are countless regimes extant today where the dissenter has no sense of security for his life, property, honour or human rights. Yet people who see this taking place in front of their own eyes try to defend Islam against this false charge by distorting the image of the divine message. They try to portray Islam as nothing more than a passive message that confronts swords and guns with nothing more than words, whether in our own time or at any other time.

This is, then, an outline of the final rulings that determine the relations between the Muslim community and the remaining idolaters in Arabia. They mean an end to the state based on peace agreements with all idolaters, after four months in some cases and at the end of their specified terms in others. The eventual outcome of these rulings is that there will only be one of two situations: either repentance, mending of ways, attending to prayers and payment of *zakāt*, which in essence means the acceptance of Islam, or fighting idolaters, taking them captive and chasing them out of their hiding places.

This termination of the state of peace based on treaties and agreements is followed by a rhetorical question stating that it is just not possible that idolaters should have such covenants with God and His Messenger. The very principle of having such agreements is rejected outright: *"How can there be a treaty with God and His Messenger for the idolaters?"* (Verse 7)

This outright denunciation, coming as it does in the verses that follow the opening ones, may be understood to abrogate the first rulings which allowed the continued observance of treaties with those who fulfilled their obligations under those rulings and did not provide any assistance to any group hostile to the Muslim community. In order to dispel any such misunderstanding, the ruling is restated once more: *"Unless it be those of them with whom you have made a treaty at the Sacred Mosque? So long as they are true to you, be true to them; for God loves those who are God-fearing."* (Verse 7)

This restatement adds a new provision. The first instruction required the Muslims to honour their obligations to those who had shown their true commitment to their peace agreements and fulfilled their own obligations under such agreements. Now the instruction to keep faith with them is qualified, making it clear that the Muslims were to honour their obligations to them for as long as they themselves continued to observe their treaties in full, as they did in the past. Here we note the careful phraseology of texts relating to dealings, transactions and relations with others. Implicit understanding is not sufficient. It is followed by a clear statement.

Considering the different aspects that prevailed in the Muslim community at the time and the way this decisive step was likely to be received by the Muslim community, the *sūrah* reminds the Muslims of the true nature of the idolaters, their feelings, intentions and attitudes towards the Muslims. We are told by God Himself that the idolaters will never respect an agreement or honour an obligation or observe a moral value or a tradition once they are sure they can get away with such treachery. Hence, they cannot be trusted to honour their obligations. The only way is for them to accept Islam and show their commitment to it.

No Peace Possible

"How can there be a treaty with God and His Messenger for the idolaters?" (Verse 7) The idolaters do not submit themselves truly to God, nor do they acknowledge His Messenger or the message he conveys to them. How could they, then, have a treaty with God and His Messenger? They do not simply deny a creature like themselves, or a constitution devised by human beings. Rather, they deny the One who has created them and continues to provide them with sustenance to preserve their lives. By so doing they place themselves in opposition to God and His Messenger. How is it conceivable, then, that they should have a treaty with them? The rhetorical question posed by the *sūrah* addresses the very principle of having such a treaty. It is not concerned with any particular application of the principle.

It may be said here that some of the idolaters had such treaties and God ordered that some of these treaties must be honoured. There were also treaties concluded after the establishment of the Muslim state in Madinah, some of which were with the idolaters and some with the Jews. Moreover, the peace agreement of al-Ḥudaybiyah was signed in the sixth year of the Islamic calendar. Earlier *sūrahs* included verses that clearly permitted such treaties, although they also permitted the termination of such treaties in case of surmised or actual treachery. So if it is the very principle of having agreements that is condemned here, how was it possible that such treaties were permitted and concluded?

Such an argument does not stand when we understand the nature of the Islamic method of operation, which we discussed in the introductions to this *sūrah* and the preceding one, The Spoils of War. These treaties dealt with existing situations with adequate means. The final ruling, however, is that the idolaters should not have any treaty with God and His Messenger. These treaties were made under provisional rulings. Otherwise, the ultimate goal of the movement which aims to establish Islam is that there should not be any idolatry on the face of the earth. All submission must be to God alone. Islam has declared this ultimate goal from the very first day, deceiving no one. The prevailing circumstances in a certain period made it necessary to conclude a peace agreement with those who wanted peace so that it could deal with those hostile forces trying to suppress its message. Islam does not lose sight of its ultimate goal. It does not overlook the fact that the idolaters themselves looked at those agreements as only temporary. They were bound to launch new aggressions against the Muslim community. They would not leave the Muslims alone when they were aware of the aim of Islam. They would not remain at peace with the Muslim community for long when they had completed their preparations for a new confrontation. God said to the believers right at the beginning: *"They shall not cease to fight you until they force you to renounce your faith, if they can."* (2: 217) This continues to be their attitude at all times. The verse describes a permanent situation, not one that applies in certain circumstances.

Although the principle itself is denounced, God has permitted the honouring of treaties with those who continued to honour their obligations. He only made the proviso that this should be reciprocated, which means that treaties were to be honoured by the Muslims as long as the idolaters continued to honour them: *"Unless it be those of them with whom you have made a treaty at the Sacred Mosque? So long as they are true to you, be true to them; for God loves those who are God-fearing."* (Verse 7)

Unlike what some contemporary commentators have understood, those people who had a treaty signed at the Sacred Mosque were the same group as they to whom reference was made earlier in the *sūrah*: *"Except for those idolaters with whom you have made a treaty and who have honoured their obligations (under the treaty) in every detail, and have not aided anyone against you. To these fulfil your obligations until their treaties have run their term. God loves those who are righteous."*

(Verse 4) The two verses refer to the same group. However, the first reference makes an exception in their case as opposed to all those whose treaties are terminated. They are mentioned again in verse 7, in connection with the denunciation of the principle of making peace agreements with idolaters. Their second mention is necessary to make it clear that there is no abrogation of the first ruling in their favour. The righteous and the God-fearing are mentioned on both occasions, using the same Arabic word for both, and highlighting the fact that God loves those who are righteous and God-fearing, to indicate that the subject matter is the same. The second statement completes the conditions stated earlier. In the first, their past attitude of honouring their obligations is mentioned, and in the second the condition of their continued observance of these obligations is made clear. The careful phraseology requires that both statements are taken together to grasp the meaning in full.

The principle of making peace with the idolaters is then denounced on historical and practical grounds, after it had been denounced on grounds of faith. Both sets of reasons are grouped together in the verses that follow: *"How (else could it be) when, should they prevail over you, they will respect neither agreement made with you, nor obligation of honour towards you? They try to please you with what they say, while at heart they remain adamantly hostile. Most of them are transgressors. They barter away God's revelations for a paltry price and debar others from His path. Evil indeed is what they do. They respect neither agreement nor obligation of honour with regard to any believer. Those indeed are the aggressors."* (Verses 8–10)

How is it conceivable that the idolaters should have a covenant with God and His Messenger when they do not make any agreement with you unless they are unable to overcome you? Should they prevail over you, they would subject you to their wrath, observing no agreement, honouring no commitment and heeding no moral or ethical value. They would respect no pledge and allow no limit in the punishment they would inflict on you if only they could prevail against you in war. They would not even respect the values of their own society, risking any criticism they might incur for not abiding by these limits. No matter what agreements they may have with you, their blind hatred of you causes them to trespass all limits and violate all commitments, if only they can prevail over you. What prevents them from doing that now is not the sort of agreements they have with you. They are only prevented by the fact that they cannot achieve victory over you in battle. Now that you are too strong for them, they try to please you with what they say and by showing that they are true to their commitments. But in truth, their hearts are full of grudges against you. With such heart-burning animosity, they will always wish you ill. They have no desire to be in a relation of friendship with you and they harbour no good intention towards you.

No Obligation Honoured

"*Most of them are transgressors. They barter away God's revelations for a paltry price and debar others from His path. Evil indeed is what they do.*" (Verses 8–9) There is a basic reason for their treacherous attitude: that they are transgressors who have deviated widely from God's guidance. They have bartered away God's revelations for a paltry price in the shape of fleeting pleasures and temporary comforts. They fear that adopting Islam will deny them some or all of these interests or that it may involve some financial cost. Hence they do not merely refuse to accept Islam, but they also try to debar others from its path. This is, then, the result of the deal they made when they exchanged God's message for a paltry price. Hence, they turn away from God's path and debar others from following it. What they do is evil indeed, as God Himself states: "*Evil indeed is what they do.*" (Verse 9)

The grudge they harbour is not directed against you personally, nor are their evil actions levelled at you as individuals or a particular group. Their grudge is against every believer, and their evil deeds shall always be levelled against every Muslim. It is an animosity directed at the very quality of faith, or indeed against faith itself. This has always been the case with the enemies of faith, in all periods of history. Thus said the sorcerers to Pharaoh when he threatened them with torture, vengeance and a woeful doom: "*You want to take vengeance on us only because we have believed in the signs of our Lord when they were shown to us.*" (7: 126) The same was said by the Prophet, on God's instructions, to the people of earlier revelations who opposed him: "*Say: People of earlier revelations! Do you find fault with us for any reason other than we believe*

75

in God alone?" (5: 59) In reference to the People of the Pit who in former times burned the believers with their women and children, God says: *"They took vengeance on them for no reason other than that they believed in God, the Almighty, the Praised One."* (85: 8)

Faith is then the cause of all their hatred for the believers. Hence their ill-will and atrocities are directed against every believer: *"They respect neither agreement nor obligation of honour with regard to any believer. Those indeed are the aggressors."* (Verse 10) It is in their nature that they are aggressors. Their aggression begins with their hatred of the divine faith and their rejection of its message. It is their aggression that leads them to stand in opposition to faith and adopt a hostile attitude to the believers, respecting no treaty or obligation of honour. Hence, should they prevail and feel that they can get away with what they want, they will resort to any atrocity without limit.

God then gives His instructions on how the believers should react to this state of affairs: *"Yet, if they repent, take to prayers and pay the zakāt, they are your brethren in faith. Clear do We make Our revelations to people of knowledge. But if they break their pledges after having concluded a treaty with you, and revile your religion, then fight these archetypes of faithlessness who have no [respect for a] binding pledge, so that they may desist."* (Verses 11–12)

In view of such a long history as well as the nature of the inevitable battle between God's message, which seeks to free mankind from subjugation by other creatures in order that they submit to God alone, and *jāhiliyyah* systems which seek to make some people tyrannize over others, God gives a very clear and decisive directive to the Muslims: *"Yet, if they repent, take to prayers and pay the zakāt, they are your brethren in faith. Clear do We make Our revelations to people of knowledge. But if they break their pledges after having concluded a treaty with you, and revile your religion, then fight these archetypes of faithlessness who have no respect for a binding pledge, so that they may desist."* (Verses 11–12)

The choice before them, then, is clear. They may accept what the Muslims have accepted and repent of whatever aggression and transgression they have committed. In this case, the Muslims will forgive them for whatever they might have committed against them in the past. A new relationship will then be established which makes these new Muslims brothers of the older Muslims and the past is forgiven and forgotten altogether: *"Clear do We make Our revelations to people of knowledge."* (Verse 11) These rulings are best appreciated and acted upon by the people of knowledge who are the believers.

Having made pledges and concluded a treaty with the believers, the other choice they had was to violate their pledges and speak ill of the Islamic faith. In such a situation they would assume the leadership of disbelief and faithlessness. No treaty would be valid in their favour and no obligation to them need be respected. The Muslims are required then to fight them, for they may, perchance, reflect on their situation and see the truth for what it is. As we have already said, the strength of the Islamic camp and its success in *jihād* may influence people to recognize its truth. They would thus see that the truth is triumphant because of its being the truth and because it relies on God's power and support. They would recognize that the Prophet (peace be upon him) was only saying the truth when he told them that God, and His Messenger, are overpowering. That should lead them to repentance for their past misdeeds and a resolve to follow divine guidance, not by force and compulsion, but through conviction that often comes as a result of seeing the truth triumphant.

An Attitude Confirmed by History

It is now pertinent to ask: to what stages of history and to what communities do these statements apply? What sort of historical and social dimensions apply to them? Are they valid only in the case of Arabia at the time of revelation? Or do they extend to other times and places? These verses reflect a situation that prevailed at the time in Arabia between the Muslims and the camp of idolatry. There is no doubt that the rulings they outline deal with that situation; the idolaters they mention are those in Arabia at that particular time. All this is true; but how far are they applicable and in which situations? In order to answer these questions, we need to review the attitudes idolaters have adopted towards the believers throughout history.

As for the Arabian stage, the events that took place during the lifetime of the Prophet are sufficient to give us a clear answer. In our commentary on this *sūrah* alone we have enough information to describe the attitude of the idolaters towards this religion and its followers ever since its early days in Makkah up to the time of the revelation of these verses. It is true that the later and much longer-lasting conflict was between Islam on the one hand and the Jews and Christians on the other, rather than between Islam and idolatry. Nevertheless, the idolaters have always adopted the same attitude towards Muslims as described in these verses: *"How [else could it be] when, should they prevail over you, they will respect neither agreement made with you, nor obligation of honour towards you? They try to please you with what they say, while at heart they remain adamantly hostile. Most of them are transgressors. They barter away God's revelations for a paltry price and debar others from His path. Evil indeed is what they do. They respect neither agreement nor obligation of honour with regard to any believer. Those indeed are the aggressors."* (Verses 8–10) As for the people of earlier revelations, i.e. the Jews and Christians, and their attitude towards the Muslims, this will be discussed at length in Chapter 2 of this volume. We need to reflect now on the history of the idolaters with the Muslims.

If we consider that Islam, which is the faith based on the principle of submission to God alone, concluded, rather than started, with the message of the Prophet Muḥammad, we are bound to recognize that the attitude of idolaters towards every one of God's Messengers and to divine messages reflects the attitude of idolatry towards faith. This should place matters in the right perspective. We see this attitude for what it is in reality, as truthfully described in these Qur'ānic verses. It is an attitude that we recognize in all periods of history.

What did the idolaters do to those noble prophets and messengers: Noah, Hūd, Ṣāliḥ, Abraham, Shu'ayb, Moses, Jesus, (peace be upon them all), each in his own time? And what did they do to the Prophet Muḥammad and his followers? They certainly respected no agreement or obligation of honour, until they had been overcome. Again, what did the idolaters do to the Muslims in the second great campaign mounted against Islam, when the banner of idolatry was this time hoisted by the Tartars? Even today, fourteen centuries after the revelation of these verses, what is being done to the Muslims by the idolaters and the atheists everywhere? They simply do what the Qur'ān states: *"They respect neither agreement nor obligation of honour with regard to any believer."* (Verse 10)

When the Tartars won victory over the Muslims in Baghdad, an unprecedented massacre took place. We will mention here only a brief account of what is recorded by the historian Ibn Kathīr in his book, *al-Bidāyah wa'l-Nihāyah,* as he describes the events of the year 656 H. (1258 CE):

> When the Tartars descended on the city of Baghdad, they killed whomever they met of men, women and children, young and old. Many people tried to hide in wells, rubbish dumps and sewers, where they stayed for several days. Some people locked themselves in inns and guesthouses, but the Tartars broke into every such house, and chased the people they found there to the roofs where they killed them. Gutters and alleys were overflowing with blood, and so were mosques and other places of worship. The only survivors were the Jews and the Christians in the city and those who sought refuge with them, and those who were given shelter in the house of Ibn al-ʿAlqamī, the Shiʿite minister. A group of businessmen were also spared and given safety after they had paid large sums of money for the purpose. Baghdad, which used to be the most friendly and peaceful of cities, was totally in ruin, inhabited only by a small portion of its original population, and even these were living in fear, hunger and humiliation.
>
> Reports on the number of the Muslims killed in Baghdad in this battle vary, with some estimating the dead to be eight hundred thousands, while other reports suggest the dead numbered a million, and still others putting the estimate at two million people. We can only say what Muslims are recommended to say at the time of a calamity: *"To God we belong and to Him do we return... All power belongs to God, the Most High, the Almighty."*
>
> The Tartars entered Baghdad towards the end of the month of Muḥarram, and continued the killing of its population for forty days. The Caliph, Al-Mustaʿṣim Billāh, was killed on Wednesday, 14 Ṣafar and his grave was erased. On the day of his death he was 46 years of age and 4 months. His reign lasted for 15 years, 8 months and a few days. His eldest son, Aḥmad Abū al-ʿAbbās, was killed at the same time at the age of 25, while his middle son, ʿAbd al-Raḥmān, who was 23, was killed a short while later. His

youngest son, Mubārak, and his three sisters, Fāṭimah, Khadījah and Maryam, were taken prisoner.

The most prominent scholar in Baghdad, Shaikh Yūsuf ibn Shaikh Abū al-Faraj ibn al-Jawzī, who was hostile to the Minister, was killed together with his three sons, 'Abdullāh, 'Abd al-Raḥmān and 'Abd al-Karīm. All the nobility in the city were killed one by one. Prominent among these were Mujāhid al-Dīn Aybak, and Shihāb al-Dīn Sulaymān Shāh and many others. Anyone who belonged to the 'Abbās ruling family might be called out, and he would have to go with his women and children to al-Khallāl graveyard, where he would be slaughtered like a sheep. The Tartars might choose some of his daughters or other women in his household to keep as prisoners. The most prominent and eldest scholar in Baghdad, 'Alī ibn al-Nayyār, who had educated the Caliph when he was young, was also killed as well as most imāms and scholars in the city. Mosques were abandoned and no congregational or Friday prayer was held in any mosque for several months in Baghdad.

After forty days, when the massacre was over, Baghdad was in total ruin, with only the odd person walking about. Dead bodies were placed in heaps in the streets. Rain had changed their colour and their bodies had begun to rot. The smell in the city was most awful and there were outbreaks of several diseases which moved far and wide, reaching as far as Syria. People were then facing scarcity of necessary commodities, an unabating massacre, as well as epidemics. Those were indeed hard times.

When safety was announced for the survivors, those who were hiding in holes and graveyards came out. They looked so pale as though they were brought back from the dead. They were practically unrecognizable, to the extent that a father might not recognize his son, and brothers might not recognize each other. They were vulnerable to any disease and many of them soon died....[12]

---

12. Ibn Kathīr, *al-Bidāyah wal-Nihāyah*, Beirut, 1996, Vol. 13, pp. 199–203.

Hostility Unabated

Such were the facts of history when the idolaters overpowered the Muslims. They respected no provision of any treaty, nor any obligation of honour. The question to be asked here is whether this was an isolated episode of ancient history, typical only of the Tartars at that particular period of time?

The answer is certainly a negative one. In modern history we find examples of similarly ghastly atrocities. What the Indian idolaters did at the time of the partition of India is by no means less hideous or appalling than what the Tartars of old did. Eight million Muslims decided to migrate to Pakistan when they were in fear of their lives as a result of the barbaric attacks launched against those Muslims who decided to stay in India. Only three million of them managed to reach the Pakistani borders. The other five million were killed on the way. They were attacked by well organized Hindu militia. These were well known to the Indian government, and indeed were controlled by some highly placed officials in the Indian government itself. Those five million Muslims were slaughtered like sheep. Their bodies were left along the roads after many of them were disfigured in a way which was no less horrendous than what the Tartars of old did in Baghdad.

The most horrible single incident was that involving the train which carried no less than 50,000 Muslim employees from different parts of India on their way to Pakistan. It was agreed at the time when the partition agreement was made that any government official who wanted to migrate to Pakistan would be allowed to do so. The train carried all those thousands of employees. It had to travel through a tunnel at the Khaybar Pass close to the borders, but when the train came out of the tunnel, it carried no living soul. Its cargo was nothing other than the dead bodies of all its passengers, having been torn to pieces. What happened was that those same Hindu militia stopped the train inside the tunnel and killed all its passengers. The train was allowed to proceed only when this most ghastly massacre was over. God certainly tells the truth as He says: *"Should they prevail over you, they will respect neither agreement made with you, nor obligation of honour towards you?"* (Verse 8) Such massacres continue to be committed in a variety of ways.

We then ask what have Communist Russia and China done to their Muslim populations? Within a quarter of a century they exterminated 26 million of them, with an average of one million a year. The policy of exterminating the Muslims is still going on. This is not to say anything about the horrible methods of torture that have become common practice in those countries. Only this year,[13] the Chinese sector of Muslim Turkmanistan witnessed events that outbid all the Tartars' atrocities. A leading figure of the Muslim community was placed in a hole specially dug for him in the middle of the road. Members of his community were forced to bring their stools, which were normally used by the state in the manufacture of fertilizers, and throw them on their leader standing in his hole. This continued for three days until the man slowly suffocated and died.

Communist Yugoslavia has also been guilty of similar atrocities against its Muslim population. One million Muslim people have been killed there since the Communist takeover in that country at the end of the Second World War. Muslim men and women were thrown into meat mincers to come out as a minced whole. This is only an example of the continuing massacres and torture being committed there.

The same sort of evil tactics are employed by all Communist and pagan countries, even today in the twentieth century. True indeed is God's statement: *"Should they prevail over you, they will respect neither agreement made with you, nor obligation of honour towards you."* (Verse 8) *"They respect neither agreement nor obligation of honour with regard to any believer. Those indeed are the aggressors."* (Verse 10)

God's description of the unbelievers' attitude towards the Muslims is not limited to a special situation that prevailed in Arabia at a particular period of history. Nor was what happened in Baghdad at the hands of the Tartars an isolated case. Indeed that statement describes a typical attitude that we meet everywhere, whenever a community of believers who submit themselves to God alone are confronted by idolaters or atheists who submit to beings other than God.

Hence, although these statements were meant to deal with a particular situation in the Arabian Peninsula, and outlined a framework for dealing with the idolaters in Arabia, they have far greater significance. They, in

---

13. This was written in 1962 or 1963. – Editor's note.

fact, address any similar situation, wherever it takes place. They are to be acted upon whenever their implementation is possible as was the case in Arabia. It is the Muslims' ability to put them into effect that counts, not the particular circumstances that led to their revelation.

Doubts Dispelled

Will you not fight against people who have broken their solemn pledges and set out to drive out the Messenger, and who were the first to attack you? Do you fear them? It is God alone whom you should fear, if you are true believers. Fight them: God will punish them at your hands, and will bring disgrace upon them; and will grant you victory over them and will grant heart-felt satisfaction to those who are believers, removing all angry feelings from their hearts. God will turn in His mercy to whom He wills. God is All-knowing and Wise. Do you think that you will be left alone, unless God takes cognizance of those of you who strive hard for His cause and establish close association with none other than God, His Messenger and the believers? God is well aware of what you do. (Verses 13–16)

These verses come immediately after questions have been raised over the very principle of a treaty or a covenant being granted to the idolaters by God and His Messenger. In the same verses the idolaters were given the choice either to accept the faith based on submission to God alone or open warfare, except for the person who may seek refuge with the Muslims. Such a person is given shelter and made to listen to God's revelations before he is given safe conduct to his place of security. The reason for questioning the principle itself is that the idolaters will never respect any agreement or obligation of honour with regard to any believer when they prevail over the Muslims.

These verses are given here to answer any doubts felt within the Muslim community, at all levels, and the reluctance of some of the believers to take such drastic action by terminating existing treaties. It also responds to the desire felt on the part of some believers that the remaining idolaters in Arabia would eventually come round to recognize the truth of the Islamic message and accept it without the need to fight them, with all that a war involves of risk to life and property.

The Qur'ān answers all these feelings and fears by reminding the Muslims of their own experiences of the idolaters' attitude to their treaties with the believers. It reminds them of the time when the idolaters tried to expel God's Messenger from Makkah before he left to settle in Madinah. It also reminds them that it was the idolaters who were the aggressors when they first attacked the Muslims in Madinah. It then arouses their sense of shame if they fear confronting the idolaters on the battlefield. If they are true believers, then they should fear God alone. It encourages them to fight the unbelievers, so that God may inflict punishment on them at their hands. This means that the believers would be the means to accomplish God's will when He determines to punish His enemies and bring about their humiliation, giving at the same time satisfaction to the believers who have suffered at their hands. These verses also answer the excuses that are made to justify a reluctance to fight those idolaters, including the hope that those unbelievers might eventually accept Islam without the need to fight them. The Muslims are told that true hope should be pinned on the victory of the Muslims in the war against them. When the idolaters are defeated by God's will, some of them may turn to God in repentance and accept Islam. Finally, these verses draw the attentions of the believers to the fact that it is only God's will that He tests believers with such duties so that they may prove themselves. Such laws which God has set in operation will continue to apply as long as human life on earth remains.

"Will you not fight against people who have broken their solemn pledges and set out to drive out the Messenger, and who were the first to attack you? Do you fear them? It is God alone whom you should fear, if you are true believers." (Verse 13) The whole history of the idolaters with the believers is one of violating solemn pledges and breaching agreements. The most recent example was the violation of the peace treaty concluded at al-Ḥudaybiyah. Acting on instructions from his Lord, the Prophet accepted in that agreement their conditions which were felt by some of his best Companions to be totally unfair to the Muslims. He fulfilled his obligations under that agreement as meticulously as possible. For their part, the idolaters did not respect their agreement, nor did they fulfil their obligations. Within two years, and at the first opportunity, they committed a flagrant breach of their obligations, extending active

support to their allies who launched a treacherous attack against the Prophet's allies.

Moreover, it was the idolaters who tried to expel the Prophet from Makkah, and who were determined finally to kill him. This was before he migrated to Madinah. It was in the Sacred Mosque, the Inviolable House of Worship, where even a murderer was sure to be unharmed. Anyone might meet there someone who had killed his father or brother and he would not lift a finger against him. In the case of Muḥammad, God's Messenger who advocated submission to God alone and the following of His guidance, they did not respect even that obligation of honour. They did not even respect their traditions which they observed even with vengeance killers. They went as far as plotting to kill him in the Sacred Mosque itself.

It was also the idolaters who tried to fight the Muslims in Madinah. Under Abū Jahl's leadership, they insisted on fighting the Muslims after their trade caravan had been able to escape. They went on the offensive in the Battles of Uḥud and the Moat, and they mobilized other tribes against the believers in the Battle of Ḥunayn. All these encounters and events were still fresh in the memories of the believers. They all confirm the persistent attitude of the idolaters which is described by God in the Qur'ān: *"They shall not cease to fight you until they force you to renounce your faith, if they can."* (2: 217) This is clear in the nature of the relationship between the camp which worships all sorts of deities and the one which worships God alone.

After this reminder, God asks them: *"Do you fear them?"* (Verse 13) They should not refrain from fighting the idolaters, after this long history of treachery, unless they were afraid of them. But this question is followed by a statement which stirs new feelings of determination and courage: *"It is God alone whom you should fear, if you are true believers."* (Verse 13) A true believer fears no creature whatsoever, because he only fears God. So they should examine their true feelings, because if they are true believers they will fear no one other than God.

An Order to Fight

The feelings of those early Muslims were heightened when they were reminded of those events: how the idolaters plotted to assassinate the

Prophet, and how they repeatedly violated their agreements with the Muslims and launched a treacherous attack against them, taking them by surprise whenever a chance presented itself. They also remembered how the idolaters, in their despotic insolence, were the first to attack them. With their feelings so heightened, they are encouraged to fight the idolaters and are promised victory over them: *"Fight them: God will punish them at your hands, and will bring disgrace upon them; and will grant you victory over them and will grant heart-felt satisfaction to those who are believers, removing all angry feelings from their hearts."* (Verses 14–15)

When you fight them, God will make you the means of the execution of His will, and He will bring about their punishment by your hands, causing them to be defeated and humiliated after they have arrogantly been demonstrating their power. With the victory He will grant you, God will make the believers who had been at the receiving end of the idolaters' repression and persecution happy. This happiness will come about as a result of the complete victory of the truth and the defeat of falsehood and its advocates.

But this is not all. There is more good news and more reward for certain people: *"God will turn in His mercy to whom He wills."* (Verse 15) When the Muslims achieve victory some of the idolaters may open their hearts to the truth. They may be able to recognize that this victory was achieved with the help of a power that is totally superior to all that human beings can muster. They may appreciate the effects faith brings about in the outlook and behaviour of the believers and feel that faith makes its followers better people. All this takes place in reality. Hence the believers receive the reward for their *jihād* and struggle against disbelief, and they are rewarded for enabling unbelievers to see the truth of faith. Islam will gain in strength as a result of those who join its ranks after the victory of the believers: *"God is All-knowing and Wise."* (Verse 15) He knows the outcome of events before they even take place, and in His wisdom, He is aware of the results and effects of forthcoming actions and moves.

The emergence of the power of Islam and its establishment as a force to be reckoned with will inevitably attract the hearts and minds of people who may prefer to turn away from Islam when it is weak or when its power and influence are not clearly demonstrated. The advocates of Islam will have a much easier task in trying to make the truth of Islam clear to people when they have the sort of power which causes their community to be held in awe by others. It must be remembered, however, that when God educated the small, persecuted Muslim community in Makkah, implanting the Qur'ānic principles in their hearts, He promised them only one thing, which was heaven, and He made only one requirement of them, which was perseverance. When they demonstrated their perseverance and sought the prize of admittance into heaven and nothing else, God granted them victory and encouraged them to achieve it so that it would soothe their hearts and bring them full satisfaction. In such circumstances, victory is not granted to the Muslim community as individuals or as a community; it is granted to God's message. The Muslims are only the means for the execution of His will.

It was also necessary that the Muslims should launch their struggle against all the idolaters as one camp, and that all treaties with all the idolaters should be terminated at the same time, and that the Muslims would form a solid, united camp against all idolaters. Thus, those who had harboured different intentions and sought excuses of business, blood relations or other interests to justify their continued dealings with the idolaters should make their true position clear, free of all ambiguity. All such excuses had to be tested so that those who make of them a means to maintain close relations with the idolaters, in preference to their association with God, His Messenger and the believers should be known. If such excuses could be made in the past when relations between different camps had not crystallized, there was no room for any ambiguity now: *"Do you think that you will be left alone, unless God takes cognizance of those of you who strive hard for His cause and establish close association with none other than God, His Messenger and the believers? God is well aware of what you do."* (Verse 16)

As happens in all communities, there was a group among the Muslims that was skilled in manoeuvres, climbing over fences and making plausible excuses. Making use of the fluid situation when relations between the different camps had not crystallized, such people continued to make contacts with the enemy behind the backs of the Muslim community, seeking to serve only their own interests. Now that the situation was finally outlined, with each camp making its standpoint very clear, all such loopholes and back doors were finally and firmly closed.

It is certainly in the interest of the Muslim community and the interest of the Islamic faith to make the situation clear and to lay all intentions bare, so that those who strive hard for no reason other than earning God's pleasure are distinguished by their sincerity. Similarly those who have different intentions, and those who try to circumvent Islamic rules in order to pursue their own interests with the unbelievers are also known.

God has known such people all the time. Nothing is added to God's knowledge as a result of any event or action. *"God is well aware of what you do."* (Verse 16) He, however, holds people to account only for what appears of their reality through their own actions. It is His method to test people so that their true feelings and what they harbour in their innermost hearts are made to appear. The best way to do this is to test them with hardship.

Who May Tend God's Houses

It is not for the idolaters to visit or tend God's houses of worship; for they are self-confessed unbelievers. Vain shall be their actions and they shall abide in the fire. God's houses of worship may be tended only by those who believe in God and the Last Day, are constant in prayers, pay zakāt *(i.e. the obligatory charity) and fear none other than God. It is those who are likely to be rightly guided. Do you, perchance, consider that the provision of drinking water to pilgrims and tending the Sacred Mosque are equal to believing in God and the Last Day and striving for God's cause? These are not equal in God's sight. God does not provide guidance for people who are wrongdoers. Those who believe, and leave their homes and strive hard for God's cause with their property and their lives stand higher in rank with God. It is they who shall triumph. Their Lord gives them the happy news of bestowing on them His grace, and acceptance, and of the gardens of eternal bliss where they shall reside for ever. God's reward is great indeed. (Verses 17–22)*

With the declaration and disavowal made at the beginning of the *sūrah* concerning the termination of the treaties with the unbelievers, there can be no excuse for anyone who refuses to fight the idolaters. Moreover, there might have been some hesitation to forbid them entry to the Sacred Mosque in Makkah, which they used to enjoy in pre-Islamic days. The *sūrah* questions the claims of the idolaters to visit the Sacred Mosque, for that is an exclusive right of the believers who attend to their duties of worshipping God alone. That the idolaters used to visit the Mosque and provide drinking water to the pilgrims did not alter the situation in any way. These verses address those troubled Muslims who might not as yet have fully understood this basic Islamic principle.

"It is not for the idolaters to visit or tend God's houses of worship, for they are self-confessed unbelievers." (Verse 17) It is totally wrong that this should ever happen because it is contrary to the nature of things. God's houses of worship belong to Him alone, and only His name should be glorified in them. No other name should be invoked beside His name. How could it be acceptable then that those who associate partners with Him should ever tend these houses of worship when they are self-confessed unbelievers. *"Vain shall be their actions."* (Verse 17) Whatever they do is without value, including their tending of the Ka'bah, the Inviolable House of Worship. That is because none of their actions is based on the fundamental principle of God's oneness. As a result of their open and clear rejection of the truth of faith, *"they shall abide in the fire."* (Verse 17)

Worship is simply an expression of faith. If the faith is wrongly based, then the worship offered on its basis is wrong as well. Hence any act of worship, including the visiting and tending of the houses of worship, is of little benefit unless hearts are full of faith which translates itself into action that is totally dedicated to God alone. *"God's houses of worship may be tended only by those who believe in God and the Last Day, are constant in prayers, pay* zakāt *(i.e. the obligatory charity) and fear none other than God."* (Verse 18) We note that the two conditions relating to belief and action are coupled with a third stipulating that those believers who do good deeds must fear none other than God. This is not an idle condition. It is important that a believer should be totally dedicated to God alone and should rid himself of all traces of idolatry in his feelings, beliefs and behaviour. To fear anyone beside God is a subtle aspect of polytheism. Hence the *sūrah* warns against it specifically so that believers may make sure that their faith is pure and that their actions are intended to earn God's pleasure. When they do that they deserve to tend houses of worship and to be graced with God's guidance: *"It is those who are likely to be rightly guided."* (Verse 18) First, concepts are formulated and beliefs are held, then action is undertaken on the basis of faith. God will then reward people with His guidance and with success and prosperity.

This is a criterion which God states clearly to the believers and unbelievers alike, because it determines who may tend God's houses and provides a basis for the evaluation of actions of worship and rituals. Those who tended the Ka'bah and provided drinking water for pilgrims in pre-Islamic days when their faith was not based on submission to God alone cannot be placed in the same position as those who have accepted the divine faith and striven hard for God's cause to help make His word supreme: *"Do you, perchance, consider that the provision of drinking water to pilgrims and tending the Sacred Mosque are equal to believing in God and the Last Day and striving for God's cause? These are not equal in God's sight."* (Verse 19) It is God's scale and His measure that are the important ones. Nothing else is of any value.

"God does not provide guidance for people who are wrongdoers." (Verse 19) The wrongdoers meant here are the idolaters who reject the true faith, even though they may tend and maintain the Ka'bah, the Sacred Mosque, and provide drinking water for pilgrims. The point here is concluded with a statement which speaks of the high position of those believers who strive hard to make God's word triumph. We are also told of the eternal bliss and great reward that await them: *"Those who believe, and leave their homes and strive for God's cause with their property and their lives stand higher in rank with God. It is they who shall triumph. Their Lord gives them the happy news of bestowing on them His grace, and acceptance, and of the gardens of eternal bliss where they shall reside for ever. God's reward is great indeed."* (Verses 20–22)

It should be pointed out here that the comparative stated in this verse, *"stand higher in rank with God,"* does not imply two positions on the same scale, or that the others have a lesser rank with God. It indicates an absolute preference. We have already been told about the others, i.e. the idolaters, and that *"vain shall be their actions and they shall abide for ever in the fire."* (Verse 17) Hence the two situations cannot be compared.

The *sūrah* continues to stress the need to purge feelings and relations within the Muslim community of any influence other than that of faith. It calls on the believers to give no importance to ties of kinship or to other interests. It groups together all worldly pleasures as well as family and social ties in order to weigh them against loving God and His Messenger and striving for His cause. The choice is then left to Muslims to make: *"Believers, do not take your fathers and brothers for allies if they choose unbelief in preference to faith. Those of you who take them for allies are indeed wrongdoers. Say: 'If your fathers, your sons, your brothers, your spouses, your clan, and the property you have acquired, and the business in which you fear a decline, and the dwellings in which you take pleasure, are dearer to you than God and His Messenger and the struggle in His cause, then wait until God shall make manifest His will. God does not provide guidance to the evildoers.'"* (Verses 23–24)

The Islamic faith cannot accept any partners in its followers' hearts and minds. A person can be either totally dedicated to it or can leave it altogether. There is no requirement here to cut off all ties with one's children, family, clan or neighbourhood, nor to reject wealth or different types of pleasure and enjoyment. That is not the point meant here. What is required is total dedication and wholehearted love. This means in practical terms that the faith becomes the prime mover and the paramount motivation. When this is the case, people may have their pleasures and enjoyment because they will be able to sacrifice all these whenever such sacrifice is required by their faith.

The determining factor is whether faith has the overall control over man's attitudes and actions or not. Would the final decision in any situation be based on considerations of faith or on some other interests or worldly matters? When a Muslim is certain that he has given all his heart to his faith then he may enjoy his family life and have all the happiness of having a wife and children. He may maintain and strengthen his social ties as he wishes and he may have his business and fine dwelling. He may enjoy all the pleasures of this world, without being too extravagant or adopting an arrogant attitude. Indeed to enjoy these pleasures is encouraged as a means of showing gratitude to God for His bounty.

Attitudes Shaped by Feelings

"Believers, do not take your fathers and brothers for allies if they choose unbelief in preference to faith." (Verse 23) All ties of blood and family relations are severed if the tie of belief does not take its place in people's hearts. Family loyalty is nullified when loyalty based on faith is non-existent. The first bond is that which exists between man and God. It is the bond which unites all humanity. When this is severed, no relationships, ties or bonds may exist. *"Those of you who take them for allies are indeed wrongdoers."* (Verse 23) The term 'wrongdoers' here means the idolaters, because to maintain ties of loyalty and alliance with family and community when they prefer unbelief to faith is a form of idolatry which believers may not entertain.

The *sūrah* does not merely state the principle. It goes on to list all types of ties, ambitions and pleasures, grouping them all together and putting them in the scale against faith and its requirements. Thus we have in the first group fathers, children, brothers, spouses and clan (i.e. ties of blood and family), property and business (i.e. the natural desire to have money), and comfortable houses and dwellings (i.e. the pleasures of affluence). Against all this is placed love of God and His Messenger and striving for God's cause. It is important to realize that striving here implies a great deal of hardship and sacrifice. It may mean suffering oppression, going to war and sacrificing one's life altogether. Moreover, all this striving must be purged of any desire to be known or to be publicly appreciated or recognized. Once this striving aims at such recognition, it earns no reward from God.

"Say: 'If your fathers, your sons, your brothers, your spouses, your clan, and the property you have acquired, and the business in which you fear a decline, and the dwellings in which you take pleasure, are dearer to you than God and His Messenger and the struggle in His cause, then wait until God shall make manifest His will.'" (Verse 24) What is required here is certainly hard, and it is certainly of great importance. But thus are God's requirements. Otherwise, *"wait until God shall make manifest*

92

His will." (Verse 24) The only alternative is to have the same fate as those who perpetrate evil: *"God does not provide guidance to the evildoers.*" (Verse 24) This requirement is not obligatory merely on individuals. The whole Muslim community, and indeed the Muslim state, are also required to make the same choice. There is no consideration or bond which may have priority over those of faith and the struggle for God's cause.

God does not impose this obligation on the Muslim community unless He knows that its nature can cope with it. It is indeed an aspect of God's grace that He has given human nature this strong ability to cope with great demands when motivated by dedication to a noble ideal. Indeed He has given it the ability to feel a more sublime pleasure which is far superior to all the pleasures of this world. This is the pleasure or the ecstasy of having a tie with God Himself and the hope of winning His pleasure. It is also the pleasure of rising above human weaknesses, family and social pressures while looking forward to a bright horizon. If human weakness sometimes pulls us down, the bright horizon that looms large will give us a renewed desire to break loose of all worldly pressures to give faith its due importance.

Reminder of a Great Event

The *sūrah* follows this with a quick reminder of some of the events that the first Muslim generation experienced. The Muslims are reminded of the many battles when they were weak and poorly equipped but where God granted them victory. They are also reminded of the Battle of Ḥunayn when they were defeated despite their numerical strength, but then God granted them His support. On that day, the army which achieved the conquest of Makkah was joined by 2,000 of its people who were pardoned by the Prophet. On that day, there was a time when, for a few seconds, the Muslims overlooked their reliance on God to admire their strength and large following. The events of that day taught the Muslims the lesson that complete dedication to God's cause and strengthening their ties with Him are the best equipment for victory. These will never fail them, while wealth, friends and even closest relatives may do so.

God has granted you His support on many a battlefield, and also in the Battle of Ḥunayn, when you took pride in your numerical strength, but it availed you nothing. For all its vastness, the earth seemed too narrow for you, and you turned back in flight. God then bestowed from on high an air of inner peace on His Messenger and on the believers, and He sent down forces whom you could not see, and punished those who disbelieved. Such is the reward for the unbelievers. God will then turn in His mercy to whom He wills, for God is Much-forgiving, Merciful. (Verses 25–27)

The victories they achieved in many battles were still fresh in their memories, requiring only a brief reference to bring them back in all clarity. The Battle of Ḥunayn took place shortly after the conquest of Makkah, in the eighth year of the Islamic calendar.

When the Prophet settled matters after Makkah had fallen to him, and its people accepted Islam and were pardoned by the Prophet, he was informed that the tribe of Hawāzin were mobilizing forces to fight him, under the leadership of Mālik ibn 'Awf al-Naḍrī. They were joined by the whole Thaqīf tribe as well as the tribes of Jusham and Sa'd ibn Bakr. Also allied with them were some forces of the clans of Hilāl, 'Amr ibn 'Āmir and 'Awf ibn 'Āmir. They marched bringing with them their women and children as well as their cattle and property to make it a battle to the bitter end.

The Prophet marched at the head of the army which conquered Makkah, estimated at the time to be around 10,000 strong, composed mostly of the *Muhājirīn* and the *Anṣār*. He was joined by 2,000 of the pardoned people of Makkah. The two hosts met at a valley known as Ḥunayn. The battle started before the break of day, as the Muslim army was going down into the valley. The Hawāzin forces had been lying in ambush. They took the Muslims by surprise and showered them with arrows and put up a determined fight. In no time, the Muslim soldiers were on the retreat, as God says here.

The Prophet remained steadfast, mounting his she-camel, with his uncle, al-'Abbās, holding its rein on the right and his cousin,

Abū Sufyān ibn al-Ḥārith holding it on the left, trying to slow her. He was calling out to his followers to come back to him, mentioning his name and saying: "You, God's servants, rally to me, for I am God's Messenger." He also said out loud: "I am the Prophet, no doubt. I am the son of 'Abd al-Muṭṭalib." A number of his Companions who might have been no more than 80 or 100, according to various reports, stood firm by him. Among these were Abū Bakr, 'Umar, al-'Abbās and his son, al-Faḍl, 'Alī, Abū Sufyān ibn al-Ḥārith, Ayman and Usāmah ibn Zayd. The Prophet then asked his uncle, al-'Abbās, who had a loud voice, to shout to the Muslims reminding them of the pledge they had given under the tree, which was a pledge to fight with him until death, and for which they earned God's pleasure. He did so, adding some variations to remind the Muslims of their position. As they heard him, they would respond verbally and rally to the Prophet in his position. If any of them found his camel unwilling to turn round in the confusion, he would take his armament and dismount to join the Prophet.

When a core group of them had rallied, the Prophet told them to fight with total dedication. Soon the idolaters were in flight, and the Muslims were chasing them, killing some of them and taking others prisoner. By the time the rest of the Muslim army had regrouped and rallied, the prisoners were in chains in front of God's Messenger.[14]

Large Forces Avail Nothing

Such was the battle in which the Muslims had for the first time an army which was 12,000 strong. They felt confident when they looked at their numbers. They overlooked the most essential cause of victory. So God allowed defeat to befall them at first so that they might remember. He then granted them victory at the hands of the small group which remained steadfast with the Prophet and defended him with all the bravery they could muster. The *sūrah* portrays some scenes

14. Ibn Kathīr, *Tafsīr al-Qur'ān al-'Aẓīm*, Beirut, Al-Maktabah al-'Aṣrīyah, 1996, Vol. 2, p. 314.

of the battle in order to recall the feelings experienced by those who were on the battlefield: *"When you took pride in your numerical strength, but it availed you nothing. For all its vastness, the earth seemed too narrow for you, and you turned back in flight."* (Verse 25)

This describes how the excessive confidence felt by a large force led to spiritual defeat causing the Muslims to feel such a heavy burden that made the vast earth seem too narrow. This then led to a physical defeat and those large forces were on the retreat. But what happened next?

"God then bestowed from on high an air of inner peace on His Messenger and on the believers." (Verse 26) This 'inner peace' seems as if it were a garment which people wore to pacify their feelings and give them tranquillity. *"And He sent down forces whom you could not see."* (Verse 26) We do not know the nature of these forces and whom they really were. No one other than God Himself knows what forces He may bring in. *"And He punished those who disbelieved. Such is the reward for the unbelievers."* (Verse 26) The killing of some of their soldiers and taking others captive, and the defeat that befell them all were part of the punishment they received in this life, which is only a fitting reward for their denial of God and rejection of the faith. However, the door to repentance is always open to receive those who wish to mend their ways. *"God will then turn in His mercy to whom He wills, for God is Much-forgiving, Merciful."* (Verse 27)

The *sūrah* refers to the Battle of Ḥunayn in order to portray the consequences of turning away from God and relying on any power other than His. The events of the battle, however, highlight the real forces on which every faith should rely. Numerical strength is of little importance. Power lies with the hard core who are totally dedicated to their faith and cannot be shaken. Sometimes the multitude may cause defeat, because some people may join in without really knowing the truth of the faith they profess. At times of hardship, courage deserts them and this may lead to confusion within the ranks of believers. Besides, large numbers may lead to a feeling of complacency which causes people to overlook the need to strengthen their ties with their Lord. The triumph of faith has always come about through the efforts of the hard core of firm believers who are ready to sacrifice all for their faith.

At this point the *surah* concludes its statement on the unbelievers who associate partners with God and gives its final verdict concerning them. This verdict remains valid for the rest of time: *"Believers, know that the idolaters are certainly impure. So, let them not come near to the Sacred Mosque after this year is ended. If you fear poverty, then in time God will enrich you with His own bounty, if He so wills. Truly, God is All-knowing, Wise."* (Verse 28)

The *surah* emphasizes the abstract impurity of the idolaters to make it their essential quality. This shows them to be totally and completely impure. This statement gives the feeling that we should seek to purify ourselves when we have anything to do with them, although their impurity is abstract. Their bodies are not really impure. In its unique style, the Qur'ān often resorts to magnification, giving abstract matters a physical shape and entity. *"The idolaters are certainly impure. So, let them not come near to the Sacred Mosque after this year is ended."* (Verse 28) Here we have the strictest injunction prohibiting their presence in the Ḥaram area. The order implies that they must not even come near it, because they are impure while the Ḥaram is a source of purity.

The whole commercial season which the people of Makkah await every year, and their business which provides livelihood for most people and the two business trips in summer and winter which are so essential for the continued prosperity of the people of Makkah will all be jeopardized as a result of banning the idolaters from pilgrimage and declaring *jihād* against them all. This may be true, but when it comes to faith, God wants people's hearts to be totally dedicated to their faith. When they do this, they will not worry about their livelihood, because God ensures that everyone gets his or her share in the normal way and through recognized means: *"If you fear poverty, then in time God will enrich you with His own bounty, if He so wills."* (Verse 28) When God wills, He may replace certain causes with others, and He may close certain doors in order to open others. *"Truly, God is All-knowing, Wise."* (Verse 28) He manages all matters and conducts all affairs in accordance with His knowledge and wisdom.

In this *surah* the Qur'ān is addressing the Muslim community as it was composed immediately after the conquest of Makkah, when standards of faith were not at the same level. We can see from reading the *surah* carefully that there were gaps in that community, and we can also see how the Qur'ān has set about filling these gaps and the great effort made to educate the Muslim community.

The method of the Qur'ān was to guide the footsteps of the Muslim community to bring it up to the high summit of total dedication to God and to the divine faith. Faith becomes the standard by which any relationship or source of pleasure in life is accepted or rejected. All this was accomplished through educating people in the real difference between God's method which makes all people serve God alone and the methods of *jāhiliyyah* which enable some people to enslave others. The two are essentially different and they cannot be reconciled.

Without this proper understanding of the nature of this religion and its method, and also the nature of *jāhiliyyah*, or the state of ignorance that Islam always comes up against, we cannot recognize the true value of Islamic rules and regulations that govern dealings and transactions between the Muslim community and other communities.

2

Relations with Other Religions

Fight against those who – despite having been given Scriptures – do not truly believe in God and the Last Day, and do not treat as forbidden that which God and His Messenger have forbidden, and do not follow the religion of truth, till they [agree to] pay the submission tax with a willing hand, after they have been humbled. (29)

قَٰتِلُوا ٱلَّذِينَ لَا يُؤْمِنُونَ بِٱللَّهِ وَلَا بِٱلْيَوْمِ ٱلْأَخِرِ وَلَا يُحَرِّمُونَ مَا حَرَّمَ ٱللَّهُ وَرَسُولُهُۥ وَلَا يَدِينُونَ دِينَ ٱلْحَقِّ مِنَ ٱلَّذِينَ أُوتُوا ٱلْكِتَٰبَ حَتَّىٰ يُعْطُوا ٱلْجِزْيَةَ عَن يَدٍ وَهُمْ صَٰغِرُونَ ﴿٢٩﴾

The Jews say: 'Ezra is the son of God,' while the Christians say: 'The Christ is the son of God.' Such are the assertions they utter with their mouths, echoing assertions made by the unbelievers of old. May God destroy them! How perverse they are! (30)

وَقَالَتِ ٱلْيَهُودُ عُزَيْرٌ ٱبْنُ ٱللَّهِ وَقَالَتِ ٱلنَّصَٰرَى ٱلْمَسِيحُ ٱبْنُ ٱللَّهِ ذَٰلِكَ قَوْلُهُم بِأَفْوَٰهِهِمْ يُضَٰهِـُٔونَ قَوْلَ ٱلَّذِينَ كَفَرُوا مِن قَبْلُ قَٰتَلَهُمُ ٱللَّهُ أَنَّىٰ يُؤْفَكُونَ ﴿٣٠﴾

They make of their rabbis and their monks, and of the Christ, son of Mary, lords besides God. Yet they have been ordered to worship none but the One God, other than whom there is no deity. Exalted be He above those to whom they ascribe divinity. (31)

أَتَّخَذُوٓا۟ أَحْبَارَهُمْ وَرُهْبَنَهُمْ أَرْبَابًا مِّن دُونِ ٱللَّهِ وَٱلْمَسِيحَ ٱبْنَ مَرْيَمَ وَمَآ أُمِرُوٓا۟ إِلَّا لِيَعْبُدُوٓا۟ إِلَهًا وَٰحِدًا لَّآ إِلَهَ إِلَّا هُوَ سُبْحَنَهُۥ عَمَّا يُشْرِكُونَ ﴿٣١﴾

They want to extinguish God's light with their mouths, but God will not allow anything but to bring His light to perfection, however hateful this may be to the unbelievers. (32)

يُرِيدُونَ أَن يُطْفِـُٔوا۟ نُورَ ٱللَّهِ بِأَفْوَٰهِهِمْ وَيَأْبَى ٱللَّهُ إِلَّآ أَن يُتِمَّ نُورَهُۥ وَلَوْ كَرِهَ ٱلْكَٰفِرُونَ ﴿٣٢﴾

It is He who has sent His Messenger with guidance and the religion of truth, so that He may cause it to prevail over all [other] religions, however hateful this may be to the idolaters. (33)

هُوَ ٱلَّذِىٓ أَرْسَلَ رَسُولَهُۥ بِٱلْهُدَىٰ وَدِينِ ٱلْحَقِّ لِيُظْهِرَهُۥ عَلَى ٱلدِّينِ كُلِّهِۦ وَلَوْ كَرِهَ ٱلْمُشْرِكُونَ ﴿٣٣﴾

Believers, some of the rabbis and monks wrongfully devour people's property and turn people away from God's path. To those who hoard up gold and silver and do not spend them in God's cause, give the news of a painful suffering, (34)

يَٰٓأَيُّهَا ٱلَّذِينَ ءَامَنُوٓا۟ إِنَّ كَثِيرًا مِّنَ ٱلْأَحْبَارِ وَٱلرُّهْبَانِ لَيَأْكُلُونَ أَمْوَٰلَ ٱلنَّاسِ بِٱلْبَٰطِلِ وَيَصُدُّونَ عَن سَبِيلِ ٱللَّهِ وَٱلَّذِينَ يَكْنِزُونَ ٱلذَّهَبَ وَٱلْفِضَّةَ وَلَا يُنفِقُونَهَا فِى سَبِيلِ ٱللَّهِ فَبَشِّرْهُم بِعَذَابٍ أَلِيمٍ ﴿٣٤﴾

on the day when it will all be heated in the fire of hell, and their foreheads, sides and backs will be branded with them. [They will be told]: 'This is what you have hoarded up for yourselves. Taste, then, what you have been hoarding.' (35)

يَوْمَ يُحْمَىٰ عَلَيْهَا فِى نَارِ جَهَنَّمَ فَتُكْوَىٰ بِهَا جِبَاهُهُمْ وَجُنُوبُهُمْ وَظُهُورُهُمْ ۖ هَٰذَا مَا كَنَزْتُمْ لِأَنفُسِكُمْ فَذُوقُوا مَا كُنتُمْ تَكْنِزُونَ ۝

Overview

This second passage of the *surah* provides the final rulings concerning the relations between the Muslim community and the people of earlier revelations, just like the first passage defined the final rulings on relations between the Muslim community and the idolaters in Arabia. However, the first passage addressed the situation that prevailed at the time in Arabia, speaking about the Arab idolaters and referring to their attitudes and events relating specifically to them. In this second passage we note that its statements are more general in phraseology and import, and are applicable to all people of earlier revelations, whether in Arabia or elsewhere.

These new rulings include a number of substantial amendments to the rules governing relations between the Muslim community and people of earlier revelations, particularly the Christians. By the time this *surah* was revealed, all encounters and military conflicts with the Jews had already taken place, but no such conflict took place with any Christian community.

The main amendment the new rulings include is the order given to fight those who deviate from the divine faith until they pay the *jizyah*, or submission tax, after they have been humbled. No peace agreement may be made with them except on this basis of submission evident by the payment of a special tax which gives them the right to live in peace with the Muslims. On the other hand, if they become convinced of the truth of Islam and accept it, they are considered part of the Muslim community.

Never will they be forced to accept the Islamic faith. A basic and definitive Islamic rule states: *"There shall be no compulsion in religion."* (2: 256) But they are not given a peaceful status unless they are bound by covenant with the Muslim community on the basis of paying the submission tax.

This last amendment cannot be clearly understood unless we are fully aware of the nature of the inevitable relations between the divine system and other systems opposed to it. We must also understand the nature of the Islamic method of action, with its progressive stages and the different means it employs to face up to a changing situation in human life.

Inevitably, coexistence between the divine system and human systems opposed to it is possible only in certain situations and under specific conditions. These ensure that no material impediments are placed in the way of the implementation of the universal Islamic declaration of the liberation of man from submission to any authority other than God. The divine system wants to prevail so that people are liberated from submission to other human beings and can submit to God alone. By contrast, the other systems want to defend their own status by crushing the movement aiming to establish the divine system in human life.

By nature, the Islamic method of action will confront this human situation with similar and more powerful action, progressing from one stage to another and employing the proper methods that suit every stage. These methods and means are represented in the provisional and final rulings governing relations between the Muslim community and other communities. In order to define the nature of these relations the *sūrah* explains in this passage the beliefs and attitudes adopted by the people of earlier revelations, making it clear that these are 'a form of idolatry, representing disbelief and are certainly false.' The passage cites the basis of this judgement. We find that it relies on the actual beliefs of those people and the similarity between these beliefs and those of the unbelievers of old. It also relies on their actions and behaviour.

The Truth of People of Earlier Revelations

The present text states that those people of earlier revelations:

1. Do not truly believe in God and the Last Day;

2. Do not forbid what God and His Messenger have made forbidden;

3. Do not follow the religion of truth;

4. The Jews among them claim that Ezra was the son of God, while the Christians claim that Jesus Christ was the son of God. In making these false claims they are merely echoing the false claims of the unbelievers of old times, Greeks, Romans, Indians and Egyptians, or other idolaters. [We will show that the concept of the Trinity was borrowed by the Christians from old idolatrous beliefs, as were the Christian and Jewish claims that God has a son. None of these was part of the origin of Christianity or Judaism.]

5. They treated their rabbis and monks, as well as Jesus himself, as lords alongside God. Thus they transgressed the principles of God's oneness they were bid to uphold. As such, they are idolaters;

6. They are hostile to God's faith, trying to put out God's light with their mouths. As such, they are unbelievers; and

7. Many of their monks and rabbis devour people's money and property against all right, and they turn people away from God's path.

It is on the basis of such beliefs and practices that the truth of the people of earlier revelations is stated, and the final rulings governing their relations with the believers who implement God's message are defined.

This definitive statement may come as a surprise and may be seen as contrary to what the Qur'ān had stated previously about the people of earlier revelations. Certainly the Orientalists and the Christian missionaries, as well as their disciples make such claims, saying that the Prophet changed his attitude when he felt he was strong enough to confront them.

However, a thorough review of Qur'ānic statements, revealed both in Makkah and Madinah, concerning the people of earlier revelations will clearly show that nothing has changed in the Islamic view about their beliefs. The Qur'ān has always made it clear that they upheld deviant, false and polytheistic beliefs, while they disbelieved in the true divine religion, or even its portion given to them. The new amendments are confined to the way the Muslim community should deal with them. This is subject to the prevailing practical conditions, which change all the time.

We will look now at some of the Qur'ānic statements about the people of earlier revelations and the concepts and beliefs they uphold. We will then consider their practical attitude to Islam and its followers which led to the final rulings on how to deal with them.

There were no Jewish or Christian communities to reckon with in Makkah. There were only some individuals whom the Qur'ān states to have been overjoyed when they heard of the new message and they believed in Islam. They confirmed that the Prophet Muḥammad was God's Messenger who confirmed what they had of God's revelations. Those must have been among the minority of Jews and Christians who continued to believe in God's oneness. It is in reference to these that Qur'ānic verses like the following ones were revealed: "*Those to whom We vouchsafed revelation in former times believe in this; and whenever it is recited to them, they say: 'We believe in it, for it is the truth from our Lord. Even before this have we surrendered ourselves to Him.'*" (28: 52–53) "*Say, 'You may believe in it or you may not.' Those who were given knowledge before it has been revealed fall down on their faces in humble prostration when it is recited to them, and say, 'Limitless in His glory is our Lord. Truly has the promise of our Lord been fulfilled.' And upon their faces they fall down, weeping, and [its recitation] increases their humility.*" (17: 107–109) "*Say, 'Consider, if this be truly [a revelation] from God and yet you deny its truth? – even though a witness from among the Children of Israel bears witness to one like it, and has believed while you glory in your arrogance.' God does not grace evildoers with His guidance.*" (46: 10) "*Thus have We bestowed this Book on you from on high. Those to whom We previously gave revelations believe in it, just as some among these do believe in it. None will reject Our revelations other than those who deny the truth.*" (29: 47) "*Am I to seek for judge anyone other than God, when it is He who has revealed the Book to you, clearly spelling out the truth. Those to whom We previously gave revelations know that it is the truth revealed by your Lord. So, do not be among the doubters."* (6: 114) *"Those to whom We have given this revelation rejoice at what has been bestowed on you from on high, but among different factions there are some who deny part of it. Say: 'I have only been bidden to worship God, and not to associate partners with Him. To Him I pray, and to Him do I return.'"* (13: 36)

Similarly, a positive response was given by a number of individuals in Madinah, and we find mention of these in some *sūrahs* revealed in Madinah. These references make it clear that those people were Christians. The Jews in Madinah, apprehensive about the rise of Islam, took a different attitude to that adopted by some individual Jews in Makkah. *"There are indeed among the people of earlier revelations some who believe in God and in what has been bestowed from on high upon you and in what has been bestowed upon them, humbling themselves before God. They do not barter away God's revelations for a trifling price. They shall have their reward with their Lord. Swift is God's reckoning."* (3: 199) *"You will certainly find that, of all people, the most hostile to those who believe are the Jews, and those who associate partners with God; and you will certainly find that the nearest of them in affection to the believers are those who say, 'We are Christians.' This is so because there are priests and monks among them and because they are not given to arrogance. When they listen to what has been revealed to God's Messenger, you see their eyes overflow with tears because of the Truth they recognize. They say: 'Our Lord, we do believe; so enrol us among those who bear witness to the truth. How could we fail to believe in God and the truth that has come to us when we dearly hope that our Lord will admit us among the righteous?' And for this their prayer God will reward them with gardens through which running waters flow, where they will abide. Such is the reward of those who do good."* (5: 82–85)

Denying a Known Truth

However, the attitude of these individuals was not representative of the attitude of the majority of the people of earlier revelations in the Arabian Peninsula, particularly the Jews. Once they felt that Islam represented a threat to them, the Jews in Madinah launched a wicked campaign against it, using all the methods mentioned in several places in the Qur'ān. Needless to say, they refused to adopt Islam, and denied the references in their own Scriptures to the Prophet Muḥammad (peace be upon him), and the fact that the Qur'ān confirmed what remained with them of their true revelations. By contrast, those goodly and honest individuals acknowledged all that openly. The Qur'ān records all their denials and points out their deviation and corruption. However, the Qur'ān also includes clear statements of the beliefs of the people of earlier revelations, such as: *"When Jesus came with all evidence of the truth, he said: 'I have now come to you with wisdom, and to make clear to you some of that on which you are at variance. Hence, fear God and pay heed to me. God is indeed my Lord and your Lord; so worship Him alone: this is a straight way!' But factions from among them began to hold divergent views. Woe, then, to the evildoers for the suffering [they will endure] on a painful day!"* (43: 63–65) *"They broke up their unity, through their own wickedness, only after knowledge was given to them. And but for a word that had already gone forth from your Lord, [postponing a decision] until an appointed term, all would have been decided between them. Those who inherited the Scriptures after them are now in grave doubt."* (42: 14) *"It was said to them: 'Dwell in this city and eat of its food whatever you may wish, and say: "Lord, relieve us of our burden," and enter the gate in humility. We will forgive you your sins, and We will richly reward those who do good.' But the wrongdoers among them substituted other words for those which they had been given. Therefore We let loose against them a scourge from heaven in requital for their wrongdoing. Ask them about the town which stood by the sea: how its people profaned the Sabbath. Each Sabbath their fish appeared before them breaking the water's surface, but they would not come near them on other than Sabbath days. Thus did We try them because of their disobedience."* (7: 161–163) *"Then your Lord declared that He would most certainly raise against them people who would cruelly oppress them till the Day of Resurrection. Your Lord is swift indeed in His retribution, yet He is certainly Much-forgiving, Merciful."* (7: 167) *"They were succeeded by generations who inherited the Book. Yet these are keen to enjoy the fleeting pleasures of this lower world and say, 'We shall be forgiven.' Should some similar pleasures come their way, they would certainly be keen to indulge them. Have they not solemnly pledged through their Scriptures to say nothing but the truth about God? And have they not studied well what is in [the Scriptures]? Surely the life in the hereafter is better for all who are God-fearing. Will you not use your reason?"* (7: 169)

The Qur'ānic *sūrahs* revealed in Madinah provide the final word about the people of earlier revelations and their attitudes. The Qur'ān describes in detail the wicked tactics and the spiteful methods they employ in their campaign against Islam. Examples of these are found in long passages of *Sūrahs* 2–5 and elsewhere in the Qur'ān. In this *sūrah* the final verdict on them is given. Here are only a few examples of what the Qur'ān says about them:

Do you hope that they will accept your message when some of them would listen to the word of God then, having understood it, knowingly distort it? When they meet the believers, they say, 'We believe,' but when they find themselves alone, they say to one another, 'Need you inform them that which God has disclosed to you? They will only use it in argument against you before your Lord? Will you not use your reason?' Do they not know that God is well aware of all that they conceal and all that they reveal? There are among them illiterate people who have no real knowledge of the Scriptures, entertaining only wishful beliefs and conjecture. Woe, then, to those who write down, with their own hands, [something which they claim to be of] the Scriptures, and then say, 'This is from God', in order to get for it a trifling price. Woe to them for what their hands have written and woe to them for what they earn. (2: 75–79)

We gave Moses the Book and caused a succession of messengers to follow him. To Jesus, son of Mary, We gave clear proofs and supported him with the Holy Spirit. Why is it that every time a messenger comes to you with a message that does not suit your fancies, you glory in your arrogance, charging some (messengers) with lying and slaying others? They say, 'Our hearts are sealed.' No! God has cursed them for their disbelief. They have but little faith. And now that a Book confirming their own has come to them from God, and they had repeatedly forecast its coming to the unbelievers, they have denied what they know to be the truth. God's curse be upon the unbelievers!

Vile is that for which they have bartered their souls, because they have denied what God has revealed, grudging that He should, by His grace, send down His revelations to whom He chooses from among His servants. Thus they have incurred God's wrath over and over again. Ignominious suffering is in store for the unbelievers. When it is said to them, 'Believe in what God has revealed,' they say, 'We believe in what has been revealed to us.' They deny everything else, although it is the truth, corroborating the revelations they have. Say, 'Why, then, did you in the past kill God's prophets, if you were true believers?' (2: 87–91)

Say: 'People of earlier revelations, why do you disbelieve in God's revelations, when God Himself is witness to all that you do?' Say: 'People of earlier revelations, why do you try to turn those who have come to believe away from the path of God, seeking to make it appear crooked, when you yourselves bear witness [to its being straight]? God is not unaware of what you do. (3: 98–99)

Are you not aware of those who, having been granted a share of Divine revelations, now believe in falsehood and arrogant deviation [from Divine faith], and they say to the unbelievers that they are better guided than the believers. These are the ones whom God has rejected; anyone whom God rejects shall find none to succour him. (4: 51–52)

Unbelievers indeed are those who say: 'God is the Christ, son of Mary.' The Christ himself said: Children of Israel, worship God, my Lord and your Lord. Whoever associates partners with God, God shall forbid him entrance into Paradise and his abode will be the Fire. Wrongdoers will have no helpers. Unbelievers indeed are those who say: 'God is the third of a trinity.' Of certain, there is no god save the One God. Unless they desist from so saying, grievous suffering will surely befall those of them who are unbelievers. Will they not, then, turn to God in repentance and seek His forgiveness? God is Much-Forgiving, Merciful. The Christ, son of Mary, was but a Messenger: other messengers have passed away before him. His mother was a saintly woman. They both ate food [like other human beings]. Behold how clear We make [Our] revelations to them and behold how perverted they are. (5: 72–75)

A review of these texts and many similar ones in the Qur'ān is sufficient to show that these latest revelations maintain the same view concerning the deviation of the people of earlier revelations from the true divine faith. Their description in this *surah* as deviant, transgressors, unbelievers and idolaters is by no means a new development. We also note that the Qur'ān continues to praise those of them who accept God's guidance and follow it. Thus we find statements like: "*Yet among the folk of Moses there are some who guide [others] by means of the truth and act justly in its light.*" (7: 159) "*Among the people of earlier revelations there is many a one who, if you trust him with a treasure, will return it to you intact; and there is among them many a one who, if you trust him with a small gold coin, will not return it to you, unless you keep standing over him. For they say: 'We have no obligation to keep faith with Gentiles.' Thus they deliberately say of God what they know to be a lie.*" (3: 75) "*Ignominy shall be pitched over them wherever they may be, save when they have a bond with God and a bond with men. They have incurred the wrath of God and humiliation shall overshadow them. That is because they persisted in denying God's revelations and killing the Prophets against all right. That is because they persisted in their disobedience and transgression. They are not all alike. Of the people of earlier revelations there are some upright people who recite the revelations of God in the depth of night, and prostrate themselves in worship. They believe in God and the Last Day and enjoin the doing of what is right and forbid what is wrong and vie with one another in doing good works. These belong to the righteous. Whatever good they do, they shall never be denied its reward. God knows those who fear Him.*" (3: 112–115)

The modifications which were introduced concerned the rules on how to deal with the people of earlier revelations. The changes occurred stage after stage, as events took place, and in line with the practical Islamic approach to other people and their behaviour towards Muslims.

There was a time when Muslims were given instructions like: "*Do not argue with the people of earlier revelations except in a most kindly manner – unless it be such of them as are bent on evildoing. And say: 'We believe in that which has been bestowed on us from on high, as well as that which has been bestowed upon you. For our God and your God is one and the same, and it is to Him that We all submit ourselves.'*" (29: 46) "*Say [all of you], 'We believe in God and in what has been revealed to us, and in what was revealed to Abraham, Ishmael, Isaac, Jacob and their descendants, and in what was given to Moses and Jesus, and in what all prophets have been given by their Lord. We make no distinction between any of them, and to God we have surrendered ourselves.' If they come to believe in the way you believe, they will be rightly guided; but if they turn away, they will be in schism, but God will protect you from them; He hears all and knows all." (2: 136–137) "Say: 'People of earlier revelations. Let us come to an agreement which is equitable between you and us: that we shall worship none but God, that we shall associate no partners with Him, and that we shall not take one another for lords beside God.' And if they turn away, then say: 'Bear witness that we have surrendered ourselves to God.'" (3: 64) "Many among the people of earlier revelations would love to lead you back to unbelief, now that you have embraced the faith. This they do out of deep-seated envy, after the truth has become manifest to them; so forgive and forbear until God makes known His decree. Indeed, God has power over all things." (2: 109)*

And then God issued His decree to the believers: events took place, rulings were modified and the practical Islamic method of action followed its course leading to the final rulings we have in this *sūrah*. Nothing was modified in the way Islam views the deviant beliefs of the people of earlier revelations, their disbelief and association of partners with God. What were modified were the rules regulating dealings with them. These are governed by the principles we have outlined at the beginning of this Overview: this last amendment cannot be clearly understood unless we are fully aware of the nature of the inevitable relations between the divine system and other systems opposed to it, and we understand the nature of the Islamic method of action, with its progressive stages and the different means it employs to face up to the changing situation in human life.

Clarity of Attitudes

We will now discuss the nature of relations between the Muslim community and the followers of earlier religions, putting it in both its substantial and historical contexts. These were the major elements in defining the final rulings governing these relations.

In order to form a clear and accurate idea of the nature of such relations, it is important first to study what God states concerning these relations in His Book which is the absolutely true word that admits no error or falsehood. Such statements are free of errors resulting from human bias and faults of reasoning and deduction. Then we have to look at the events and attitudes which confirm these statements.

The nature of the attitude of the people of the earlier revelations towards the Muslims is stated several times in the Qur'ān. On certain occasions, God speaks of them alone, while on others, He groups them with the unbelievers, since the two groups are united in their attitudes towards Islam and the Muslim community. At times, the Qur'ān speaks of certain positions they have taken which expose their alliance against Islam. The statements themselves are too clear and decisive to require any comment: *"Neither the unbelievers among the people of earlier revelations nor the idolaters would like to see any blessing ever bestowed upon you by your Lord."* (2: 105) *"Many among the people of earlier revelations would love to lead you back to unbelief, now that you have embraced the faith. This they do out of deep-seated envy, after the truth has become manifest to them."* (2: 109) *"Never will the Jews nor yet the Christians be pleased with you unless you follow their faith."* (2: 120) *"A party of the people of earlier revelations would love to lead you astray."* (3: 69) *"A party of the people of earlier revelations say [to one another]: 'Declare at the beginning of the day that you believe in what has been revealed to the believers, and then deny it at the end of the day, so that they may go back on their faith. But do not really trust anyone who does not follow your own faith."* (3: 72–73) *"Believers, if you pay heed to some of those who have been given revelations, they will cause you to renounce the truth after you have accepted the faith."* (3: 100) *"Are you not aware of those who, having been granted a share of divine revelations, now barter it away for error, and want you too to lose your way? But God knows best who are your enemies."* (4: 44–45) *"Are you not aware of those who, having been granted a share of divine revelations, now believe in falsehood and arrogant deviation [from divine faith], and they say to the unbelievers that they are better guided than the believers."* (4: 51)

These examples are sufficient to make the attitude of the people of earlier revelations towards the believers absolutely clear. They would dearly love the believers to sink back into disbelief, although they know them to be following the truth. Their only motive is selfishness. They define their final and irrevocable attitude towards the believers in terms of insistence that they must become Jews or Christians. They will not enter into true peace with them unless the believers do so and thus abandon their faith altogether. They go further than this and testify to the idolaters that their idolatry is better guided than Islam.

To determine the ultimate objectives of their attitudes towards Islam and the Muslims, we may recall the following statements God has revealed in the Qur'ān: *"They shall not cease to fight you until they force you to renounce your faith, if they can."* (2: 217) *"The unbelievers would love to see you oblivious of your weapons and your equipment, so that they might swoop on you with one assault."* (4: 102) *"If they could overcome you, they would surely remain your enemies, and would stretch forth their hands and their tongues against you with evil intent. They dearly desire that you should disbelieve."* (60: 2) *"Should they prevail over you, they will respect neither agreement made with you, nor obligation of honour towards you."* (Verse 8) *"They respect neither agreement nor obligation of honour with regard to any believer."* (Verse 10)

When we review God's statements, we find that the unbelievers' ultimate objectives towards the believers are identical to the objectives of those who are described as the people of earlier revelations. Indeed both sets of statements are expressed in more or less the same words. This shows that the nature of the attitudes of both groups is exactly the same.

The Qur'ānic statements concerning both groups are expressed as if they are stating established facts. God says about the unbelievers: *"They shall not cease to fight you until they force you to renounce your faith, if they can."* (2: 217) He also says about the people of earlier revelations: *"Never will the Jews nor yet the Christians be pleased with you unless you follow their faith."* (2: 120) This method of expression suggests that these are definitive statements describing permanent attitudes not individual or temporary cases.

When we cast a quick glance at the history of these relations, on the basis of the attitudes adopted by the Jews and the Christians towards Islam and the Muslims in all periods of history, we will appreciate the full import of these true statements by God Himself. We also realize that such hostile attitudes are the rule, not the exception.

There have certainly been some exceptions. Indeed the Qur'ān reports, and historical facts speak of, the cases of certain individuals or small communities who have been friendly to the Muslims, and who made it clear that they believed in the truth preached by the Prophet Muḥammad, and in his message. They eventually adopted Islam. However, beyond these instances, we find nothing but a long history of determined hostility to, and wicked scheming against, this faith of Islam which have continued unabated ever since God vouchsafed His message to His final Messenger, the Prophet Muḥammad (peace be upon him).

Jewish Attitudes towards Islam

Several *sūrahs* in the Qur'ān refer to the Jews' hostility towards Islam which manifested itself in wicked scheming and conspiracies aiming to undermine the Muslim community. Indeed this hostility has always been manifest, ever since their first confrontation with Islam in Madinah up to the present moment. It is beyond the scope of this commentary to provide a full account of such a hostile history, but we will make only a few brief references to episodes of the unabating war the Jews have launched against Islam.

When the Prophet migrated to Madinah, the Jews there gave him the worst reception that could have been given by the followers of a divine message to a Messenger of God whom they knew to be honest and conveying a true message. They invented lies and raised doubts among the followers of the new faith, resorting to the most devious means to spread these fabrications. They expressed doubts about the Prophet himself when they were certain of his honesty and true position. They allied themselves with the hypocrite Arabs and taught them how to make false accusations and spread them around. They manipulated every possible event, such as the change in direction when Muslims offer their prayers and the false accusations levelled against the Prophet's wife, as well as numerous other instances. Several comments in the Qur'ān, in *Sūrahs* 2, 3, 4, 5, 9, 33 and 59, refer directly to such incidents. Here are some examples:

> *And now that a Book confirming their own has come to them from God, and they had repeatedly forecast its coming to the unbelievers,*

they have denied what they know to be the truth. God's curse be upon the unbelievers! Vile is that for which they have bartered their souls, because they have denied what God has revealed, grudging that He should, by His grace, send down His revelations to whom He chooses from among His servants. Thus they have incurred God's wrath over and over again. Ignominious suffering is in store for the unbelievers. (2: 89–90)

Now that a Messenger from God has come to them, confirming what is already in their possession, some of those who had been given the Scriptures cast God's Book behind their backs as though they know nothing. (2: 101)

The weak-minded among people will say, 'What has turned them away from the direction of prayer which they have so far observed?' Say, 'To God belong the east and the west. He guides whomever He wills to a straight path.' (2: 142)

People of earlier revelations! Why do you disbelieve in God's revelations when you yourselves bear witness [to their truth]? People of earlier revelations! Why do you cloak the truth with falsehood, and knowingly conceal the truth? A party of the people of earlier revelations say [to one another]: 'Declare at the beginning of the day, that you believe in what has been revealed to the believers, and then deny it at the end of the day, so that they might go back on their faith.' (3: 70–72)

There are some among them who twist their tongues when quoting the Scriptures, so that you may think that [what they say] is from the Scriptures, when it is not from the Scriptures. They say: 'It is from God,' when it is not from God. Thus, they deliberately say of God what they know to be a lie. (3: 78)

Say: 'People of earlier revelations, why do you disbelieve in God's revelations, when God Himself is witness to all that you do?' Say: 'People of earlier revelations, why do you try to turn those who have come to believe away from the path of God, seeking to make it appear crooked, when you yourselves bear witness [to its being straight]? God is not unaware of what you do.' (3: 98–99)

The people of earlier revelations ask you to have a book sent down to them from heaven. They asked Moses for something even greater than that, when they said: 'Make us see God with our own eyes.' The thunderbolt smote them for this their wrongdoing. After that, they took to worshipping the calf, even after clear evidence of the truth had come to them. (4: 153)

They want to extinguish God's light with their mouths, but God will not allow anything but to bring His light to perfection, however hateful this may be to the unbelievers. (Verse 32)

History witnessed repeated violations by the Jews of their treaties with the Muslim state in Madinah, as also their scheming against the Muslims. These violations led to the encounters with the Jewish tribes of Qaynuqāʻ, al-Naḍīr and Qurayẓah and also the Battle of Khaybar. Their efforts to bring together all the forces hostile to Islam in an unholy alliance, with the aim of exterminating Islam altogether, are well known.

They have continued to scheme against Islam and the Muslim community ever since. They were instrumental in the chaotic events that led to the assassination of the third rightly-guided Caliph, ʻUthmān ibn ʻAffān, and to the emergence of division in the Muslim community. They were the main culprits in the conflict that took place between ʻAlī and Muʻāwiyah. They led the way in the fabrication of false statements attributed to the Prophet, historical reports and baseless interpretations of Qurʼānic statements. They also paved the way to the victory of the Tartars and their conquest of Baghdad and the fall of the Islamic Caliphate.

In modern history, the Jews have been behind every calamity that has befallen the Muslim communities everywhere. They give active support to every attempt to crush the modern Islamic revival and extend their protection to every regime that suppresses such a revival.

History Tells its Tale

The other people of earlier revelations, the Christians, have been no less hostile. Enmity between the Byzantines and the Persians went back for centuries. Nevertheless, as soon as the Church felt that Islam, the new faith, represented a threat to its concocted version of Christianity, which was no more than a collection of ancient pagan legends, misguided inventions and a handful of statements from the Prophet Jesus, both camps buried all their past enmity and age-old hatred to confront the new faith together.

The Byzantines, and their puppet Arab regime of Ghassān, started to raise forces to fight the new faith. They killed the Prophet's messenger, when messengers were traditionally given full protection. When the Prophet sent a force of 3,000 men to stop the provocation, they were confronted by an army that included, according to historical reports, 100,000 of the Byzantines and a similar force of Christian Arabs under their rule. This was the Battle of Mu'tah, which took place in year 8 H, corresponding to 630 CE, and in which three Muslim commanders, Zayd ibn Ḥārithah, Jaʿfar ibn Abī Ṭālib and ʿAbdullāh ibn Rawāḥah, fell as martyrs.

Then the expedition to Tabūk, which is the major subject of discussion in this *sūrah*, took place, followed by the march of the army commanded by Usāmah ibn Zayd. This was prepared by the Prophet and dispatched by his successor, Abū Bakr, in a demonstration of power to confront the Byzantine forces being mobilized to suppress the voice of Islam. Then the Muslims achieved a great victory in the Battle of Yarmūk against the Byzantines. This ushered in the liberation of wide areas of Syria, Egypt, North Africa and the Mediterranean from Byzantine colonialism, and the consolidation of an Islamic base in Andalusia. From then on the hostility of the Crusaders to Islam was in full swing.

Everybody has heard of the campaigns known as the Crusades, but these were not the only ones launched by the Church against Islam. Indeed there were much earlier campaigns, which started when the Byzantines patched up their long hostility with the Persians to lend them a helping hand against Islam in the southern areas of Arabia. The Battle of Mu'tah was another early confrontation, but there were more battles to come after the great victory achieved by the Muslims in Yarmūk. This hostility was at its most brutal when Europe, motivated by Crusader zeal, swept over the Islamic base in Spain and committed atrocities without parallel in history. The same sort of hatred and unscrupulous brutality were demonstrated during the Crusades that showed no respect for any value or pledge of honour.

Gustav Le Bon, a French Christian author who wrote a book speaking favourably of the Arab Civilization refers to the compassionate treatment Muslims extended to their enemies. He states that during the Crusades, the first thing Richardo did was that he killed at the Muslim camp 3,000 prisoners who had surrendered to him after he had given them his pledges of honour to spare them. He then ran riot with his soldiers killing and looting. This angered Saladin who had extended noble and compassionate treatment to the Christians in Jerusalem, and went as far as sending medicines, drinks and provisions to Philip and Richard, the Lion-Heart when they were ill.

Another Christian writer also quoted in Arabic sources reflects that the Crusaders made the worst start to their march to Jerusalem. A group of Christian pilgrims went about killing those whom they found in the palaces that fell to them. They demonstrated their brutality by opening their victims' stomachs to look for any gold articles they might have swallowed. In contrast, when Saladin conquered Jerusalem, he granted security to the Crusaders, and fulfilled all his pledges to them. The Muslims showed their beaten enemies unparalleled magnanimity. King al-ʿĀdil, Saladin's brother, set 1,000 prisoners free, and ensured the safety of all the Armenians. He allowed the Patriarch to hold and carry the Cross and all church ornaments. The Queen and the princesses were also allowed to visit their husbands.

A proper examination of the long line of Christian hostility to Islam over the centuries is beyond the scope of this commentary. We will only say, however, that this hostility has never ended. We need only recall what happened recently in Zanzibar, when an extermination campaign was launched against the Muslims there. About 12,000 were killed and the remaining 4,000 Muslims were put to sea to go into exile. We may also recall the brutality witnessed in Cyprus where neither food nor drink was allowed to reach the Muslim areas, with the aim of starving the Island's Muslim inhabitants to death. We only need to remember the atrocities committed by Ethiopia in Eritrea and other Muslim areas, and the persecution of about 100,000 Muslims of Somali origin in Kenya, only because they wanted to join their people in Somalia. Indeed we need go no further than what the Christian missionaries have been trying to do in the south of the Sudan.[1]

To describe the Christians' hostile view of Islam we may quote the following paragraph by a European author, George Brown, writing in 1944:[2]

> We used to be warned against dangers posed by different nations, but experience has shown that there is no cause for worry. We were warned against the Jewish threat and the threat of the yellow races and the Bolshevik threat. But none of these warnings has come true. We have found the Jews to be very good friends, which means that anyone who persecutes them is our enemy. We have also found out that the Bolsheviks are our allies. The yellow races are being taken care of by powerful democracies. The only real threat is that of Islam because of its dynamism and ability to spread and attract new followers. It is the only real obstacle that stands up to Western imperialism.

We cannot go much further than this to review the various aspects of the determined war that continues to be launched by Christianity against Islam. We have referred on various occasions to the nature of this age-long war and its various aspects. The preceding remarks should be sufficient and further details may be sought elsewhere.

Let us now recall that, on the one hand, Islam represents a general declaration for the liberation of mankind and that, on the other, the camp of *jāhiliyyah* the world over seeks to crush any implementation of this declaration. With this in mind, we realize that the final rulings contained in this *sūrah* on the relationship between Islam and other

---

1. The author is referring here to events that took place in the early 1960s in these different places. For example, a *coup* took place in Zanzibar against its Muslim rulers, encouraged by the government of Tanganyika, and shortly afterwards the Island of Zanzibar joined its African mainland neighbour to form Tanzania. In Cyprus, persecution of the Muslim minority continued after the Island's independence. In Sudan, a very large contingent of Christian missionaries were encouraging civil strife, which forced the government of General Abboud to expel 300 missionaries. – Editor's note.

2. As quoted by Muṣṭafā Khālidī and 'Umar Farrūkh in *Al-Tabshīr wa'l-Isti'mār fī al-Bilād al-'Arabīyah.*

camps are the cumulative and natural reaction to all these facts. They are not limited to a particular period or a special case. At the same time, the earlier provisional rulings are partially abrogated, in the sense that they can be implemented in situations and conditions similar to those which prevailed at the time of their revelation. It is in the nature of Islam that real situations are faced with attitudes and actions that are suited to them.

These final rulings, as they are stated in this *sūrah*, deal with a specific situation that obtained in Arabia, and serve, in a sense, as a legislative prelude to the Tabūk campaign, the central issue of the *sūrah*, which sought to confront the Byzantine mobilization close to the Arabian borders. But the attitude of the people of earlier revelations and their hostility to Islam and the Muslim community were not the result of any particular historical event, or limited to any stage. That is a permanent reality. They will continue to be at war with Islam until the Muslims have abandoned their faith altogether. This hostility and the war it launches will continue to be fed by all possible means. Hence, the rulings outlined in this *sūrah* remain in full effect, unlimited to a particular period of history. However, implementation of rulings must come within the framework of putting into effect the proactive Islamic approach. People must study this approach fully before they start to talk about the rulings themselves and before those latter-day Muslims, who know nothing about Islam except its name, blame Islam for their weakness and subjugation.

Legal Islamic rulings have always been, and will continue to be, the result of action taken in accordance with the Islamic method and approach. There is a great deal of difference between looking at Qur'ānic statements as theoretical models and looking at them within the context of action taken according to the Islamic approach. This last qualification, 'according to the Islamic approach', is extremely important. We are not talking here about any action, in which any situation is acceptable as a basis. Any human situation will become an important factor if it results from the implementation of Islam.

If we keep this rule in mind, we can see the final rulings determining the relationship between the people of earlier revelations and the Muslim community. We will now look more closely at the verses included in the present passage.

A Fight Until Submission

Fight against those who – despite having been given Scriptures – do not truly believe in God and the Last Day, and do not treat as forbidden that which God and His Messenger have forbidden, and do not follow the religion of truth, till they [agree to] pay the submission tax with a willing hand, after they have been humbled. (Verse 29)

This verse and the ones that follow were meant to prepare the Muslims for their expedition to Tabūk and the confrontation with the Byzantines and their puppet regime of Christian Arabs, known as the Ghassānīd. This suggests that the descriptions we have here were true of the people on the other side of the confrontation. They simply show the reality of those people. These descriptions are not mentioned here as conditions for fighting the people of earlier revelations, but as qualities inherent in their distorted beliefs and the actual reality of those people. Hence they provide the justification for fighting them. The ruling also applies to all those who share the same beliefs and characteristics.

This verse specifies three such characteristics. (1) They do not believe in God and the Last Day; (2) they do not treat as forbidden what God has forbidden; and (3) they do not believe in the religion of truth. The verses that follow show how these characteristics apply to them.

Firstly, the Jews claim that Ezra is the son of God, and the Christians assert that Christ is His son. These claims echo similar ones made by the pagans of former times. Hence, they are to be treated on the same basis as people who do not believe in God and the Last Day.

Secondly, they treat their rabbis and their monks, as well as Jesus Christ, as their Lords, in place of God. This is in total conflict with the principles of the faith of truth which is based on total submission to God alone, who has no partners. As they make such claims they demonstrate that they are idolaters who do not follow the true faith.

Thirdly, they try to put out the light of God's guidance with their mouths. In other words, they are at war with the divine faith. No one is ever at war with the divine faith if he truly believes in God.

Fourthly, many of their monks and rabbis devour people's property without any justification. They do so knowing that their claims to such property are false. Hence they do not treat as forbidden what God and His Messenger have made forbidden, whether we take this statement as referring to the Messenger sent to them or to the Prophet Muḥammad.

All these characteristics were true of the Christians in Syria and the Byzantines, as well as other Christians ever since Church Synods distorted the faith preached by Jesus Christ and claimed that he was the son of God and invented the concept of the Trinity, the conflict between the different sects and churches over the concept of Trinity notwithstanding.

What we have here then is a general order stating a universal rule that applies to all those among the people of earlier revelations who share the same characteristics as the Christians of Syria and Byzantium. This general application is not restricted by the exceptions the Prophet made with regard to how Muslims behave in war towards women, children, the elderly, or monks who stay in places of worship, on account of the fact that these are not fighters. Islam indeed does not allow attacks against such non-fighters whatever their religion may be.

These exceptions were not made by the Prophet because such groups did not launch an aggression, but rather because they do not normally launch any aggression at all. Therefore it is not right to try to interpret this exception as restricting the general order by saying that it applies only to aggressors, as done by those who adopt an apologetic attitude in trying to defend Islam. Aggression has been committed in the first place, against God's Lordship of the universe and against human beings who are forced to submit to deities other than God. As Islam tries to defend God's Lordship and human dignity, ignorance will try to stop it by aggression and war. This is the reality we have to realize.

This Qur'ānic verse commands the Muslims to fight against those among the people of earlier revelations who "do not believe in God and the Last Day." A person who claims that Ezra or Jesus is the son of God cannot be described as a believer in God. The same applies to a person who says that the Christ is the Lord, or that God is one of a Trinity, or that He manifested Himself in Jesus. It further applies to all concepts formulated by the Synods, diverse as these concepts are.

121

Nor can we describe as believers in God and the Last Day those who say that they will suffer God's punishment only for a few days no matter what sins they may commit because God loves them as His sons and daughters, or because they are God's chosen people. The same applies to those who claim that all sins are forgiven through a holy communion with Jesus Christ, which is the only way to achieve forgiveness. Neither of these two groups can be described as believers in God or in the Last Day.

This verse also describes the people of earlier revelations as ones who do not treat as forbidden what God and His Messenger have made forbidden. Whether the term 'His Messenger' refers to the Messenger whom God sent to them in particular or to the Prophet Muḥammad, the import is the same. The following verses explain this by saying that they devour other people's property by false claims, an action which has been forbidden in all divine messages and by all God's messengers. Some of the clearest examples of this are usurious transactions, the sale of bonds of forgiveness by the Church, opposition to the divine faith with brutal force as well as trying to turn believers away from their faith. Another clear example is forcing people to submit to beings other than God, and forcing them to implement laws other than those revealed by God. All these examples are covered by the description: *'who do not treat as forbidden what God and His Messenger have forbidden.'* All this applies today to the people of earlier revelations as was applicable to them when this verse was revealed.

The Qur'ānic verse also describes them as not following 'the religion of truth.' This is clear from what we have already said. It is not part of the religion of truth to believe in the Lordship of anyone other than God, or to apply a law different from God's law, or to accept legislation enacted by any authority other than God, or to submit to anyone other than Him. All these qualities are today true of the people of earlier revelations, as it was true of them then.

When Scriptures are Ignored

The condition which the Qur'ānic verse lays down for not fighting them is not that they should accept Islam. No. There is simply no compulsion in matters of faith, and no one is forced to accept Islam at any time. The condition is simply that they should pay the tribute, or the submission tax, with a willing hand and that they be utterly subdued. What is the purpose of this condition, and why is it the end at which all fighting must stop?

The answer is found in the fact that with such characteristics, the people of earlier revelations place themselves at war with the divine faith, both in belief and in practical terms. They are also at war with Islamic society because of the inherent conflict between the codes of living derived from the divine faith on the one hand and ignorance, or *jāhiliyyah*, on the other. As described in these verses, the people of earlier revelations belong to *jāhiliyyah* in both beliefs and practices. History also proves the nature of conflict, and the impossibility of co-existence between the two codes. The people of earlier revelations were determined in their opposition to the Islamic faith in the period preceding the revelation of this verse, and in the period following it, up to the present day.

As the only religion of truth that exists on earth today, Islam takes appropriate action to remove all physical and material obstacles that try to impede its efforts to liberate mankind from submission to anyone other than God. That submission is translated in following the religion of truth, provided that every human being is given free choice. There must be no pressure either from the religion itself or from those forces putting up the physical obstacles.

The practical way to ensure the removal of those physical obstacles while not forcing anyone to adopt Islam is to smash the power of those authorities based on false beliefs until they declare their submission and demonstrate this by paying the submission tax. When this happens, the process of liberating mankind is completed by giving every individual the freedom of choice based on conviction. Anyone who is not convinced may continue to follow his faith. However, he has to pay the submission tax to fulfil a number of objectives:

Firstly, by paying this tax, known as *jizyah*, he declares that he will not stand in physical opposition to the efforts advocating the true Divine faith. Secondly, he contributes to the defence expenses for himself, his property, honour and family. Islam guarantees such protection for those who pay the *jizyah* to place themselves under Islamic protection. To ensure this, Islam defends those under its protection against all internal and external enemies with its own soldiers. Thirdly, he contributes to the treasury of the Muslim state which guarantees a decent standard of living for all those who are unable to work, including those who pay the submission tax, without any distinction between them and those Muslims who pay *zakāt*. We do not here want to enter into polemics on who should pay the submission tax and who are exempt from it, and how much each one or each category should pay, and the methods of imposing this tax and its collection. The whole question is not under discussion today as it was at the time when Muslim scholars gave their different rulings on these matters on the basis of scholarly discretion, or *ijtihād*. So today this question is considered historic rather than practical. Nowadays Muslims do not engage in *jihād*, because there is practically no Muslim community in the real sense of the term. Indeed the issue to be discussed is that of the existence of Islam and Muslims.

As we have said on several occasions, Islam takes a very serious approach which refuses to enter into any discussion of hypothetical matters. It is simply against the nature of this approach to engage in academic discussion on matters that have no practical relevance, since there is no single Islamic society that conducts all its affairs in accordance with God's law. Indeed Islam has little time for people who occupy themselves with issues that are far removed from the realities of the present day. Such people are given a funny Arabic nickname which means 'the hypothesists', because they are always putting forward hypotheses and trying to find answers to them.

The starting point today is the same as it was in the early days of Islam. There must be a group of people, living in a certain area, who believe in the religion of truth and declare that they believe in God's oneness and in Muḥammad as God's Messenger. They also believe that all sovereignty belongs to God, which means that He alone has the authority to legislate. They implement all this in their lives and move on to implement Islam's general declaration to liberate mankind. Only when this happens will there be a chance to implement Islamic rules governing the relations between the Muslim community and other societies and communities. At that time it is possible to enter such discussions about the rules that are applicable to situations that the Muslim community face in practice.

We have only discussed this verse in principle because it relates to a question of faith and to the nature of the Islamic approach. We limit our discussion to this aspect, without entering into the legal differences out of respect for the Islamic approach which is always serious, practical and realistic.

A Claim Only Unbelievers Make

As we have seen, God issued His order to the Muslims to fight the people of earlier revelations, i.e. the Jews and the Christians, "*till they pay the submission tax with a willing hand, after they have been humbled.*" (Verse 29) When this order was given certain circumstances, discussed in the Prologue to this *sūrah*, affected the Muslim community in Madinah at that time. These circumstances required that this order should be reiterated and emphasized. Its reasons needed to be clarified. The uneasiness felt by some Muslims about its purpose required reassurance. To obey this order meant opposing the Byzantines in southern Syria. Before the advent of Islam, the Arabs held the Byzantines in awe, particularly because they held control over the north of Arabia for a long time. Some Arab tribes collaborated with them, and they had a puppet state where the Ghassān tribe assumed power.

This was not the first encounter the Muslims had with the Byzantines. With Islam, God gave the Arabs a sense of dignity which enabled them to stand up to both the Persians and the Byzantines. Formerly, all the bravery they demonstrated was in internal conflict and the looting raids they launched against one another, tribe against tribe. Yet there was still a lingering fear of the Byzantines, particularly among those who had not yet acquired the true Islamic attitude. Moreover, the last major encounter with the Byzantines had not gone in favour of the Muslims. In that battle, the Byzantines and their Arab stooges marshalled large forces which some reports put at no less than 200,000 men.

All these circumstances, whether relating to the structure of the Muslim community at the time, or to the old fear of the Byzantines, or to the expedition itself which was termed 'the expedition of hardship,' and also the feeling that the Byzantines and the Christian Arabs allied with them followed earlier Scriptures required further clarification and more categorical statements to show that the fight against them was inevitable. All doubts had to be removed and unease needed to be countered with reassurance by explaining the reasons for that inescapable eventuality.

In this verse, the Qur'ān makes it clear why those people of earlier revelations were following deviant beliefs which echoed those of the Arab idolaters, Roman idolaters of old as also other nations and communities. They had not maintained the right faith which was outlined in their Scriptures. Hence they could not be considered as followers of any divine message, since they held beliefs contrary to all messages revealed by God. What is worth noting is the mention of the Jews and their assertion that Ezra was the son of God when these verses are meant to prepare the Muslims for a confrontation with the Byzantines and their Arab Christian allies. Most probably there are two reasons for this:

The first relates to the fact that these verses are given as a general statement, and the order to fight the people of earlier revelations until they pay the submission tax with a willing hand and are subdued is also of general import. In view of this it is necessary to outline the ideological basis of this general order that applies to both Christians and Jews.

The second reason is that the Jews had to be included in this order because they were in a position to put up obstacles to impede the Muslim expansion into southern Syria. They had moved from Madinah to areas close to Syria after a hard fight against the Muslims which had led to the evacuation of the tribes of Qaynuqā' and al-Naḍīr.

The Christian claim that Jesus Christ is the son of God is well known. This has been their belief ever since Paul distorted the Christian faith. On the other hand, the claim by the Jews that Ezra was the son of God is not known today. What we find today in Jewish religious writings about Ezra is a description which shows him as a skilful scribe of the Torah and that he dedicated himself to the pursuit of knowledge of the Lord's law. Nevertheless, the fact that the Qur'ān attributes to them this assertion that Ezra was the son of God is irrefutable evidence that at least some of them, particularly the Jews of Madinah, used to believe so and that this was commonly accepted among them. The

Qur'ān faced the Jews and the Christians in an open and clear way. Had there been anything untrue in what it attributed to them, they would have found in it a valid argument to support their denial of the truth of the Prophet's message.

The late Shaikh Rashīd Riḍā' gives a useful summary about Ezra's position and status as viewed by the Jews and adds his own comments. It is useful to quote a few of these paragraphs here so that we have an insight into what the Jews believe.[3]

> The Jewish Encyclopaedia (1903 edition) mentions that Ezra marks the springtime in the national history of Judaism. "The flowers appear on the earth" refers to Ezra and Nehemiah. Ezra was worthy of being the vehicle of the Law, had it not been already given through Moses. It was forgotten but Ezra restored it. But for its sins, Israel in the time of Ezra would have witnessed miracles as in the time of Joshua... Ezra re-established the text of the Pentateuch, introducing therein the Assyrian or square characters, apparently as a polemical measure against the Samaritans. He showed his doubts concerning the correctness of some words of the text by placing points over them... the beginnings of the Jewish calendar are traced back to him.

> In the Dictionary of the Bible, Dr George Box says that Ezra was a Jewish priest, a famous scribe who lived for a time in Babylon in the reign of Artaxerxes, of the long hands. In the seventh year of his reign he permitted Ezra to take a large number of the Jewish people to Jerusalem around 457 BC. (Ezra p. 7) The journey took them four months...

> 'In Jewish tradition, Ezra's position is comparable to that of Moses and Iliya. It is said that he founded the large assembly, collected the books of the Holy Book, introduced the Chaldean alphabet

---

3. This quotation is translated from Arabic. It contains portions which were originally in English or other languages. I have tried hard to find the quoted parts in their original language, but I met with only little success. What also hampered my efforts was the fact that in the early part of the twentieth century, when Shaikh Riḍā' was writing, referencing in Arabic writings lacked any standard pattern. Besides, we often find a quoted text unmarked because it was sufficient that an author mentions the name of the author he was quoting. Moreover, the spelling of many of the names mentioned could be easily mistaken. – Editor's note.

in place of the old Hebrew alphabet, and wrote the books of Chronicles, Ezra and Nehemiah of the Old Testament. The book of Ezra (pp. 4: 8, 6: 19 and 7: 1–27) is written in the Chaldean language because when the people returned from exile, they could understand Chaldean better than Hebrew.'

It is widely known to historians, including Jews and Christians, that the Torah which Moses wrote and kept in or near the casket was lost before the time of Solomon. When the casket was opened during his reign, there was nothing in it other than the two tablets containing the ten commandments,[4] as seen in the first book of Kings. It was Ezra who, after the end of slavery, wrote the Torah and other things in Chaldean letters, and the Chaldean language mixed with whatever was left of the old Hebrew, which the Jews had largely forgotten. The people of earlier revelations maintain that Ezra wrote it as it originally was, having been inspired by God. But this is not accepted by other communities. Many objections are raised which we find at the appropriate place in specialized books, even those authored by them, such as *Dhakhīrat al-Albāb* for Catholics, written originally in French. The author devotes Chapters 11 and 12 to objections to the view that the five books were those of Moses. Concerning this, he says:

'It is mentioned in the book of Ezra (4: 14.21) that all holy books were burnt with fire at the time of Nebuchadnezzar, when he said: "The Law is burnt, and no one knoweth the works that thou hast done,[5] or what thou art about to do."[6] It is added that with inspiration by the Holy Spirit, Ezra re-wrote the five books burnt with fire, and he was assisted by five contemporary scribes. Therefore, we see St Thertholianus, St Irinaous, St Ironemus, St John the Golden, St Basilius and others call Ezra 'the one who revived Jewish holy books'[7]

---

4. As regards this event, the Qur'ān says: "*The portent of his kingship is that a casket shall be brought to you, wherein you shall have peace of reassurance from your Lord, and a legacy left behind by the House of Moses and the House of Aaron. It will be borne by angels.*" (2: 248)

5. G.H. Box, *The Apocalypse of Ezra*, London, 1917, p. 110.

6. We say that what the Qur'ān mentions is the truth, and the Qur'ān states that a 'legacy' was left behind.

7. M.R. Riḍā', *Tafsīr al-Manār*, Dār al-Ma'rifah, Beirut, Vol. 10, 1930, pp. 322–324.

Shaikh Rashīd Riḍā' further:

This is sufficient for our purposes. We wish to make it clear that all the people of earlier revelations are indebted to Ezra with regard to the foundation of their faith and their holy books. We wish also to show that this foundation is feeble, relying on weak support. This has been clearly shown by European free-thinking scholars.[8] Under his entry in the *Encyclopaedia Britannica* his writing of the law – confirmed in the books of Ezra and Nehemiah – is mentioned. Then the entry says that later reports claim that he did not merely re-write for them the law that had been burnt, but also all the Hebrew books which had been lost. He further re-wrote 70 unauthorized books. The writer of the entry comments that this legend about Ezra has been written by some historians of their own accord, relying on no other reference. Hence, modern writers consider it as mere fabrication.

To sum up, the Jews venerated and still venerate Ezra, to the extent that some of them call him the son of God. We do not know if using this description was a kind of honouring Ezra, in the same way as Israel, David and others were honoured, or it was akin to what their philosopher Philo later claimed. This latter claim is close to Indian philosophy, which is the origin of Christian beliefs.[9] Qur'ānic commentators are in agreement that the claim attributed to the Jews about Ezra being the son of God was made by some Jews, not all of them.

---

8. Perhaps we should say here that terms like 'free-thinking scholars' are used by writers who followed Shaikh Muḥammad 'Abduh and his way of thinking. This school was generally influenced by Western ideas and thoughts that are alien to the Islamic approach. It is this influence that made this school praise opponents to the Church and those who advocated freedom and democracy as free-thinking. It also spoke approvingly of the European way of life, saying that we should adopt 'what is good of European ideas and traditions.' This is a very slippery road. It should be said that Lord Cromer and other colonialists encouraged this trend. The matter requires much more careful consideration, based on an independent Islamic approach.

9. For our part we find no justification for this uncertainty. The Qur'ānic statement makes it clear that the Jewish claim, 'Ezra is the son of God,' is the same as the Christian assertion that 'Jesus is the son of God.' Both echo the assertions of the unbelievers of old times, alleging that God has a son. Anyone who makes such a claim takes himself out of the fold of divine religion and joins the unbelievers and the idolaters.

The Jews who said this were some of those who lived in Madinah. It is the same as the Qur'ānic reference: "*The Jews say: 'God's hand is shackled!' It is their own hands that are shackled. Rejected [by God] are they for what they say. Indeed, both His hands are outstretched. He bestows [His bounty] as He wills.*" (5: 64) The same applies to others whom the Qur'ān mentions in the following verse: "*God has certainly heard the words of those who said: 'God is poor, and we are rich.'*" (3: 181) These people uttered this mouthful in reply to God's invitation: "*Who is it that will offer up to God a goodly loan, which He will amply repay?*" (57: 11) It may be that some earlier ones said the same thing, but it was not reported to us.

Ibn Isḥāq and others report: "Sallām ibn Mishkam, Nu'mān ibn Awfā, Abū Anas, Shās ibn Qays and Mālik ibn al-Ṣayf said to the Prophet: 'How can we follow you when you have abandoned our *qiblah* [i.e. the direction faced in prayer] and you do not accept that Ezra was the son of God."

It is well known that some Christians who claimed that Jesus was the son of God were originally Jews. Philo, a Jewish philosopher from Alexandria who was a contemporary of Jesus, says that God has a son who is His word with which He creates all things. Hence, it is perfectly possible that some Jews claimed prior to the advent of Islam that Ezra was the son of God.[10]

By quoting this Jewish assertion in this context the Qur'ān makes clear that some of the people of earlier revelations held such distorted beliefs as could not fit with their being believers in God or their following the religion of truth. These are the main characteristics which form the basis for the ruling given to the Muslims to fight them. The purpose of such a fight is not to compel them to be Muslims, but to subdue them so that they do not stand in opposition to Islam and so that they accept its authority. Thus individuals would be free of all influences restricting their freedom to make a choice to believe in God and follow His message.

---

10. Muḥammad Rashīd Riḍā', op.cit., pp. 326–327.

As we have said, the Christian assertion about Jesus being the son of God is very widely known. Indeed all Christian churches have been making this assertion ever since Paul distorted the message of Jesus Christ which, like all divine messages, was based on God's oneness. The Church Synods carried the distortion further and practically killed the concept of God's oneness.

For a summary of Christians' beliefs we will similarly quote from Shaikh Muḥammad Rashīd Riḍā"s commentary on the Qur'ān, *Al-Manār*. Under the heading 'Trinity', we read:

> The Trinity is a term used by Christians to refer to three manifestations of God. These are the Father, the Son and the Holy Spirit. This is part of the teachings of the Catholic and Eastern Churches, as well as almost all Protestants. Those who adhere to this concept allege that it is absolutely in line with the Holy Bible. Scholars of Divinity have written extensively in interpreting and explaining this concept, based on the teachings of the old Synods and the writings of the former fathers of the Church. Much of their writings discuss the way the second manifestation was born and how the third manifestation came about, and the relationships of the three manifestations, their distinctive qualities, names and titles. The term, 'Trinity', is not used in the Bible. No verse of the Old Testament specifically mentions the Trinity. Yet old Christian writers cite many verses that refer to a collective presence of God. The point here is that if these verses admit more than one interpretation, they cannot be cited as clear evidence in support of the concept of the Trinity. They are used as reference to clear revelations they believe to be included in the New Testament. Two large sets of verses from the New Testament are quoted in support of this concept. The first set consists of verses that mention the Father, Son and Holy Spirit together, and the second mentions them separately, emphasizing some of their attributes and the relationship between them.

> Dispute about the three persons of the Trinity started at the time of the Apostles. Most probably it emanated from the ideas of Hellenic philosophers. Theophilus, the second century Bishop of Antioch, used the Greek word *trinus*, while subsequently

Tertiliyanus was the first to use its synonym *trinitas*, which means three. Much dispute about this concept took place prior to the Council of Nicea, particularly in the East. The Church branded many views as heretic. Among these were the views of the Abionians who believed that Christ was no more than a human being, the Sabilians who believed that the Father, the Son and the Holy Spirit were three different manifestations by which God shows Himself to people, the Airisis who believed that the Son was not ever present like the Father; rather, the Father created the Son before creating the universe. Hence, the Son has a lower status and is subject to the Father's will, and the Macedonians deny that the Holy Spirit is a person of God.

The Church concept was approved by the Council of Nicea in 325 CE, and the Constantinople Synod in 381. Both ruled that the Son and the Holy Spirit are equal to the Father in the Trinity, and while the Son was born through the father before the start of time, the Holy Spirit emanated from Him. The Toledo Synod of 589 CE also ruled that the Holy Spirit emanated from the Father. The Latin Church unanimously accepted this addition and held on to it. As for the Greek Church, it showed little resistance at the beginning, but later gave its argument against changing the law, considering that as heresy.

The phrase 'And also from the Son' continues to be a barrier preventing the unity between the Greek and Catholic Churches. The writings of the followers of Martin Luther and the Reformist churches adopt the same concept of the Trinity as the Catholic Church. However, beginning with the thirteenth century, a large number of divinity specialists have opposed this, as also some new groups such as the Susinians, Germans, Unitarians and the Universalists, who all consider that concept contrary to the Holy Bible and to reason. Suweid Tiragh makes the Trinity the Christ given a tri-mark. He speaks of one in three, not three in one. What he understands is that the divine in Christ is the Father, while the divine which is in union with the human in Christ is the Son, and the divine that emanated from Him is the Holy Spirit. The influence of the rationalists on the Protestant and

Reformist churches weakened the Trinity concepts among many German divines.

Kant considers that the Father, the Son and the Holy Spirit signify three essential attributes of God, which are power, wisdom and love, or three main activities, which are creation, protection and control. Both Higgins and Shling tried to establish an abstract basis to the concept of the Trinity, and they were followed by later German divines who tried to defend the concept on abstract lines. Some divines who rely on the Scriptures do not strictly follow the Church line as stated by the Nicea and Constantinople Councils. In later years many tried to defend the views of the Sabilians in particular.[11]

Indeed, no longer do any Christian churches believe in the religion of truth based on God's oneness; nor do they accept that nothing and no one is similar to Him in any way, or that He does not beget anyone; limitless indeed is He in His glory.

It is often mentioned that some groups of Christians, particularly those referred to in Islamic literature as the Arīsīs, believed in God's oneness. To say this is inaccurate. This group is not unitarian in the sense we find in the divine faith. Their concepts are rather confused. While they state that, unlike God, Jesus Christ is not eternal – which is true – they also claim that he is the Son, and that he has been created by the Father before the universe. All this has nothing to do with the proper concept of God's oneness.

Indeed a clear verdict has been given by God that those who say that Christ is the son of God, or say that Christ is God, or say that God is one of a Trinity are unbelievers. The same faith cannot lead to belief and unbelief at the same time. No one can simultaneously be a believer and an unbeliever.

Clear Order and Perverse Response

Commenting on the assertions by the Jews and the Christians that Ezra or Jesus is the son of God, the Qur'ān emphasizes that they echo

---

11. M.R. Riḍā', ibid., pp. 329–331.

the assertions and concepts of unbelievers in former times: *"Such are the assertions they utter with their mouths, echoing assertions made by the unbelievers of old."* (Verse 30) First of all this comment emphasizes that these assertions were made by them and not reported by others. This is the reason for mentioning 'their mouths' to add a physical image, following the Qur'ānic method of expression. It is evident that whatever they say or assert must be said by word of mouth. The deliberate mention of their mouths is neither redundant – far be it from God to unnecessarily add what is redundant – nor does it make the statement verbose. The Qur'ānic style pictures how they make their assertions and gives us a very real image that we can see as we listen to the statement. There is also an additional connotation stressing that the words do not describe any thing that exists in reality. These are merely words uttered and have no real significance.

Then we have another aspect of the uniqueness of the Qur'ān which points to its origin and that it is God's revelation. This we find in the statement: *"echoing assertions made by the unbelievers of old."* (Verse 30) Commentators on the Qur'ān used to say that this means that their assertions about God having a son are similar to what the Arab idolaters used to say that the angels were God's daughters. The similarity between the two assertions is true, but this statement has a wider implication which has transpired only recently when the faiths of idolaters in India, ancient Egypt and Greece were studied. The study has brought to light the origins of the distorted beliefs of the people of earlier revelations, particularly the Christians. They were simply derived from those forms of pagan faiths which found their way firstly into Paul's teachings and finally into those of the Church Synods.

The Egyptian trinity of Osiris, Isis and Horus forms the basis of Pharaonic idolatry, with Osiris representing the 'father' while Horus represents the 'son'. In the Alexandrian divinity, which was taught many years before Christ, the assertion is made that "the word is the second deity," and it is also called "the first son of God".

The Indians believed that God might take three different states: Brahma which signified creation, Vishnu which signified lordship and the provision of sustenance, and Siva which signified destruction. In this faith Vishnu is considered the son of Brahma.

The Assyrians believed in the 'Word' which they called Mardookh whom they described as the first son of God.

The Greeks also believed in three states of God. When their priests slaughtered for sacrifice, they sprinkled the alter with holy water three times, and they handled incense from the censer with three fingers, and they splashed those around the alter with the holy water three times. All these rituals are symbols of the trinity. Together with the pagan beliefs they represented, these rituals were introduced by the Church into Christianity, to echo the beliefs of the unbelievers of old times.

A careful look at the ideologies of the ancient idolaters, which were not known to people at the time when the Qur'ān was revealed, in the light of this Qur'ānic statement: *"echoing assertions made by the unbelievers of old,"* (Verse 30) will prove two points. It shows that the people of earlier revelations do not follow the faith of truth and do not have the right concepts of God. It also reveals a certain aspect of the uniqueness of the Qur'ān, pointing to its source and that it is revealed by God whose knowledge is perfect, absolute.

This verse, which makes it clear that the people of earlier revelations have adopted idolatrous beliefs, is concluded with these words: *"May God destroy them! How perverse they are!"* (Verse 30) Yes indeed. "May God destroy them!" How they overlook the simple truth which is clear and straightforward to adopt ambiguous and complex idolatrous concepts which have no logical or coherent basis.

The *sūrah* then describes another type of deviation from the truth manifested by the people of earlier revelations. This time the deviation is not confined to verbal statements and beliefs only; it translates itself into practices based on erroneous beliefs: *"They make of their rabbis and their monks, and of the Christ, son of Mary, lords besides God. Yet they have been ordered to worship none but the One God, other than whom there is no deity. Exalted be He above those to whom they ascribe divinity."* (Verse 31)

This verse comes at its most appropriate place in this passage which dispels all lingering doubts that those people may still be following a divine faith. For this verse states that they are no longer following any religion revealed by God. This is proven by their beliefs and practices. They were ordered to worship God alone, but they took their rabbis and monks as lords besides God. They also made Jesus Christ the Lord. All this is a form of idolatry which associates partners with God. From the standpoint of beliefs, they are not true believers in God, and in practice, they do not follow the religion of truth.

An Order and its Distorted Application

Before we explain how they took their monks and rabbis for lords, we wish to mention some authentic reports which include the Prophet's own interpretation. His is undoubtedly the correct and final interpretation.

Al-Tirmidhī and several major scholars of *Ḥadīth* report on the authority of 'Adiy ibn Ḥātim, who was a Christian before he met the Prophet and adopted Islam: "When I first came to see the Prophet, he was reciting this verse of the *sūrah* entitled Repentance: *'They make of their rabbis and their monks, and of the Christ, son of Mary, lords besides God.'* He explained: "They certainly did not worship these (rabbis and monks). But when they permitted them something they treated it as permissible, and when they prohibited something they treated it as forbidden."

A second authentic report is transmitted by Imām Aḥmad, al-Tirmidhī and al-Ṭabarī on the authority of 'Adiy ibn Ḥātim:

> When 'Adiy, who in pre-Islamic days was a Christian, heard of the Islamic message, he fled to Syria. His sister was taken prisoner together with a group of his tribesmen. The Prophet treated his sister kindly, granted her freedom and gave her some gifts. She went to her brother and urged him to adopt Islam and to meet the Prophet. 'Adiy took his sister's advice and travelled to Madinah. He used to be the chief of his tribe, Ṭayyi', and his father was widely renowned for his unparalleled generosity. People were speaking about his arrival in Madinah. When he went to see the Prophet he was wearing a silver crucifix which he hung around his neck. The Prophet was reading this verse: *'They make of their rabbis and their monks...lords besides God.'* 'Adiy said: 'They have not worshipped them.' The Prophet said: 'Yes, indeed they did. They followed them when they forbade them what was lawful

and permitted them what was forbidden. That is how they worshipped them.'

Al-Suddī, a learned commentator on the Qur'ān says: "They have sought the advice of human beings and abandoned God's Book. Hence He says: *'Yet they have been ordered to worship none but the One God,'* which means the One who may forbid something and it is treated by all as forbidden and may permit another and it is treated as lawful. His law is to be obeyed and His verdict is final."

In his commentary on the Qur'ān, al-Ālūsī, a scholar of the modern period says: "That they made them lords does not mean that they treated them as if they were gods in control of the universe. What is meant is that they obeyed them in what they have bidden and forbidden."

From the very clear Qur'ānic statement and its interpretation by the Prophet, which provides the ultimate judgement, and also from the observations of scholars, old and new, we may deduce a number of very important conclusions concerning religion and beliefs which we will state here very briefly:

- According to the Qur'ān and the Prophet's interpretation, worship means the following of the law. The Jews and the Christians did not make their rabbis and monks as lords in the sense that they treated them as gods or that they offered their worship rituals to them. Yet God describes them in this verse as 'associating partners with Him' and, in a later verse in the *sūrah*, as 'unbelievers' only because they followed the laws they devised for them. This alone, regardless of beliefs and rituals, is sufficient to make anyone who does it a person who associates partners with God, which takes him out of faith altogether and puts him in the category of unbelievers.

- The Qur'ānic statement attaches the descriptions of 'associating partners with God' and 'unbelief' to both the Jews who accepted the laws made for them by their rabbis and put those laws into practice and the Christians who believe that Christ is their Lord and offer worship rituals to him. Both actions are the same in the sense that both make their perpetrators polytheists ascribing lordship to beings other than God.

- Polytheism, or idolatry, comes into being merely by assigning the authority to legislate to anyone other than God, even though this is not accompanied by a belief that such a legislator is a deity or by offering worship rituals to it.

The primary aim of pointing out these facts is to deal with the circumstances of the Muslim society at the time, particularly the reluctance to confront the Byzantines and the feeling that they were believers on account of their having received revelations. Yet these facts are of general application and serve to emphasize the nature of the true religion.

The religion of truth which is the only one that is acceptable to God from any human being is 'self surrender'. Such surrender is manifested by implementing God's law, after having believed in His oneness, and offering worship to Him alone. If people are to implement a law other than that of God, then what God has said about the Jews and the Christians will apply to them as well. In other words, they would be idolaters and unbelievers, no matter how emphatically they assert that they believe in God. Those descriptions will apply to them once they willingly implement a law devised by human beings in total disregard of God's law, unless they protest that they only follow such laws against their will and they have no power to repel that compulsion.

The term 'religion' has nowadays lost much of its significance in the minds of most people, so much so that they confine it to beliefs to which they may hold and rituals they may offer. This was exactly the situation of the Jews who are described by this categorical verdict, as interpreted by the Prophet (peace be upon him), as unbelievers, associating partners with God and disobeying His clear command not to worship anyone besides Him. This same Qur'ānic statement tells us that they have taken their rabbis as lords besides God.

The most essential meaning of 'religion' is 'to submit and to follow'. This is most clearly evidenced by following the law as it is proven by offering worship. The matter is very serious. It admits no ambiguity of the sort that considers people who follow laws other than God's law, without being compelled to do so, as believers and as Muslims, simply because they profess to believe in God and because they offer their worship to Him.

This ambiguity is perhaps the most serious threat to this religion of Islam at the present time. It is the worst weapon levelled at it by its enemies who depict some people and situations as Muslim and Islamic, even though these people are similar to the ones God describes as unbelievers taking as lords beings other than God and turning away from the religion of truth. If the enemies of this religion try to associate such people and situations with Islam, then it is the duty of the advocates of Islam to deny them that description and to uncover their reality. They would thus show them as they are: people who do not believe in God's oneness and who take for themselves lords other than God when *"they have been ordered to worship none but the One God, other than whom there is no deity. Exalted be He above those to whom they ascribe divinity."* (Verse 31)

A True Promise

The *sūrah* goes a step further in encouraging the believers to fight: *"They want to extinguish God's light with their mouths, but God will not allow anything but to bring His light to perfection, however hateful this may be to the unbelievers. It is He who has sent His Messenger with guidance and the religion of truth, so that He may cause it to prevail over all [other] religions, however hateful this may be to the idolaters."* (Verses 32–33)

The people of earlier revelations do not stop at mere deviation from the religion of truth and worshipping lords and other beings instead of God, as well as refusing to believe in God and the Last Day in the true sense of such a belief. They go further by declaring war against the religion of truth and trying hard to extinguish God's light, represented by this religion, the movement advocating it and the system it provides for human life.

"They want to extinguish God's light with their mouths." (Verse 32) So, they are hostile to God's light, trying to prevent its spread. They fabricate lies and sew the seeds of discord and division. They also mobilize their followers to stand in opposition to this religion and its followers, as was the case when these verses were revealed. This has continued to be the case ever since. Although this statement aimed primarily at enhancing the determination of the Muslims at the time,

it also describes the true nature of the attitude the people of earlier revelations always adopt towards God's light as reflected by His true faith providing guidance for mankind.

"*But God will not allow anything but to bring His light to perfection, however hateful this may be to the unbelievers.*" (Verse 32) This is a true promise by God reflecting His permanent law which ensures that His light will always be perfected and that His religion will always prevail in spite of the unbelievers' attempts to stifle it. This promise will reassure the believers and motivate them to continue along their way, full as it may be with hardships, and to stand up to all the unbelievers' wicked scheming. In this instance, the term 'unbelievers' refers to those people who were given Scriptures in former times. The promise also implies a clear threat to those unbelievers and all who follow in their footsteps.

The *sūrah* re-emphasizes the promise and the threat at the same time: "*It is He who has sent His Messenger with guidance and the religion of truth, so that He may cause it to prevail over all (other) religions, however hateful this may be to the idolaters.*" (Verse 33)

It is clear from this statement that the religion of Islam, preached by God's last Messenger, is the one to which reference is made in the previous Qur'ānic statement: "*Fight against those who – despite having been given Scriptures – do not truly believe in God and the Last Day, and do not treat as forbidden that which God and His Messenger have forbidden, and do not follow the religion of truth, till they [agree to] pay the submission tax with a willing hand, after they have been humbled.*" (Verse 29) It is also clear that this order to fight is targeted against those who do not believe in this religion.

This is true however we may interpret this verse. Generally speaking, the religion of truth means submission to God alone as reflected in beliefs, worship rituals and laws. This is the basic foundation of all divine faith which takes its final form in the message of the Prophet Muḥammad (peace be upon him). Any individual and any community who do not clearly submit totally to God alone in beliefs, worship and laws may be described as ones who do not believe in the religion of truth. Therefore, they are included among those to whom the verse of fighting applies. However, we have always to consider the nature of the Islamic method of action, and the different stages the message of Islam may go through and the tools and means it may employ.

"It is He who has sent His Messenger with guidance and the religion of truth, so that He may cause it to prevail over all [other] religions, however hateful this may be to the idolaters." (Verse 33) This statement confirms God's first promise: *"But God will not allow anything but to bring His light to perfection, however hateful this may be to the unbelievers."* (Verse 32) The confirmation, however, takes a much more specific form. The light which God, who is limitless in His glory, has decided to bring to full perfection is the religion of truth with which He has sent His last Messenger so that He may cause it to prevail over all other religions.

As we have already explained, the religion of truth is submission to God in beliefs, worship and laws altogether. It is represented in every divine message given to any former prophet. Needless to say, it does not include any form of the distorted versions that the Jews and Christians of today profess, as these have been adulterated with pagan beliefs. Nor can be included under it any situation that raises the banner of faith while at the same time assigning lordship to beings other than God, and associating partners with God in the form of following laws and legislations enacted by those partners without reference to God's law.

God, limitless is He in His glory, says that He has sent His Messenger with guidance and the religion of truth in order to make it prevail over all other religions. We must take the term 'religion' in its broader sense which we have outlined in order to appreciate the scope of God's promise. Since 'religion' means 'submission', then it includes every creed and system which requires people to submit to its edicts and follow its rules. God also declares His ruling that the religion of truth will surely prevail over all religion, in this broad sense of the word. This means that all submission will be to God alone, and the final triumph will be for the system which reflects this total submission.

This promise was fulfilled once at the hands of God's Messenger (peace be upon him) and his successors, as well as those who succeeded them, for a very long period of time when the religion of truth was the one which prevailed. All other religions, which were not based on

141

true submission to God alone, stood in awe. Then there followed a time when those who professed to believe in the religion of truth started to abandon it, step by step, due to various factors relevant to the internal structure of Muslim societies on the one hand, and to the long war against this religion by its different enemies. In this war a wide variety of weapons and tactics are employed in order to suppress Islam. But this is not the end of the road. God's promise will always come true. It will be fulfilled by the Muslim community which will raise the banner of Islam and start its activities at the very beginning where the Prophet himself started when he began his call, preaching the religion of truth and guided by God's light.

The *sūrah* takes the final step in this passage, describing how the people of earlier revelations do not treat as forbidden what God and His Messenger have declared forbidden. A reference to this fact has already been made in the statement: *"They make of their rabbis and monks, and of the Christ, son of Mary, lords besides God."* (Verse 31) We have already mentioned the Prophet's explanation of this statement: "They (i.e. the rabbis and monks) permitted them what is forbidden and forbade them what is lawful, and they followed them." This means that they listen to their monks and rabbis, not to God and His Messenger, in determining what is lawful and what is forbidden.

Hoarding Gold and Silver

This last step in exposing the reality of those people of earlier revelations who have distorted God's message is given in two verses addressed to the believers: *"Believers, some of the rabbis and monks wrongfully devour people's property and turn people away from God's path. To those who hoard up gold and silver and do not spend them in God's cause, give the news of a painful suffering, on the day when it will all be heated in the fire of hell, and their foreheads, sides and backs will be branded with them. [They will be told]: 'This is what you have hoarded up for yourselves. Taste, then, what you have been hoarding.'"* (Verses 34–35)

The first verse elaborates on the roles of the rabbis and monks whom those people of earlier revelations have made as lords, following their bidding in their day-to-day transactions, and also in their worship.

Indeed the rabbis and monks enjoy being treated as lords whose orders are always obeyed. In what they legislate for their followers, they devour people's property on the basis of false claims and they also turn people away from God's path.

Devouring people's property always takes various forms. One of these is the money they receive in return for issuing rulings that make lawful what is really forbidden and prohibiting what is permissible. Such rulings are always meant to serve the interests of those who possess wealth or power or both. Another way is what a priest might receive for listening to people's confessions and his forgiveness of their sins, using the authority allegedly given to the Church. The worst and most common way of devouring people's property without lawful basis is usury. There are, however, many other methods.

Another method of such wrongful devouring of people's wealth is the raising of funds which they use to fight the religion of truth. Many were the priests, bishops, cardinals and popes who raised millions and millions to finance the successive Crusades. They continue to do so in order to finance missionary work and Orientalist research, all of which aim at turning people away from God's path.

It is important to note here the care exercised in giving an accurate and honest statement which is characteristic of divine justice. In this verse, God says: *"Many of the rabbis and monks..."* This is to guard against making a generalization that would be unfair to the few who do not indulge in such wrongful practices. In any community there will always be good individuals who maintain virtuous and honest practices. God will never do any injustice to anyone.

Many of those rabbis and monks hoard up the wealth they acquire by wrongful means. The history of those communities has seen great wealth amassed by rabbis, clerics and churches. In certain periods of history they were wealthier than despotic kings and emperors. The Qur'ān describes in detail how they will be punished in the hereafter and the suffering of all those who hoard up gold and silver and do not spend them to serve God's cause. This is portrayed in a very vivid way that produces an awesome effect: *"To those who hoard up gold and silver and do not spend them in God's cause, give the news of a painful suffering, on the day when it will all be heated in the fire of hell, and their foreheads, sides and backs will be branded with them. [They will be told]: 'This is what you have hoarded up for yourselves. Taste, then, what you have been hoarding.'"* (Verses 34–35)

The scene is portrayed in full detail, with the whole operation described from its first step to its conclusion. Thus the scene is deliberately made to linger in our minds so that we contemplate it longer.

The description starts with a general statement: *"To those who hoard up gold and silver and do not spend them in God's cause, give the news of a painful suffering."* (Verse 34) The verse ends here with a general reference to the punishment of the hereafter. But then the full details are given: *"On the day when it will all be heated in the fire of hell."* (Verse 35) As we listen we wait for the heating up to be completed, then we see it red hot and gathered in readiness. Now the suffering starts with foreheads being branded with all that gold and silver. When all foreheads have been branded, those who are being punished are made to turn on their sides so that they can be branded there as well. With that over, they are made to turn yet again in order to brand them a third time with the red hot gold and silver on their backs. When this type of their punishment is completed, they are severely rebuked: *"This is what you have hoarded up for yourselves."* (Verse 35) It is the very thing you were keen to have and keep for your pleasure and enjoyment. It is now a means to inflict on you this grievous suffering: *"Taste, then, what you have been hoarding."* (Verse 35) Taste it in reality, because it is the very thing which is branding your foreheads, sides and backs.

It is a horrifying scene, portrayed at length, in full detail, so as to bring the image it describes in sharp relief. The scene is portrayed here in order to explain first the destiny that awaits many of the rabbis and monks. It also describes in detail the destiny of those who hoard gold and silver without spending to serve God's cause. Portraying it at this juncture also serves as a prelude to the 'expedition of hardship', which is the subject matter of the longer part of the *sūrah*.

We need to pause a little here to comment on God's statement which explains the true nature of the faith of the people of earlier revelations, the religion to which they adhere, the moral values they adopt and also their practices. We have referred to these previously, but we need to add more here.

Making the reality of the people of earlier revelations clear is a more pressing need than showing the truth of the idolaters who openly admit their idolatry, and participate in rituals based on such beliefs. Exposing the reality that those people of earlier revelations are devoid of any true belief in God is necessary because the Muslims will not whole-heartedly confront *jāhiliyyah* unless they are aware of its absolute reality. Such a reality is well known in the case of the idolaters, but it is not so commonly accepted in the case of the people of earlier revelations. (This also applies to people who similarly claim to follow the divine faith, as is the case with the majority of today's Muslims.)

Setting out to confront the idolaters has required that a long portion of this *sūrah* be devoted to explaining their true situation and attitude. We have explained the reasons for this in the Prologue and in the Overview of Chapter 1. In the opening passage, God says to the believers:

> *How can there be a treaty with God and His Messenger for the idolaters, unless it be those of them with whom you have made a treaty at the Sacred Mosque? So long as they are true to you, be true to them; for God loves those who are God-fearing. How [else could it be] when, should they prevail over you, they will respect neither agreement made with you, nor obligation of honour towards you? They try to please you with what they say, while at heart they remain adamantly hostile. Most of them are transgressors. They barter away God's revelations for a paltry price and debar others from His path. Evil indeed is what they do. They respect neither agreement nor obligation of honour with regard to any believer. Those indeed are the aggressors.* (Verses 7–10)

> *Will you not fight against people who have broken their solemn pledges and set out to drive out the Messenger, and who were the first to attack you? Do you fear them? It is God alone whom you should fear, if you are true believers. Fight them: God will punish them at your hands, and will bring disgrace upon them; and will grant you victory over them and will grant heart-felt satisfaction to those who are believers, removing all angry feelings from their hearts. God will turn in His mercy to whom He wills. God is All-knowing and Wise.* (Verses 13–15)

145

It is not for the idolaters to visit or tend God's houses of worship; for they are self-confessed unbelievers. Vain shall be their actions and they shall abide in the fire. (Verse 17)

Believers, do not take your fathers and brothers for allies if they choose unbelief in preference to faith. Those of you who take them for allies are indeed wrongdoers. (Verse 23)

The Truth will Out

Although the reality of the idolaters was very clear, confronting them on the battlefield required a carefully prepared campaign by the Muslim community. By contrast, the confrontation with the people of earlier revelations required an even stronger and more profound campaign which aimed, at the outset, to expose the reality of those people. It also required the removal of their nameplate which no longer reflected their reality. They needed to appear as they truly were: unbelievers, associating partners with God, and at war with God and His message. Moreover, they were too far astray, devouring people's wealth and property without justification and turning people away from God's path. This exposure comes in statements like the following:

Fight against those who – despite having been given Scriptures – do not truly believe in God and the Last Day, and do not treat as forbidden that which God and His Messenger have forbidden, and do not follow the religion of truth, till they [agree to] pay the submission tax with a willing hand, after they have been humbled. The Jews say: 'Ezra is the son of God,' while the Christians say: 'The Christ is the son of God.' Such are the assertions they utter with their mouths, echoing assertions made by the unbelievers of old. May God destroy them! How perverse they are! They make of their rabbis and their monks, and of the Christ, son of Mary, lords besides God. Yet they have been ordered to worship none but the One God, other than whom there is no deity. Exalted be He above those to whom they ascribe divinity. They want to extinguish God's light with their mouths, but God will not allow anything but to bring His light to perfection, however hateful this may be to the unbelievers. It is He who has sent His Messenger with guidance and the religion of truth, so that He may cause it to prevail over all [other] religions, however hateful this may be to the idolaters. Believers, some of the rabbis and monks wrongfully devour people's property and turn people away from God's path... (Verses 29–34)

To this should be added all the decisive statements in several *sūrahs*, some of which are of the Makkah period while others were revealed in Madinah. These explain the ultimate reality of the people of earlier revelations and that they no longer belong to the divine faith preached by their prophets. Added to this must be their attitude to God's final message. It is on the basis of this attitude that it may be determined whether they are believers or not.

Earlier *sūrahs* confronted them with the fact that they no longer had any solid foundation of divine faith to support their claims to be believers: *"Say: 'People of earlier revelations, you have no ground to stand upon unless you observe the Torah and the Gospel and that which has been revealed to you by your Lord.' That which is revealed to you by your Lord is bound to make many of them even more stubborn in their arrogance and disbelief. But do not grieve for unbelieving folk."* (5: 68)

Other Qur'ānic statements describe them, Jews or Christians or both, as having no belief in God and group them with the idolaters. As examples of these we may cite the following: *"The Jews say: 'God's hand is shackled!' It is their own hands that are shackled. Rejected [by God] are they for what they say. Indeed, both His hands are outstretched. He bestows [His bounty] as He wills. But that which has been revealed to you by your Lord is bound to make many of them more stubborn in their overweening arrogance and unbelief."* (5: 64) *"Unbelievers indeed are those who say: 'God is the Christ, son of Mary.'"* (5: 72) *"Unbelievers indeed are those who say: 'God is the third of a trinity.'"* (5: 73) *"Those who disbelieve among the people of earlier revelations and the idolaters could have never departed [from their erring ways] until there had come to them the Clear Proof."* (98: 1) We have also cited other examples. Indeed statements of this nature are numerous in the Qur'ān.

It is true that the Qur'ān also gives certain privileges to the people of earlier revelations which are not given to the idolaters, such as allowing the Muslims to eat of their food and to marry their chaste women. Such privileges are not based on any acknowledgement that the beliefs they profess have any basis in divine faith. Most probably, they have been given such privileges because originally they had divine Scriptures and a true faith, although they no longer implemented that faith. It is then possible to deal with them on the basis of that original code they claim to follow. In this respect, they are different from the idolaters who have no scriptures and no original faith to be taken as a basis. As to the present beliefs and religion of the people of earlier revelations, the Qur'ānic statements are very clear and decisive in maintaining that they have nothing to do with the faith revealed by God. They had indeed abandoned that in order to follow their rabbis, clerics, monks, synods and churches in what they had devised for them. What God says is the final verdict which may not be subject to any argument.

The Reality Outlined

What does this exposure by God of the beliefs of the people of earlier revelations signify?

The deceptive front they present acts as a check on the advocates of the Islamic message in their confrontation with the *jāhiliyyah*. Hence, it must be removed, so that they can no longer present a false image. We must not overlook the importance of the prevailing circumstances of the Muslim community at the time, including the organic structure of that community and the fact that the Tabūk Expedition took place at a time of economic hardship which was not made any easier by the extreme heat of the Arabian summer. Moreover, the Muslims were reluctant to confront the Byzantines in open warfare, because the Arabs had always held them in awe. They were even more uneasy about the general order given to them to fight the people of earlier revelations, when they were following divine Scriptures revealed by God.

The enemies of this faith who are watching carefully the Islamic revivalist movements of today are fully aware of what may influence human nature, and of the history of Islam as well. Therefore, they are keen to give an outward 'Islamic' appearance to the regimes, movements, values, traditions and philosophies they nurture and support in order to crush the Islamic revivalist movements the world over. They do so, because this outward 'Islamic' appearance may prevent the true advocates of Islam from confronting the *jāhiliyyah* reality that lies behind this false appearance.

They were forced, in certain instances, to reveal the reality of such regimes and movements and their hostility to Islam. The clearest example of these was in the case of Ataturk and his movement in Turkey which was uncompromising in its enmity to everything Islamic. They needed to reveal its reality because of the urgency they felt to bury the Caliphate system which was the last aspect of Muslim unity. Although it was merely a formal aspect, they needed to do away with it before they could attack more fundamental aspects such as worship and prayer. This reminds us of the Prophet's statement: "This religion will be undermined, one aspect after another. The first aspect to be undermined is government and the last is prayer."

Once the need for open hostility was over, those atheists and self-proclaimed followers of earlier religions, who revive their alliance only when they fight Islam, reverted to their secret ways. They were now even keener to give an Islamic appearance to other regimes which were in reality of the same orientation in opposing Islam as Ataturk's. They have become so inventive in hiding the reality of these regimes which they support politically, economically and culturally. Their intelligence services, wide-reaching media and other resources are all used to protect such regimes. Atheists and religious enemies of Islam alike cooperate in supporting such regimes which try to achieve for them the task left unfulfilled by the Crusades, old and new.

Some Muslims, including many of those who advocate the need for an Islamic revival, are deceived by this 'Islamic' appearance which is portrayed by present-day *jāhiliyyah*. Hence they are reluctant to unmask these hostile regimes and show them as they truly are. All this impedes an open confrontation with *jāhiliyyah*. Thus the false 'Islamic' appearance exercises a sedative influence on the Islamic revivalist movements. It creates a barrier that prevents the launching of a determined effort to stand up to contemporary *jāhiliyyah* which tries to pull out the last remaining roots of this faith.

In my view, those naïve advocates of Islam present a more serious threat to the Islamic revivalist movement than the sly enemies of Islam who give a false 'Islamic' appearance to regimes, set-ups, movements, values, traditions and social trends which they manipulate so that they can crush Islam for them.

This religion of Islam will always be victorious when its advocates, in any generation and any place, achieve a certain degree of awareness of its reality and the reality of the *jāhiliyyah* trying to suppress it. The real danger to this religion does not come from strong and skilful open enemies. The real danger is that posed by naïve friends who allow its enemies to wear an Islamic mask while they mount their unwavering efforts to uproot it. Indeed the first duty of the advocates of Islam is to remove these masks so that the reality of regimes and set-ups hostile to Islam and determined to crush it is laid bare. Indeed the starting point for every truly Islamic movement is to remove the false attire of *jāhiliyyah* and expose it for what it is: unbelief and idolatry. It must describe people as they really are. Only then can the Islamic movement go onwards to achieve its goals. Indeed, these people themselves will only then be aware of their own situation, which is similar to that with which the people of earlier revelations ended up, as we are told by the One who is aware of all things and who knows the reality of all situations. Who knows but such a new awareness may provide such people with a motive to mend their ways hoping that God will then replace their misery and suffering with happiness and bliss.

This unnecessary reluctance and unwise acceptance of false appearances can only delay the initial march of any Islamic movement. Consequently, it serves the goals of the enemies of Islam for which they have given such regimes a false 'Islamic' appearance. Such enemies are well aware that when Ataturk and his movement were exposed and appeared for what they truly were, they could not serve any new purpose after they had ended the last forum to unite the Muslims of the world on the basis of faith. Indeed a very sly, shrewd and cunning Orientalist has tried to give Ataturk's movement a cover to hide its reality. In his book, *Islam in Modern History*, Wilfred Cantwell Smith tries to deny that the Ataturk movement was of atheistic orientation. He describes it as the greatest and wisest movement of Islamic revival in modern history.

3

A Higher Degree of Unbelief

The number of months, in God's sight, is twelve as set by God's decree on the day when He created the heavens and the earth. Of these, four are sacred, according to the ever-true law [of God]. Therefore, do not wrong yourselves by violating them. But fight against the idolaters all together as they fight against you all together, and know that God is with those who are God-fearing. (36)

إِنَّ عِدَّةَ ٱلشُّهُورِ عِندَ ٱللَّهِ ٱثْنَا عَشَرَ شَهْرًا فِى كِتَبِ ٱللَّهِ يَوْمَ خَلَقَ ٱلسَّمَوَتِ وَٱلْأَرْضَ مِنْهَآ أَرْبَعَةٌ حُرُمٌ ذَٰلِكَ ٱلدِّينُ ٱلْقَيِّمُ فَلَا تَظْلِمُوا فِيهِنَّ أَنفُسَكُمْ وَقَٰتِلُوا ٱلْمُشْرِكِينَ كَآفَّةً كَمَا يُقَٰتِلُونَكُمْ كَآفَّةً وَٱعْلَمُوٓا أَنَّ ٱللَّهَ مَعَ ٱلْمُتَّقِينَ ۝

The postponement [of sacred months] is only an excess of unbelief, in which the unbelievers are led astray. They declare it permissible one year and forbidden another year, so that they may make up the number of the months which God has sanctified, and thus they make lawful what God has forbidden. The evil of their deeds thus seems fair to them. God does not guide those who are unbelievers. (37)

إِنَّمَا ٱلنَّسِىٓءُ زِيَادَةٌ فِى ٱلْكُفْرِ يُضَلُّ بِهِ ٱلَّذِينَ كَفَرُوا يُحِلُّونَهُ عَامًا وَيُحَرِّمُونَهُ عَامًا لِّيُوَاطِـُٔوا عِدَّةَ مَا حَرَّمَ ٱللَّهُ فَيُحِلُّوا مَا حَرَّمَ ٱللَّهُ زُيِّنَ لَهُمْ سُوٓءُ أَعْمَٰلِهِمْ وَٱللَّهُ لَا يَهْدِى ٱلْقَوْمَ ٱلْكَٰفِرِينَ ۝

Overview

These two verses form a short passage that continues the process of removing obstacles that impeded the fight against the Byzantines and their Christian Arab allies in the northern parts of Arabia. Mobilization for this expedition took place in the month of Rajab, which is one of the four sacred months. However, due to a certain ploy, Rajab in that year did not fall at its right time because of postponement, which is denounced in the second verse of this passage. According to reports, the month of Dhu'l-Ḥijjah that year was also out of place, and it was meant to fall in the preceding month of Dhu'l-Qa'dah, which meant that Rajab was actually in Jumādā II. This mess was due to the fact that the *jāhiliyyah* society had played about with its traditions and only outwardly honoured sanctities. There will always be interpretations and views to support any transgression as long as the question of permissibility and prohibition is assigned to human beings, as is the case in all *jāhiliyyah* societies.

It may be useful to give a more detailed account of how this situation arose. God has made four months in the year sacred: three consecutive ones which are Dhu'l-Qa'dah, Dhu'l-Ḥijjah and al-Muḥarram and a single one occurring later, which is the month of Rajab. It is clear that this sanctity started when the pilgrimage was ordained as a duty at its appointed time every year since the time of Abraham and Ishmael. Much as the Arabs have distorted the faith of Abraham and wide as their deviation from its teachings was, they continued to treat these months as sacred because their sanctity related to the pilgrimage which was a season so vital to the livelihood of the Arabs of Hijaz, particularly the people of Makkah. In these sacred months Arabia was free from all fighting. Peace was observed and this allowed pilgrims to travel and conduct useful business during the season.

However, at times certain needs were so important to some Arab tribes and these could not be met while observing the sanctity of these sacred months. Here personal needs came into play, and there would have been no shortage of advocates for making one of the sacred months unsacred by postponing it one year or putting it forward in another. In this way they kept the sacred months as four in number, although their identity changed, in order to keep the numbers as God had ordained. However, this process meant in effect making lawful what God had forbidden. In the ninth year of the Islamic calendar, the true month of Rajab and the true month of Dhu'l-Ḥijjah did not fall at their respective times. Rajab was observed when the month was that of Jumādā II and Dhu'l-Ḥijjah was in Dhu'l-Qaʿdah. Thus mobilization for this expedition truly took place in Jumādā II which was nominally declared to be Rajab because of the practice of postponing months.

These verses outlaw the practice of postponement and show it, in essence, to be a violation of the divine faith which assigns the authority to make things lawful or forbidden to God alone. For human beings to practise this authority in any way which is not sanctioned by God is actually an act of unbelief, and indeed *"an excess of unbelief,"* as God describes. Thus this passage in the *sūrah* removes any reluctance to mobilize felt by some Muslims because it gave the impression of violating the sanctity of Rajab. At the same time, the passage establishes a basic principle of Islam which gives the authority to legislate and make things lawful or forbidden to God alone. It also relates this principle to the basic truth on which the whole structure of the universe is founded ever since God created the heavens and the earth. What God legislates for mankind is only part of His overall legislation for the universe and all His creation. Deviating from it is, then, a violation of the basic principle on which the universe is founded. Hence it is *"an excess of unbelief, in which the unbelievers are led astray."* (Verse 37)

Another fundamental fact stated here relates to what has been explained in the preceding passage which made it clear that the people of earlier revelations are unbelievers. They are grouped together with the idolaters as hostile people whom the Muslims should fight as one united community, as they themselves do fight the Muslims all together. This assertion is borne out by historical events exactly as it is stated by God. It shows that they are all united by their goals of suppressing Islam and crushing its followers. It also shows that they all stand in the same camp when the battle is against Islam and the Muslims. They find it easy to overlook their differences and work together to stem Islamic *jihād* and destroy the Muslim community.

These two verses express two basic facts. The first is that the people of earlier revelations have sunk into idolatry and have joined the idolaters in fighting the Muslims so as to form one united front. Hence all Muslims must fight them together. The second fact is that the postponement of sacred months is an excess of unbelief because it involves legislating for mankind things that God has not legislated. Hence it adds a practical aspect to unbelief. It is by these two basic facts that this passage is linked to what precedes it and what follows it in this *sūrah* which addresses various factors impeding a general mobilization to confront all opponents, be they idolaters or people of earlier revelations.

Changing the Order of Time

> *The number of months, in God's sight, is twelve as set by God's decree on the day when He created the heavens and the earth. Of these, four are sacred, according to the ever-true law [of God].*
> (Verse 36)

This Qur'ānic statement refers the origin of time and the way it runs to the nature of the universe and how God created it, and to the origin of creation of both the heavens and the earth. It tells us that there is a permanent cycle of time consisting of twelve months. That it is permanent is evident from the fact that in every cycle there are twelve months. This is included in God's decree, which means that it is part of the divine law for the universe. Hence, the cycle is permanent and the months are twelve, without any possibility of increase or decrease. Its movement is in accordance with the divine law set into operation when God created the heavens and the earth.

The reference to the fact that this time cycle is permanent serves as a prelude to making certain months sacred. Their selection and sanctity is part of God's decree or His law which cannot be changed at will. It simply cannot be made subject to people's desires who may wish to bring one month forward and put another back. Its permanence is similar to that of the seasons which follow one another according to a constant law: *"according to the ever-true law of God."* (Verse 36) This religion is, then, in perfect harmony with the law which governs the creation of the heavens and the earth and their functions.

This short passage refers to a series of important aspects that follow and strengthen one another. It includes certain universal facts which contemporary scientific research tries hard to explain through its own experiments. It establishes a firm link between the laws of nature and the requirements and obligations of this religion of Islam, so that people truly appreciate its solid foundation and deep roots. In the Arabic text of the Qur'ān, all this takes no more than 21 simple words which are easy to understand.

All this about the number of months and those of them which are sacred is *"according to the ever-true law [of God]. Therefore do not wrong yourselves by violating them."* (Verse 36) You should not wrong yourselves in these four sacred months, the sanctity of which relates to a law of nature which applies to the whole universe. This law makes it clear that God is the Legislator in human life and in the universe at large. Do not wrong yourselves by violating the sanctity of these months which God has willed to be a period of peace and security for all. Whenever human beings violate God's rules they wrong themselves because they actually expose themselves to punishment in the life to come and to fear and worry in this life when all months become a period of war without intermission.

"But fight against the idolaters all together as they fight against you all together." (Verse 36) This obviously applies throughout the rest of the year, not in the sacred months, except when the unbelievers launch an attack, in which case the Muslims must repel the aggression in these months. To take a unilateral decision not to fight will weaken the forces of goodness which are required to defend sanctities and repel aggression by forces of evil. It will also lead to the spread of corruption in the land and the disruption of the laws of nature. Repelling aggression in the sacred months is a means to preserve their sanctity and prevent their violation.

"But fight against the idolaters all together as they fight against you all together." (Verse 36) Fight them all without exception, because they do not make any exception of any single person or community when they fight you. The battle is truly between idolatry and believing in God's oneness, between proper guidance and going astray. It is a battle

between two clearly distinguished camps which cannot come to a complete agreement or make permanent peace because the differences between them are not over details or over conflicting interests where a compromise could be worked out, or over borders which may be demarcated anew. The Muslim community would be deluded if it believes, or is led to understand, that its battle with the idolaters, whether pagan or people who had distorted their Scriptures, is over issues of politics or economics, national independence or strategy. It is first of all an ideological battle, and it is over the system laid down by this ideology, which means religion. Such a battle cannot be sorted out by compromises worked out through negotiations. It is sorted out only by *jihād* and dedicated struggle. This is God's law which never changes, and over which the whole universal system is founded. It is the law at the core of the divine faith and which controls the operation of conscience. It has been set in operation on the day when God created the heavens and the earth.

"And know that God is with those who are God-fearing." (Verse 36) Those who fear to violate God's sanctities or to make lawful what He has forbidden, or to disrupt His laws are the ones who will be granted victory. Muslims then must never hesitate to fight the unbelievers all together, or fear to engage in an all-out campaign of *jihād*. Theirs is a campaign of struggle for God's cause, in which they do not violate its rules or moral standards. They dedicate their struggle to God and watch Him when they are alone as much as they do when they are with other people. Victory is theirs because God is with them, and whoever is on God's side shall certainly be victorious.

A Change Not Sanctioned by God

The postponement [of sacred months] is only an excess of unbelief, in which the unbelievers are led astray. They declare it permissible one year and forbidden another year, so that they may make up the number of the months which God has sanctified, and thus they make lawful what God has forbidden. The evil of their deeds thus seems fair to them. God does not guide those who are unbelievers. (Verse 37)

156

Mujāhid, an authoritative commentator on the Qur'ān, says that a man from the tribe of Kinānah used to come every year to the pilgrimage riding his donkey and say: "I am not one who may be criticised or return with failure. No one may reject what I say. We have made al-Muḥarram sacred and let Ṣafar come later." The following year he would come again and say: "We have made Ṣafar sacred and let al-Muḥarram come later." This is the reference in God's statement to their making up the number of months God has sanctified, which are four. When they delay a sacred month they actually make lawful what God has forbidden.

'Abd al-Raḥmān ibn Zayd ibn Aslam, another leading commentator on the Qur'ān, mentions that this was done in pre-Islamic days by a man from the tribe of Kinānah called al-Qulummus. In those days the Arabs would stop fighting or launching raids on one another in the sacred month. A man would meet his father's killer and he would not lift a hand to harm him. One day this man gave orders to set out for a raid. When he was told that it was the month of al-Muḥarram, he said: "We will delay it this year. There are two Ṣafar months this year. Next year we will compensate for this by making them two Muḥarrams." Indeed the following year, he told them not to launch any raid in Ṣafar, so that it too was made sacred.

These are two interpretations of the verse and two versions of postponement. In the first version Ṣafar is made sacred in place of al-Muḥarram to make the sacred months four in number, but not the ones which God has specified since al-Muḥarram is made unsacred. In the other version three months are made sacred one year and five the next year to make up eight, with an average of four a year. This means in effect that the sanctity of al-Muḥarram is lost one year and Ṣafar is made sacred in another. Both actions represent a violation of God's law, making lawful what He has forbidden. Both are, as God says, "*an excess of unbelief*," because they involve an assumption of the authority to legislate which is an act of unbelief that is added to the actual rejection of the faith.

In this act which is described as an 'excess of unbelief,' "*the unbelievers are led astray.*" (Verse 37) They actually deceive themselves with their ploys and tricks. "*The evil of their deeds thus seems fair to them.*"

(Verse 37) They see as fair what is evil and they think deviation from the truth to be a virtue. They are totally unaware of how far astray they have gone and to what depths of unbelief they have sunk.

"God does not guide those who are unbelievers." (Verse 37) They have placed a shield between their hearts and divine guidance. Hence God abandons them to their unbelief in which they live in total darkness, far removed from God's guidance.

4

The Supreme Word of God

Believers, what is amiss with you that, when it is said to you: 'Go forth to fight in God's cause,' you cling heavily to the earth? Are you content with the comforts of this world in preference to the life to come? Paltry indeed are the enjoyments of life in this world when compared with those to come. (38)

If you do not go forth to fight [in God's cause], He will punish you severely and replace you by other people. You will not harm Him in any way, for God has power over all things. (39)

If you do not help him [the Prophet]; God [will, as He] supported him at the time when the unbelievers drove him away. He was only one of two. When these two were alone in the cave, he said to his companion: 'Do not grieve, for God is with us.'

يَٰٓأَيُّهَا ٱلَّذِينَ ءَامَنُوا مَا لَكُمْ إِذَا قِيلَ لَكُمُ ٱنفِرُوا فِى سَبِيلِ ٱللَّهِ ٱثَّاقَلْتُمْ إِلَى ٱلْأَرْضِ أَرَضِيتُم بِٱلْحَيَوٰةِ ٱلدُّنْيَا مِنَ ٱلْأَخِرَةِ فَمَا مَتَٰعُ ٱلْحَيَوٰةِ ٱلدُّنْيَا فِى ٱلْأَخِرَةِ إِلَّا قَلِيلٌ ۝

إِلَّا تَنفِرُوا يُعَذِّبْكُمْ عَذَابًا أَلِيمًا وَيَسْتَبْدِلْ قَوْمًا غَيْرَكُمْ وَلَا تَضُرُّوهُ شَيْئًا وَٱللَّهُ عَلَىٰ كُلِّ شَىْءٍ قَدِيرٌ ۝

إِلَّا تَنصُرُوهُ فَقَدْ نَصَرَهُ ٱللَّهُ إِذْ أَخْرَجَهُ ٱلَّذِينَ كَفَرُوا ثَانِىَ ٱثْنَيْنِ إِذْ هُمَا فِى ٱلْغَارِ إِذْ يَقُولُ لِصَٰحِبِهِ لَا تَحْزَنْ إِنَّ ٱللَّهَ مَعَنَا فَأَنزَلَ ٱللَّهُ سَكِينَتَهُ

Thereupon God bestowed on him the gift of inner peace, and sent to his aid forces which you did not see. He brought the word of the unbelievers utterly low, while the word of God remained supreme. God is Mighty, Wise. (40)

عَلَيْهِ وَأَيَّدَهُۥ بِجُنُودٍ لَّمْ تَرَوْهَا وَجَعَلَ كَلِمَةَ ٱلَّذِينَ كَفَرُواْ ٱلسُّفْلَىٰ وَكَلِمَةُ ٱللَّهِ هِيَ ٱلْعُلْيَا وَٱللَّهُ عَزِيزٌ حَكِيمٌ ﴿٤٠﴾

Go forth, whether you be lightly or heavily armed, and strive in God's cause with your wealth and your lives. This will be best for you if you but knew it. (41)

ٱنفِرُواْ خِفَافًا وَثِقَالًا وَجَٰهِدُواْ بِأَمْوَٰلِكُمْ وَأَنفُسِكُمْ فِي سَبِيلِ ٱللَّهِ ذَٰلِكُمْ خَيْرٌ لَّكُمْ إِن كُنتُمْ تَعْلَمُونَ ﴿٤١﴾

Overview

It is perhaps most likely that the present passage was revealed after the order was given for general mobilization for the Tabūk Expedition. The Prophet received intelligence that the Byzantines were deploying large forces in southern Syria near the borders with Arabia. He was also informed that the Byzantine Emperor had ordered that all soldiers taking part should be given their salaries a year in advance. A number of Arab tribes in the area, such as Lukham, Judām, 'Āmilah and Ghassān had also joined the Byzantine forces, and advance units had already been deployed in al-Balqā' in Palestine. Therefore, the Prophet issued an order to prepare for war against the Byzantines.

It was the Prophet's standard strategy when he set out of Madinah to confront an enemy that he kept his destination unknown in order to maintain an element of surprise. This time, however, he made his objective very clear because of the long travelling expected and the difficult circumstances. The timing of this expedition coincided with the burning heat of summer, when people would seek the shade and be keen to enjoy the summer fruits. At such a time all physical activity, let alone military confrontation a long way from home, was to be avoided. Hence, the symptoms we mentioned in the Prologue started to appear among the Muslims. The hypocrites felt this to be their chance to dissuade the Muslims from joining the Prophet. They advised them not to march in the hot summer, and warned them against the might of the Byzantines and the long, weakening travel they would have to endure. Hence some people began to feel uneasy. This passage, then, deals with this type of reluctance.

A Slackening Resolve

The passage begins with a word of reproach and a warning against the reluctance to join the campaign of *jihād*, or struggle for God's cause. The believers are reminded of the help God gave to His Messenger even before any one of them had joined him, and also of His ability to help him to victory without them. In such an eventuality they would have nothing except their disobedience of God and their failure to support His Messenger.

Believers, what is amiss with you that, when it is said to you: 'Go forth to fight in God's cause,' you cling heavily to the earth? (Verse 38)

Such reluctance to march forth in support of God's cause is only motivated by worldly considerations and ambitions. People may fear for their lives and their property. They are keen to protect their interests and preserve their pleasures, and would prefer a settled life of ease and comfort. They think primarily of their present life, immediate objectives, close relatives and physical needs. The words chosen here give a vivid impression of "clinging heavily to the earth". It is as if we are looking at a heavy object that has been in its position for a long time. It is lifted up by a group of people, but it soon falls down with a strong gravitational pull.

Joining a *jihād* campaign for God's cause represents freedom from the shackles of this earthly life and physical pleasures. It emphasizes the yearning for freedom after the shedding of narrow needs, and the expanse of eternity after getting rid of this limited worldly life: *"Are you content with the comforts of this world in preference to the life to come? Paltry indeed are the enjoyments of life in this world when compared with those to come."* (Verse 38)

No one who believes in God would hesitate to set out to fight for God's cause unless there is some weakness in his faith. The Prophet says: "A person who dies without having ever joined an expedition fighting for God's cause or having thought about joining such an expedition must surely have a characteristic of hypocrisy." Hypocrisy, which is essentially a weakness of faith, is the characteristic which holds a person who claims to believe in God from joining a fight for God's cause, because he fears death or poverty when life and death are determined by God, and all provisions and wealth are granted by Him. Besides, all the comforts and pleasures of this life are petty and meaningless when compared with what is in store for the believers in the life to come.

A stern threat then follows:

> If you do not go forth to fight [in God's cause], He will punish you severely and replace you by other people. You will not harm Him in any way, for God has power over all things. (Verse 39)

The address here is made to certain people at a certain period of time, but its import applies to all those who believe in God. The punishment with which they are threatened is not limited to the life to come, but it also includes a punishment in this life. They will suffer the humiliation which afflicts all those who refrain from fighting for God's cause when their enemies have power over them. They are also deprived of the enjoyments and comforts of this life which will be taken up by their enemies. In addition their loss of life and property is far greater than what they will lose when they fight in support of God's cause. Whenever a community abandons *jihād* and refuses to fight for God's cause, it is bound to suffer humiliation. Its eventual loss is much greater than it would need to sacrifice when it fights with the spirit of *jihād*.

"He will ... replace you by other people," (Verse 39) who will guard their faith and who are prepared to make the necessary sacrifices without ever submitting to God's enemies. "You will not harm Him in any way," (Verse 39) and you can have no effect on the outcome. "For God has power over all things." (Verse 39) He can easily cause you to perish and bring about a different community to take your place. In the final balance you will count for nothing.

To elevate oneself above the shackles of the earth and over one's own weaknesses is to enhance one's noble existence. It represents the higher meaning of life. To give in to fears for one's life and the attractions of this worldly life is to condemn one's humanity to extinction. This is the real death knell of the spiritual aspect which distinguishes human life.

The Best Choice for Believers

God then gives them an example of the history which they themselves had witnessed, showing them how He supported His Messenger and gave him a great victory without need for their support. After all, victory is granted by God to whom He pleases:

> If you do not help him [the Prophet]; God [will, as He] supported him at the time when the unbelievers drove him away. He was only one of two. When these two were alone in the cave, he said to his Companion: 'Do not grieve, for God is with us.' Thereupon God bestowed on him the gift of inner peace, and sent to his aid forces which you did not see. He brought the word of the unbelievers utterly low, while the word of God remained supreme. God is Mighty, Wise. (Verse 40)

This is a reference to the time when the Quraysh had lost all patience with Muḥammad and his message. It is the same with every tyrannical authority when it loses patience with the message of the truth after it realizes that it cannot stifle or suppress it. They held their consultations and decided to assassinate Muḥammad. God then informed the Prophet of what the Quraysh had plotted and instructed him to leave. He set out of Makkah alone except for his trusted Companion, Abū Bakr. He had neither troops nor weapons with which to confront his numerous enemies. The odds were heavily against him.

The *sūrah* describes vividly the situation of the Prophet and his friend: *"When these two were alone in the cave,"* (Verse 40) with several bands of the Quraysh chasing them in all directions. Abū Bakr had no fear for his own life, but he feared for the Prophet. The pursuers were so close to them at one point that he said to the Prophet: "Should any one of them look down where he is standing, he would surely see us." But the Prophet had all the calmness of the inner peace bestowed on him by God. He reassured his Companion, saying to him: "Abū Bakr, what do you think of two men who have God on their side?"

What was the result of this confrontation when all the material power was on one side while the Prophet and his Companion stood alone with no such power? A fantastic victory was granted, employing troops whom no human being could see. A humiliating defeat engulfed the unbelievers: *"He brought the word of the unbelievers utterly low."* (Verse 40) God's word remained mighty, victorious, supreme: *"while the word of God remained supreme."* (Verse 40) God is certainly *"Mighty"* and those who advocate His cause will never be humiliated, and He is *"Wise,"* which means here that He determines when to grant victory to those who deserve it.

That confrontation was an example of God's help to His Messenger and how His word remains supreme. God is certainly able to repeat such a victory at the hands of other people who do not cling heavily to the earth and who are not reluctant to fight for His cause. This is an example from the near history which the Muslims themselves had witnessed. Yet no evidence is needed when God has stated His word.

They are then called upon to mobilize their forces and not to allow any impediment to stand in their way. If they wish to attain what is best for them in this life as well as in the life to come, then they should not allow any factor to interfere with their response to such a call:

> Go forth, whether you be lightly or heavily armed, and strive in God's cause with your wealth and your lives. This will be best for you if you but knew it. (Verse 41)

They must march whatever the circumstances, and must strive hard, and be ready to sacrifice their wealth and their lives, seeking no excuses and allowing no impediments to stand in their way: *"This will be best for you if you but knew it."* (Verse 41)

The sincere believers realized that this is best and they set forth on their campaign in support of God's cause. All sorts of impediments stood in their way and they had no shortage of excuses if they wished to justify staying behind, but they sought none and marched on. Hence, God enabled them to liberate the hearts and minds of other communities and to liberate their lands as well. He allowed His word to triumph at their hands and enhanced their position by being its advocates. He thus enabled them to achieve miraculous victories, unparalleled in history.

Abū Ṭalḥah, one of the Prophet's Companions, after reading this verse, said to his sons: "I see that God has ordered us to go on *jihād* whether we are young or elderly. Prepare my equipment." His sons protested: "You fought in all the battles with the Prophet until he passed away, and you fought with Abū Bakr until he died, then with 'Umar until his death. Now let us fight on your behalf." He refused and insisted on doing his share. He joined an expedition by sea, but soon he died. No island was near where he could be buried. His body remained in the boat for nine days without showing any change of colour. They then came to an island where he was buried.

Abū Rāshid al-Ḥarrānī reports: "I visited al-Miqdād ibn al-Aswad, a great warrior and a Companion of the Prophet. I found him sitting on a wooden box, looking so thin, but he nevertheless wanted to join an army on an expedition. I said to him: 'You are certainly excused by God.' He said: 'I have been reading this *sūrah* and read God's order, *Go forth, whether you be lightly or heavily armed, and strive in God's cause with your wealth and your lives.'" (Verse 41)

Al-Ṭabarī, the famous historian also reports on the authority of Ḥayyān ibn Zayd al-Shar'abī: "We went on a campaign with Ṣafwān ibn 'Amr, the Governor of Ḥums, until we reached a place called al-Jarājimah when I saw a man looking very old with his eyebrows practically covering his eyes. He was from Damascus, riding his camel and taking part in the fight. I went to him and said, 'Uncle, God has certainly excused those who are like you.' He lifted his eyebrows and said: 'Nephew, God has called upon us to go forth and strive in His cause, whether we be lightly or heavily armed. God will test a person whom He loves, and then He will let him live. God tests those of His servants who thank and praise Him and those who remain steadfast in adversity, as well as those who worship God alone.'"

It is with such a serious attitude to God's words that Islam was able to march on in the land, carrying its message which sought to liberate mankind from submission to other creatures so that they would submit to God alone. The result was the greatest victories ever achieved in the history of mankind.

5

Manifestations of Hypocrisy

Had there been [a prospect of] an immediate gain, and a short journey, they would certainly have followed you; but the distance was too far for them. Yet they will swear by God: 'Had we been able, we would surely have joined you.' They bring ruin upon themselves. God knows indeed that they are liars. (42)

لَوۡ كَانَ عَرَضًا قَرِيبًا وَسَفَرًا قَاصِدًا لَّاتَّبَعُوكَ وَلَٰكِنۢ بَعُدَتۡ عَلَيۡهِمُ ٱلشُّقَّةُ وَسَيَحۡلِفُونَ بِٱللَّهِ لَوِ ٱسۡتَطَعۡنَا لَخَرَجۡنَا مَعَكُمۡ يُهۡلِكُونَ أَنفُسَهُمۡ وَٱللَّهُ يَعۡلَمُ إِنَّهُمۡ لَكَٰذِبُونَ ﴿٤٢﴾

May God forgive you [Prophet]! Why did you grant them permission [to stay behind] before you had come to know who were speaking the truth and who were the liars (43)

عَفَا ٱللَّهُ عَنكَ لِمَ أَذِنتَ لَهُمۡ حَتَّىٰ يَتَبَيَّنَ لَكَ ٱلَّذِينَ صَدَقُواْ وَتَعۡلَمَ ٱلۡكَٰذِبِينَ ﴿٤٣﴾

Those who believe in God and the Last Day will not ask you to exempt them from striving with their property and with their lives. God has full knowledge as to who are the God-fearing. (44)

لَا يَسۡتَـٔۡذِنُكَ ٱلَّذِينَ يُؤۡمِنُونَ بِٱللَّهِ وَٱلۡيَوۡمِ ٱلۡأٓخِرِ أَن يُجَٰهِدُواْ بِأَمۡوَٰلِهِمۡ وَأَنفُسِهِمۡ وَٱللَّهُ عَلِيمٌۢ بِٱلۡمُتَّقِينَ ﴿٤٤﴾

Only those who do not truly believe in God and the Last Day ask you for exemption. Their hearts are filled with doubt; and troubled by doubt, they do waver. (45)

إِنَّمَا يَسْتَأْذِنُكَ ٱلَّذِينَ لَا يُؤْمِنُونَ بِٱللَّهِ وَٱلْيَوْمِ ٱلْأَخِرِ وَٱرْتَابَتْ قُلُوبُهُمْ فَهُمْ فِى رَيْبِهِمْ يَتَرَدَّدُونَ ﴿٤٥﴾

Had they really intended to set out [with you], they would surely have made some preparations for that. But God was averse to their going, so He caused them to hold back; and it was said to them: 'Stay behind with those who stay.' (46)

وَلَوْ أَرَادُوا ٱلْخُرُوجَ لَأَعَدُّوا لَهُۥ عُدَّةً وَلَٰكِن كَرِهَ ٱللَّهُ ٱنبِعَاثَهُمْ فَثَبَّطَهُمْ وَقِيلَ ٱقْعُدُوا مَعَ ٱلْقَٰعِدِينَ ﴿٤٦﴾

Had they set out with you, they would have added nothing to you but trouble, and would have scurried to and fro in your midst, seeking to sow discord among you. There are among you some who would have lent them ear. Certainly God has full knowledge of the wrongdoers. (47)

لَوْ خَرَجُوا فِيكُم مَّا زَادُوكُمْ إِلَّا خَبَالًا وَلَأَوْضَعُوا خِلَٰلَكُمْ يَبْغُونَكُمُ ٱلْفِتْنَةَ وَفِيكُمْ سَمَّٰعُونَ لَهُمْ وَٱللَّهُ عَلِيمٌۢ بِٱلظَّٰلِمِينَ ﴿٤٧﴾

They had, even before this time, tried to sow discord, and devised plots against you, until the truth was revealed and the will of God prevailed, no matter how hateful it is to them. (48)

لَقَدِ ٱبْتَغَوُا ٱلْفِتْنَةَ مِن قَبْلُ وَقَلَّبُوا لَكَ ٱلْأُمُورَ حَتَّىٰ جَآءَ ٱلْحَقُّ وَظَهَرَ أَمْرُ ٱللَّهِ وَهُمْ كَٰرِهُونَ ﴿٤٨﴾

There is among them [many a] one who may say: 'Give me leave to stay behind, and do not expose me to temptation.' Surely they have succumbed to temptation. Hell is certain to engulf the unbelievers. (49)

وَمِنْهُم مَّن يَقُولُ ٱئْذَن لِّي وَلَا تَفْتِنِّيٓ أَلَا فِي ٱلْفِتْنَةِ سَقَطُواْ وَإِنَّ جَهَنَّمَ لَمُحِيطَةٌ بِٱلْكَٰفِرِينَ ﴿٤٩﴾

Your good fortune grieves them; but if a disaster befalls you, they will say: 'We are lucky to have taken our precautions.' Thus they turn away rejoicing. (50)

إِن تُصِبْكَ حَسَنَةٌ تَسُؤْهُمْ وَإِن تُصِبْكَ مُصِيبَةٌ يَقُولُواْ قَدْ أَخَذْنَآ أَمْرَنَا مِن قَبْلُ وَيَتَوَلَّواْ وَّهُمْ فَرِحُونَ ﴿٥٠﴾

Say: 'Nothing will befall us except what God has decreed. He is our Guardian. In God alone should the believers place their trust.' (51)

قُل لَّن يُصِيبَنَآ إِلَّا مَا كَتَبَ ٱللَّهُ لَنَا هُوَ مَوْلَىٰنَا وَعَلَى ٱللَّهِ فَلْيَتَوَكَّلِ ٱلْمُؤْمِنُونَ ﴿٥١﴾

Say: 'Are you waiting for something [bad] to happen to us?; but [nothing may happen to us except] one of the two best things. On our part we are waiting for God to inflict upon you a scourge, either directly from Himself or by our hands. Wait, then, if you will; we shall also be waiting.' (52)

قُلْ هَلْ تَرَبَّصُونَ بِنَآ إِلَّا إِحْدَى ٱلْحُسْنَيَيْنِ وَنَحْنُ نَتَرَبَّصُ بِكُمْ أَن يُصِيبَكُمُ ٱللَّهُ بِعَذَابٍ مِّنْ عِندِهِۦٓ أَوْ بِأَيْدِينَا فَتَرَبَّصُوٓاْ إِنَّا مَعَكُم مُّتَرَبِّصُونَ ﴿٥٢﴾

Say: 'Whether you spend willingly or unwillingly, it will not be accepted from you; for you are indeed wicked people.' (53)

قُلْ أَنفِقُواْ طَوْعًا أَوْ كَرْهًا لَّن يُتَقَبَّلَ مِنكُمْ إِنَّكُمْ كُنتُمْ قَوْمًا فَٰسِقِينَ ﴿٥٣﴾

169

What prevents their spending from being accepted from them is that they have disbelieved in God and His Messenger, and they only come to prayer with reluctance, and never donate anything [for a righteous cause] without being resentful. (54)

وَمَا مَنَعَهُمْ أَن تُقْبَلَ مِنْهُمْ نَفَقَتُهُمْ إِلَّا أَنَّهُمْ كَفَرُوا۟ بِٱللَّهِ وَبِرَسُولِهِۦ وَلَا يَأْتُونَ ٱلصَّلَوٰةَ إِلَّا وَهُمْ كُسَالَىٰ وَلَا يُنفِقُونَ إِلَّا وَهُمْ كَٰرِهُونَ ﴿٥٤﴾

Let neither their riches nor their children rouse your admiration. God only wishes to punish them by means of these in this worldly life, and that their souls perish while they are unbelievers. (55)

فَلَا تُعْجِبْكَ أَمْوَٰلُهُمْ وَلَآ أَوْلَٰدُهُمْ إِنَّمَا يُرِيدُ ٱللَّهُ لِيُعَذِّبَهُم بِهَا فِى ٱلْحَيَوٰةِ ٱلدُّنْيَا وَتَزْهَقَ أَنفُسُهُمْ وَهُمْ كَٰفِرُونَ ﴿٥٥﴾

They swear by God that they belong to you, when certainly they do not belong to you, but are people overwhelmed by fear. (56)

وَيَحْلِفُونَ بِٱللَّهِ إِنَّهُمْ لَمِنكُمْ وَمَا هُم مِّنكُمْ وَلَٰكِنَّهُمْ قَوْمٌ يَفْرَقُونَ ﴿٥٦﴾

If only they could find a place of shelter, or cavern, or any hiding place, they would rush headlong into it. (57)

لَوْ يَجِدُونَ مَلْجَـًٔا أَوْ مَغَٰرَٰتٍ أَوْ مُدَّخَلًا لَّوَلَّوْا۟ إِلَيْهِ وَهُمْ يَجْمَحُونَ ﴿٥٧﴾

Among them there are those who speak ill of you concerning the distribution of charity. If they are given a share of it, they are pleased, but if no share is given to them, they are enraged. (58)

وَمِنْهُم مَّن يَلْمِزُكَ فِى ٱلصَّدَقَٰتِ فَإِنْ أُعْطُوا۟ مِنْهَا رَضُوا۟ وَإِن لَّمْ يُعْطَوْا۟ مِنْهَآ إِذَا هُمْ يَسْخَطُونَ ﴿٥٨﴾

Yet [how much better it would have been for them] had they contented themselves with what God and His Messenger have given them, and said: 'God is sufficient for us. God will give us out of His bounty, and so too will His Messenger. To God alone do we turn in hope.' (59)

وَلَوْ أَنَّهُمْ رَضُوا مَآ ءَاتَىٰهُمُ ٱللَّهُ وَرَسُولُهُ وَقَالُواْ حَسْبُنَا ٱللَّهُ سَيُؤْتِينَا ٱللَّهُ مِن فَضْلِهِ وَرَسُولُهُ إِنَّا إِلَى ٱللَّهِ رَٰغِبُونَ ۞

Charitable donations are only for the poor and the needy, and those who work in the administration of such donations, and those whose hearts are to be won over, for the freeing of people in bondage and debtors, and to further God's cause, and for the traveller in need. This is a duty ordained by God, and God is All-knowing, Wise. (60)

إِنَّمَا ٱلصَّدَقَٰتُ لِلْفُقَرَآءِ وَٱلْمَسَٰكِينِ وَٱلْعَٰمِلِينَ عَلَيْهَا وَٱلْمُؤَلَّفَةِ قُلُوبُهُمْ وَفِي ٱلرِّقَابِ وَٱلْغَٰرِمِينَ وَفِي سَبِيلِ ٱللَّهِ وَٱبْنِ ٱلسَّبِيلِ فَرِيضَةً مِّنَ ٱللَّهِ وَٱللَّهُ عَلِيمٌ حَكِيمٌ ۞

And among them are others who hurt the Prophet and say: 'He is all ear.' Say: 'He is an ear listening to what is good for you. He believes in God, trusts the believers and he is a mercy to those of you who are true believers.' Those who hurt God's Messenger shall have painful suffering. (61)

وَمِنْهُمُ ٱلَّذِينَ يُؤْذُونَ ٱلنَّبِيَّ وَيَقُولُونَ هُوَ أُذُنٌ قُلْ أُذُنُ خَيْرٍ لَّكُمْ يُؤْمِنُ بِٱللَّهِ وَيُؤْمِنُ لِلْمُؤْمِنِينَ وَرَحْمَةٌ لِّلَّذِينَ ءَامَنُواْ مِنكُمْ وَٱلَّذِينَ يُؤْذُونَ رَسُولَ ٱللَّهِ لَهُمْ عَذَابٌ أَلِيمٌ ۞

171

They swear to you by God in order to please you. Yet it is God and His Messenger that they should strive to please, if indeed they are believers. (62)

يَحْلِفُونَ بِٱللَّهِ لَكُمْ لِيُرْضُوكُمْ وَٱللَّهُ وَرَسُولُهُۥٓ أَحَقُّ أَن يُرْضُوهُ إِن كَانُوا۟ مُؤْمِنِينَ ۝

Do they not know that anyone who defies God and His Messenger shall have the fire of hell, therein to abide? That is the ultimate disgrace. (63)

أَلَمْ يَعْلَمُوٓا۟ أَنَّهُۥ مَن يُحَادِدِ ٱللَّهَ وَرَسُولَهُۥ فَأَنَّ لَهُۥ نَارَ جَهَنَّمَ خَٰلِدًا فِيهَا ذَٰلِكَ ٱلْخِزْىُ ٱلْعَظِيمُ ۝

The hypocrites dread lest a *sūrah* be revealed about them, making clear to them what is really in their hearts. Say: 'Scoff, if you will; God will surely bring to light the very thing you are dreading.' (64)

يَحْذَرُ ٱلْمُنَٰفِقُونَ أَن تُنَزَّلَ عَلَيْهِمْ سُورَةٌ تُنَبِّئُهُم بِمَا فِى قُلُوبِهِمْ قُلِ ٱسْتَهْزِءُوٓا۟ إِنَّ ٱللَّهَ مُخْرِجٌ مَّا تَحْذَرُونَ ۝

Should you question them, they will say: 'We have only been indulging in idle talk and jesting.' Say: 'Was it, then, at God, His revelations and His Messenger that you have been mocking?' (65)

وَلَئِن سَأَلْتَهُمْ لَيَقُولُنَّ إِنَّمَا كُنَّا نَخُوضُ وَنَلْعَبُ قُلْ أَبِٱللَّهِ وَءَايَٰتِهِۦ وَرَسُولِهِۦ كُنتُمْ تَسْتَهْزِءُونَ ۝

Make no excuses. You have disbelieved after you have professed to be believers. Though We may pardon some of you, We shall punish others, on account of their being guilty. (66)

لَا تَعْتَذِرُوا۟ قَدْ كَفَرْتُم بَعْدَ إِيمَٰنِكُمْ إِن نَّعْفُ عَن طَآئِفَةٍ مِّنكُمْ نُعَذِّبْ طَآئِفَةًۢ بِأَنَّهُمْ كَانُوا۟ مُجْرِمِينَ ۝

The hypocrites, both men and women, are all of a kind. They enjoin what is wrong and forbid what is right, and tighten their fists. They have forgotten God and so He has chosen to forget them. Surely the hypocrites are the transgressors. (67)

اَلْمُنَٰفِقُونَ وَالْمُنَٰفِقَٰتُ بَعْضُهُم مِّنۢ بَعْضٍ يَأْمُرُونَ بِالْمُنكَرِ وَيَنْهَوْنَ عَنِ الْمَعْرُوفِ وَيَقْبِضُونَ أَيْدِيَهُمْ نَسُوا اللَّهَ فَنَسِيَهُمْ إِنَّ الْمُنَٰفِقِينَ هُمُ الْفَٰسِقُونَ ۝

God has promised the hypocrites, both men and women, and the unbelievers the fire of hell, where they shall abide. It shall be sufficient for them. God has rejected them, and theirs is a lasting torment. (68)

وَعَدَ اللَّهُ الْمُنَٰفِقِينَ وَالْمُنَٰفِقَٰتِ وَالْكُفَّارَ نَارَ جَهَنَّمَ خَٰلِدِينَ فِيهَا هِيَ حَسْبُهُمْ وَلَعَنَهُمُ اللَّهُ وَلَهُمْ عَذَابٌ مُّقِيمٌ ۝

Yours is just like the case of those before you. They were more powerful than you and had greater wealth and more children. They enjoyed their share. And you have been enjoying your share, just as those who preceded you enjoyed their share; and you have been indulging in idle talk just like they did. Their works have come to nothing in this world and shall come to nothing in the life to come. They are indeed the losers. (69)

كَالَّذِينَ مِن قَبْلِكُمْ كَانُوا أَشَدَّ مِنكُمْ قُوَّةً وَأَكْثَرَ أَمْوَٰلًا وَأَوْلَٰدًا فَاسْتَمْتَعُوا بِخَلَٰقِهِمْ فَاسْتَمْتَعْتُم بِخَلَٰقِكُمْ كَمَا اسْتَمْتَعَ الَّذِينَ مِن قَبْلِكُم بِخَلَٰقِهِمْ وَخُضْتُمْ كَالَّذِي خَاضُوا أُوْلَٰٓئِكَ حَبِطَتْ أَعْمَٰلُهُمْ فِي الدُّنْيَا وَالْآخِرَةِ وَأُوْلَٰٓئِكَ هُمُ الْخَٰسِرُونَ ۝

173

Have they not heard the histories of those who preceded them, such as Noah's people, 'Ād and Thamūd, and Abraham's people, and the folk of Madyan and the ruined cities? Their messengers came to them with clear evidence of the truth. It was not God who wronged them; it was they who wronged themselves. (70)

أَلَمْ يَأْتِهِمْ نَبَأُ ٱلَّذِينَ مِن قَبْلِهِمْ قَوْمِ نُوحٍ وَعَادٍ وَثَمُودَ وَقَوْمِ إِبْرَٰهِيمَ وَأَصْحَٰبِ مَدْيَنَ وَٱلْمُؤْتَفِكَٰتِ أَتَتْهُمْ رُسُلُهُم بِٱلْبَيِّنَٰتِ فَمَا كَانَ ٱللَّهُ لِيَظْلِمَهُمْ وَلَٰكِن كَانُوٓا۟ أَنفُسَهُمْ يَظْلِمُونَ ۝

The believers, men and women, are friends to one another: they enjoin what is right and forbid what is wrong; they attend to their prayers, and pay their *zakāt*, and obey God and His Messenger. It is on these that God will have mercy. Surely, God is Almighty, Wise. (71)

وَٱلْمُؤْمِنُونَ وَٱلْمُؤْمِنَٰتُ بَعْضُهُمْ أَوْلِيَآءُ بَعْضٍ يَأْمُرُونَ بِٱلْمَعْرُوفِ وَيَنْهَوْنَ عَنِ ٱلْمُنكَرِ وَيُقِيمُونَ ٱلصَّلَوٰةَ وَيُؤْتُونَ ٱلزَّكَوٰةَ وَيُطِيعُونَ ٱللَّهَ وَرَسُولَهُۥٓ أُو۟لَٰٓئِكَ سَيَرْحَمُهُمُ ٱللَّهُ إِنَّ ٱللَّهَ عَزِيزٌ حَكِيمٌ ۝

God has promised the believers, men and women, gardens through which running waters flow, where they will abide, and goodly dwellings in the garden of Eden. Yet God's acceptance is the greatest blessing of all. This is indeed the supreme triumph. (72)

وَعَدَ ٱللَّهُ ٱلْمُؤْمِنِينَ وَٱلْمُؤْمِنَٰتِ جَنَّٰتٍ تَجْرِى مِن تَحْتِهَا ٱلْأَنْهَٰرُ خَٰلِدِينَ فِيهَا وَمَسَٰكِنَ طَيِّبَةً فِى جَنَّٰتِ عَدْنٍ وَرِضْوَٰنٌ مِّنَ ٱللَّهِ أَكْبَرُ ذَٰلِكَ هُوَ ٱلْفَوْزُ ٱلْعَظِيمُ ۝

Prophet, strive hard against the unbelievers and the hypocrites, and press hard on them. Their ultimate abode is hell, and how vile a journey's end. (73)

يَٰٓأَيُّهَا ٱلنَّبِىُّ جَٰهِدِ ٱلْكُفَّارَ وَٱلْمُنَٰفِقِينَ وَٱغْلُظْ عَلَيْهِمْ وَمَأْوَىٰهُمْ جَهَنَّمُ وَبِئْسَ ٱلْمَصِيرُ ۝

They swear by God that they have said nothing [wrong]. Yet they certainly uttered the word of unbelief, and disbelieved after they had professed to submit to God, for they aimed at something which they could not attain. They had no reason to be spiteful, except that God and His Messenger had enriched them out of His bounty. If they repent, it will be for their own good; but if they turn away, God will cause them to endure grievous suffering both in this world and in the life to come. They shall find none on this earth to be their friend or to give them support. (74)

يَحْلِفُونَ بِٱللَّهِ مَا قَالُوا۟ وَلَقَدْ قَالُوا۟ كَلِمَةَ ٱلْكُفْرِ وَكَفَرُوا۟ بَعْدَ إِسْلَٰمِهِمْ وَهَمُّوا۟ بِمَا لَمْ يَنَالُوا۟ وَمَا نَقَمُوٓا۟ إِلَّآ أَنْ أَغْنَىٰهُمُ ٱللَّهُ وَرَسُولُهُۥ مِن فَضْلِهِۦ فَإِن يَتُوبُوا۟ يَكُ خَيْرًا لَّهُمْ وَإِن يَتَوَلَّوْا۟ يُعَذِّبْهُمُ ٱللَّهُ عَذَابًا أَلِيمًا فِي ٱلدُّنْيَا وَٱلْءَاخِرَةِ وَمَا لَهُمْ فِي ٱلْأَرْضِ مِن وَلِيٍّ وَلَا نَصِيرٍ ۝

Some of them have pledged to God: 'If He gives us of His bounty, we will certainly spend in charity, and we will be among the righteous.' (75)

وَمِنْهُم مَّنْ عَٰهَدَ ٱللَّهَ لَئِنْ ءَاتَىٰنَا مِن فَضْلِهِۦ لَنَصَّدَّقَنَّ وَلَنَكُونَنَّ مِنَ ٱلصَّٰلِحِينَ ۝

But when He had given them of His bounty they grew niggardly and turned away, heedless [of their pledges]. (76)

فَلَمَّآ ءَاتَىٰهُم مِّن فَضْلِهِۦ بَخِلُوا۟ بِهِۦ وَتَوَلَّوا۟ وَّهُم مُّعْرِضُونَ ۝

In consequence, He caused hypocrisy to take root in their hearts till the Day on which they will meet Him, because they have been untrue to the pledges they made to God, and because of the lies they used to tell. (77)

فَأَعْقَبَهُمْ نِفَاقًا فِي قُلُوبِهِمْ إِلَىٰ يَوْمِ يَلْقَوْنَهُۥ بِمَآ أَخْلَفُوا۟ ٱللَّهَ مَا وَعَدُوهُ وَبِمَا كَانُوا۟ يَكْذِبُونَ ۝

Do they not realize that God knows both their secret thoughts and what they talk about in private, and that God has full knowledge of all things that are hidden away? (78)

It is those hypocrites that taunt the believers who donate freely, as well as those who have nothing to give except what they earn through their toil, and deride them all. God derides them, and grievous suffering awaits them. (79)

You may pray for their forgiveness or may not pray for them, [for it will all be the same]. Even if you were to pray seventy times for their forgiveness, God will not forgive them, for they have denied God and His Messenger. God does not guide those who are transgressors. (80)

Those who were left behind rejoiced at having stayed at home after [the departure of] God's Messenger, for they were averse to striving with their property and their lives in God's cause. They said [to one another]: 'Do not go to war in this heat.' Say: 'The fire of hell is far hotter.' Would that they understood. (81)

أَلَمْ يَعْلَمُوٓاْ أَنَّ ٱللَّهَ يَعْلَمُ سِرَّهُمْ وَنَجْوَىٰهُمْ وَأَنَّ ٱللَّهَ عَلَّٰمُ ٱلْغُيُوبِ ۝

ٱلَّذِينَ يَلْمِزُونَ ٱلْمُطَّوِّعِينَ مِنَ ٱلْمُؤْمِنِينَ فِى ٱلصَّدَقَٰتِ وَٱلَّذِينَ لَا يَجِدُونَ إِلَّا جُهْدَهُمْ فَيَسْخَرُونَ مِنْهُمْ سَخِرَ ٱللَّهُ مِنْهُمْ وَلَهُمْ عَذَابٌ أَلِيمٌ ۝

ٱسْتَغْفِرْ لَهُمْ أَوْ لَا تَسْتَغْفِرْ لَهُمْ إِن تَسْتَغْفِرْ لَهُمْ سَبْعِينَ مَرَّةً فَلَن يَغْفِرَ ٱللَّهُ لَهُمْ ذَٰلِكَ بِأَنَّهُمْ كَفَرُواْ بِٱللَّهِ وَرَسُولِهِۦ وَٱللَّهُ لَا يَهْدِى ٱلْقَوْمَ ٱلْفَٰسِقِينَ ۝

فَرِحَ ٱلْمُخَلَّفُونَ بِمَقْعَدِهِمْ خِلَٰفَ رَسُولِ ٱللَّهِ وَكَرِهُوٓاْ أَن يُجَٰهِدُواْ بِأَمْوَٰلِهِمْ وَأَنفُسِهِمْ فِى سَبِيلِ ٱللَّهِ وَقَالُواْ لَا تَنفِرُواْ فِى ٱلْحَرِّ قُلْ نَارُ جَهَنَّمَ أَشَدُّ حَرًّا لَّوْ كَانُواْ يَفْقَهُونَ ۝

They shall laugh but a little, and they will weep much, in return for what they have earned. (82)

فَلْيَضْحَكُواْ قَلِيلًا وَلْيَبْكُواْ كَثِيرًا جَزَآءَ بِمَا كَانُواْ يَكْسِبُونَ ﴿٨٢﴾

If God brings you back and you meet some of them, and then they ask leave to go forth with you, say: 'Never shall you go forth with me, nor shall you fight an enemy with me. You were happy to stay behind on the first occasion, so you stay now with those who remain behind.' (83)

فَإِن رَّجَعَكَ ٱللَّهُ إِلَىٰ طَآئِفَةٍ مِّنْهُمْ فَٱسْتَـٔذَنُوكَ لِلْخُرُوجِ فَقُل لَّن تَخْرُجُواْ مَعِىَ أَبَدًا وَلَن تُقَٰتِلُواْ مَعِىَ عَدُوًّا إِنَّكُمْ رَضِيتُم بِٱلْقُعُودِ أَوَّلَ مَرَّةٍ فَٱقْعُدُواْ مَعَ ٱلْخَٰلِفِينَ ﴿٨٣﴾

You shall not pray for any of them who dies, and you shall not stand by his grave. For they have denied God and His Messenger and died as hardened sinners. (84)

وَلَا تُصَلِّ عَلَىٰٓ أَحَدٍ مِّنْهُم مَّاتَ أَبَدًا وَلَا تَقُمْ عَلَىٰ قَبْرِهِ إِنَّهُمْ كَفَرُواْ بِٱللَّهِ وَرَسُولِهِ وَمَاتُواْ وَهُمْ فَٰسِقُونَ ﴿٨٤﴾

Let neither their riches nor their children excite your admiration. God only wishes to punish them by means of these in the life of this world, and that their souls perish while they are unbelievers. (85)

وَلَا تُعْجِبْكَ أَمْوَٰلُهُمْ وَأَوْلَٰدُهُمْ إِنَّمَا يُرِيدُ ٱللَّهُ أَن يُعَذِّبَهُم بِهَا فِى ٱلدُّنْيَا وَتَزْهَقَ أَنفُسُهُمْ وَهُمْ كَٰفِرُونَ ﴿٨٥﴾

When a *surah* was revealed from on high calling on them to believe in God and to strive alongside His Messenger, those of them who were well able to do so asked you to give them leave and said to you: 'Allow us to stay with those who remain behind.' (86)

وَإِذَآ أُنزِلَتْ سُورَةٌ أَنْ ءَامِنُواْ بِٱللَّهِ وَجَٰهِدُواْ مَعَ رَسُولِهِ ٱسْتَـٔذَنَكَ أُوْلُواْ ٱلطَّوْلِ مِنْهُمْ وَقَالُواْ ذَرْنَا نَكُن مَّعَ ٱلْقَٰعِدِينَ ﴿٨٦﴾

They are well-pleased to remain with those who are left behind. And their hearts are sealed, so that they are unable to understand the truth. (87)

رَضُواْ بِأَن يَكُونُواْ مَعَ ٱلْخَوَالِفِ وَطُبِعَ عَلَىٰ قُلُوبِهِمْ فَهُمْ لَا يَفْقَهُونَ ﴿٨٧﴾

But the Messenger and those who have believed with him strive hard in God's cause with their property and their lives. These shall have all the good things. These shall certainly prosper. (88)

لَٰكِنِ ٱلرَّسُولُ وَٱلَّذِينَ ءَامَنُواْ مَعَهُۥ جَٰهَدُواْ بِأَمْوَٰلِهِمْ وَأَنفُسِهِمْ وَأُوْلَٰٓئِكَ لَهُمُ ٱلْخَيْرَٰتُ وَأُوْلَٰٓئِكَ هُمُ ٱلْمُفْلِحُونَ ﴿٨٨﴾

God has prepared for them gardens through which running waters flow, where they shall abide. That is the supreme triumph. (89)

أَعَدَّ ٱللَّهُ لَهُمْ جَنَّٰتٍ تَجْرِى مِن تَحْتِهَا ٱلْأَنْهَٰرُ خَٰلِدِينَ فِيهَا ذَٰلِكَ ٱلْفَوْزُ ٱلْعَظِيمُ ﴿٨٩﴾

Some of the Bedouins who had excuses to offer turned up, begging to be granted exemption; while those who denied God and His Messenger stayed behind. Grievous suffering shall befall those of them that disbelieved. (90)

وَجَآءَ ٱلْمُعَذِّرُونَ مِنَ ٱلْأَعْرَابِ لِيُؤْذَنَ لَهُمْ وَقَعَدَ ٱلَّذِينَ كَذَبُواْ ٱللَّهَ وَرَسُولَهُۥ سَيُصِيبُ ٱلَّذِينَ كَفَرُواْ مِنْهُمْ عَذَابٌ أَلِيمٌ ﴿٩٠﴾

No blame shall be attached to the weak, the sick or those who do not have the means, if they are sincere towards God and His Messenger. There is no cause to reproach those who do good. God is Much-forgiving, Merciful. (91)

لَّيْسَ عَلَى ٱلضُّعَفَآءِ وَلَا عَلَى ٱلْمَرْضَىٰ وَلَا عَلَى ٱلَّذِينَ لَا يَجِدُونَ مَا يُنفِقُونَ حَرَجٌ إِذَا نَصَحُواْ لِلَّهِ وَرَسُولِهِۦ مَا عَلَى ٱلْمُحْسِنِينَ مِن سَبِيلٍ وَٱللَّهُ غَفُورٌ رَّحِيمٌ ﴿٩١﴾

178

Nor shall those be blamed who, when they came to request you for transport and you said: 'I have no means of transporting you', turned away with their eyes overflowing with tears, sad that they did not have the means to cover their expenses. (92)

وَلَا عَلَى ٱلَّذِينَ إِذَا مَا أَتَوْكَ لِتَحْمِلَهُمْ قُلْتَ لَا أَجِدُ مَا أَحْمِلُكُمْ عَلَيْهِ تَوَلَّوا وَّأَعْيُنُهُمْ تَفِيضُ مِنَ ٱلدَّمْعِ حَزَنًا أَلَّا يَجِدُوا مَا يُنفِقُونَ ۞

But blame shall certainly attach only to those who ask you for exemption even though they are rich. They are well pleased to be with those who are left behind. God has sealed their hearts, so that they have no knowledge. (93)

إِنَّمَا ٱلسَّبِيلُ عَلَى ٱلَّذِينَ يَسْتَئْذِنُونَكَ وَهُمْ أَغْنِيَاءُ رَضُوا بِأَن يَكُونُوا مَعَ ٱلْخَوَالِفِ وَطَبَعَ ٱللَّهُ عَلَى قُلُوبِهِمْ فَهُمْ لَا يَعْلَمُونَ ۞

They shall come to you with their excuses when you return to them. Say: 'Do not offer any excuses, for we shall not believe you. God has already enlightened us about you. God will see how you act, and so will His Messenger; and in the end you shall be brought before Him who knows all that is beyond the reach of human perception, and all that is manifest when He will tell you what you used to do.' (94)

يَعْتَذِرُونَ إِلَيْكُمْ إِذَا رَجَعْتُمْ إِلَيْهِمْ قُل لَّا تَعْتَذِرُوا لَن نُّؤْمِنَ لَكُمْ قَدْ نَبَّأَنَا ٱللَّهُ مِنْ أَخْبَارِكُمْ وَسَيَرَى ٱللَّهُ عَمَلَكُمْ وَرَسُولُهُۥ ثُمَّ تُرَدُّونَ إِلَى عَالِمِ ٱلْغَيْبِ وَٱلشَّهَادَةِ فَيُنَبِّئُكُم بِمَا كُنتُمْ تَعْمَلُونَ ۞

When you return to them they will swear to you by God so that you may let them be. Let them be, then: they are unclean. Hell shall be their abode in recompense for what they used to do. (95)

سَيَحْلِفُونَ بِاللَّهِ لَكُمْ إِذَا ٱنقَلَبْتُمْ إِلَيْهِمْ لِتُعْرِضُوا عَنْهُمْ فَأَعْرِضُوا عَنْهُمْ إِنَّهُمْ رِجْسٌ وَمَأْوَىٰهُمْ جَهَنَّمُ جَزَآءَ بِمَا كَانُوا يَكْسِبُونَ ۝

They swear to you trying to make you pleased with them. Should you be pleased with them, God shall never be pleased with such transgressing folk. (96)

يَحْلِفُونَ لَكُمْ لِتَرْضَوْا عَنْهُمْ فَإِن تَرْضَوْا عَنْهُمْ فَإِنَّ ٱللَّهَ لَا يَرْضَىٰ عَنِ ٱلْقَوْمِ ٱلْفَٰسِقِينَ ۝

Distinguishing True Believers from Liars

At this point the *surah* speaks about certain groups that demonstrated weakness, but it reserves more space for exposing the hypocrites who pretended to believe in order to join the Muslim ranks after Islam had shown its strength and looked certain to triumph. They felt it safer to bow their heads to Islam so as to acquire whatever they might by way of other gain. Simultaneously, and with open hostility no longer feasible, they could also undermine the Muslim community from within. Here, then, we will encounter all those aspects of weakness to which we referred in the Prologue.

Had there been [a prospect of] an immediate gain, and a short journey, they would certainly have followed you; but the distance was too far for them. Yet they will swear by God: 'Had we been able, we would surely have joined you.' They bring ruin upon themselves. God knows indeed that they are liars. May God forgive you [Prophet]! Why did you grant them permission [to stay behind] before you had come to know who were speaking the truth and who were the liars. Those who believe in God and the Last Day will not ask you to exempt them from striving with their property and with their lives. God has full knowledge as to who are the God-fearing. Only those who do not truly believe in God and the

180

Last Day ask you for exemption. Their hearts are filled with doubt; and troubled by doubt, they do waver. Had they really intended to set out [with you], they would surely have made some preparations for that. But God was averse to their going, so He caused them to hold back; and it was said to them: 'Stay behind with those who stay.' Had they set out with you, they would have added nothing to you but trouble, and would have scurried to and fro in your midst, seeking to sow discord among you. There are among you some who would have lent them ear. Certainly God has full knowledge of the wrongdoers. They had, even before this time, tried to sow discord, and devised plots against you, until the truth was revealed and the will of God prevailed, no matter how hateful it is to them. (Verses 42–48)

The first thing highlighted here is that had the situation involved the prospect of immediate gain or the undertaking of a short journey, which represented no serious risk, they would have joined the Prophet. But the undertaking was not an easy one. The destination was much too far for those with a weak resolve and a frail aptitude for glory. The effort required was not for those with weak hearts. People were called upon to rise to a great occasion, one which would prove their metal. Hence we find in the community a type of people that we encounter across all generations: *"Had there been [a prospect of] an immediate gain, and a short journey, they would certainly have followed you; but the distance was too far for them."* (Verse 42)

Countless people turn their backs when they see a road leading to a high summit. When they realize that it is a long way that they must traverse, they withdraw, preferring to seek immediate gain, petty as it may be. Such people are found in every community and in all generations. They are not a small group found in the Madinah community only; they are encountered everywhere. They languish on the margins of life, although they may think that they have attained their goals without having to pay a hefty price. A paltry price can only buy what is trivial, worthless.

"They will swear by God: 'Had we been able, we would surely have joined you.'" (Verse 42) Lying goes hand in hand with cowardice and weakness. Only the weak and faint-hearted resort to lies, even though

181

they may occasionally appear to command considerable power. A strong person will not hesitate to face any eventuality head on, while the weak will always remain evasive. It is a rule that never fails. *"They bring ruin upon themselves."* (Verse 42) They certainly ruin themselves by their false swearing which they imagine will save them in the eyes of other people. However, God knows the truth and He reveals it to mankind. Thus the liar is ruined in this life by the effects of his falsehood and he ruins himself in the hereafter when he cannot deny his true motives before God, because *"God knows indeed that they are liars."* (Verse 42)

"May God forgive you [Prophet]! Why did you grant them permission [to stay behind] before you had come to know who were speaking the truth and who were the liars?" (Verse 43) Here we have an example of God's kindness as He begins with stating His pardon before His reproach. Those hypocrites who stayed behind were able to hide their true colours when the Prophet allowed them to stay behind after they had presented their excuses. This was a chance to expose their falsehood, because they would have stayed behind anyway, even though the Prophet would have withheld his permission. They would have been seen as they truly were, without their false guise.

But since this did not happen, the Qur'ān exposes them and states clearly the rules which distinguish the true believers from the hypocrites: *"Those who believe in God and the Last Day will not ask you to exempt them from striving with their property and with their lives. God has full knowledge as to who are the God-fearing. Only those who do not truly believe in God and the Last Day ask you for exemption. Their hearts are filled with doubt; and troubled by doubt, they do waver."* (Verses 44–45)

This is the rule which will never fail. Those who believe in God and in the Day of Judgement do not wait for permission in order to fight for God's cause. They will not hesitate to answer the call to strive hard, offering their wealth and their lives. They will rush to respond, whether they are lightly or heavily armed, as God has commanded. They obey Him, assured that they will meet Him on the Day of Judgement, certain of His reward, and hoping to win His pleasure. They are quick to volunteer, and so they do not need any encouragement, let alone special permission. Those who seek permission are the ones whose hearts have little faith. Hence they slacken, seeking all kinds of excuses. Indeed they hope for something to happen which will prevent them from fulfilling the tasks required by the faith they pretend to have, when they are waverers, full of doubt.

The way leading to God's pleasure is straight and clearly marked. Only a person who does not know the way, or one who knows it but tries to avoid its hardship, is reluctant to follow it. Those who stayed behind at the time of the Tabūk Expedition were able to join the army, had they wished to do so. They had all the means at their disposal. Among them were people like ʿAbdullāh ibn Ubayy and al-Jadd ibn Qays, both of whom were rich and from among the nobility. "*Had they really intended to set out [with you], they would surely have made some preparations for that. But God was averse to their going.*" (Verse 46)

This is due to what He knew of their nature and their hypocrisy, as well as their ill intentions towards the believers, as we will see. Hence, "*He caused them to hold back,*" and did not give them the motivation to set forth with the believers. So, "*it was said to them: 'Stay behind with those who stay.'*" (Verse 46) Thus they stayed behind with the elderly, the women and the children who were not required to fight. This is the right place for faint-hearted waverers who lack faith.

However, this was certainly better for Islam and the Muslims: "*Had they set out with you, they would have added nothing to you but trouble, and would have scurried to and fro in your midst, seeking to sow discord among you. There are among you some who would have lent them ear. Certainly God has full knowledge of the wrongdoers.*" (Verse 47)

Wavering hearts are likely to spread cowardice and reluctance to meet the enemy. Traitors are a real danger to any army. Had those hypocrites set out with the Muslim army, they would not have added to the strength of the Muslims. Indeed they would only have added chaos and trouble, and they would have scurried to and fro, sewing discord and counselling retreat. At that time, there were among the Muslims some who would listen to them, thinking them to be honest in their counsel. However, God who takes care of His message and extends His protection to those who are dedicated believers, spared the Muslims all this by letting the hypocrites stay behind: *'Certainly God has full knowledge of the wrongdoers."* (Verse 47) The description, wrongdoers, in this instance means 'the idolaters,' which in effect means that they also belong to the idolaters.

Their past confirms their evil intentions and their lack of faith. They had opposed God's Messenger exerting their utmost in such opposition. When all their opposition and schemes were foiled, they declared their acceptance of his message, but deep at heart they lacked belief: *"They had, even before this time, tried to sow discord, and devised plots against you, until the truth was revealed and the will of God prevailed, no matter how hateful it is to them."* (Verse 48)

This was at the time the Prophet Muḥammad (peace be upon him) migrated to Madinah and before God enabled him to achieve victory over his enemies. Then the truth triumphed and God's word was supreme. The hypocrites had to bow before it, hateful as that was to them. However, they remained on the look out for a chance to cause trouble for the Muslims.

Absurdity Carried Too Far

The *sūrah* goes on to report some of their fabricated excuses and to expose their ill intentions towards the Prophet and the Muslim community: *"There is among them [many a] one who may say: 'Give me leave to stay behind, and do not expose me to temptation.' Surely they have succumbed to temptation. Hell is certain to engulf the unbelievers. Your good fortune grieves them; but if a disaster befalls you, they will say: 'We are lucky to have taken our precautions.' Thus they turn away rejoicing. Say: 'Nothing will befall us except what God has decreed. He is our Guardian. In God alone should the believers place their trust.' Say: 'Are you waiting for something [bad] to happen to us?; but [nothing may happen to us except] one of the two best things. On our part we are waiting for God to inflict upon you a scourge, either directly from Himself or by our hands. Wait, then, if you will; we shall also be waiting.'"* (Verses 49–52)

It is authentically reported by several authorities that one day when the Prophet was making preparations for the Tabūk Expedition, he said to al-Jadd ibn Qays, of the Salamah clan: "What would you say,

Jadd, to a confrontation with the Byzantines?" He answered: "Or would you rather excuse me, Messenger of God, so that I am not exposed to temptation? My people are aware that no one is more fond of women than me. I fear that should I see the Byzantine women, I would not be able to resist them." The Prophet turned away from him and said: "You are excused." It is to al-Jadd ibn Qays that this verse refers.

This is typical of the absurd excuses proffered by the hypocrites. What answer has the Qur'ān for them? *"Surely they have succumbed to temptation. Hell is certain to engulf the unbelievers."* (Verse 49) The *sūrah* portrays here a scene in which temptation is shown like an abyss in which the tempted fall, and behind them stands hell ready to engulf them, blocking all openings for escape. This image suggests that they have committed an unmitigated sin and that their punishment is inevitable. It is a punishment for their falsehood, staying behind at a time of war and offering such absurd excuses. It confirms their total lack of faith, despite the fact that they were keen to pretend that they believed in God and His Messenger.

They certainly do not wish the Prophet or the Muslims well. They are grieved when the Prophet and the Muslims meet good fortune: *"Your good fortune grieves them."* (Verse 50) Indeed they are so happy when misfortune or a disaster befalls the believers, or when they encounter hardship: *"If a disaster befalls you, they will say: 'We are lucky to have taken our precautions.'"* (Verse 50) Thus they consider having stayed behind when the Muslims left to fight the Byzantines a wise precaution. *"Thus they turn away rejoicing."* (Verse 50) They are so pleased that they have ensured their own safety and did not expose themselves to the hardship the Muslims endured.

Their attitude shows their superficial outlook. They consider any hardship to be evil which must be avoided at all costs. They think that they make great gain by staying behind. Their hearts are devoid of any element of submission to God and accepting His will, believing it to be for their own good. A true believer does his best, fearing no outcome, because he believes that whatever good or evil he experiences is tied to God's will, and that God will help him and grant him success: *"Say: 'Nothing will befall us except what God has decreed. He is our Guardian. In God alone should the believers place their trust.'"* (Verse 51)

God has promised the Muslims eventual victory. Therefore whatever hardship they are made to suffer, and however hard their test appears to be, they are being prepared for their promised victory. The believers will certainly have their victory after they have passed their test. It will come by the means God has ordained so that it is treated as a valuable, not a cheap, victory. Thus the Muslims will defend their position of honour, ready to give any sacrifice for it. It is God who gives help and grants victory: *"In God alone should the believers place their trust."* (Verse 51)

To believe in God's will and to rely on Him totally are in no way contradictory with making all the necessary preparations. God gives us a very clear order when He says: *"Make ready against them whatever force and war mounts you can muster."* (8: 60) Placing one's trust in God truly means carrying out His orders, taking all necessary precautions, and understanding the laws He has set into operation without allowing them to deviate from their respective courses in order to please any human being.

It should be mentioned that a believer will only get what is good for him, whether he achieves victory or martyrdom. An unbeliever will only end up with what is evil, whether he is made to taste God's punishment directly or at the hands of the believers: *"Say: 'Are you waiting for something [bad] to happen to us?; but [nothing may happen to us except] one of the two best things. On our part we are waiting for God to inflict upon you a scourge, either directly from Himself or by our hands. Wait, then, if you will; we shall also be waiting."* (Verse 52)

What do the hypocrites expect to happen to the believers? It will be something good anyway. They will either achieve victory which causes God's word to triumph, and this would be the believers' reward in this life; or else, they will achieve martyrdom, which secures for them the highest position with God. What do the believers expect to happen to the hypocrites? It will only be a calamity which overpowers them as happened to earlier unbelievers; or else, they will be defeated and humiliated at the hands of the believers, as happened to the idolaters. They are to wait, then, because the Muslims will be waiting as well. The end will certainly be in favour of the believers.

Possessed by Fear

Some of the hypocrites who tried to stay behind, hoping to spare themselves hardship, offered to help finance the campaign. In this way, they were holding the stick in the middle, like all hypocrites do at all times. God foiled their attempt and instructed His Messenger to declare that their spending was unacceptable by God. Their offers were motivated by fear and hypocrisy, not by genuine faith. Hence, even if the offer were made voluntarily to deceive the Muslims, or they were forced to make it for fear of being exposed for what they truly were, it was of no value. It was rejected by God and earned them no reward whatsoever: *"Say: 'Whether you spend willingly or unwillingly, it will not be accepted from you; for you are indeed wicked people.' What prevents their spending from being accepted from them is that they have disbelieved in God and His Messenger, and they only come to prayer with reluctance, and never donate anything [for a righteous cause] without being resentful."* (Verses 53–54)

This detailed description is true of all hypocrites wherever they happen to be. They are always full of fear, sly, deviant, making pretences that are void of all substance. They are keen to give a false impression in order to escape confrontation. The Qur'ān describes them very accurately: *"They only come to prayer with reluctance."* (Verse 54) They only put up false appearances, and do not approach prayer with sincerity which would enhance their honesty. Hence, they are reluctant when they pray, because they are forced to do it. They have no real motivation to pray, except to impress the Muslims that they belong to them, when in reality they do not. The same is the case with what they spend. It is all a question of appearances.

God does not accept such false pretences which are not motivated by true faith. Indeed it is the motive which gives value to any action, and the intention behind it provides the standard by which it is judged.

Many of those hypocrites were people of affluence, having many children and occupying positions of nobility and honour in their tribes. All this counts for nothing with God and so it should be with His Messenger and the community of believers. Such privileges were not a bounty given to them by God to enjoy; they were only a means of trial which would ensure their punishment: *"Let neither their riches nor their children rouse your admiration. God only wishes to punish them by means of these in this worldly life, and that their souls perish while they are unbelievers.* (Verse 55)

Wealth and children may be a blessing that God grants to any one of His servants when He guides them to be grateful for what they have been granted and to use it for good purposes. Whatever they do with God's bounty, it is motivated by their desire to please God, and this gives them a feeling of security and reassurance. They are thus certain of the outcome: whenever they donate something they feel it a saving for their life to come, and when a calamity befalls their children or their wealth, they accept it with resignation. This gives them new reassurance and hope that God will replace their loss with something better.

On the other hand, wealth and children may be a trial by means of which God tests any of His servants whom He knows to be wicked at heart. Concerns about his wealth and children will soon give him a taste of hell, while his desire to protect what he has been given and to increase it gives him many a sleepless night. He spends his money on what will hurt him and cause his soul to perish. He will be miserable when his children fall ill, and he will be miserable when they recover. Numerous indeed are the ones who suffer in different ways on account of their children.

The hypocrites at the time of the Prophet, and those who are like them everywhere, may have plenty of wealth and plenty of children, which people may admire. Yet to them they are only a cause of suffering in one way or another. This suffering is their lot in this life. What is worse is that, because of their hypocrisy which is perfectly known to God, they are certain to end up dying as unbelievers. This abyss is the worst outcome that any human being can experience.

The statement, *"and that their souls perish,"* imparts its connotations to give us a sense of restless, perturbed souls, lacking all sense of security. They try to escape but are lost, perished. This impression fits in well with that of suffering as a result of having wealth and children. It is, then, all worry and misery in this life as well as the life to come. No one can be envied for such appearances which involve a very hard test indeed.

The hypocrites tried to place themselves in the ranks of believers, not because of their faith – for they had none – but because of fear coupled with hope and expectation. Hence they would swear that they were believers and that they were convinced of the truth of Islam. This *sūrah* exposes their reality. Hence it is described as 'the *sūrah* which reveals the reality,' since it shatters falsehood and tears off the mask of hypocrisy: "*They swear by God that they belong to you, when certainly they do not belong to you, but are people overwhelmed by fear. If only they could find a place of shelter, or cavern, or any hiding place, they would rush headlong into it.*" (Verses 56–57)

They are indeed cowards, and here we are presented with a very vivid picture of their cowardice. It is painted in a physical and mental sweep: "*If only they could find a place of shelter, or cavern, or any hiding place, they would rush headlong into it.*" (Verse 57) They will always look for a shelter, whatever it may be, a fort or a cave or even a tunnel, as long as it gives them protection from an imminent calamity. They are in terrible fear, chased by internal and spiritual cowardice. Hence, "*They swear by God that they belong to you,*" (Verse 56) using all means of emphasis and assertion in order to cover up what they harbour at heart. They only hope to ensure their safety. It is a very miserable picture of cowardly fear which only the unique style of the Qur'ān can depict as it shows the inner feelings of hearts vividly brought before our eyes.

Contented with God's Gifts

The *sūrah* continues its discussion of the hypocrites' attitude and what they may say or do, betraying their real feelings and intentions, hard as they may try to hide them. Some of them speak ill of the Prophet's way of distributing charitable donations, with an implicit accusation of injustice, when he always maintained the highest moral standard. Some say that he listens to any speaker and believes whatever is said to him, when he is in fact most discerning, wise and thoughtful. Some utter a wicked mouthful in private, and when it becomes known, he tries to shelter himself by lies, making false oaths to escape punishment. Some are always in fear lest revelations should give them away, and their reality become known to all Muslims.

Here, the *sūrah* exposes the true nature of both hypocrisy and the hypocrites. Their case is linked to that of the unbelievers which was discussed earlier. Those unbelievers were destroyed after having enjoyed their portion for a time. Thus the difference between them and the believers is clearly shown.

> *Among them there are those who speak ill of you concerning the distribution of charity. If they are given a share of it, they are pleased, but if no share is given to them, they are enraged. Yet [how much better it would have been for them] had they contented themselves with what God and His Messenger have given them, and said: 'God is sufficient for us. God will give us out of His bounty, and so too will His Messenger. To God alone do we turn in hope.' Charitable donations are only for the poor and the needy, and those who work in the administration of such donations, and those whose hearts are to be won over, for the freeing of people in bondage and debtors, and to further God's cause, and for the traveller in need. This is a duty ordained by God, and God is All-knowing, Wise.* (Verses 58–60)

Some of the hypocrites may hurt the Prophet accusing him of injustice when it comes to the distribution of charitable donations, implying that he favours certain people. They do not say this for any love of justice, or to express their enthusiasm for the truth and the values of faith. They only make their claims for vested interests and ulterior motives: *"If they are given a share of it, they are pleased."* (Verse 58) They would not care then about justice, the rights of others or about religious values, because they would have had their share, and that is all that counts with them. *"But if no share is given to them, they are enraged."* (Verse 58)

There are several reports about the immediate incident which led to the revelation of this verse. They refer to particular people who spoke ill of the Prophet and his undoubtedly fair distribution of material benefits. One of these reports is related by al-Bukhārī and al-Nasā'ī on the authority of Abū Sa'īd al-Khudrī who said: "The Prophet was sharing out something when Dhu'l-Khuwayṣir al-Tamīmī came forward and said: "Be fair, Messenger of God." The Prophet said to him: "Who would be fair if I am unfair?" 'Umar ibn al-Khaṭṭāb said to the Prophet: "Allow me to strike his head off." The Prophet said: "Leave him alone. He has companions compared to whom you may think very little of your prayer and fasting, yet they split away from the faith as an arrow penetrates into game." Abū Saʿīd says that it is concerning them that this verse was revealed.

Another report quotes ʿAbdullāh ibn Masʿūd, the Prophet's Companion, as saying: "When the Prophet distributed the spoils of war after the Battle of Ḥunayn, I heard a man saying, 'This distribution has not been done for God's sake.' I went to the Prophet and mentioned this to him. He said: 'May God bestow His mercy on Moses. He was accused of what is worse than this, but he tolerated it patiently.' Following this incident this verse was revealed: *"Among them there are those who speak ill of you concerning the distribution of charity."* (Verse 58)

Another report attributed to Dāwūd ibn Abī ʿĀṣim says: "A sum of money given in charity was brought to the Prophet and he sent a share of it here and a share there until it was all gone. A man from the *Anṣār* who saw this said: 'This is unfair.' This verse was then revealed."

Qatādah, a leading commentator on the Qurʾān, says in his explanation of this verse: "Some of them would criticize the Prophet as to the distribution of charity. It has been mentioned that a Bedouin who had only recently embraced Islam came to the Prophet when he was sharing out some gold and silver. He said to him: 'Muḥammad, if God has ordered you to be fair, then you have not been fair.' The Prophet said: 'Look what you are saying! Who would be fair to you if I am not?'"

Be that as it may, the Qurʾān tells us that the statement was made by some hypocrites who had no qualms about the implementation of religious values. They only expressed their anger at not having been given a share. This is the clearest proof of their hypocrisy. No one who truly believes in Islam would entertain any doubt about the fairness of the Prophet Muḥammad (peace be upon him) who was renowned for his truthfulness and honesty long before he started to receive the divine message. Fairness and justice is a branch of the trust God has assigned to all believers, but more so to His messengers who call on mankind to be believers. It is clear that these Qurʾānic statements refer to certain events and incidents that had happened earlier. However, they relate these within the context of the expedition to Tabūk in order to describe the nature of all hypocrites at all times.

Within the same context, the *sūrah* outlines the attitude that befits true believers: "*Yet [how much better it would have been for them] had they contented themselves with what God and His Messenger have given them, and said: 'God is sufficient for us. God will give us out of His bounty, and so too will His Messenger. To God alone do we turn in hope.'*" (Verse 59)

Such are the attitudes and the manners that befit true believers. They accept with complete satisfaction whatever division is made by God and His Messenger. It is not a forced acceptance. They feel that whatever God gives them is good and sufficient, and He will certainly give His servants what will satisfy them. They hope for God's grace and bounty, and seek His pleasure with complete devotion, free from any expectation of material gain. Such are the proper manners of true believers. Of course these manners are unknown to hypocrites who have never experienced the happiness generated by faith in God and His Messenger. Never had the light of faith shined in their hearts.

Fair Distribution Ordered by God

Having established the right attitude a Muslim should have towards God and His Messenger, which is an attitude of total acceptance of their judgement in all situations, the *sūrah* makes clear that the final decision on the distribution of charity does not belong to the Prophet. It is all God's decision, and it is He who determines which groups of people are entitled to receive a share. The Prophet's role is only to execute what God has ruled. Obligatory donations are taken from the rich in fulfilment of God's commandment, and they are given to the poor also in fulfilment of His same commandment. Its beneficiaries are certain groups of people specified in the Qur'ān. There can be no addition to, or reduction from, these groups by anyone, not even the Prophet himself.

Charitable donations are only for the poor and the needy, and those who work in the administration of such donations, and those whose hearts are to be won over, for the freeing of people in bondage and

debtors, and to further God's cause, and for the traveller in need.
This is a duty ordained by God, and God is All-knowing, Wise.
(Verse 60)

Thus *zakāt*, which is referred to here as 'charitable donations',
occupies its important position in Islamic law and the Islamic social
system. It is not given as a favour by those from whom it is due, but is
rather an incumbent duty. Nor is it given as a gift in an amount
determined by the one who distributes it, but rather its amount is
properly calculated. It is a major Islamic duty collected by the state in
order to fulfil a particular social service. The one who gives it does not
hold a favour for doing so, and the beneficiary does not have to beg
for it. No, the Islamic social system could never be based on begging.

The basis of the Islamic system is work, in all its various ways. It is
the duty of the Muslim state to make sure that anyone who is able to
work has a job. It should provide training opportunities, and it should
take the necessary measures for job creation. Furthermore, it should
ensure that those who work receive fair wages. Those who are able to
work have no claim to *zakāt*, because *zakāt* is a social security tax that
functions between those who are able and those who are deprived.
The state administers its collection and distribution when any society
runs its affairs on the basis of Islam, putting God's law into effect,
seeking no law or social system other than that devised by God.

'Abdullāh ibn 'Umar quotes the Prophet as saying: "Charity is not
lawful to be given to anyone who is rich or to anyone who is strong
and fit." Two men came to the Prophet and asked him to give them a
share of *zakāt*. When he looked at them carefully, he found them
strong and able. He said to them: "If you wish I will give you, but you
should know that no one who is rich or able to work and earn has any
claim to a share in it."

Zakāt is a branch of the Islamic system of social security, and this
system is far wider and more comprehensive than *zakāt*, because it
works along several lines that comprise all aspects of life and all sides
of human ties. *Zakāt* is only an important one of these lines.

Zakāt is collected at the rate of one-tenth, or a half or a quarter of
one-tenth of the principal property, depending on the type of property
held. It is collected from everyone who owns more than the threshold

of *zakāt* when a year has passed since he or she has had that threshold. This means that most members of the community make their contribution to the *Zakāt* Fund. The proceeds are then spent according to the system outlined in the verse we are discussing. The first groups of its beneficiaries are the poor and the needy. The poor are those who have less than what they need to live on. The needy are also in the same position, but they do not show their need or ask for help.

Some among the people who qualify as *zakāt* payers and pay their *zakāt* one year may find their position has changed the following year. Their property may have decreased and they may not have enough for their needs. Thus they qualify as *zakāt* beneficiaries. Some may not have ever paid any *zakāt* but they nevertheless qualify as beneficiaries. In both these cases we see *zakāt* as a means of social security. However, it is first and foremost a duty imposed by God. A human soul is purified as one pays *zakāt* as a form of worship. It is purged of all traces of miserliness, and it triumphs over its love to retain money and property.

The Beneficiaries of *Zakāt*

Let us now look at the groups who should benefit by *zakāt*. *"Charitable donations are only for the poor and the needy, and those who work in the administration of such donations."* (Verse 60) We have already explained who the poor and the needy are. The third group of beneficiaries are the people who actually work in the collection and distribution of *zakāt*.

"And those whose hearts are to be won over." This description applies to several groups of people. Among them may be people who are newcomers to Islam and it is felt that they may be helped to consolidate their conviction of its truth. Also included in this category are those whom we hope to win over to the faith. Similarly, we may include here people who have already become Muslim, but we may give them *zakāt* money to win over some of their colleagues and friends who may start to think about Islam when they see that those who have become Muslim are being given gifts.

There are differences among scholars as to whether this category of beneficiaries still exists, given the fact that Islam has firmly established itself. The fact is that, given the nature of the Islamic system and the various situations in which the Muslim community may find itself, there may often be a need to pay *zakāt* to some individuals or group of people under this heading. The purpose may be either to strengthen their resolve to follow Islam, if they are being subjected to discrimination on account of having adopted Islam, or to help them formulate a favourable idea about Islam. This may apply to people who are not Muslim themselves, but may render some service to Islam by speaking favourably of it in their own circles. When we consider this we recognize how God's wisdom takes good care of the Muslims in all situations.

"For the freeing of people in bondage." In olden days, slavery was an international system where captives of war were enslaved. There was no escape from this system where it had to be applied on the basis of 'an eye for an eye,' until the world could get rid of that system and replace it with something that does not involve enslaving anyone. This portion of *zakāt* funds was used to help anyone who could buy his own freedom in return for a sum of money which he would pay to his master. Alternatively, slaves would be bought with *zakāt* funds and then set free by the Muslim authorities.

"And debtors." This category includes anyone who has incurred debts for a purpose that does not involve committing a sin. They are helped in the repayment of their debts, instead of forcing them to go bankrupt, as happens in a materialistic civilization where business people who are unable to repay their debts have no other option. Islam is a system based on social security, where no honourable human being is left to go by the wayside, and no honest person is lost. Under man-made law, or should we say the law of the jungle, people are allowed to eat one another like fish, although they give the process a legal guise.

"To further God's cause." Under this heading any activity which brings benefit to the Muslim community and serves the advancement of God's cause may be included.

"And for the traveller in need." This includes anyone who might have spent or lost his money while on a journey. He is given what will see him home, even though he may be rich in his hometown.

This is then the *zakāt* system which some people criticize these days, describing it as a system of begging and handouts. It is simply a social duty, discharged in the form of an act of Islamic worship, to purge people's hearts of all traces of miserliness and a grudging love of money. It establishes a bond of mutual care and compassion between all people in the Muslim community. It gives human life an element of loving care while providing a comprehensive system of social security. It retains at the same time its essential nature of being an act of worship which strengthens the bond between man and God, as well as the social human bond.

It is after all: *"a duty ordained by God,"* who knows what is good for humanity and who provides the best system for it based on His wisdom. For, *"God is All-knowing, Wise."*

The Prophet's Care

This explanation of the *zakāt* system and how *zakāt* is to be distributed shows at the same time how ignorant and ill-mannered were those people who criticized the Prophet and made unfavourable remarks about his honesty. The *sūrah* gives further examples of hypocrites and what they used to say and do: *"And among them are others who hurt the Prophet and say: 'He is all ear.' Say: 'He is an ear listening to what is good for you. He believes in God, trusts the believers and he is a mercy to those of you who are true believers.' Those who hurt God's Messenger shall have painful suffering."* (Verse 61)

Here their extremely bad manners in their dealings with the Prophet appear in a different way. They find him extremely accessible, listening to all people with full attention, and always making them welcome. He treats them as they profess to be, without judging their intentions, as he is indeed required to do according to the principles of his faith. They describe his exemplary attitude and refined manners by the wrong adjectives. Describing the Prophet (peace be upon him), they say: *"He is all ear."* By this they mean that he listens to all people, and that he can easily be taken in by lies and false assertions. He believes anyone who is ready to swear to him, and he accepts whatever is being said to him with a false air of conviction.

They say this to one another in order to reassure themselves that he will not see their reality or discover their hypocrisy. They may also say it in criticism of the Prophet because he believes the true believers who would report to him whatever they might come to learn of the reality of the hypocrites and what they might say about Islam, or about God's Messenger and his genuine Companions. Various reports confirm both attitudes as a reason for the revelation of this verse. Indeed it may be taken to refer to either attitude. As for the hypocrites, they said these words intending either meaning at different times.

The Qur'ān uses their very words to silence them with its reply: *"And among them are others who hurt the Prophet and say: 'He is all ear.'"* (Verse 61) Yes, indeed, but what sort of ear? *"Say: 'He is an ear listening to what is good for you.'"* (Verse 61) He is a good ear, listening to what God reveals and communicating it to you as it is. In it you have what is most beneficial to you, ensuring a very good outcome for you. Besides, he listens to you most politely, without confronting you with your hypocrisy and scheming, aware of all that as he certainly is.

Moreover, he *"believes in God."* (Verse 61) He certainly believes what God tells him about you and about any other people. He also *"trusts the believers,"* (Verse 61) and he believes what they tell him. He knows them to be true believers and he knows that true faith deters its adherents from saying anything false or putting up any false appearance. But above all the Prophet is: *"a mercy to those of you who are true believers."* (Verse 61) He leads them by the hand to all that is good. *"Those who hurt God's Messenger shall have painful suffering."* (Verse 61) That suffering will undoubtedly be inflicted by God on anyone who hurts His Messenger. He will not allow anyone who hurts His Messenger to escape punishment.

Dreading Exposure

"They swear to you by God in order to please you. Yet it is God and His Messenger that they should strive to please, if indeed they are believers." (Verse 62) They are always ready to swear by God in order to persuade others to believe them. Here the aim of their swearing is also to please the believers. This is typical of the hypocrites everywhere. They say and do whatever they want behind people's backs, but they are too cowardly to admit to their real attitude. They will not say openly what should be said. Hence, they try to seek every sort of cover and put on any false appearance in the hope of pleasing other people.

197

"Yet it is God and His Messenger that they should strive to please, if indeed they are believers." (Verse 62) Why should they care about other human beings? What power or influence do they have? But a person who does not believe in God and does not submit to Him will always fear and submit to a human being like him. He would be much better off submitting to God in front of whom all people are alike. A person who submits to God will never suffer any humiliation. The only people who are humiliated and who feel their own inadequacy are those who turn away from God and fear their fellow human beings.

"Do they not know that anyone who defies God and His Messenger shall have the fire of hell, therein to abide? That is the ultimate disgrace." (Verse 63) This is a question of censure and rebuke. They profess to be believers, and a believer knows for certain that there can be no offence greater than defying God and His Messenger and taking a stand in opposition to Him. Hell stands in waiting for anyone who commits such an offence. Moreover, humiliation is the fitting reward of rebellion. If they are truly believers, as they claim to be, how is it then that they do not know such an elementary fact?

They fear God's creatures and swear to them in order to please them and to deny what the others have heard about them. How is it, then, that they do not fear the Creator when they hurt His Messenger and oppose the faith He has chosen for human beings? Their attitude is the same as being at war with God Himself. Most sublime is God for anyone to choose to be at war with Him. These verses, then, simply magnify their wickedness and aim to strike fear into the hearts of those who hurt God's Messenger and scheme against His faith.

They are much too cowardly to confront the Prophet and the believers openly. They fear that God will expose their reality and reveal their intentions to His Messenger: *"The hypocrites dread lest a sūrah be revealed about them, making clear to them what is really in their hearts. Say: 'Scoff, if you will; God will surely bring to light the very thing you are dreading.' Should you question them, they will say: 'We have only been indulging in idle talk and jesting.' Say: 'Was it, then, at God, His revelations and His Messenger that you have been mocking?' Make no excuses. You have disbelieved after you have professed to be believers. Though We may pardon some of you, We shall punish others, on account of their being guilty."* (Verses 64–66)

This is a general statement that applied to all hypocrites who feared that revelations might be sent down to expose what they entertained in their hearts. They would then be out on a limb, with all that they had carefully concealed being brought out into the open. However, we have several reports of certain events that led to the revelation of these verses.

One report tells that one of the hypocrites said: "I see that those among us who are most keen to read the Qur'ān are gluttons, liars and cowardly." This was reported to the Prophet. When the man learned of this, he went to the Prophet to find him having mounted his camel, ready to depart. He said to him: "Messenger of God, we were only engaged in idle talk and jesting." The Prophet said to him: *"Was it, then, at God, His revelations and His Messenger that you have been mocking? Make no excuses. You have disbelieved after you have professed to be believers. Though We may pardon some of you, We shall punish others, on account of their being guilty."* (Verses 65–66) As the Prophet replied, he did not face the man who kept holding on to the Prophet's sword, his feet hitting the rocks.

Another report mentions that a group of hypocrites, including Wadī'ah ibn Thābit, as well as a man called Makhshī ibn Ḥimyar, an ally of the tribe of Salamah, were with the Muslim army when the Prophet headed for Tabūk. Some of them tried to frighten the believers and spread doubt in their ranks. They said: "Do you think fighting the Byzantines the same as internal warfare between Arabian tribes? We can even now see how you will all be taken captive tomorrow and be put in chains." Makhshī said: "I wish we could escape with only 100 lashes each, without having verses of the Qur'ān revealed to expose us as a result of what you have said."

The Prophet was informed of this and he said to 'Ammār ibn Yāsir: "Rush to those people for they are burnt. Ask them about what they have said and if they deny it, tell them that they have said these very words." 'Ammār went to them and told them exactly what the Prophet said. They came to the Prophet to apologize. Wadī'ah ibn Thābit said to the Prophet as he mounted his camel, and Wadī'ah holding its reins: "Messenger of God, we were only talking idly and jesting." Makhshī said: "Messenger of God, my name and my father's name prevented me from leaving these people." (This is a reference to the fact that he was only an ally occupying a weak position.) He was the one, among those to whom this verse refers, who was pardoned. He changed his name to 'Abd al-Raḥmān and appealed to God to grant him martyrdom where his body would not be found. He was killed when he was fighting with the Muslim army at Yamāmah against the apostates. His body was lost without trace.

Another report says that a group of hypocrites were in the army going to Tabūk, and some of them said: "Does this man (meaning the Prophet) hope to take hold of the palaces and forts of Syria? Far be it from him." God informed His Messenger of what they said. The Prophet ordered his Companions to have them isolated and he came to them and confronted them with what they had said. They replied: "Messenger of God, we were only engaged in idle talk and jesting." God then revealed these verses.

"We have only been indulging in idle talk and jesting." (Verse 65) As if such important matters which are closely related to the very fundamentals of faith can at all be the subject of idle talk and careless jesting. Hence the reply: "Say: 'Was it, then, at God, His revelations and His Messenger that you have been mocking?'" (Verse 65) Their offence is grave indeed. Hence they are confronted with the reality that they have disbelieved after they had professed to be believers. They are warned of grave suffering which some of them might escape because they have hastened to declare their repentance and were keen to maintain the path of the faithful. Others who remained hypocrites and continued to mock at God's revelations as well as His Messenger and His faith could never escape that torment, on account of their being genuinely guilty.

The Trodden Path of Hypocrisy

So far, the *sūrah* has given us a number of examples of what the hypocrites said and did, as well as the way their concepts and views are formulated. Now it moves on to describe their true nature and their distinctive qualities which set them as a class apart from true believers. It also defines the punishment awaiting all hypocrites: "*The hypocrites, both men and women, are all of a kind. They enjoin what is wrong and forbid what is right, and tighten their fists. They have forgotten God and so He has chosen to forget them. Surely the hypocrites are the transgressors. God has promised the hypocrites, both men and women, and the unbelievers the fire of hell, where they shall abide. It shall be sufficient for them. God has rejected them, and theirs is a lasting torment."* (Verses 67–68)

So, all the hypocrites have the same nature and the same characteristics, regardless of the time and the place where they are found. Their actual actions and statements may differ but they all share the same essence and go back to the same roots. They all have the same essential characteristics: wickedness at heart, ill intentions towards others, and evil scheming against them, because they feel themselves to be too weak and cowardly to enter into an open confrontation, etc. Their behaviour is similarly wicked: they urge others to do what they know to be wrong, and discourage them from doing what is right. They are also tight-fisted with their money. They will not give financial support to any good cause except when they need to do so in order to give a false impression about themselves.

At the same time, they deride those who do right and belittle the committing of wrong deeds. But in all that, they conceal their motives and notions. Whatever they say about right and wrong, they say it in whispers, or sly remarks, ridiculing people and slandering them, because they have no courage to confront anyone with their true convictions. Only when they feel secure do they come out with what is truly in their hearts.

"They have forgotten God," (Verse 67) so they only consider their own interests and weigh up other people's reactions. They only fear those who are powerful among fellow human beings. With such, they are humble and submissive. They try their best to please them and to curry favour with them. As a result, God *"has chosen to forget them."* (Verse 67) He gives them no weight and no consideration. Such indeed is their situation in this life, and so it is in the life to come. People only give due importance to those who are strong, ready to speak up and make their position clear, defending their beliefs and trying to impress others with their ideas, and who fight or make peace in open daylight. Such people pay little attention to human beings in order to give all importance to the Lord of mankind. As they take their position in

support of the truth, they fear no one. Such people are given their due respect by others.

"*Surely the hypocrites are the transgressors.*" (Verse 67) They have abandoned the path of faith, and chosen the path of error. Hence God promises them the same fate as that He promised the unbelievers. That is indeed a sorrowful destiny: "*God has promised the hypocrites, both men and women, and the unbelievers the fire of hell, where they shall abide. It shall be sufficient for them.*" (Verse 68) It is a fitting recompense for their crimes. There is no need for any other punishment. Nevertheless, they are denied access to God's mercy: "*God has rejected them, and theirs is a lasting torment.*" (Verse 68)

Such a wicked nature is not something new; it has its parallels and forerunners in history. Previous communities had their own cases of hypocrisy. Those hypocrites of old faced a doom which befitted their offences, after they had their apportioned share of what this earthly life had to offer. Despite the fact that those were even more powerful than the hypocrite Arabs and possessed greater wealth and had more numerous children, nothing of all this was of any use to them when God inflicted His punishment on them.

Hence the Qur'ān reminds those Arabs of what happened to those communities before them, and warns them that as they follow the same route, they are likely to face the same outcome. If heeded, such warnings should be enough to guide them to follow the message of truth: "*Yours is just like the case of those before you. They were more powerful than you and had greater wealth and more children. They enjoyed their share. And you have been enjoying your share, just as those who preceded you enjoyed their share; and you have been indulging in idle talk just like they did. Their works have come to nothing in this world and shall come to nothing in the life to come. They are indeed the losers.*" (Verse 69)

They are deluded by the fact that they have power, wealth and children. Hence they adopt such an attitude. However, those who recognize the greatest power of God have no such delusions about any earthly or material power. They only fear the One who has the greatest power, and, therefore, they use their own power in demonstrating their obedience to Him and ensuring that His word reigns supreme. Their wealth and children do not give them any false sense of power, because they realize that it is God who has given them these. They are keen to show their gratitude to Him and to use what He has given them in what pleases Him. It is only those who have taken themselves away from the source of real power that are ungrateful and arrogant. Their style of life is that of eating and enjoyment, just like animals.

"*Their works have come to nothing in this world and shall come to nothing in the life to come.*" (Verse 69) Indeed whatever they do is worthless, because it is the same as a plant which has no roots: it cannot stand, grow or blossom. "*They are indeed the losers.*" (Verse 69) They have ended with complete loss with nothing left for them.

The *sūrah* now makes a general address, wondering at those who follow in the footsteps of those communities which suffered God's punishment without learning the lesson: "*Have they not heard the histories of those who preceded them, such as Noah's people, 'Ād and Thamūd, and Abraham's people, and the folk of Madyan and the ruined cities? Their messengers came to them with clear evidence of the truth. It was not God who wronged them; it was they who wronged themselves.*" (Verse 70)

The *sūrah* then puts a question with regard to those who just seek enjoyment and tread the path of destroyed nations: "*Have they not heard the histories of those who preceded them?*" There were many of them who suffered painful doom. There were first the people of Noah, destroyed by the great flood; and the people of 'Ād, victims of a furious wind storm, and the people of Thamūd, overwhelmed by a stunning blast. There were also the people of Abraham whose despotic ruler was destroyed, while Abraham himself was saved by God. The folk of Madyan suffered the violent quake and were suffocated, and the people of Lot had their cities ruined. Now have these latter day hypocrites not heard the histories of those communities to whom "*their messengers came to them with clear evidence of the truth.*" (Verse 70) But they choose to deny such clear evidence and follow the path of error instead. Hence God punished them for what they did: "*It was not God who wronged them; it was they who wronged themselves.*" (Verse 70)

Yet the lessons of the past benefit only those who open their hearts and minds for the contemplation of the working of the laws God has set in operation. These laws make allowances for no one, regardless of

203

their position. Many of those whom God tests with power and affluence choose to overlook what happened to those before them. So they are doomed when God's law applies to them, and God takes them with a mighty hand. It is often the case that those given power and wealth are blinded to realities. Only those who serve God sincerely are spared such a blinding attitude which spells a miserable doom.

The Believers' Dwelling Place

In contrast to the unbelievers and the hypocrites stand the true believers. They are characterized by their totally different nature, different behaviour and different destiny: "*The believers, men and women, are friends to one another: they enjoin what is right and forbid what is wrong; they attend to their prayers, and pay their zakāt, and obey God and His Messenger. It is on these that God will have mercy. Surely, God is Almighty, Wise. God has promised the believers, men and women, gardens through which running waters flow, where they will abide, and goodly dwellings in the garden of Eden. Yet God's acceptance is the greatest blessing of all. This is indeed the supreme triumph.*" (Verses 71–72)

While the hypocrites are all of a kind, having the same characteristics, the believers are by nature a community united in furthering every good thing and promoting what is right. Despite having the same qualities, the hypocrites cannot achieve a status of friends or community. That requires mutual solidarity which is alien to the nature of hypocrisy. Such solidarity cannot be achieved even within a group of hypocrites, who remain weak individuals, despite their identical qualities and behaviour. The Qur'ān points this out in describing both groups: "*The hypocrites, both men and women, are all of a kind.*" (Verse 67) "*The believers, men and women, are friends to one another.*" (Verse 71) An individual believer has the same qualities of the community, where the values of solidarity and mutual care are upheld to promote what is good and prevent what is wrong: "*They enjoin what is right and forbid what is wrong.*" (Verse 71)

To achieve the goals of promoting what is good, enjoining what is right and fighting what is wrong and evil requires close ties within the community, mutual solidarity and true co-operation. Thus the community stands united allowing no divisive element to have any influence on it.

Whenever division appears within the community, it must be a signal pointing to the existence of a strange factor which is alien to its nature and its faith. There must be a purpose or an ailment which prevents the first characteristic of the Muslim community from taking root. That characteristic is described by God, the All-knowing who is aware of all details: *"The believers, men and women, are friends to one another."* Their friendship motivates them to enjoin what is right and to censure and forbid what is wrong. Their aim is to make God's word reign supreme, and to make their community fulfil its role in human life.

"They attend to their prayers," for prayer gives them their bond with God. *"And pay their* zakāt," for *zakāt* is the duty which cements the bonds within the Muslim community. It reflects the material and spiritual solidarity within this community. *"And obey God and His Messenger."* (Verse 71) They have no desire other than to discharge God's orders and obey Him and His Messenger. They have no law other than that revealed by God, and no constitution other than the faith revealed by God to His Messenger. When God and His Messenger determine something concerning their affairs, they accept it realizing that this is the choice they have. This gives them unity of goals, approaches and methods of action. They have a single course which they follow, paying no attention to other courses of action which may cause disunity in their ranks.

"It is on these that God will have mercy." (Verse 71) Mercy is not bestowed only in the hereafter. It is first bestowed in this life, and it is granted first to the individual who fulfils his duties of enjoining what is right and forbidding what is evil, attends to his prayer and pays his *zakāt.* It is also granted to the community which is made up of individuals of such qualities. It is manifested in the reassurance felt by such people and in their bond with God who looks after them and spares them much strife and friction. God's mercy is also seen in the unity and co-operation which are characteristic of such a community where every individual enjoys a contented life, and is reassured by God's acceptance.

These four characteristics of the believers: enjoining what is right, forbidding what is wrong, attending to prayer and paying *zakāt* are contrasted with four characteristics of the hypocrites, namely, enjoining what is wrong, forbidding what is right, forgetting God and tightening their fists. God's mercy which He bestows on the believers is shown here in contrast to His rejection of the hypocrites and the unbelievers. It is for maintaining these characteristics that God has promised the believers victory and establishment in the land. Thus they will be able to put them into effect when they exercise their role as the leaders of mankind.

"*Surely, God is Almighty, Wise.*" (Verse 71) He is able to give power to the believers so that they can help one another to discharge their duties. His wisdom is also seen in granting victory to such a community which sets human life on the right footing, and ensures that God's word reigns supreme.

As we have seen, suffering in hell is the destiny awaiting the hypocrites and unbelievers. They cannot escape God's curse. The fact that He will forget them shows that they are of little importance, suffering deprivation. In contrast, the happiness of being in heaven is what awaits the believers: "*God has promised the believers, men and women, gardens through which running waters flow, where they will abide, and goodly dwellings in the garden of Eden.*" (Verse 72) That is then their dwelling place.

But there is something much greater that awaits them: "*Yet God's acceptance is the greatest blessing of all.*" (Verse 72) Indeed, heaven and all the bliss and happiness that are assured for those who are admitted into it appear to be so small when compared to being accepted by God: "*Yet God's acceptance is the greatest blessing of all.*" Indeed one moment of being in communion with God, contemplating His majesty; a moment of release from the restraints of a physical constitution, and the limitations of this earth and its petty concerns; a moment when a ray of that light which cannot be seen by our eyes lightens our hearts; a moment when the human soul is enlightened by a glimpse of God's mercy; any moment of these which are experienced only by a small number of people when they have clear, undisturbed vision is far greater than all enjoyments and all aspirations. How do people feel when His acceptance overwhelms their souls and they receive it without interruption? Hence these verses conclude with a highly appropriate comment: "*This is indeed the supreme triumph.*" (Verse 72)

All Out Effort to Fight Unbelievers

Thus the *sūrah* has given us a clear outline of the essential characteristics of true believers and those of the hypocrites who claim to be believers. This is now followed by an order from God to His Messenger to strive against the unbelievers and the hypocrites. The Qur'ān makes it clear that the hypocrites certainly disbelieved after they had claimed to be Muslims. They tried something that only their disbelief could have led them to contemplate, but God foiled their attempts. It wonders at their hostile attitude to the Prophet when they have gained nothing but good from his message. It invites them to repent and change their attitude.

> *Prophet, strive hard against the unbelievers and the hypocrites, and press hard on them. Their ultimate abode is hell, and how vile a journey's end. They swear by God that they have said nothing [wrong]. Yet they certainly uttered the word of unbelief, and disbelieved after they had professed to submit to God, for they aimed at something which they could not attain. They had no reason to be spiteful, except that God and His Messenger had enriched them out of His bounty. If they repent, it will be for their own good; but if they turn away, God will cause them to endure grievous suffering both in this world and in the life to come. They shall find none on this earth to be their friend or to give them support.* (Verses 73–74)

The Prophet had been very lenient with the hypocrites, turning a blind eye to much of what they did and forgiving them much. At this point, however, such leniency is no longer useful. He is commanded by his Lord to start a new phase in his dealings with them. They are grouped here with the unbelievers; and the Prophet is ordered to strive against both as hard as he can. There are times when it is more suitable to take a hardened attitude while at others it is wiser to take the side of leniency. When a period of patience and tolerance is no longer advisable, then it is time to be tough. A practical movement has different requirements at different times, and its method of action may move from one stage to another. A soft attitude may sometimes bring about more harm than good.

207

Early scholars differ on what is meant by pressing hard in striving against the hypocrites, and whether it means fighting them with arms as suggested by 'Alī ibn Abī Ṭālib, or by general treatment and clear disapproval which make the reality of their position clear to all. This latter view is expressed by Ibn 'Abbās. In practical terms, the Prophet did not kill any hypocrite.

"*They swear by God that they have said nothing [wrong]. Yet they certainly uttered the word of unbelief, and disbelieved after they had professed to submit to God, for they aimed at something which they could not attain.*" (Verse 74) Taken in general terms, this statement portrays the consistent attitude of the hypocrites reflected in a whole range of incidents. It also refers to various attempts they made to cause harm to the Prophet and the Muslim community. There are, however, several reports which mention a specific incident in connection with the revelation of this verse.

Qatādah says: "This verse refers to 'Abdullāh ibn Ubayy concerning an event when a man from the tribe of Juhaynah quarrelled with a man from the *Anṣār*, with the first gaining the upper hand. 'Abdullāh said to the *Anṣārī* man: 'Will you not support your brother? Our position with Muḥammad is similar to that of a man who feeds his dog until the dog becomes so fat and eats him.' He further said: 'When we go back to Madinah, the honourable among us will drive out the humble.' A Muslim heard what he said and informed the Prophet who sent someone to ask him about it and he swore that he did not utter those words. God then revealed this verse making clear that he did.

Al-Ṭabarī reports that the Prophet was once sitting in the shade of a tree when he said to his Companions who were with him: "A man will come soon, looking at you with the eye of the devil. Do not talk to him." Shortly afterwards a blue looking man came over. The Prophet asked him: "Why do you and your friends speak ill of me?" The man went away and brought his friends who repeatedly swore that they had said nothing, until the Prophet pardoned them. God then revealed the verse which quotes their assertions: "*They swear by God that they have said nothing wrong.*" (Verse 74)

'Urwah ibn al-Zubayr and others report that this verse concerns a man called Al-Jallās ibn Suwayd who had a stepson called 'Umayr ibn

Sa'd. Al-Jallās once said: "If what Muḥammad says be true, then we are worse than these donkeys of ours." 'Umayr said: "You know that you are the dearest of all people to me, and I would rather spare you all harm. But you have said something which would put me in a very bad light if I report it, and would destroy me if I keep it to myself. One of these alternatives is easier than the other." He went to the Prophet and told him, but al-Jallās denied having said it and swore to that effect. When these verses were revealed, he retracted and said: "I have certainly said this, but I am offered a chance to repent. I regret what I said and turn to God in repentance." This was accepted.

All these reports, however, do not take account of the next statement in this verse, *"They aimed at something which they could not attain."* (Verse 74) This supports the other reports which say that the verse refers to a group of hypocrites who plotted to kill the Prophet on his way back from Tabūk. It is useful to mention one of these reports.

Imām Aḥmad reports: "When the Prophet was on his way back from the expedition to Tabūk, he ordered someone to announce that he himself had taken a narrow climbing route and no one else should take it. The Prophet went along with the help of two of his Companions, Ḥudhayfah and 'Ammār. A group of masked men soon came and attacked 'Ammār as he was leading the Prophet's camel, but 'Ammār chased them hitting the faces of their camels. The Prophet told Ḥudhayfah to be patient with his camel until he dismounted. When 'Ammār came back to the Prophet, he asked him whether he was able to recognize those people. 'Ammār said: 'I could recognize most of the camels but the people themselves were masked.' The Prophet asked him whether he could find out what they wanted. 'Ammār said: 'God and His Messenger know best.' The Prophet said: 'They wanted to frighten the camel of God's Messenger so that he would fall to the ground.' 'Ammār went to one of the Prophet's Companions and said: 'I appeal to you by God Almighty, do you know how many people were in that narrow route?' The man said that they were fourteen. 'Ammār said to him: 'If you were with them, then they were fifteen.' The Prophet named three of them who said: 'By God we did not hear the Prophet's announcer when he made the announcement and we were totally unaware what those people were up to.' 'Ammār said: 'I bear witness that the other twelve are enemies of God and His Messenger in this life and on the Day of Judgement.'

This event betrays what those people harboured of ill intentions. Whether this event or a similar one is meant here, it remains very surprising that they should be so treacherous. The Qur'ān wonders at their attitude: "*They had no reason to be spiteful, except that God and His Messenger had enriched them out of His bounty.*" (Verse 74) Islam had caused them no harm to justify such hostility. The only reason that could be thought of was perhaps the wealth they were able to gain as a result of the advances made by Islam. It may be that the easy life they were able to lead accounted for their hostility!

This is followed by a clear verdict concerning their case: "*If they repent, it will be for their own good; but if they turn away, God will cause them to endure grievous suffering both in this world and in the life to come. They shall find none on this earth to be their friend or to give them support.*" (Verse 74)

The door to repent and mend one's ways remains wide open. Whoever is keen to do himself good, let him get in through that open door. But those who wish to continue along their evil path should also know their fate. They will be made to suffer God's severe punishment in this life and in the life to come, while they can rely on no one's support in this whole world. Since the alternatives have been made clear, they can make their choice.

Lying to God

The *sūrah* goes on to portray more cases of hypocrisy and how the hypocrites behave. "*Some of them have pledged to God: 'If He gives us of His bounty, we will certainly spend in charity, and we will be among the righteous.' But when He had given them of His bounty they grew niggardly and turned away, heedless [of their pledges].*" (Verses 75–76)

Some of these hypocrites pledge solemnly to God that if He would bestow His grace on them and give them some of His bounty, they would be very charitable to the poor and behave in the way expected of righteous people. Such a pledge, however, is given at a time when those people are poor, when their poverty makes them yearn for a time of plenty. Yet when God answers their prayers, and favours them with His bounty, they forget all about their pledges, and behave like misers. They turn away unwilling to honour their pledges. This violation of their promises and lying to God make hypocrisy take root in their hearts. Hence they continue to be hypocrites until they die.

Human beings are weak and niggardly, except for the few who manage, by God's grace, to elevate themselves. They cannot rid themselves of their miserliness unless their hearts become full of faith, raising them above the needs of this world and freeing them of their eagerness to protect their immediate interests. This is easy if they hope to achieve something better in the hereafter, and aspire to receive God's acceptance, which is far superior to all comforts and enjoyments. A believer's heart is reassured by faith, does not fear to be poor as a result of spending in charity or for God's cause, because he knows that what people may have will be exhausted and what God has in store is inexhaustible. His knowledge motivates him to pay in furthering God's cause willingly, without any fear that he will be left in need. Even if he becomes without money, what he hopes to receive from God is infinitely better and far greater.

When a person's heart is devoid of true faith, his natural instinct to keep his wealth for himself is aroused whenever he is called upon to give in charity or to spend something for God's cause. The fear of poverty overrides his weaker desire to respond to such a call. He is imprisoned within his niggardliness, feeling insecure. A person who makes a pledge to God and then reneges on his pledge and lies to God is not free from hypocrisy. The Prophet is authentically quoted as saying: "The mark of a hypocrite is threefold: he lies when he speaks, reneges on his promises and betrays his trust."

Hence their deliberately unfulfilled pledges and their repeated lies breed hypocrisy which settles permanently in their hearts, as the Qur'ānic verse describes: "*In consequence, He caused hypocrisy to take root in their hearts till the Day on which they will meet Him, because they have been untrue to the pledges they made to God, and because of the lies they used to tell.*" (Verse 77)

"*Do they not realize that God knows both their secret thoughts and what they talk about in private, and that God has full knowledge of all things that are hidden away?*" (Verse 78) Since they claim to be believers, do they not know that God knows all that there is in people's innermost hearts, and what they may say to each other even in the most private of situations? He is certainly aware of all that is kept hidden, and aware of the most secret of intentions. Since they know all this, they should not try to conceal any bad intention, hoping that God will not be aware of it. They should not have harboured any thoughts of leaving their pledges unfulfilled, or of lying to Him.

There are several reports on the incident or incidents which led to the revelation of this verse. Whichever one is correct,[1] the statement is general in its import. It describes a general condition and a pattern of people who have not let faith establish its roots in their hearts. If we compare the attitude of such people with that of the early Muslims, we find that those Muslims considered the payment of *zakāt* an aspect of God's grace. If a person did not pay it or if it was not accepted from him, he was the loser who should be pitied for his loss. They fully understood the meaning of the following verse which gives this order to the Prophet: *"Take a portion of their money as charity, so that you may cleanse and purify them thereby."* (Verse 103) Indeed the payment of *zakāt* was a gain not a loss. This is the difference between a duty fulfilled for the sake of God in the hope of earning His pleasure and a tax which is imposed by the law and paid to avoid punishment under the law.

The *sūrah* then describes another version of the hypocrites' view of *zakāt* which is contrary to that of the true believers. It also shows how the hypocrites are always given to taunting and slandering others, an indication of their perverted nature: *"It is those hypocrites that taunt*

---

1. The author mentions one of these reports, concerning Tha'labah ibn Ḥāṭib. It is a long and detailed story which is often quoted. It shows that Tha'labah pledged to give much in charity if he were given wealth. When his wealth was enormous, he refused to pay *zakāt* at first, but when he repented and tried to pay it, it was not accepted from him. However, a piece of scholarly research has clearly concluded that the story is greatly lacking in authenticity. Moreover, it runs against the established Islamic principle that God accepts genuine repentance, and in the story Tha'labah appears to have genuinely repented. Since the story is clearly suspect with regard to its authenticity, and since the person involved is one of the Prophet's Companions, I feel it is better left out, since the message of the verses is, as the author says, general and abundantly clear. Perhaps I should add that the research I have referred to was published long after the author's death. Nevertheless, the author seems doubtful about its authenticity. – Editor's note.

the believers who donate freely, as well as those who have nothing to give except what they earn through their toil, and deride them all. God derides them, and grievous suffering awaits them." (Verse 79)

The story associated with the revelation of this verse describes the hypocrites' crooked outlook on spending for God's cause. It is reported that the Prophet encouraged the believers to spend freely for equipping the army which was to go to Tabūk. 'Abd al-Raḥmān ibn 'Awf carried 4,000 dirhams and said to the Prophet: "Messenger of God, I have 8,000, of which I have brought you half and kept half for my family." The Prophet said to him: "May God bless you for what you have kept and what you have given." Abū 'Aqīl came with a small quantity of dates and said: "Messenger of God, all I have is some dates of which I have brought half and kept the other half for my family." The hypocrites derided them both and said: "'Abd al-Raḥmān only gave that much to show off; but do God and His Messenger need such a small quantity of dates?" Other reports suggest that they scoffed at Abū 'Aqīl suggesting that he only brought his dates to remind the Prophet of his poverty.

This is how they scoffed at the believers who were prompt in giving what they could, willingly and generously, eager to contribute as best as they could to the *jihād* campaign. They simply do not understand the motives of any true believer and why he gives willingly, nor do they understand that a believer's conscience urges him to do so. They do not appreciate the pure feelings which respond readily to the call to sacrifice. Hence, they describe the one who gives much as showing off and say of the one who has only little to give away that he reminds others of his poverty. They thus abuse the rich person because he gives generously, and deride the poor person because he has only very little to give. Thus, no one who gives freely is immune from their derision. They do all this while they themselves stay behind, give nothing and remain niggardly. If they give anything away, they do it only out of hypocrisy. That is the only motive they understand.

Hence they are given the decisive answer: *"God derides them, and grievous suffering awaits them."* (Verse 79) What a painful ridicule which they will suffer. How can we imagine a few weak individuals suffering the ridicule of the Almighty and destined for His punishment. That is a woeful end no doubt.

Never to be Forgiven

You may pray for their forgiveness or may not pray for them, [for it will all be the same]. Even if you were to pray seventy times for their forgiveness, God will not forgive them, for they have denied God and His Messenger. God does not guide those who are transgressors. (Verse 80)

This verse refers to the hypocrites who deride the true believers when they come forward with their contributions and donations. Such people have a well-known destiny which will not change. They shall not benefit by any request for forgiveness. *"God will not forgive them,"* whether such requests are made on their behalf or not. It seems that the Prophet used to pray to God to forgive those who committed mistakes or sins in the hope that they would mend their ways and earn God's forgiveness. As for the hypocrites, their fate has been sealed. There is no going back, and that is for a very good reason: *"For they have denied God and His Messenger. God does not guide those who are transgressors."* (Verse 80)

These are the ones who have deviated so widely that there can be no hope of them ever mending their ways. Hence, God tells His Messenger: *"Even if you were to pray seventy times for their forgiveness, God will not forgive them."* (Verse 80) The number seventy is normally mentioned to indicate a large, not specific, number. Hence the statement means that they cannot hope for forgiveness, because there is no way they will repent and mend their ways. That is because when a human heart reaches a certain stage of corruption, it becomes impossible to reform. Similarly when a person has gone so far astray, he cannot follow guidance. It is God who knows best how hearts respond.

Pleased with One's Misdeeds

The *sūrah* resumes its comments on the attitude of those who stayed behind when the Prophet had marched to Tabūk:

Those who were left behind rejoiced at having stayed at home after [the departure of] God's Messenger, for they were averse to striving with their property and their lives in God's cause. They said [to one another]: 'Do not go to war in this heat.' Say: 'The fire of hell is far hotter.' Would that they understood. They shall laugh but a little, and they will weep much, in return for what they have earned. If God brings you back and you meet some of them, and then they ask leave to go forth with you, say: 'Never shall you go forth with me, nor shall you fight an enemy with me. You were happy to stay behind on the first occasion, so you stay now with those who remain behind.' You shall not pray for any of them who dies, and you shall not stand by his grave. For they have denied God and His Messenger and died as hardened sinners. Let neither their riches nor their children excite your admiration. God only wishes to punish them by means of these in the life of this world, and that their souls perish while they are unbelievers. (Verses 81–85)

Such people are so keen to ensure their continued personal comfort and are unwilling to spend anything of their wealth for God's cause. They are devoid of all desire to strive because their hearts are devoid of faith. The adjective used in the Arabic text to refer to them has the added connotation of showing them to be left behind as if they were dispensable articles of little value. They are delighted at having secured their own safety when they stayed at home after the Prophet and his Companions had departed on their blessed mission. They spared themselves the toil and hardship willingly undertaken by the believers who were ready to strive for God's cause, thinking that personal safety is a goal coveted by all men. Hence: "*They were averse to striving with their property and their lives in God's cause. They said [to one another]: 'Do not go to war in this heat.'*" (Verse 81) Such words are only said by a person who is keen to indulge himself in every luxury. Such a person is not fit to do anything which only men of endurance can undertake.

They are a fitting example of people with no will power. Numerous indeed are those who dislike to go through any hardship and turn away when they are required to make a real effort, preferring cheap comfort to noble effort and humble safety to a position of honour that involves taking risks. They collapse in utter exhaustion behind the rows of believers who move on with seriousness, knowing that the advocacy of the true message requires great sacrifices. Nevertheless, those believers march forth and pay little attention to the size of the opposition or the tough impediments they face, because they know that it is part of human nature to try to overcome impediments. This is far more befitting and satisfying to man than staying behind, betraying ineptitude and lack of will.

The *sūrah* answers them coupling the truth with sarcasm: "*They said [to one another]: 'Do not go to war in this heat.' Say: 'The fire of hell is far hotter.' Would that they understood.*" (Verse 81) If they fear the heat of the summer and prefer the comfort of staying in the shade, how will they tolerate the heat of the fire of hell, when it is much more intense and longer lasting? Although this sounds like a remark full of derision, it only states the truth. The choice they had to make was between striving for a certain period in defence of God's cause, tolerating the heat of the earthly summer or being thrown in hell for an extended period the length of which is known to God alone.

"*They shall laugh but a little, and they will weep much, in return for what they have earned.*" (Verse 82) Their laughter takes place in this life which lasts only for a certain number of days, but their tears are poured in the hereafter with its much longer days. Indeed each one of God's days is equal to one thousand years of ours. Their tears are "*in return for what they have earned.*" It is then a befitting and just reward.

Those hypocrites who preferred to stay behind during a time of hardship, when all Muslims were called upon to join the *jihād* campaign, are not fit to join any campaign or to take part in any effort undertaken for God's cause. Hence, leniency is not the proper policy to follow with them. They are not to be given the chance of earning the honour of participating in *jihād* at any time. The Prophet is directed to make this clear to them whenever the occasion arises: "*If God brings you back and you meet some of them, and then they ask leave to go forth with you, say: 'Never shall you go forth with me, nor shall you fight an enemy with me. You were happy to stay behind on the first occasion, so you stay now with those who remain behind.'*" (Verse 83)

Every message or ideology is in need of people who are dedicated, willing to undertake any effort in their support and advocacy. When the ranks of any such ideology are infiltrated by weak elements, it cannot tolerate hardship. Hence, such weaklings must be isolated from its ranks which need to remain steadfast. If those who join the ranks at a time of ease and desert them at a time of hardship are to be easily tolerated, their continued presence will work to the detriment of the whole message and its true advocates. Hence, the Prophet is instructed to make it clear to them that they have no place in the ranks of the believers: *"Say: 'Never shall you go forth with me, nor shall you fight an enemy with me.'"* (Verse 83) And the reason for this attitude is also made clear: *"You were happy to stay behind on the first occasion."* (Verse 83) That deprived them of the privilege of being able to join the ranks of the fighters for God's cause and the honour of going forth with the Prophet. Going on *jihād* is a responsibility which may only be shouldered by those who are fit to undertake it. This religion of Islam does not admit any partiality or favouritism. Hence they are told: *"Stay now with those who remain behind."* (Verse 83) You may stay with such people as are like you in their attitude. You all prefer to absent yourselves when the occasion requires sacrifices.

This way of continuous striving, marked out by God Himself for His Messenger, remains the one to be followed by the advocates of this religion of Islam for as long as life continues on earth. Advocates of Islam should remain aware of this at all times.

Staying Behind at a Time of Mobilization

This last instruction to the Prophet meant that he was not to allow those hypocrites who stayed behind when he called on all Muslims to join him on the expedition to Tabūk to be part of any subsequent campaign. They were to be deprived of the privilege of joining any effort aimed at defending God's cause. The Prophet is also commanded not to give such people any semblance of honour: *"You shall not pray for any of them who dies, and you shall not stand by his grave. For they have denied God and His Messenger and died as hardened sinners."* (Verse 84)

Commentators on the Qur'ān have mentioned certain events to which this verse relates, but the message of this verse is much wider in application than any individual event. The verse sets out a principle which denies any aspect of honour in the system implemented by a community which strives for God's cause to those who prefer laziness to struggle, and comfort to making an effort. There is to be no favouritism in giving each individual his rank in the community. The

217

standard by which this is determined is based on dedication, steadfastness, perseverance and unwavering determination.

The *sūrah* gives here the reason for this instruction: "*For they have denied God and His Messenger and died as hardened sinners.*" (Verse 84) This explanation applies to the order not to pray for the dead among them and for the Prophet not to stand at any of their graves. But the principle itself has a wider application. Prayer and standing at the grave of a deceased person are aspects of honour. The Muslim community must not accord such an honour to anyone who stays behind at a time of *jihād*. The standing of any person in the Muslim community is related to what that person is ready to give, do or sacrifice at the time when he is called upon to do so. True Muslims give their all, remain steadfast at times of hardship and are always ready to strive with their wealth and persons. Hence they receive the honour they deserve.

On the other hand, those who stay behind deserve neither the apparent honour seen by everyone in the community, nor the type of mental appreciation that is felt by people though may not be demonstrated in any action: "*Let neither their riches nor their children excite your admiration. God only wishes to punish them by means of these in the life of this world, and that their souls perish while they are unbelievers.*" (Verse 85) The general meaning of this verse has already been explained when a similar one was mentioned earlier in the *sūrah*. It is repeated here for a different reason. What is meant here is that no significance should be attached by the Muslim community to the wealth or the children of these hypocrites, because to admire these is to give such people a degree of mental honour or appreciation which they do not deserve. The only thing they deserve is to be ignored and looked upon with contempt.

When a sūrah *was revealed from on high calling on them to believe in God and to strive alongside His Messenger, those of them who were well able to do so asked you to give them leave and said to you: 'Allow us to stay with those who remain behind.' They are well-pleased to remain with those who are left behind. And their hearts are sealed, so that they are unable to understand the truth. But the Messenger and those who have believed with him strive hard in*

God's cause with their property and their lives. These shall have all the good things. These shall certainly prosper. God has prepared for them gardens through which running waters flow, where they shall abide. That is the supreme triumph. (Verses 86–89)

These verses tell of two different natures, one of hypocrisy, weakness, and self-abasement, and another full of faith, strength and sacrifice. These give rise to two different attitudes: one of deviousness, humbleness and lack of self-respect, and another which is straightforward, dignified and ready to sacrifice.

When a *sūrah* or a passage of the Qur'ān is revealed from on high, giving an explicit order to the believers to strive for God's cause, then those who have the means to give physical and financial sacrifices come forward. They do not show up in order to take their positions in the front, as their ability and gratitude to God would require. They come forward to make stupid excuses and to request exemption so that they can stay behind with women, doing nothing to defend sanctity or home. They do not realize how abject and humiliating their request is. They are only interested in their own safety. Those who make their own safety paramount do not feel any shame, because "*they are well-pleased to remain with those who are left behind. And their hearts are sealed, so that they are unable to understand the truth.*" (Verse 87) Had they been able to understand it, they would have realized that it is when one strives for God's cause that one feels strong, leading a life of dignity and honour, and when one stays behind, one lives in weakness and abject humiliation.

Humility imposes its tax on human beings like dignity does. However, the tax imposed by humility is often heavier by far. Weak people may think that the tax of dignity is much too heavy, and try to evade it by accepting an abject position of humility. They live in fear and anxiety, thinking each loud cry a call to attack them. They remain in constant fear for their lives. Such people pay a far heavier tax than that which would have been required by a dignified life. The tax they pay for their humble living is taken from their honour, prestige, social standing, reputation, security and often also from their lives, although they may not readily perceive this. But who are these? They are the ones who "*are well-pleased to remain with those who are left behind, and their hearts are sealed, so that they are unable to understand [the truth]."* (Verse 87)

"*But the Messenger and those who have believed with him*" are a totally different type of people. These "*strive in God's cause with their property and their lives.*" (Verse 88) They fulfil the duties imposed on them by their faith and work hard to achieve the dignity which cannot be attained while one stays behind. Hence, "*these shall have all the good things.*" (Verse 88) Such good things are of both the type enjoyed here in this life and the one attained in the life to come. In this world they enjoy dignity, honour and a position which guarantees that people respect what they say. In the hereafter, they receive the best and fullest reward, as they attain God's acceptance. "*These shall certainly prosper.*" (Verse 88) They prosper in this life as they enjoy good living, and they prosper in the life to come as they receive their mighty reward. "*God has prepared for them gardens through which running waters flow, where they shall abide. That is the supreme triumph.*" (Verse 89)

> *Some of the Bedouins who had excuses to offer turned up, begging to be granted exemption; while those who denied God and His Messenger stayed behind. Grievous suffering shall befall those of them that disbelieved.* (Verse 90)

The first group are the ones who have real excuses which merit their exemption. Hence no blame is attached to them for their request. The others have no real excuse. They stay behind and lie to God and His Messenger. The unbelievers among these have grievous punishment awaiting them. Those who repent and do not disbelieve are not discussed here because they may face a different fate.

Eager but Without Means

The *sūrah* then provides a definitive statement with regard to who should join the army when there is a general call of mobilization. It is not obligatory that all people, whether able or not, should fight. Islam is a religion that does not overburden people. God does not charge anyone with more than he or she can bear. Those without the means or the ability to fight cannot be blamed because of their situation:

No blame shall be attached to the weak, the sick or those who do not have the means, if they are sincere towards God and His Messenger. There is no cause to reproach those who do good. God is Much-forgiving, Merciful. Nor shall those be blamed who, when they came to request you for transport and you said: 'I have no means of transporting you', turned away with their eyes overflowing with tears, sad that they did not have the means to cover their expenses. (Verses 91–92)

Those who are weak because of a certain disability or old age, and those who are ill and do not have the physical strength to move and make the sort of effort required in war, and those who do not have the financial means to pay for their food and transport will not be blamed if they stay behind. They are, however, required to be sincere, providing honest advice and making whatever effort they can to protect the land of Islam, such as keeping guard or looking after the women and children of the fighters, or any other jobs that are of benefit to the community. No blame can be attached to them because they do the best they can. Blame is only attached to those who do wrong.

Nor is there any blame to be attached to those who may be physically able to fight but have no means of transport to take them to the battlefield. When they realize that they are unable to join the army for this reason, their eyes overflow with tears of sadness. Their feelings are genuine as they grieve at their inability to take part in a struggle for God's cause. This was true of a number of people at the time of the Prophet whose names are variously given in different reports but which all agree that the event was real indeed.

A report attributed to Ibn 'Abbās mentions that "the Prophet ordered his Companions to get ready for a campaign. A group of his Companions, among whom was 'Abdullāh ibn Mughaffil al-Māzinī, went to him and said: 'Messenger of God, could you give us some mounts, for we have none.' The Prophet said to them: "*I have no means of transporting you.*" (Verse 92) They were weeping as they went away, because it hurt them not to be able to join the campaign and they could not find any means of transport nor cover their own expenses. Hence God states their exemption in His revelation.

Mujāhid says that this verse refers to a group from Muqarrin, a clan of Muzaynah.

Muḥammad ibn Ka'b mentions seven people whom he lists by name and tribe. Ibn Isḥāq says in his report on the expedition to Tabūk: "A group of Muslims, seven in number, including Sālim ibn 'Umayr, 'Ilyah ibn Zayd, 'Abd al-Raḥmān ibn Ka'b, 'Amr ibn al-Ḥamām ibn al-Jamūḥ, 'Abdullāh ibn Mughaffal, Ḥaramī ibn 'Abdullāh and 'Iyāḍ ibn Sāriyah, requested the Prophet for mounts as they were too poor to be able to find their own transport. He said to them: "*I have no means of transporting you.*" (Verse 92) When they heard this they left with tears in their eyes, saddened at their inability to cover their own expenses.

With this spirit Islam was able to be victorious and establish its power. We should reflect on our own commitment in comparison to such people. If we believe that we possess some of their attributes, we may appeal to God for victory. Otherwise we should concentrate on improving our situation.

The issue is clear, then. The weak, disabled, ill and also those who are too poor to pay their own expenses and for whom the Prophet cannot provide transport will not be blamed for staying behind. The real blame attaches to those who come to the Prophet with their thinly disguised excuses, when they have the means to go to battle and have no real reason for staying behind. "*But blame shall certainly attach only to those who ask you for exemption even though they are rich.*" (Verse 93)

It is the ones happy to stay behind that are to be blamed, because they have no real desire to take part in a struggle for God's cause. They do not give what is due to God when He has given them wealth and ability, nor do they fulfil their duties to Islam when it has given them power and dignity, or to their community which gives them protection and honour. Hence God's description of them: "*They are well pleased to be with those who are left behind.*" (Verse 93) They are then weak of heart, spineless, and content, though without reason, to remain with those who stay behind for valid reasons such as women, children and disabled men who are exempt from *jihād*.

In view of this: "*God has sealed their hearts, so that they have no knowledge.*" (Verse 93) With what they have preferred for themselves of laziness and inactivity, staying away from active participation in efforts that open new horizons for the Islamic cause, God has sealed their means of reception, feeling and understanding. No one prefers idle safety and miserable inactivity unless he has no aspiration for higher things and no motivation to participate in a community which seeks to make its mark on life and influence its direction. Indeed idleness and cheap comforts seal minds and hearts and inactivate feelings and interaction. Action is the mark of life and it also inspires life. Facing danger heightens senses, taps latent capabilities, enhances physical ability and makes use of all potential. It makes human beings better able to utilize all their resources whenever there is a need to do so. All these may be included under the heading of knowledge of which those who prefer lazy comfort are deprived.

Hollow Excuses

The *sūrah* continues its description of those people of plentiful means who prefer to stay behind at a time when the Prophet and the Muslim community are marching to face a powerful enemy. There is something behind such preference with what it entails of adopting a humiliating attitude and being always evasive when asked to come clean and state their position openly.

"*They shall come to you with their excuses when you return to them.*" (Verse 94) This is a piece of information which God gives to His Messenger and the faithful among his Companions. It tells them of what those hypocrites will be doing when the Muslims return from their arduous expedition. This confirms that these verses were revealed when the Muslim army was on its way back from the expedition, and before they had arrived in Madinah. The hypocrites would come with their excuses, because they would be ashamed to let their action be seen in its true light. It would be disgraceful to let it be seen with its real motives, which were a weak faith, a preference for personal safety and an unwillingness to fight a great power: "*Say: 'Do not offer any excuses, for we shall not believe you. God has already enlightened us about you.'*" (Verse 94) The Prophet is instructed to tell them to spare themselves the trouble of offering excuses, because they are not to be believed. It is no longer the case that these hypocrites can be taken on the basis of appearances. God has revealed the truth about them to

His Messenger and He has informed him of their motives which are now seen for what they truly are. The Arabic expression used here is highly significant. The words indicating refusal to accept the excuses of the hypocrites are identical to those used in reference to being believers. This connotes verbal acceptance, rational trust, and inner faith and reassurance. It also involves a believer's trust in his Lord, and a mutual trust between all believers.

Those offering their excuses are told not to do so, because words are of no use. They need to show what they do. If their action confirms what they say, then their assertions will be true. If not, there can be no trust or acceptance. "*God will see how you act, and so will His Messenger.*" (Verse 94) God sees every action and knows every secret hidden in every heart. He knows the real intentions of all His creation. The Prophet was to take what people say in conjunction with what they do. That would be the basis of internal relationships in the Muslim community.

Moreover, matters will not end in this life on earth. There will eventually come the reckoning and the reward which will be based on God's absolute knowledge of what is done openly and what remains in people's hearts: "*In the end you shall be brought before Him who knows all that is beyond the reach of human perception, and all that is manifest when He will tell you what you used to do.*" (Verse 94)

The phrase '*beyond the reach of human perception*' means what people do not know, while '*what is manifest*' refers to what they see and what comes to their knowledge. God knows all this when the statement is read in this simple sense, but it also has a wider and more profound sense. God knows everything in this world which is seen and experienced, and He knows everything in the worlds beyond, of which we know nothing. There is an intended meaning in what God says to those whom He addresses in this verse: "*He will tell you what you used to do.*" (Verse 94) They know what they do, but God – limitless is He in His glory – knows their doings better than they, and He will tell them about these. It is often the case that a person may not be aware of an inner motive for something he does. God knows it better than he. An action may very often produce an outcome that may remain unknown to the person who performed it. What is meant here is that God gives people the results of what they used to do. That is the reward they will have for their actions. Here, though, they are only informed and the reward itself is not specified.

When you return to them they will swear to you by God so that you may let them be. Let them be, then: they are unclean. Hell shall be their abode in recompense for what they used to do. (Verse 95)

This is another piece of information given by God to His Messenger, telling him what the hypocrites will be doing when he and his faithful Companions return to Madinah; an encounter the hypocrites thought they would never return from. God knew, and He told His Messenger as much, that they would try to make their excuses easier to accept by swearing to their truth. By doing so, they hoped to make the Muslims overlook what they had done so that they might forgive them their negligence without question.

God instructs His Messenger to leave them alone, not as a sign of forgiveness, but as a sign of turning away from them, because they are abominable: "*Let them be, then: they are unclean.*" (Verse 95) This gives a physical expression of mental impurity. They are not physically or bodily unclean, but they are unclean mentally, as a result of their actions. The physical description gives an image that is much more abominable, revolting and contemptible. They are more concerned with their personal safety than striving for the cause of the community and are hence described as unclean. Their impurity contaminates souls, spreads disease and fills people with disgust, just like a rotten, dead body left in their midst.

"*Hell shall be their abode in recompense for what they used to do.*" (Verse 95) They feel that they gain by staying behind, securing their safety and comfort and enjoying their wealth. The fact is that in this life they are unclean, while they waste their share of the life to come. They end up in utter loss. God certainly tells the truth.

The *sūrah* goes on to tell more of what they will do after the Muslim fighters return home: "*They swear to you trying to make you pleased with them. Should you be pleased with them, God shall never be pleased with such transgressing folk.*" (Verse 96) They first request the Muslims to overlook what they have done. Then, they gradually ask for more, trying to make the Muslims feel easy with them so that they can secure their own safety within the community. They want to ensure that the Muslims continue to accept their outward appearances, treating them on that basis, and not mounting a campaign against them as God has ordered them in this final, definitive description of relations between Muslims and hypocrites.

God makes it clear that they have transgressed by staying behind because their action is motivated by their lack of faith. He also tells the Muslim community that He will never be pleased with wrong-doing people, even though they may be able to win acceptance with the Muslims through their swearing and excuses. It is God's verdict that is final. People's acceptance, though they may be Muslims, will not change their position with God and will avail them nothing. The only way to win God's acceptance is to change their attitude and to embrace the true faith leading to God's pleasure.

God has thus revealed the true situation of those living among the Muslim community and staying behind without having any real cause for exemption. He has also defined the sort of relations that should prevail between the Muslim community and the hypocrites in the same way as He defined the relationship between this community and the idolaters on the one hand, and between it and the followers of earlier revelations on the other. This *sūrah* gives the details of this final verdict.

6

A Mosque for the Hypocrites

The desert Arabs are more tenacious in unbelief and hypocrisy, and more likely to be ignorant of the ordinances which God has revealed to His Messenger. But God is All-knowing, Wise. (97)

ٱلْأَعْرَابُ أَشَدُّ كُفْرًا وَنِفَاقًا وَأَجْدَرُ أَلَّا يَعْلَمُوا۟ حُدُودَ مَآ أَنزَلَ ٱللَّهُ عَلَىٰ رَسُولِهِۦ وَٱللَّهُ عَلِيمٌ حَكِيمٌ ۞

Some desert Arabs regard what they may spend [for God's cause] as a loss, and wait for some misfortune to befall you. The evil turn of fortune will be theirs. God hears all and knows all. (98)

وَمِنَ ٱلْأَعْرَابِ مَن يَتَّخِذُ مَا يُنفِقُ مَغْرَمًا وَيَتَرَبَّصُ بِكُمُ ٱلدَّوَآئِرَ عَلَيْهِمْ دَآئِرَةُ ٱلسَّوْءِ وَٱللَّهُ سَمِيعٌ عَلِيمٌ ۞

Still other desert Arabs believe in God and the Last Day, and regard what they spend [for God's cause] as a means to bring them closer to God and of [their being remembered] in the Messenger's prayers. It shall certainly be for them a means of drawing near to God. God will admit them to His grace, for God is Much-forgiving, Merciful. (99)

وَمِنَ ٱلْأَعْرَابِ مَن يُؤْمِنُ بِٱللَّهِ وَٱلْيَوْمِ ٱلْأَخِرِ وَيَتَّخِذُ مَا يُنفِقُ قُرُبَـٰتٍ عِندَ ٱللَّهِ وَصَلَوَٰتِ ٱلرَّسُولِ أَلَآ إِنَّهَا قُرْبَةٌ لَّهُمْ سَيُدْخِلُهُمُ ٱللَّهُ فِي رَحْمَتِهِۦٓ إِنَّ ٱللَّهَ غَفُورٌ رَّحِيمٌ ۞

As for the first to lead the way, of the *Muhājirīn* and the *Anṣār*, as well as those who follow them in [the way of] righteousness, God is well-pleased with them, and well-pleased are they with Him. He has prepared for them gardens through which running waters flow, where they shall abide for ever. That is the supreme triumph. (100)

وَٱلسَّٰبِقُونَ ٱلْأَوَّلُونَ مِنَ ٱلْمُهَٰجِرِينَ وَٱلْأَنصَارِ وَٱلَّذِينَ ٱتَّبَعُوهُم بِإِحْسَٰنٍ رَّضِىَ ٱللَّهُ عَنْهُمْ وَرَضُوا۟ عَنْهُ وَأَعَدَّ لَهُمْ جَنَّٰتٍ تَجْرِى تَحْتَهَا ٱلْأَنْهَٰرُ خَٰلِدِينَ فِيهَآ أَبَدًا ذَٰلِكَ ٱلْفَوْزُ ٱلْعَظِيمُ ﴿١٠٠﴾

Some desert Arabs around you are hypocrites, and so are some of the people from Madinah, who are indeed persistent in their hypocrisy. You do not know them, but We know them. Twice shall We punish them, and then they will be given over to a grievous suffering. (101)

وَمِمَّنْ حَوْلَكُم مِّنَ ٱلْأَعْرَابِ مُنَٰفِقُونَ وَمِنْ أَهْلِ ٱلْمَدِينَةِ مَرَدُوا۟ عَلَى ٱلنِّفَاقِ لَا تَعْلَمُهُمْ نَحْنُ نَعْلَمُهُمْ سَنُعَذِّبُهُم مَّرَّتَيْنِ ثُمَّ يُرَدُّونَ إِلَىٰ عَذَابٍ عَظِيمٍ ﴿١٠١﴾

There are others who have acknowledged their sins, after having mixed righteous deeds with evil ones. It may well be that God will accept their repentance. God is Much-forgiving, Merciful. (102)

وَءَاخَرُونَ ٱعْتَرَفُوا۟ بِذُنُوبِهِمْ خَلَطُوا۟ عَمَلًا صَٰلِحًا وَءَاخَرَ سَيِّئًا عَسَى ٱللَّهُ أَن يَتُوبَ عَلَيْهِمْ إِنَّ ٱللَّهَ غَفُورٌ رَّحِيمٌ ﴿١٠٢﴾

Take a portion of their money as charity, so that you may cleanse and purify them thereby; and pray for them: for your prayers are a source of comfort for them. God hears all and knows all. (103)

خُذْ مِنْ أَمْوَٰلِهِمْ صَدَقَةً تُطَهِّرُهُمْ وَتُزَكِّيهِم بِهَا وَصَلِّ عَلَيْهِمْ إِنَّ صَلَوٰتَكَ سَكَنٌ لَّهُمْ وَٱللَّهُ سَمِيعٌ عَلِيمٌ ﴿١٠٣﴾

Do they not know that it is God alone who accepts repentance from His servants, and He is truly the One who takes charitable offerings, and that God is the only One to accept repentance and bestow mercy? (104)

أَلَمْ يَعْلَمُوٓاْ أَنَّ ٱللَّهَ هُوَ يَقْبَلُ ٱلتَّوْبَةَ عَنْ عِبَادِهِۦ وَيَأْخُذُ ٱلصَّدَقَٰتِ وَأَنَّ ٱللَّهَ هُوَ ٱلتَّوَّابُ ٱلرَّحِيمُ ١٠٤

Say to them: 'Do as you will. God will see your deeds, and so will His Messenger, and the believers; and in the end you shall be brought before Him who knows all that is beyond the reach of human perception and all that is manifest when He will tell you what you used to do.' (105)

وَقُلِ ٱعْمَلُواْ فَسَيَرَى ٱللَّهُ عَمَلَكُمْ وَرَسُولُهُۥ وَٱلْمُؤْمِنُونَ وَسَتُرَدُّونَ إِلَىٰ عَٰلِمِ ٱلْغَيْبِ وَٱلشَّهَٰدَةِ فَيُنَبِّئُكُم بِمَا كُنتُمْ تَعْمَلُونَ ١٠٥

And yet there are others who must await God's judgement. He will either punish them or turn to them in His mercy. God is All-knowing, Wise. (106)

وَءَاخَرُونَ مُرْجَوْنَ لِأَمْرِ ٱللَّهِ إِمَّا يُعَذِّبُهُمْ وَإِمَّا يَتُوبُ عَلَيْهِمْ وَٱللَّهُ عَلِيمٌ حَكِيمٌ ١٠٦

And there are those who have established a house of worship out of mischievous motives, to promote unbelief and disunity among the believers, and to provide an outpost for those who have already been warring against God and His Messenger. They will certainly swear: 'We have only the best of intentions.' God bears witness that they certainly are liars. (107)

وَٱلَّذِينَ ٱتَّخَذُواْ مَسْجِدًا ضِرَارًا وَكُفْرًا وَتَفْرِيقًا بَيْنَ ٱلْمُؤْمِنِينَ وَإِرْصَادًا لِّمَنْ حَارَبَ ٱللَّهَ وَرَسُولَهُۥ مِن قَبْلُ وَلَيَحْلِفُنَّ إِنْ أَرَدْنَآ إِلَّا ٱلْحُسْنَىٰ وَٱللَّهُ يَشْهَدُ إِنَّهُمْ لَكَٰذِبُونَ ١٠٧

Never set a foot there. Only a house of worship that from the very first day has been founded on piety is worthy of you standing to pray there. In it are men who love to grow in purity, for God loves those who purify themselves. (108)

لَا تَقُمْ فِيهِ أَبَدًا لَّمَسْجِدٌ أُسِّسَ عَلَى التَّقْوَىٰ مِنْ أَوَّلِ يَوْمٍ أَحَقُّ أَن تَقُومَ فِيهِ فِيهِ رِجَالٌ يُحِبُّونَ أَن يَتَطَهَّرُوا وَاللَّهُ يُحِبُّ الْمُطَّهِّرِينَ ۝

Who is better: a man who founds his building [motivated by a sense of] being God-fearing and seeking His goodly acceptance, or one who founds his building on the edge of a crumbling precipice, so that it tumbles with him in the fire of hell? God does not guide the wrongdoers. (109)

أَفَمَنْ أَسَّسَ بُنْيَـٰنَهُ عَلَىٰ تَقْوَىٰ مِنَ اللَّهِ وَرِضْوَانٍ خَيْرٌ أَم مَّنْ أَسَّسَ بُنْيَـٰنَهُ عَلَىٰ شَفَا جُرُفٍ هَارٍ فَانْهَارَ بِهِ فِي نَارِ جَهَنَّمَ وَاللَّهُ لَا يَهْدِى الْقَوْمَ الظَّالِمِينَ ۝

The structure which they have built will continue to be a source of disquiet in their hearts, until their hearts are torn to pieces. God is All-knowing, Wise. (110)

لَا يَزَالُ بُنْيَـٰنُهُمُ الَّذِى بَنَوْا رِيبَةً فِي قُلُوبِهِمْ إِلَّا أَن تَقَطَّعَ قُلُوبُهُمْ وَاللَّهُ عَلِيمٌ حَكِيمٌ ۝

Overview

This new passage gives an account of the different groups and classes that lived within the Muslim community at the time of the Tabūk Expedition. It describes those groups which were part of its overall structure and their true attitudes to faith as well as their deeds and distinctive characteristics.

We have outlined, in the Prologue to this *sūrah*, the historical causes that led to the presence of such different standards of acceptance of the faith among the Muslim community in Madinah. We will quote here the last few paragraphs in that introduction in order to remind ourselves of the general situation at the time and the circumstances influencing it in this way.

The stubborn opposition of the Quraysh continued to act as a barrier preventing the advance of Islam into the rest of Arabia. The Quraysh tribe had the ultimate say in all religious matters in Arabia, and it exercised a very strong influence over economic, political and social matters. Hence its determined and uncompromising opposition to the new faith ensured that the rest of Arabia turned away from it, or at least adopted a wait-and-see attitude until the fight between the Quraysh and one of its children had produced a clear winner. When the Quraysh declared its submission, followed by the major tribes of Hawāzin and Thaqīf, and when the three main Jewish tribes in Madinah had previously been subdued, and those of Khaybar had been defeated, people embraced the new faith in flocks. The whole of Arabia submitted to Islam within one year.

This rapid expansion in the geographical area of Islam heralded the resurgence, on an even more intensive scale, of all the symptoms experienced after the resounding victory the Muslims achieved in the Battle of Badr. The Muslim community had almost managed to rid itself of those, thanks to the seven-year-long education process it had enjoyed after that battle. The rapid geographical expansion of Islam in Arabia could have had some serious negative effects, had it not been for the fact that Madinah had become, in its entirety, the solid base of Islam. It was God Almighty who looked after the new faith and charted its course. He had prepared the first core of believers, the *Muhājirīn* and the *Anṣār*, to be the first solid base of Islam after the relatively important expansion that followed the victory at Badr. He also made the whole of Madinah the solid base which would withstand the great expansion brought about by the splendid triumph achieved when Makkah was won over to Islam. God certainly knows what forces to mobilize in support of His message.

The first symptom of the new dangers appeared on the day of the Battle of Ḥunayn, mentioned in this *sūrah*: "*God has granted you*

His support on many a battlefield, and also in the Battle of Ḥunayn,
when you took pride in your numerical strength, but it availed
you nothing. For all its vastness, the earth seemed too narrow for
you, and you turned back in flight. God then bestowed from on
high an air of inner peace on His Messenger and on the believers,
and He sent down forces whom you could not see, and punished
those who disbelieved. Such is the reward for the unbelievers."
(Verses 25–26)

One of the apparent reasons for the defeat at the beginning of the
battle was that 2,000 of those the Prophet had pardoned in
Makkah, and who embraced Islam after the fall of that city, had
joined the 10,000-strong army which originally travelled from
Madinah to subdue the Quraysh in Makkah. The presence of
those 2,000 men alongside the others who came from Madinah
was a cause of imbalance in the Muslim ranks. There was also the
fact that the Hawāzin took the Muslims by surprise. What that
meant was that the army did not wholly belong to the solid,
well-knit base which had been nurtured over the several years
separating the Battle of Badr and the conquest of Makkah.

Similarly, the negative symptoms that appeared at the time of the
Tabūk Expedition were a natural result of this rapid expansion
and the great influx of new Muslims with varying standards of
faith. These symptoms are discussed fully in this *sūrah* in a long
exposition with varied styles and methods of treatment.

Where Hypocrisy is Hardest

Bearing this in mind, we can now discuss the verses included in this
passage: "*The desert Arabs are more tenacious in unbelief and hypocrisy,*
and more likely to be ignorant of the ordinances which God has revealed
to His Messenger. But God is All-knowing, Wise. Some desert Arabs regard
what they may spend [for God's cause] as a loss, and wait for some
misfortune to befall you. The evil turn of fortune will be theirs. God
hears all and knows all. Still other desert Arabs believe in God and the
Last Day, and regard what they spend [for God's cause] as a means to
bring them closer to God and of [their being remembered] in the

Messenger's prayers. It shall certainly be for them a means of drawing near to God. God will admit them to His grace, for God is Much-forgiving, Merciful." (Verses 97–99)

These verses begin with mentioning different classes of desert Arabs, some of whose tribes lived close to Madinah. Earlier, they had attacked the land of Islam in Madinah, but later, when they accepted Islam, they belonged to either one of the two groups mentioned in this passage. The descriptive outline of these groups begins with establishing a rule about their general nature: *"The desert Arabs are more tenacious in unbelief and hypocrisy, and more likely to be ignorant of the ordinances which God has revealed to His Messenger. But God is All-knowing, Wise."* (Verse 97)

This description outlines a constant characteristic of desert and nomadic people, or bedouins. It is in their nature that they should be more tenacious in their unbelief and hypocrisy, and that they should be ignorant of God's directives as He reveals these to His Messenger. Their ignorance stems from their life circumstances and the way these affect them. Thus they grow up rather hostile, having little knowledge and less inclination to abide by rules and regulations, developing a strongly materialistic outlook. Faith modifies their nature, elevates their values and brings them to a wider and more sublime horizon.

There are countless reports which mention the bedouin's lack of refinement. Ibn Kathīr mentions some of these in his commentary on the Qur'ān:

> A bedouin attended the circle of Zayd ibn Ṣūḥān, a scholar who had a hand injured in the Battle of Nihāwand.[1] The bedouin said to him: "What you say is admirable, but your hand makes me worried." Zayd said: "What worries you about my hand? It is my left hand anyway." The bedouin said: "I am not sure which hand they cut, the right or the left." [He was referring to the punishment for theft which implied his suspicion that this respected scholar might have been punished for stealing.] Zayd said: "God certainly tells the truth, and so does His Messenger: *"The desert Arabs are more tenacious in unbelief and hypocrisy, and more likely to be*

---

1. The Battle of Nihāwand was a major battle the Muslims fought against the Persian Empire only a few years after the Prophet had passed away.

ignorant of the ordinances which God has revealed to His Messenger." (Verse 97)

Imām Aḥmad relates on the authority of Ibn 'Abbās that the Prophet said: "Whoever lives in the desert develops a rough edge, and whoever chases game loses concentration, and whoever attends rulers may yield to temptation." Because desert people are rough, God has not selected His Messengers from among them. Prophets have always been chosen from among city dwellers: *"We have only sent before you men from among city dwellers to whom We send down Our revelations."* (12: 109)

When a bedouin gave a present to the Prophet, the Prophet gave him back a much more valuable gift so that he was well pleased. He then said: "I feel I should not accept any gift unless it comes from a man from the Quraysh, Thaqīf, the Anṣār or the Daws." Needless to say that these were far more gentle in character and behaviour, because they were the dwellers of the main centres in Arabia at the time, Makkah, Ṭā'if, Madinah and in Yemen respectively.

Muslim reports on the authority of 'Ā'ishah: "Some desert Arabs came in a delegation to meet God's Messenger. They asked whether the people of Madinah used to kiss their sons. When they were given an answer in the affirmative, they said: 'But we definitely would not kiss our sons.' The Prophet said: 'What can I do for you if God has taken mercy out of your hearts?'"[2]

The rough nature of the desert Arabs is well established, even after they had accepted Islam. It is only natural, therefore, that they would be harder in their stubborn rejection of the faith or in their hypocrisy. They were too brutal when victorious, and very hypocritical when subdued. They were aggressive and would observe no limits.

"God is All-knowing, Wise." (Verse 97) He knows His creation, their circumstances, characteristics and nature. He has given them a variety of talents, capabilities and specialities, and He made them

---

2. Ibn Kathīr, *Tafsīr al-Qur'ān al-'Aẓīm*. Al-Maktabah al-'Aṣrīyah, Beirut, 1996, Vol. 2, pp. 348–349.

into races, communities and nations. All this is in manifestation of His wisdom.

The Gap Separating Faith and Hypocrisy

Having given a general description of the desert Arabs, the *sūrah* classifies them further on the basis of what changes in their characteristics the faith has produced, and the gap that has emerged between hearts that have experienced the happiness generated by faith and those that remained unbelieving, hypocritical. This description is drawn against the background of the situation of the Muslim community at that time: *"Some desert Arabs regard what they may spend [for God's cause] as a loss, and wait for some misfortune to befall you. The evil turn of fortune will be theirs. God hears all and knows all."* (Verse 98) Most probably the hypocrites among the desert people are mentioned first in order to group them with the hypocrites in Madinah who were the subject of discussion in the previous passage. This complements the discussion of hypocrites from both areas.

"Some desert Arabs regard what they may spend [for God's cause] as a loss." (Verse 98) Such a person needs to give some of his money in *zakāt* and to contribute to the *jihād* campaigns. In this way he gives evidence of his being a Muslim and is thus able to enjoy the comforts of life in the Muslim community. He is also able to win favour with the Muslims who were the major power in Arabia. To him, what he spends is a clear loss which he is forced to pay. He does not give it out of any good will towards Islam or the Muslims. He does not like that they are victorious. Indeed his real attitude is quite different. He *"waits for some misfortune to befall you."* (Verse 98) He would love to see the Muslims return from battle soundly defeated. He would be thrilled if misfortune befell them.

Hence a supplication against them is stated here. A supplication by God signifies certainty. Hence the supplication is given here in the form of a statement: *"The evil turn of fortune will be theirs."* (Verse 98) The Arabic expression describes evil as if it has a circle which closes in on them and from which they can have no escape. It turns them round and they are seized in the middle with no let up. This abstract notion, described in vivid and concrete terms, brings the meaning closer

235

to our minds. *"God hears all and knows all."* (Verse 98) His hearing and knowledge are attributes which fit in perfectly with the atmosphere of ill intention, the waiting for misfortune to befall the Muslim community, and the hypocrisy that fills their hearts, although they try hard to conceal it. God certainly hears what they say, and He knows what they hide and what they keep in the open.

Another group however have experienced the happiness and delight that come with faith: *"Still other desert Arabs believe in God and the Last Day, and regard what they spend [for God's cause] as a means to bring them closer to God and [of their being remembered] in the Messenger's prayers. It shall certainly be for them a means of drawing near to God. God will admit them to His grace, for God is Much-forgiving, Merciful."* (Verse 99) What motivates these people to spend their money is their belief in God and the Day of Judgement. They have no fear of people, and they feel no need to flatter those in power. They make no calculation of profit and loss which they are likely to make in this world.

This group of believers wish that what they spend of their wealth will bring them closer to God and are eager to be remembered in the Prophet's prayers. That remembrance would demonstrate that he is pleased with them. His prayers are certainly answered by God as he devotes them to believers who spend their money for God's sake. The *sūrah* states clearly that what they give is indeed a means to give them what they wish of being close to God: *"It shall certainly be for them a means of drawing near to God."* (Verse 99) They are further given the news of an even happier destiny as a certain promise by God: *"God will admit them to His grace."* (Verse 99) Again mercy is described in rather concrete terms to set it in contrast with the 'evil turn'. Mercy is described here as if it is a house into which they are admitted. *"God is Much-forgiving, Merciful."* (Verse 99) He accepts repentance and charity. He forgives past sins and bestows His mercy on those who seek it.

Those Who Lead the Way

Having classified the desert Arabs, now the *sūrah* classifies the whole community, in urban and desert areas alike, into four groupings: the vanguard who took the lead among the *Muhājirīn* and the *Anṣār* as

well as those who followed in their footsteps, those who were hardened
in their hypocrisy whether they lived in Madinah or in the desert nearby,
those who combined good deeds with bad ones, and those whose cases
were deferred for judgement. These groups are outlined in the following
verses:

As for the first to lead the way, of the Muhājirīn *and the* Anṣār, *as
well as those who follow them in [the way of] righteousness, God is
well-pleased with them, and well-pleased are they with Him. He
has prepared for them gardens through which running waters flow,
where they shall abide for ever. That is the supreme triumph.*

*Some desert Arabs around you are hypocrites, and so are some of the
people from Madinah, who are indeed persistent in their hypocrisy.
You do not know them, but We know them. Twice shall We punish
them, and then they will be given over to a grievous suffering.*

*There are others who have acknowledged their sins, after having
mixed righteous deeds with evil ones. It may well be that God will
accept their repentance. God is Much-forgiving, Merciful. Take a
portion of their wealth as charity, so that you may cleanse and purify
them thereby; and pray for them: for your prayers are a source of
comfort for them. God hears all and knows all. Do they not know
that it is God alone Who accepts repentance from His servants, and
He is truly the One who takes charitable offerings, and that God is
the only One to accept repentance and bestow mercy? Say to them:
'Do as you will. God will see your deeds, and so will His Messenger,
and the believers; and in the end you shall be brought before Him
who knows all that is beyond the reach of human perception and all
that is manifest when He will tell you what you used to do.'*

*And yet there are others who must await God's judgement. He will
either punish them or turn to them in His mercy. God is All-knowing,
Wise.* (Verses 100–106)

It appears that these verses, making this classification, were revealed
after the Prophet's return from Tabūk. By that time, different people,
most of whom were hypocrites, had presented their excuses. The true
believers who did not join the expedition made their real regret

237

apparent, and some of them tied themselves to a pillar in the mosque declaring that they would not release themselves until the Prophet himself released them. Others did not make any excuses, hoping that God would accept their sincere repentance. These were three of the Prophet's Companions whose cases were not settled until God accepted their repentance, as will be discussed in full in Chapter 7. Together these groups represented the total variety of people around the Muslim area in Arabia after the expedition. God wanted to reveal the whole of the battlefield in front of His Messenger and the true believers with him. They would then understand the situation that prevailed at the time, which was close to the end of the first epoch, close to the time and birth place of this religion of Islam.

Such a revelation was necessary before the Islamic message made its move to liberate the whole of mankind throughout the globe. All communities needed to be liberated from serving any deities other than God, and from submitting themselves to anyone beside God. Before making such a move, the Muslim community needed to fully understand the prevailing situation so that it would be able to chart its course of action with clarity and a thorough perception of what was needed.

"*As for the first to lead the way, of the* Muhājirīn *and the* Anṣār, *as well as those who follow them in [the way of] righteousness, God is well-pleased with them, and well-pleased are they with Him. He has prepared for them gardens through which running waters flow, where they shall abide for ever. That is the supreme triumph.*" (Verse 100) This class of Muslims, with its three groupings, the *Muhājirīn*, the *Anṣār* and those who followed closely in their footsteps, formed the hard core of the Muslim community in Arabia after the conquest of Makkah. This was the group that ensured the unity of the Muslim community in every hardship as well as every period of ease and comfort. It is often the case that a trial of ease and comfort is more difficult to overcome than a trial of hardship.

In our view, this description of '*the first to lead the way*' refers to those of the *Muhājirīn* who migrated to Madinah before the Battle of Badr and the *Anṣār* who embraced Islam in the same period as well. Those who '*follow them in the way of righteousness*' refers to those who followed the same course, were true believers, strove hard for God's cause and shared with them the sublime heights of faith. The earlier ones still enjoy a higher position on account of their response to the call of Islam in the early, hard period that preceded Badr.

Scholars have expressed different views about who were the 'first to lead the way.' Some suggest that they were the ones to migrate or give their support before Badr, and others say they were the ones who were believers before the direction of prayer was changed from Jerusalem to Makkah. Some also say that these were the ones who fought at Badr, while others are of the opinion that they were the believers before the signing of the peace agreement at al-Ḥudaybiyah, and still others say that they were the ones who accepted to fight to the finish in the pledge known as Riḍwān. In our close study of the various stages of the building of the Muslim community, we feel that the view which we expressed earlier is the correct one, but God knows best.

We will quote here a few pages from the Prologue describing the different stages of building the first Muslim community for ease of reference:

> The Islamic movement in Makkah encountered difficulties right from the time when it was born. *Jāhiliyyah*, represented in this instance by the Quraysh, soon sensed the danger it was facing from the message declaring that 'there is no deity other than God, and Muhammad is God's Messenger.' It realized that this new message was an outright revolution against all authority not derived from God's own. It was a rebellion against all tyranny, seeking God's protection. *Jāhiliyyah* also sensed that the new message, led by God's Messenger, began to form a new organic grouping pledging sole and complete allegiance to God and His Messenger. Thus, it rebelled against the leadership of the Quraysh and the situation prevailing under *jāhiliyyah*. No sooner did the Quraysh sense this danger than it launched a determined attack on the new message, grouping and its leadership. It utilized in this attack all its power to inflict physical harm and to sow discord through intrigue and wicked designs.

> In fact this *jāhiliyyah* society sought every means to defend itself against a danger it felt to threaten its very existence. This is the normal state of affairs whenever a movement begins to advocate

God's Lordship in a community where Lordship is exercised by some people over others. Whenever such advocacy is undertaken by an organized movement that has its own leadership, it will be in direct confrontation with *jāhiliyyah* society, as the two cannot be accommodated within the same community.[3]

At this stage, every individual in the new Islamic grouping was subjected to oppression and persecution in every way, to the extent that many were killed. At the time, only a person who had dedicated himself and his life to God, and who was willing to endure persecution, hunger and even a ghastly death would join the new group, declaring his belief that there is no deity other than God and that Muḥammad is God's Messenger.

In this way a solid foundation was established for Islam, comprising the most determined individuals in Arabian society. Others who could not endure the hardship succumbed to the pressure and reverted to unbelief. But there were very few of these because the issues were clear at the outset. It was only people of distinction that were willing to take the decisive step and join Islam, despite the great danger that such a move involved.

This is how God chose those rare elements to be the early supporters of His message and to form the solid foundation of Islam in Makkah, i.e. the *Muhājirīn*, then to join the early *Anṣār* to form its core group in Madinah. Although the *Anṣār* were not subjected to the same pressures and persecution as the *Muhājirīn*, the pledge they gave to the Prophet at 'Aqabah indicated that they were equal to the task required by Islam. On that night when the pledge was given, as Ibn Kathīr reports, 'Abdullāh ibn Rawāḥah said to the Prophet: 'Stipulate whatever you wish for your Lord and yourself.' He said: 'As for my Lord, my condition is that you worship Him alone, associating no partners with Him. And as for myself, my condition is that you protect me as you would protect yourselves and your property.' They asked: 'What will be our reward in return?' He said: 'Paradise.' They said: 'It is a

---

3. For a full discussion of this, refer to the commentary of Verses 8: 72–75, in Vol. 7, Chapter 4, pp. 204–220

profitable deal. We accept no going back and we will not go back on it ourselves.'

Those who made this deal with God's Messenger, seeking no reward other than Paradise, and declaring that they would accept no going back, either by themselves or the Prophet, were aware that it was no easy option they were undertaking. In fact, they were certain that the Quraysh would fight them determinedly, supported by all the other Arabs. They realized that they would never again be able to live in peace with *jāhiliyyah* which had its roots deep in the whole of Arabia, including the areas adjoining Madinah...

The *Anṣār*, then, were fully aware of the likely consequences of their pledge once they had given it. They were also aware that they were not promised anything in this world in return for their efforts. They were not even promised victory over their enemies. The only reward they were promised was admittance into heaven. Yet they were still keen to offer their pledges. Hence, they were definitely with the early *Muhājirīn* in taking the necessary preparations so that they would constitute the solid foundation of the first Islamic society in Madinah.

Early Indications of Weakness

But the Madinah society did not maintain this level of purity despite the spread of Islam. Many people, especially those who were in positions of influence, felt they had to take a similar stand to their people in order to maintain their positions. When the Battle of Badr took place, the leading figure among these, 'Abdullāh ibn Ubayy ibn Salūl, thought that Islam had established firm roots and could not be easily dislodged. Hence, he pretended to be a Muslim. It was perhaps inevitable that many accepted Islam in order to keep abreast of their people. They were not hypocrites, but they had not fully understood Islam or moulded themselves according to it. This meant that the community in Madinah had different levels of commitment to the new faith.

At this point, the unique Islamic method of education began its work under the Prophet's supervision in order to mould these new elements. It aimed to achieve coherence within the Muslim community at the ideological, moral and behavioural levels.

When we read the *sūrahs* revealed in Madinah, in the approximate order of their revelation, we note the great effort that aimed to absorb and remould the new elements in the Muslim community, particularly because there were always newcomers. This was the case despite the determined opposition of the Quraysh and its attempts to win other Arabian tribes to its side, and despite the wicked designs of the Jews and their efforts to marshal hostile forces to the new faith and its advocates. Hence, the effort to bring newcomers to the same level as the elite, for this was needed if they were to continue with determination.

Nonetheless, weaknesses continued to surface, particularly in times of difficulty. There were indications of hypocrisy, reluctance, unwillingness to make physical or financial sacrifices, and a general turning away from danger. There were also signs of confusion concerning the relationship between a Muslim and his non-Muslim relatives. Qur'ānic texts in different *sūrahs* provide a clear idea of these phenomena and the method the Qur'ān employed to deal with them....

The Process of Integration

However, the structure of the Muslim community in Madinah remained generally sound, because it essentially relied on its solid foundation, made up of the elite of the *Muhājirīn* and the *Anṣār*. This foundation gave the Muslim community its strong constitution that withstood all weakening elements and overcame all hazards that might have been brought in by newcomers who had not yet been integrated into it.

Gradually, these new elements were integrated into the solid core, and the numbers of the weak, the hypocrites, and those who lacked the ideological clarity that serves as the basis of all relations and ties dwindled. Shortly before the conquest of Makkah, the Muslim

242

community in Madinah was very close to complete integration, providing the closest model of society Islamic education seeks to bring into existence.

There undoubtedly remained different levels of participation according to the various actions different individuals undertook for Islam. Some groups were distinguished by the dedication, work and sacrifice they made to serve God's cause. Examples of these were the earliest to believe in Islam among the *Muhājirīn* and the *Anṣār*, the people of Badr, those who were party to the pledge given to the Prophet at al-Ḥudaybiyah, and generally those who donated and fought before the conquest of Makkah. Qur'ānic and *ḥadīth* texts, as well as the practical situation in the Muslim community confirmed these distinctions that resulted from action taken for Islam...

That there were these different grades on the basis of strength of faith was no barrier to bridging the gap between them in the Madinah society before the conquest of Makkah. In fact, most of the apparent weaknesses within the ranks of the Muslim community were remedied, and their symptoms disappeared. Hence the whole of Madinah society could be considered as forming a solid Islamic basis.

However, when Makkah fell to Islam in year 8, followed by the surrender of the Hawāzin and the Thaqīf tribes, which were the last two large tribes to put up resistance to Islam, this ushered in a great influx of new Muslims. Needless to say, these were of different levels with regard to their outlook. Some among them were hypocrites, while others simply adopted Islam, the new overpowering force. Others still needed to be won over to Islam. Mostly, however, these were people who had not yet understood the fundamentals of Islam and their souls had not yet interacted with its values and principles.

This account clearly shows the position of the *Muhājirīn* and the *Anṣār* and those who followed them with regard to their strength of faith and readiness to sacrifice their all for God's cause. Theirs is a highly significant role in the building of the structure of the Muslim community and giving the message of Islam a practical manifestation. Their role will continue to influence every group of people who want to live their lives in accordance with the teachings of Islam.

"*God is well-pleased with them and well-pleased are they with Him.*" (Verse 100) That God is pleased with them means that He will be rewarding them generously. Indeed His pleasure with them is the highest reward to which they may aspire. That they are pleased with Him means that they are reassured by being on His side, confident that whatever He determines for them is right and good. They are grateful when they receive His bounty and they remain steadfast when they endure hardship. However, usage of the term '*well-pleased*' in both conditions imparts an air of total happiness, which is mutual between God and this elite group of His servants. It elevates this group to a high position in which they reciprocate God's feelings towards them when He is their supreme Lord and they are His servants whom He created. Language cannot adequately describe such a situation; it is merely felt as we read the Qur'ānic expression and reflect on it with an open mind and a spirit that aspires to the sublime.

That is their situation with their Lord. It is a permanent situation: "*God is well-pleased with them and well-pleased are they with Him.*" The signs of this mutual pleasure await them: "*He has prepared for them gardens through which running waters flow, where they shall abide for ever. That is the supreme triumph.*" (Verse 100) What triumph can be greater than this? It is indeed the supreme triumph.

Mixing Good Deeds with Bad Ones

The second group is in total contrast with the one we have just described: "*Some desert Arabs around you are hypocrites, and so are some of the people from Madinah, who are indeed persistent in their hypocrisy. You do not know them, but We know them. Twice shall We punish them, and then they will be given over to a grievous suffering.*" (Verse 101) We have discussed at length the nature of the hypocrites, whether they lived in Madinah or in the Arabian desert. The *sūrah* has given numerous examples of their attitude. Here, however, it points to a special type of hypocrite who acquired great skill in hiding their true attitude to the extent that they remain unknown to the

Prophet, despite his profound insight and great experience. What is so special about such hypocrites?

God declares that such hypocrites were in Madinah, as well as among the nearby desert Arabs. He reassures His Messenger and the believers that the hypocrites' scheming will come to nothing. He also warns the hypocrites who were adept at hiding their true position that they will not escape God's punishment. Indeed their punishment will be doubled in this life as well as in the life to come. "*You do not know them, but We know them. Twice shall We punish them, and then they will be given over to a grievous suffering.*" (Verse 101) Perhaps the closest interpretation of the double punishment in this life is that they worry lest their reality be discovered by the Muslim community, and the punishment inflicted on them by the angels when they gather their souls, hitting them on their faces and backs. Alternatively, it refers to the pain they feel when they see the Muslims triumph over the forces of falsehood and their fear lest their true feelings are discovered. God knows best the precise meaning of His statement.

If those were the two extreme groups, there is a third one in between: "*There are others who have acknowledged their sins, after having mixed righteous deeds with evil ones. It may well be that God will accept their repentance. God is Much-forgiving, Merciful. Take a portion of their wealth as charity, so that you may cleanse and purify them thereby; and pray for them: for your prayers are a source of comfort for them. God hears all and knows all. Do they not know that it is God alone who accepts repentance from His servants, and He is truly the One who takes charitable offerings, and that God is the only One to accept repentance and bestow mercy? Say to them: 'Do as you will. God will see your deeds, and so will His Messenger, and the believers; and in the end you shall be brought before Him who knows all that is beyond the reach of human perception and all that is manifest when He will tell you what you used to do.'*" (Verses 102–105)

The fact that God instructs His Messenger to take a certain action with this group suggests that they were known in person to the Prophet. It is reported that these verses refer to a particular group who did not join the Prophet on the Tabūk Expedition, but soon regretted their action, admitted their guilt and repented. Their bad action was to stay behind, and their good action was their regret and repentance.

Al-Ṭabarī reports in his commentary on this verse: "It refers to Abū Lubābah and his companions who did not join the Prophet when he set out to Tabūk. When the Prophet approached Madinah on his way back they blamed themselves for staying behind. They said: 'Do we stay behind enjoying food, comfort and the company of our women while the Prophet strives for God's cause enduring much hardship!' They tied themselves to pillars, determining not to release themselves unless the Prophet himself untied them. Only three among them did not tie themselves to pillars. When the Prophet saw what they did, he was told of their regret and their determination that they would be released only by him. He said: 'I will not release them until I am commanded to do so, and I will not excuse them until God has accepted their regrets. They preferred to spare themselves the hardship of joining a campaign of Muslims.' God then revealed the verse: "*There are others who have acknowledged their sins, after having mixed righteous deeds with evil ones. It may well be that God will accept their repentance. God is Much-forgiving, Merciful.*" (Verse 102) When God uses the expression '*it may well be*', it signifies certainty.

There are several other reports, one of which suggests that it refers only to Abū Lubābah who alerted the Jews of Qurayẓah to the death sentence awaiting them by making a sign of cutting his throat. This is highly unlikely, because these verses were revealed long after what happened then. Other reports suggest that it refers to the desert Arabs.

Al-Ṭabarī comments on these reports: "Perhaps the nearest to the truth is that which suggests that they refer to those who acknowledged their mistake when they stayed behind and did not join the *jihād* campaign with the Prophet when he marched out to face the Byzantines. Those were a group of people among whom was Abū Lubābah. We say that this is the closest to the truth because God – limitless is He in His glory – refers in this verse to a group of people who acknowledged their guilt. This means that they were not one person. All the reports we have make it clear that the only group to do so consisted of people who did not join the Prophet when he went on his expedition to Tabūk. We say that Abū Lubābah was among them because all commentators say so."

Having described this group of people who regretted their staying behind and repented having done so, the *sūrah* goes on to say: "*It may well be that God will accept their repentance. God is Much-forgiving, Merciful.*" (Verse 102) As al-Ṭabarī has explained, when God says, '*it may well be,*' the expression suggests realization. It is a prospect raised by the One Who can fulfil it. The acknowledgement of error in this way and feeling one's guilt are indications of an alert and sensitive conscience. Hence, repentance is likely to be accepted and forgiveness is likely to follow. God has certainly accepted their repentance and forgiven them.

God says to His Messenger, Muḥammad (peace be upon him): "*Take a portion of their money as charity, so that you may cleanse and purify them thereby; and pray for them: for your prayers are a source of comfort for them. God hears all and knows all.*" (Verse 103) Those were people with alert consciences which prompted their regret and repentance for what they had done. Hence they deserved to be reassured and to receive the sympathy which opened up for them hopeful prospects. As the Prophet was moulding a whole community and establishing a system, he felt he needed to wait for instructions from God regarding their cases. Al-Ṭabarī reports on the authority of Ibn 'Abbās: "When the Prophet released Abū Lubābah and his two Companions, they brought him some money and said: 'Take this money of ours and give it away as *Ṣadaqah*, i.e. charity, and pray for us.' In other words they requested him to pray for their forgiveness and for the purity of their souls. The Prophet said: 'I am not taking any of it until I have received instructions.' God then revealed this verse: '*Take a portion of their money as charity, so that you may cleanse and purify them thereby; and pray for them: for your prayers are a source of comfort for them.*' (Verse 103) The Prophet then did as he was instructed."

Thus we see how God favoured them with His acceptance as He knew that they were good at heart, sincere in their repentance. He ordered His Messenger to take some of their money for charitable uses, and to pray for them. Taking charity from them brought them back as full members of the Muslim community. They could once again share in its duties and participate in meeting its responsibilities. They were thus neither rejected nor expelled. Their charitable donation added to the purity of their hearts. The Prophet's prayer on their behalf gave them reassurance.

"*God hears all and knows all.*" (Verse 103) He hears supplications and prayers, and He knows what is in peoples' hearts. He judges all in accordance with what He hears and knows, for He is indeed the One who hears all and knows all. It is He who makes the final judgement on His servants, accepting their repentance and their charity. His Messenger, the Prophet Muḥammad (peace be upon him), carries out what God commands. He does not initiate any part of this himself.

To establish this fact God says in the following verse: "*Do they not know that it is God alone who accepts repentance from His servants, and He is truly the One who takes charitable offerings, and that God is the only One to accept repentance and bestow mercy?*" (Verse 104) This is a form of question which signifies an emphatic statement, meaning: let them know that it is God who accepts repentance, takes charitable offerings and bestows mercy on His servants. None of this belongs to anyone beside God. As al-Ṭabarī says: "When the Prophet refused to release those who tied themselves to the pillars after they had stayed behind, and when he did not accept their charity after their release, he was simply making it clear to all that none of this was within his authority. It all belonged to God alone. The Prophet himself would only do these things if he were authorized to do so."

Finally those who had repented after they had stayed behind are addressed directly: "*Say to them: 'Do as you will. God will see your deeds, and so will His Messenger, and the believers; and in the end you shall be brought before Him who knows all that is beyond the reach of human perception and all that is manifest when He will tell you what you used to do.'*" (Verse 105) The Islamic system is based on faith as well as action that gives credence to professed beliefs. The real proof of their repentance is their action which is apparent to all. It is seen by God, His Messenger and the believers. In the hereafter, they are returned to the One whose knowledge encompasses what is manifest and what is thought to be hidden, as well as physical actions and inner feelings.

Regretting slips and mistakes and repenting past errors do not represent the end. It is the action that follows such repentance that counts. It may either give credence to such feelings of regret and build new actions on their basis or undermine them and deprive them of their value.

Islam is a practical code of living in which feelings and intentions count for little unless they are transformed into real action. A good intention has its place, but the final verdict is not determined on its basis. A good intention is added to the action following it in order to determine its value. This is the import of the *ḥadīth* in which the Prophet says: "Actions are but by intentions." So intention on its own is of little value unless it is acted upon.

Awaiting God's Judgement

The fourth group of people in the society that lived in Madinah and its surrounding area at the time of the revelation of this *sūrah* are left to God to judge in their case: "*And yet there are others who must await God's judgement. He will either punish them or turn to them in His mercy. God is All-knowing, Wise.*" (Verse 106)

This is the fourth group of people who did not join the expedition, and whose cases were deferred for judgement. These were different from the hypocrites, the apologetic, and the repentant who admitted their error. Until the revelation of these verses, nothing had been determined in the case of this group. Their cases were left to God for judgement. Neither they nor anyone else were aware of what decision would be taken. It is reported that this verse speaks specifically about Murārah ibn al-Rabīʿ, Kaʿb ibn Mālik and Hilāl ibn Umayyah. These three did not take part in the expedition out of laziness and in preference for the comforts of life at home to marching in the desert heat. They were treated differently by the Prophet, and their cases will be discussed in full later.

Al-Ṭabarī reports on the authority of Ibn ʿAbbās: "After the revelation of the verse which says, "*Take a portion of their money as charity, so that you may cleanse and purify them thereby,*" the Prophet took money from Abū Lubābah and his companions and gave it away in charity on their behalf. There remained three more who did not chain themselves like Abū Lubābah. They were neither excused nor given any mention. They were in dire trouble and felt the whole earth too tight for them. It is in reference to these that God says: "*And yet there are others who must await God's judgement. He will either punish them or turn to them in His mercy. God is All-knowing,*

Wise." (Verse 106) Some people said that these people were ruined as no acceptance of their repentance had been mentioned, while others continued to hope that they would be forgiven by God. Thus, their cases were deferred for judgement by God Himself. Then the later verses were revealed which state: "*God has assuredly turned in His mercy to the Prophet, the* Muhājirīn *and the* Anṣār, *who followed him in the hour of hardship, when the hearts of a group of them had almost faltered. Then again He turned to them in mercy; for He is compassionate towards them, merciful. And [so too] to the three who were left behind.* " (Verses 117–118) Thus they were included among those to whom God has turned in His mercy. This report sounds more authentic.

Since their cases were deferred for judgement, we prefer to postpone discussion of their cases till we discuss these later verses, God willing.

A Mosque to Promote Unbelief

And there are those who have established a house of worship out of mischievous motives, to promote unbelief and disunity among the believers, and to provide an outpost for those who have already been warring against God and His Messenger. They will certainly swear: 'We have only the best of intentions.' God bears witness that they certainly are liars. Never set a foot there. Only a house of worship that from the very first day has been founded on piety is worthy of you standing to pray there. In it are men who love to grow in purity, for God loves those who purify themselves. Who is better: a man who founds his building [motivated by a sense of] being God-fearing and seeking His goodly acceptance, or one who founds his building on the edge of a crumbling precipice, so that it tumbles with him in the fire of hell? God does not guide the wrongdoers. The structure which they have built will continue to be a source of disquiet in their hearts, until their hearts are torn to pieces. God is All-knowing, Wise. (Verses 107–110)

The story of this mosque intended for mischief is prominent in the events of the expedition to Tabūk. This is the reason for making specific mention of the hypocrites who built it. Their case is discussed at length after completing the discussion of the various groups of people in the Muslim society at the time.

In his commentary on the Qur'ān, Ibn Kathīr reports:

The reason for the revelation of these verses is that before the Prophet's arrival in Madinah, there lived in it a man from the tribe of the Khazraj called Abū 'Āmir and nicknamed al-Rāhib. He had adopted Christianity and read the Bible. He used to be a man of devotion before the advent of Islam, and he enjoyed a position of great honour among the Khazraj. When the Prophet arrived in Madinah and the Muslims there rushed to his support, Islam began to gather strength. Then the Prophet and his Companions achieved their resounding victory in the Battle of Badr, but Abū 'Āmir was in distress at their success and he was now open with his hostility. He then left Madinah secretly and joined the unbelievers in Makkah encouraging them to fight God's Messenger. They gathered their forces and were joined by other tribes to attack Madinah for the Battle of Uḥud which was a test for the believers and the final outcome was in favour of those who were God-fearing.

This evil man dug large holes in the ground in the area separating the two hosts. The Prophet fell into one of them and received an injury to his face, and his right lower front tooth was broken. There was a cut on his forehead. At the beginning of the battle, Abū 'Āmir stepped forward and addressed his clansmen among the *Anṣār*, calling on them to support him. When they recognized him and understood his purpose, they abused him, describing him as an enemy of God. He went back to the Quraysh saying some evil had befallen his people after he had left them.

Before Abū 'Āmir left Madinah, the Prophet had called on him to believe in God and he recited the Qur'ān to him, but he stubbornly refused. The Prophet then prayed that he would die in a far away land, without support. That was indeed his end. When the Battle of Uḥud was over and the Muslims were able to overcome its effects, he felt that the Prophet would move from strength to strength. He then fled to join Hercules, the Byzantine

Emperor, and tried to persuade him to fight the Prophet. He promised him something to satisfy him and Abū 'Āmir stayed in his court. He started to write to a group of hypocrites from his tribe, promising them that he would come at the head of a large army to defeat the Prophet. He asked them to establish an outpost where anyone he would be sending could stay, and where he himself would establish residence when he came. They started to build what ostensibly was a mosque at a place not far away from the Qubā' Mosque.

The building was completed before the Prophet marched towards Tabūk. The hypocrites who built it came to the Prophet and asked him to come over and pray in their mosque, hoping that they would use that prayer as an endorsement of their action. They told the Prophet that they intended it to be used by the weak and the ill on a rainy night. However, God protected him against praying in such a place. He said to them: "We have embarked on a travel. So let it be until we come back, God willing." When the Prophet was on his way back from Tabūk, and at a distance of one day's travel from Madinah, or even less, the Angel Gabriel came down with the true story of this mosque intended for evil and to sow seeds of discord among the believers who used to pray in the Qubā' Mosque which was founded right from the first day on piety. The Prophet dispatched some of his Companions to pull this other mosque down before he arrived in Madinah.[4]

This is then the story of the mosque which was built by the hypocrites to further their designs against Islam. The Prophet was instructed not to pray there, but to pray in the first mosque built in the Islamic period, i.e. the Qubā' Mosque which was founded on piety right from the first day. It was frequented by people who were keen to do everything that helped them to grow in purity, and "*God loves those who purify themselves.*" (Verse 108)

---

4. Ibn Kathīr, op.cit., p. 353.

Houses of False Worship

It was then at the time of the Prophet that a mosque for mischief making was built by the hypocrites, intended to scheme against Islam and to undermine the position of the Muslims. Its purpose was to promote unbelief and to provide a cover for those who plotted against the Muslim community, co-operating with the enemies of Islam while pretending to be believers. The same types of mosque are still being established in a great variety of forms, making use of advanced evil. These may take the form of an activity which ostensibly seeks to promote Islam, but works in reality to obliterate or disform it or to deprive it of its true character. They may also establish regimes or social orders which raise a false religious banner, when in reality they undermine Islam. They can also take the form of organizations, books and research which take on a religious guise in order to pacify those who feel ill at ease as they see Islam being attacked by its enemies. These organizations and books try to quieten their worries, reassuring them that Islam is still in a healthy position.

Because there are so many masks and disguised places of mischief, it is important that they should be known and identified. They should be made to appear in their true colours, and their reality laid bare. If we do this, we will only be doing what was done to this mosque once its true nature was unmasked so clearly and powerfully: *"And there are those who have established a house of worship out of mischievous motives, to promote unbelief and disunity among the believers, and to provide an outpost for those who have already been warring against God and His Messenger. They will certainly swear: 'We have only the best of intentions.' God bears witness that they certainly are liars. Never set a foot there. Only a house of worship that from the very first day has been founded on piety is worthy of you standing to pray there. In it are men who love to grow in purity, for God loves those who purify themselves. Who is better: a man who founds his building [motivated by a sense of] being God-fearing and seeking His goodly acceptance, or one who founds his building on the edge of a crumbling precipice, so that it tumbles with him in the fire of hell? God does not guide the wrongdoers. The structure which they have built will continue to be a source of disquiet in their hearts, until their hearts are torn to pieces. God is All-knowing, Wise."* (Verses 107–110)

The inimitable Qur'ānic style draws here a very vivid picture showing the end which awaits every deceptive structure built close to a real mosque or centre of piety, and intended to play the same role as that of the first such mosque built by the hypocrites of Madinah. It reassures the true advocates of faith who are keen to purge themselves of the evil designs of the enemies of Islam: "*Who is better: a man who founds his building [motivated by a sense of] being God-fearing and seeking His goodly acceptance, or one who founds his building on the edge of a crumbling precipice, so that it tumbles with him in the Fire of Hell? God does not guide the wrongdoers.*" (Verse 109)

Let us pause for a moment to look at the solid foundations of a building established on fear of God. It is firm, solid and well established. Let us then look at the other side and see the swift and violent movement which shakes the deceptive structure. It is founded on the edge of a precipice which is crumbling, about to collapse. We see it now shaking, sliding and falling into a deep precipice. And that precipice is the fire of hell. For God provides no guidance for the unbelievers who have built this edifice to use it as a place of scheming against Islam and the Muslims.

This remarkably vivid scene which is full of movement is painted and brought alive with just a few words, which reassure the advocates of the truth that the scheming of the hypocrites and the unbelievers will come to nought. Thus those who build their structure on a proper foundation of fear of God will be able to face up to others who scheme against this religion of Islam.

The *sūrah* paints another remarkable scene showing the effects on the evil builders of their deceptive structure: "*The structure which they have built will continue to be a source of disquiet in their hearts, until their hearts are torn to pieces. God is All-knowing, Wise.*" (Verse 110) The edge has crumbled and the ill-intended structure built on it has collapsed and fallen into the precipice, into the fire of hell, and good riddance! Yet the effects of that building remain in the hearts of its builders in the form of doubt, worry and confusion. It will continue to deprive them of any comfort and stability until their hearts are torn into pieces and collapse from their positions.

The image of a collapsing building is complementary to that of doubt, instability and worry. The first depicts a physical picture and the other a mental one. Both are held side by side in the remarkable scene painted by the inimitable Qur'ānic style. They also complement each other in practical human situations in every age. The deviant schemer will always be shaken, confused, unstable, worried lest his reality is unmasked. This is perhaps the secret of the surpassing excellence of the Qur'ān. It depicts feelings with artistic beauty and remarkable complementarity and contrast. At the same time it maintains simplicity and clarity of expression and vividness in its imagery.

Beyond all this there is a definite purpose served by the unmasking of the true nature of the mosque built by the hypocrites, and by the classifying of the community into those levels of belief. Thus the path is charted for the Islamic movement and its field of operation is clearly drawn.

As it was revealed, the Qur'ān was providing leadership, direction and education for the Muslim community, and preparing it to undertake its great task. The Qur'ān will not be properly understood unless it is taken within its great field of operation. It will only be understood by people who undertake to move with it along its clear path.

7

The Earth's Suffocating Expanse

God has bought of the believers their lives and their property, promising them heaven in return: they fight for the cause of God, kill and be killed. This is a true promise which He has made binding on Himself in the Torah, the Gospel and the Qur'ān. Who is more true to his promise than God? Rejoice, then, in the bargain you have made with Him. That is the supreme triumph. (111)

إِنَّ ٱللَّهَ ٱشْتَرَىٰ مِنَ ٱلْمُؤْمِنِينَ أَنفُسَهُمْ وَأَمْوَٰلَهُم بِأَنَّ لَهُمُ ٱلْجَنَّةَ يُقَـٰتِلُونَ فِى سَبِيلِ ٱللَّهِ فَيَقْتُلُونَ وَيُقْتَلُونَ وَعْدًا عَلَيْهِ حَقًّا فِى ٱلتَّوْرَىٰةِ وَٱلْإِنجِيلِ وَٱلْقُرْءَانِ وَمَنْ أَوْفَىٰ بِعَهْدِهِۦ مِنَ ٱللَّهِ فَٱسْتَبْشِرُوا۟ بِبَيْعِكُمُ ٱلَّذِى بَايَعْتُم بِهِۦ وَذَٰلِكَ هُوَ ٱلْفَوْزُ ٱلْعَظِيمُ ۝

[It is a triumph for] those who turn to God in repentance, who worship and praise Him, who contemplate [God and His creation], who bow down and prostrate themselves, who enjoin the doing of what is right and forbid the doing of what is wrong, and keep within the limits set out by God. Give you [Prophet] glad tidings to the believers. (112)

ٱلتَّـٰٓئِبُونَ ٱلْعَـٰبِدُونَ ٱلْحَـٰمِدُونَ ٱلسَّـٰٓئِحُونَ ٱلرَّٰكِعُونَ ٱلسَّـٰجِدُونَ ٱلْءَامِرُونَ بِٱلْمَعْرُوفِ وَٱلنَّاهُونَ عَنِ ٱلْمُنكَرِ وَٱلْحَـٰفِظُونَ لِحُدُودِ ٱللَّهِ وَبَشِّرِ ٱلْمُؤْمِنِينَ ۝

It is not for the Prophet and the believers to pray for the forgiveness of those who associate partners with God, even though they may be their close relatives, after it has become clear that they are destined for the blazing fire. (113)

مَاكَانَ لِلنَّبِيِّ وَٱلَّذِينَ ءَامَنُوٓاْ أَن يَسْتَغْفِرُواْ لِلْمُشْرِكِينَ وَلَوْكَانُوٓاْ أُوْلِي قُرْبَىٰ مِنۢ بَعْدِ مَا تَبَيَّنَ لَهُمْ أَنَّهُمْ أَصْحَٰبُ ٱلْجَحِيمِ ﴿١١٣﴾

Abraham prayed for the forgiveness of his father only because of a promise he had made to him. But when it became clear to him that he was God's enemy, he disowned him; Abraham was most tender-hearted, most clement. (114)

وَمَاكَانَ ٱسْتِغْفَارُ إِبْرَٰهِيمَ لِأَبِيهِ إِلَّا عَن مَّوْعِدَةٍ وَعَدَهَآ إِيَّاهُ فَلَمَّا تَبَيَّنَ لَهُۥٓ أَنَّهُۥ عَدُوٌّ لِّلَّهِ تَبَرَّأَ مِنْهُ إِنَّ إِبْرَٰهِيمَ لَأَوَّٰهٌ حَلِيمٌ ﴿١١٤﴾

Never will God let people go astray after He has given them guidance until He has made plain to them all that they should avoid. God has perfect knowledge of all things. (115)

وَمَاكَانَ ٱللَّهُ لِيُضِلَّ قَوْمًۢا بَعْدَ إِذْ هَدَىٰهُمْ حَتَّىٰ يُبَيِّنَ لَهُم مَّا يَتَّقُونَ إِنَّ ٱللَّهَ بِكُلِّ شَىْءٍ عَلِيمٌ ﴿١١٥﴾

To God belongs the kingdom of the heavens and the earth; He alone gives life and causes death. Besides God, you have none to protect or support you. (116)

إِنَّ ٱللَّهَ لَهُۥ مُلْكُ ٱلسَّمَٰوَٰتِ وَٱلْأَرْضِ يُحْيِۦ وَيُمِيتُ وَمَا لَكُم مِّن دُونِ ٱللَّهِ مِن وَلِيٍّ وَلَا نَصِيرٍ ﴿١١٦﴾

God has assuredly turned in His mercy to the Prophet, the *Muhājirīn* and the *Anṣār*, who followed him in the hour of hardship, when the hearts of a group of them had almost faltered. Then again He turned to them in mercy; for He is compassionate towards them, Merciful. (117)

And [so too] to the three who were left behind: when the earth, vast as it is, seemed to close in upon them, and their own souls had become too constricted, they realized that there was no refuge from God except by returning to Him. He then turned to them in mercy, so that they might repent. God is indeed the One who accepts repentance, the merciful. (118)

Believers, have fear of God and be among those who are truthful. (119)

It does not behove the people of Madinah and the bedouins who live around them to hold back from following God's Messenger, or to care for themselves more than for him; for, whenever they endure thirst, stress, or hunger for the sake of God, or take any step which would irritate the un-

لَّقَد تَّابَ ٱللَّهُ عَلَى ٱلنَّبِيِّ وَٱلْمُهَٰجِرِينَ وَٱلْأَنصَارِ ٱلَّذِينَ ٱتَّبَعُوهُ فِى سَاعَةِ ٱلْعُسْرَةِ مِنۢ بَعْدِ مَا كَادَ يَزِيغُ قُلُوبُ فَرِيقٍ مِّنْهُمْ ثُمَّ تَابَ عَلَيْهِمْ إِنَّهُۥ بِهِمْ رَءُوفٌ رَّحِيمٌ ﴿١١٧﴾

وَعَلَى ٱلثَّلَٰثَةِ ٱلَّذِينَ خُلِّفُوا۟ حَتَّىٰٓ إِذَا ضَاقَتْ عَلَيْهِمُ ٱلْأَرْضُ بِمَا رَحُبَتْ وَضَاقَتْ عَلَيْهِمْ أَنفُسُهُمْ وَظَنُّوٓا۟ أَن لَّا مَلْجَأَ مِنَ ٱللَّهِ إِلَّآ إِلَيْهِ ثُمَّ تَابَ عَلَيْهِمْ لِيَتُوبُوٓا۟ إِنَّ ٱللَّهَ هُوَ ٱلتَّوَّابُ ٱلرَّحِيمُ ﴿١١٨﴾

يَٰٓأَيُّهَا ٱلَّذِينَ ءَامَنُوا۟ ٱتَّقُوا۟ ٱللَّهَ وَكُونُوا۟ مَعَ ٱلصَّٰدِقِينَ ﴿١١٩﴾

مَا كَانَ لِأَهْلِ ٱلْمَدِينَةِ وَمَنْ حَوْلَهُم مِّنَ ٱلْأَعْرَابِ أَن يَتَخَلَّفُوا۟ عَن رَّسُولِ ٱللَّهِ وَلَا يَرْغَبُوا۟ بِأَنفُسِهِمْ عَن نَّفْسِهِۦ ذَٰلِكَ بِأَنَّهُمْ لَا يُصِيبُهُمْ ظَمَأٌ وَلَا نَصَبٌ وَلَا مَخْمَصَةٌ فِى سَبِيلِ ٱللَّهِ وَلَا يَطَـُٔونَ مَوْطِئًا يَغِيظُ ٱلْكُفَّارَ

believers, or inflict any loss on the enemy, a good deed is recorded in their favour. God does not suffer the reward of those who do good to be lost. (120)

وَلَا يَنَالُونَ مِنْ عَدُوٍّ نَّيْلًا إِلَّا كُتِبَ لَهُم بِهِۦ عَمَلٌ صَٰلِحٌ إِنَّ ٱللَّهَ لَا يُضِيعُ أَجْرَ ٱلْمُحْسِنِينَ ۝

And whenever they spend anything for the sake of God, be it little or much, or traverse a valley [in support of God's cause], it is recorded for them, so that God will give them the best reward for what they do. (121)

وَلَا يُنفِقُونَ نَفَقَةً صَغِيرَةً وَلَا كَبِيرَةً وَلَا يَقْطَعُونَ وَادِيًا إِلَّا كُتِبَ لَهُمْ لِيَجْزِيَهُمُ ٱللَّهُ أَحْسَنَ مَا كَانُوا۟ يَعْمَلُونَ ۝

It is not desirable that all the believers should go out to fight. From every section of them some should go forth, so that they may acquire a deeper knowledge of the faith and warn their people when they return to them, so that they may take heed. (122)

وَمَا كَانَ ٱلْمُؤْمِنُونَ لِيَنفِرُوا۟ كَآفَّةً فَلَوْلَا نَفَرَ مِن كُلِّ فِرْقَةٍ مِّنْهُمْ طَآئِفَةٌ لِّيَتَفَقَّهُوا۟ فِي ٱلدِّينِ وَلِيُنذِرُوا۟ قَوْمَهُمْ إِذَا رَجَعُوٓا۟ إِلَيْهِمْ لَعَلَّهُمْ يَحْذَرُونَ ۝

Believers, fight those of the unbelievers who are near you, and let them find you tough; and know that God is with those who are God-fearing. (123)

يَٰٓأَيُّهَا ٱلَّذِينَ ءَامَنُوا۟ قَٰتِلُوا۟ ٱلَّذِينَ يَلُونَكُم مِّنَ ٱلْكُفَّارِ وَلْيَجِدُوا۟ فِيكُمْ غِلْظَةً وَٱعْلَمُوٓا۟ أَنَّ ٱللَّهَ مَعَ ٱلْمُتَّقِينَ ۝

Whenever a *sūrah* is revealed, some of them say: 'Which of you has this strengthened in faith?' It certainly strengthens the believers in their faith, and so they rejoice. (124)

وَإِذَا مَآ أُنزِلَتْ سُورَةٌ فَمِنْهُم مَّن يَقُولُ أَيُّكُمْ زَادَتْهُ هَٰذِهِۦٓ إِيمَٰنًا فَأَمَّا ٱلَّذِينَ ءَامَنُوا۟ فَزَادَتْهُمْ إِيمَٰنًا وَهُمْ يَسْتَبْشِرُونَ ۝

But as for those whose hearts are diseased, it only adds wickedness to their wickedness, and so they die unbelievers. (125)

وَأَمَّا الَّذِينَ فِي قُلُوبِهِم مَّرَضٌ فَزَادَتْهُمْ رِجْسًا إِلَىٰ رِجْسِهِمْ وَمَاتُوا وَهُمْ كَافِرُونَ ﴿١٢٥﴾

Do they not see that they are tested once or twice every year? Yet they do not repent, and they do not take warning. (126)

أَوَلَا يَرَوْنَ أَنَّهُمْ يُفْتَنُونَ فِي كُلِّ عَامٍ مَّرَّةً أَوْ مَرَّتَيْنِ ثُمَّ لَا يَتُوبُونَ وَلَا هُمْ يَذَّكَّرُونَ ﴿١٢٦﴾

Whenever a *surah* is revealed, they look at one another [as if to say]: 'Is anyone watching?' Then they turn away. God has turned their hearts away, for they are people devoid of understanding. (127)

وَإِذَا مَا أُنزِلَتْ سُورَةٌ نَّظَرَ بَعْضُهُمْ إِلَىٰ بَعْضٍ هَلْ يَرَاكُم مِّنْ أَحَدٍ ثُمَّ انصَرَفُوا صَرَفَ اللَّهُ قُلُوبَهُم بِأَنَّهُمْ قَوْمٌ لَّا يَفْقَهُونَ ﴿١٢٧﴾

Indeed there has come to you a Messenger from among yourselves: one who grieves much that you should suffer; one who is full of concern for you; and who is tender and full of compassion towards the believers. (128)

لَقَدْ جَاءَكُمْ رَسُولٌ مِّنْ أَنفُسِكُمْ عَزِيزٌ عَلَيْهِ مَا عَنِتُّمْ حَرِيصٌ عَلَيْكُم بِالْمُؤْمِنِينَ رَءُوفٌ رَّحِيمٌ ﴿١٢٨﴾

Should they turn away, then say to them: "God is enough for me! There is no deity other than Him. In Him have I placed my trust. He is the Lord of the Mighty Throne. (129)

فَإِن تَوَلَّوْا فَقُلْ حَسْبِيَ اللَّهُ لَا إِلَٰهَ إِلَّا هُوَ عَلَيْهِ تَوَكَّلْتُ وَهُوَ رَبُّ الْعَرْشِ الْعَظِيمِ ﴿١٢٩﴾

Overview

This final passage of the *sūrah* outlines a number of final rulings that govern the Muslim community's relations with other groups and communities. It starts with defining the relationship between a Muslim and his Lord, the nature of Islam and an outline of Islamic duties and methods of action.

- Embracing Islam is described as a deal in which the buyer is God while the believer is the seller. Since it is a sale to God, believers have no say over anything in their lives. Neither their property nor their person can be withheld from serving God's cause. The final product is that God's word should be supreme, and all submission is made to God alone. The price a believer receives in this deal is admittance into heaven, which is far superior in value to the commodity he offers. Therefore, he receives it as a favour from God: "*God has bought of the believers their lives and their property, promising them heaven in return: they fight for the cause of God, kill and be killed. This is a true promise which He has made binding on Himself in the Torah, the Gospel and the Qur'ān. Who is more true to his promise than God? Rejoice, then, in the bargain you have made with Him. That is the supreme triumph.*" (Verse 111)

- The people who enter into this deal are a select few with distinctive qualities, some of which apply to them in their direct relationship with God, their feelings and the worship they offer. Their other qualities are concerned with the duties under this deal, which requires them to work for the establishment of the divine faith on earth, enjoin what is right and forbid what is wrong, and to see to it that God's bounds are respected: "*[It is a triumph for] those who turn to God in repentance, who worship and praise Him, who contemplate [God and His creation], who bow down and prostrate themselves, who enjoin the doing of what is right and forbid the doing of what is wrong, and keep within the limits set out by God. Give you [Prophet] glad tidings to the believers.*" (Verse 112)

- The verses that follow in this passage show that relations between the believers who make this deal and all others, including their close relatives, are severed. The two groups move in opposite directions, towards opposite ends. Those who are party to this deal go to heaven, while the others go to hell. The two meet neither in this world nor in the next. Hence, blood relationships cannot establish a bond between the two: "*It is not for the Prophet and the believers to pray for the forgiveness of those who associate partners with God, even though they may be their close relatives, after it has become clear that they are destined for the blazing fire. Abraham prayed for the forgiveness of his father only because of a promise he had made to him. But when it became clear to him that he was God's enemy, he disowned him; Abraham was most tender-hearted, most clement.*" (Verses 113–114)

- A believer's loyalty must be purely to God. It is on the basis of this unified loyalty that all ties and bonds are established. Here we have a clear statement by God clarifying all issues and leaving no room for error. It is more than enough for the believers that they have God's protection and support. With these promised by the One who is the master of the universe, they need nothing from anyone else: "*Never will God let people go astray after He has given them guidance until He has made plain to them all that they should avoid. God has perfect knowledge of all things. To God belongs the kingdom of the heavens and the earth; He alone gives life and causes death. Besides God, you have none to protect or support you.*" (Verses 115–116)

- With the nature of the deal being such, reluctance to join an expedition serving God's cause is a very serious matter. However, God has pardoned those whom He knew to have good intentions and a firm resolve to do their duty after having once failed. Thus, He turned to them in mercy: "*God has assuredly turned in His mercy to the Prophet, the* Muhājirīn *and the* Anṣār, *who followed him in the hour of hardship, when the hearts of a group of them had almost faltered. Then again He turned to them in mercy; for He is compassionate towards them, merciful. And [so too] to the three who were left behind: when the earth, vast as it is, seemed to close in upon them, and their own souls had become too constricted, they realized that there was no refuge from God except by returning to Him. He then turned to them in mercy, so that they might repent. God is indeed the One who accepts repentance, the Merciful."* (Verses 117–118)

- This is followed by a clear definition of the duties of the people of Madinah and the Bedouins that live nearby on account of their pledges given to the Prophet. It should be remembered that those formed the solid base of the Muslim community that was the standard-bearer of Islam. Strong objections are raised to staying behind, coupled with a clear statement of the terms of the deal and the actions to be taken in fulfilment of those pledges: *"It does not behove the people of Madinah and the bedouins who live around them to hold back from following God's Messenger, or to care for themselves more than for him; for, whenever they endure thirst, stress, or hunger for the sake of God, or take any step which would irritate the unbelievers, or inflict any loss on the enemy, a good deed is recorded in their favour. God does not suffer the reward of those who do good to be lost. And whenever they spend anything for the sake of God, be it little or much, or traverse a valley [in support of God's cause], it is recorded for them, so that God will give them the best reward for what they do."* (Verses 120–121)

- This encouragement to go forth on *jihād* for God's cause is coupled with a clarification that shows the limits of general mobilization, particularly after the land area of the Muslim state had become much bigger and the number of Muslims increased manifold. It is now feasible that only some of them should go to fight the enemy and acquire a more profound knowledge of the faith. The rest should stay behind to look after the needs of the community, provide logistic support and discharge other duties. All these efforts converge at the end: *"It is not desirable that all the believers should go out to fight. From every section of them some should go forth, so that they may acquire a deeper knowledge of the faith and warn their people when they return to them, so that they may take heed."* (Verse 122)

- The next verse defines the line the *jihād* movement should follow after the entire Arabian Peninsula has become the base of Islam. Now *jihād* should mean fighting the unbelievers all together, so that all oppression is ended and people submit only to God. The same applies to *jihād* against the people of earlier revelations until they pay the submission tax: *"Believers, fight those of the unbelievers who are near you, and let them find you tough; and know that God is with those who are God-fearing."* (Verse 123)

- Now that a full clarification of the pledge and the responsibilities it lays down, and the line the Muslim community should follow is given, the *sūrah* provides two contrasting pictures showing the opposite attitudes of the believers and unbelievers towards the Qur'ān as it is being revealed. Needless to say, the Qur'ān opens up positive responses to faith within people's hearts, outlines practical duties, and censures the hypocrites for their paying no heed to reminders and tests: *"Whenever a sūrah is revealed, some of them say: 'Which of you has this strengthened in faith?' It certainly strengthens the believers in their faith, and so they rejoice. But as for those whose hearts are diseased, it only adds wickedness to their wickedness, and so they die unbelievers. Do they not see that they are tested once or twice every year? Yet they do not repent, and they do not take warning."* (Verses 124–126)

- The final two verses of the *sūrah* describe the Prophet's concern and compassion for the believers. The Prophet himself is directed to place his trust totally in God and to pay little heed to those who reject God's guidance: *"Indeed there has come to you a Messenger from among yourselves: one who grieves much that you should suffer [in the life to come]; one who is full of concern for you; and who is tender and full of compassion towards the believers. Should they turn away, then say to them: 'God is enough for me! There is no deity other than Him. In Him have I placed my trust. He is the Lord of the Mighty Throne.'"* (Verses 128–129)

This brief outline of this final passage reflects the strong emphasis placed on *jihād*, the alignment of loyalties on the basis of faith, the advocacy of the Islamic faith throughout the world, in line with the terms of the pledge of loyalty required of believers. This pledge is shown here as a deal by which believers sell their lives and property in return for heaven. This means fighting to establish the divine order, with the emphasis on God's sovereignty over people and land. No acknowledgement of sovereignty to anyone else can be condoned.

Perhaps this quick outline of the passage shows the extent of defeatism that overwhelms people who try hard to explain the Qur'ān in such a way that limits *jihād* to the narrow sense of defending the 'land of Islam'. Yet the verses here declare very clearly the need to fight unbelievers who live next to this land of Islam, without reference to any aggression they might have perpetrated. Indeed their basic aggression is the one they perpetrate against God as they submit themselves and other people to deities other than Him. It is this type of aggression that must be fought through *jihād* by all Muslims.

A Very Special Contract

God has bought of the believers their lives and their property, promising them heaven in return: they fight for the cause of God, kill and be killed. This is a true promise which He has made binding on Himself in the Torah, the Gospel and the Qur'ān. Who is more true to his promise than God? Rejoice, then, in the bargain you have made with Him. That is the supreme triumph. (Verse 111)

I have heard this verse recited and have read it myself countless times over a long period starting from when I first memorized the Qur'ān and later when I used to recite and study it over a period of more than a quarter of a century. But when I began to reflect on it in order to write about it in this commentary, I began to understand it in a way that did not occur to me previously.

It is an inspiring verse, revealing the nature of the relationship between the believers and God, and the nature of the deal they make with God when they adopt Islam and which remains in force throughout their lives. Whoever makes this deal and remains true to it is the one who may truly be described as a believer reflecting the nature of faith. Otherwise his claim to be a believer remains short of proof.

The nature of this deal, or this contract of sale, as God graciously describes it, is that He has taken for Himself the souls and property of the believers, leaving them nothing of all that. They do not retain any part of that which they would feel too dear to sacrifice for His cause. They no longer have any choice whether to spend it in furthering His cause or not. It is indeed a deal that has been concluded and sealed. The buyer may do what He likes, as He pleases, with what He has bought. The seller has no option other than to fulfil the terms of the deal. He cannot argue or make any choices. He can only do what the deal specifies. The price given for this purchase is paradise, and the way to be followed by the sellers is that of *jihād*, fighting and sacrificing their lives, and the end result is either victory or martyrdom.

"*God has bought of the believers their lives and their property, promising them heaven in return: they fight for the cause of God, kill and be killed.*" (Verse 111) Whoever is party to this deal, signing the contract, paying the price agreed is a true believer. It is with the believers that God has made this deal of purchase. He has bestowed His grace on them by specifying a price. He is, after all, the One who gives life and property to all His creation, and He has also given human beings the ability to make a choice. He then bestowed further grace on human beings by making them able to make contracts, even with God Himself, and holding them to their contracts. He makes the honouring of their contract an evidence of their humanity, while going back on it is evidence of sinking back to the level of animals, and the worst of animals: "*Indeed, the worst of all creatures in God's sight are the ones who have denied the truth, and therefore will not believe; those with whom you have concluded a treaty, and then they break their treaty at every occasion, entertaining no sense of fearing God.*" (8: 55–56) He has also made the honouring or violation of such deals the criterion of reckoning and reward.

It is indeed an awesome deal, but it remains binding on every believer who is able to honour its terms. He is not to be exempt from it unless he goes back on his faith. Hence the sense of dread that I feel now as I am writing these words. *"God has bought of the believers their lives and their property, promising them heaven in return: they fight for the cause of God, kill and be killed."* (Verse 111) My Lord, we certainly need Your help. The deal fills us with awe. Yet those who are claiming to be Muslims everywhere, from the far east to the far west are sitting idle, unwilling to strive hard in order to establish the fundamental truth of God's Lordship on earth, or to remove the tyranny which usurps the qualities of Lordship over human life on earth. They are unwilling to fight, kill and be killed for God's cause, and unwilling to undertake a struggle that does not involve fighting and sacrificing one's life.

These words touched the hearts of the early Muslims at the time of the Prophet and were transformed into a reality that they would experience in life. They were not mere words carrying certain abstract meanings for contemplation and reflection. They were meant for immediate implementation. This is how 'Abdullāh ibn Rawāḥah felt at the time of the second pledge given by the *Anṣār* to the Prophet at 'Aqabah as reported by Muḥammad ibn Ka'b al-Quraẓī and others: "'Abdullāh ibn Rawāḥah asked God's Messenger to specify God's conditions and his own conditions. The Prophet said: 'As for God, the condition is that you worship Him alone, associating no partners with Him. And as for myself, the condition is that you protect me like you protect yourselves and your property.' He said: 'What do we get in return if we fulfil these terms?' The Prophet said: 'Paradise.' They all said: 'This is a profitable deal. We accept no going back and we will not go back on it ourselves.'"

That is how they felt about the whole contract: it was a profitable deal that allows no going back by either party. They treated it as a final deal concluded and sealed, with no opting out clause. The price, which is paradise, is paid, not deferred. Is it not a promise made by God Himself? Is He not the purchaser? Is He not the One who has made an old promise specifying the price in all His revelations: *"This is a true promise which He has made binding on Himself in the Torah, the Gospel and the Qur'ān."* (Verse 111)

"Who is more true to his promise than God?" (Verse 111) Indeed a promise by God is certain to be honoured. No one fulfils his promises like He does.

Jihād, or striving for God's cause, is a deal made by every believer, ever since the first Messenger was sent to mankind with a religion setting out the principles of faith. It is a course of action that is necessary to put life on a proper footing. Without it human life will not follow its right course. It is as God says in the Qur'ān: "*Had it not been for the fact that God repels one group of people by another, the earth would have been utterly corrupted.*" (2: 251) And He also says: "*Had it not been for the fact that God repels one group of people by another, monasteries, temples, houses of worship and mosques, wherein God's name is often praised, would have been pulled down.*" (22: 40)

A True Promise and a Profitable Deal

The truth must certainly move along its well-known way, and it is inevitable that falsehood should try to obstruct its march. The true faith revealed by God must set forth to liberate all mankind from submission to other creatures and to return them to serve and submit to God alone. Tyranny is certain to try to stop it and foil its efforts. The aim of the faith is to reach all corners of the world and liberate all mankind. The truth must set out along its way, without hesitation in order to prevent falsehood from gaining access to it. As long as unbelief and falsehood continue to exist anywhere in the world, and as long as people continue to submit to beings other than God, thus causing man to be humiliated, then striving for God's cause must continue. The deal made by every believer must be fulfilled, or else he is not a believer. The Prophet is quoted as saying: "Whoever dies without having joined a campaign of *jihād*, or at least considered joining it, betrays an aspect of hypocrisy." [Related by Aḥmad, Muslim, Abū Dāwūd and al-Nasā'ī.]

"*Rejoice, then, in the bargain you have made with Him. That is the supreme triumph.*" (Verse 111) Yes, people should rejoice at having dedicated their souls and their property for God's cause in return for admittance into heaven, as God Himself has promised. What does a believer miss out on when he honours his part of the deal? He certainly does not miss out on anything. He is certain to die anyway, and his wealth is certain to go, whether he spends it to serve God's cause or in any other way. Being in paradise is a great gain which a believer actually gets for nothing, since the price he offers would be gone anyway, whichever course of action he follows.

We need not mention the position of honour man attains when he conducts his life in line with what God requires of him. If he attains victory, then it is a victory achieved to make God's word supreme, to establish the faith God has revealed and to liberate God's servants from subjugation by human beings. If he attains martyrdom, then he is a martyr sacrificing his life for God's cause, making a testimony that he values his faith as more precious than his life. At every moment and at every step he feels himself to be stronger than the shackles and bonds of life, and that the burdens of this earthly life cannot stop his march. His faith triumphs over pain, and over life itself.

On its own this is a great victory, because it represents the fulfilment of man's humanity through his release from the burdens of his needs. When admittance to heaven is added as a reward, then the sale he has made calls for him to rejoice as it represents a great triumph indeed: "*Rejoice then in the bargain you have made with Him. That is the supreme triumph.*" (Verse 111)

We need to pause here a little to reflect on God's statement which says: "*This is a true promise which He has made binding on Himself in the Torah, the Gospel and the Qur'ān.*" (Verse 111) The promise God has made in the Qur'ān to those who strive for His cause is well known and is repeated several times. It leaves no room for any doubt about the fact that striving for God's cause is an essential part of the Islamic way of life as revealed by God Himself. Such striving is indeed the means to counter any human situation, at any place or time. It is to be remembered that the state of ignorance, or *jāhiliyyah*, is found in a human grouping or community that resorts to physical force to protect itself. It is not a theoretical concept standing in opposition to another. It takes practical steps to resist the divine faith and to overcome any Islamic grouping that upholds it. It prevents people from listening to the general declaration Islam makes which emphasizes that God is the only Lord to whom all human beings should submit; the declaration that ensures the liberation of all mankind throughout the world from submission to creatures of any sort. It actually stops people from joining the liberated Islamic community. Hence Islam has no choice but to confront the physical power that protects *jāhiliyyah* groupings, which, in turn, try their utmost to crush the Muslim revivalist groups and suppress their declaration announcing the liberation of mankind.

God's promise in the Torah and the Gospel to those who strive for His cause needs clarification. The Torah and the Gospel that are today in circulation cannot be described as the ones which God – limitless is He in His glory – revealed to His Messengers, Moses and Jesus (peace be upon them both). Even the Jews and the Christians do not claim that. They agree that the original versions of these Scriptures are not in existence. What they have today was written long after the revelation of these books, when all that was left was the little committed to memory after more than one generation. Much was added to that small memorized portion.

Nevertheless there remain in the Old Testament clear references to *jihād* and much encouragement to the Jews to fight their pagan enemies in order to ensure the triumph of their faith. Having said that, we should remember that distortion has crept into their concept of God and what striving for His cause means.

On the other hand, the Gospels that circulate among Christians today do not include any reference to *jihād*. We must, however, revise the concepts people have of the nature of Christianity, because these are taken from those Gospels which are not authentic, a fact conceded by Christian scholars. Besides, their lack of authenticity has been stated by God Himself in His last book, the Qur'ān, which admits no falsehood whatsoever. And in the Qur'ān God says clearly that His promise to grant heaven to those who strive for His cause, kill and be killed, was spelled out in the Torah, the Gospel and the Qur'ān. This is, then, the true fact which no counter argument can disprove.

What this statement means is that *jihād*, or striving for God's cause, is a deal binding on everyone who believes in God, ever since God sent messengers to mankind to preach His faith. But striving for God's cause does not mean rushing to fight the enemy. It is the practical translation of a principle of faith which influences the feelings, attitudes, behaviour and worship of the believers. Those with whom God has made this deal reflect their faith by their true characteristics outlined in the next verse.

The Characteristics of True Believers

Those who turn to God in repentance, who worship and praise Him, who contemplate [God and His creation], who bow down and prostrate themselves, who enjoin the doing of what is right and forbid the doing of what is wrong, and keep within the limits set out by God. Give you [Prophet] glad tidings to the believers. (Verse 112)

The first of these qualities is that they "turn to God in repentance." They appeal to Him for forgiveness, regretting any slip they may make and resolving to turn to Him and follow His guidance in their future days. They will not revert to sin. They will endeavour to do only good actions in order to make their repentance a reality. It is then a means of purging themselves of the effects of temptation and of mending their ways so that they can earn God's acceptance.

"Who worship and praise Him." (Verse 112) They submit and dedicate their worship to Him alone, acknowledging that He is God, the only Lord. This is a basic quality of theirs which is manifested by their worship, and also by their dedicating all their actions and statements to the pursuit of God's pleasure. Their worship, then, is meant as a practical confirmation of their belief in God's oneness. They praise God acknowledging His grace which He bestows on them. They praise Him continuously, in times of happiness and in times of adversity. When they are happy they praise God for His blessings, and when they go through difficult times they praise Him because they know that the difficulty is a test which they need to pass. They realize that God will show them His mercy when they prove their metal by going through the test with their faith unshaken. True praise is not that expressed only in times of ease and happiness. It is the praise genuinely expressed in times of adversity, recognizing that God, the Just and Merciful, would not put a believer through a trial unless it is eventually for his own good. A believer may not know that at the time, but God certainly knows it.

"Who contemplate [God and His creation.]" (Verse 112) The meaning of the Arabic term which is translated here in this fashion is not readily apparent. There are several interpretations of what it means.

Some people suggest that it refers to those who leave their homes to support God's cause, while others suggest that it refers to those who strive hard for its triumph. Other scholars suggest that it refers to those who travel in pursuit of knowledge, and still others say that it refers to people who fast. We feel that the interpretation we have chosen is closer to its meaning. It is in reference to such a quality that God says elsewhere in the Qur'ān: *"In the creation of the heavens and the earth, and in the succession of night and day, there are indeed signs for men endowed with insight, who remember God when they stand, sit and lie down, and reflect on the creation of the heavens and the earth: 'Our Lord, You have not created all this in vain. Limitless are You in Your glory. Guard us, then, against the torment of the fire.'"* (3: 190–191) The quality of contemplation and reflection is better suited to the context here. With repentance, worship and praising of God comes the quality of reflecting on God and His dominion which will inevitably lead to turning to Him, acknowledging His wisdom manifested in all His creation. The contemplation and reflection are not meant for their own sake or for gaining more knowledge of the world around us, but they should be made the basis on which human society is built.

"Who bow down and prostrate themselves." (Verse 112) They attend to their prayers which becomes an essential part of their life. Praying is thus made one of their distinctive characteristics.

"Who enjoin the doing of what is right and forbid the doing of what is wrong." (Verse 112) When a Muslim community that conducts its life in accordance with God's law is established, making clear that it submits to God and no one else, then the quality of enjoining the doing of what is right and forbidding what is wrong is seen to be fully operative within this community. It addresses any errors of implementation of, or deviation from, the code of living God has revealed. But when there is no Islamic community which gives supremacy to the implementation of God's law, then this quality of enjoining what is right should be addressed totally to the most important thing, which is acceptance of God's oneness, submission to His authority and the establishment of a truly Islamic community.

Similarly, the forbidding of what is wrong should also address the greatest wrong, namely, submission to authorities other than God's through enforcing laws that are at variance with His law. Those who responded to the Prophet Muḥammad (peace be upon him) and believed in his message, migrated, and strove to establish the Muslim state that implements God's law and a Muslim community that is governed on its basis. When this was achieved, they continued to enjoin what is right and forbid what is wrong, addressing matters that related to the details of worship or violation of the Islamic code of living. They never spent any time addressing these details before the establishment of the Islamic state and its Muslim community, because these details only arose as a later and practical development. The concept of doing what is right and forbidding what is wrong must be understood in the light of reality. No matter of detail, whether right or wrong, need be addressed before the basic and essential one is completed, as happened when the first Islamic community came into being.

"And keep within the limits set out by God." (Verse 112) That is to say, they make sure of the implementation of God's law in their own life and in the life of the community, and they resist anyone who tries to forestall it. Like the previous one, this quality can only work in a Muslim community governed by God's law in all its affairs. By definition, such a community acknowledges God's sovereignty as the only God, Lord and Legislator, and rejects any authority which seeks to implement laws that are not revealed by God. Efforts must concentrate first of all on the establishment of such a community. Only when it comes into being, will those who *"keep within the limits set out by God"* have their rightful place in it, as happened in the first Islamic community.

Such is the Islamic community with whom God has made this deal, and such are its distinctive qualities: repentance brings a human being back to God's way, stops him from committing sin and motivates him to do what is right; worship maintains a close relationship with God and sets the winning of His pleasure as people's aim; praising God in times of happiness and in adversity is a manifestation of total submission to Him alone and complete trust in His justice and wisdom; reflecting on God's attributes and the signs that indicate His wisdom and perfection of creation; enjoining what is right and forbidding what is wrong to expand people's role so as to ensure that the whole community is set on the right course; and keeping within the limits set out by God to ensure their implementation and to prevent any violation.

Such is the believing community which is bound by a deal with God which guarantees heaven in return for their lives and property which they sell to God. It thus implements a rule that has been in force since the start of the divine faith, and the revelation of God's first message to mankind. The deal means fighting for God's cause with the aim of making His word supreme, killing those who stand in opposition to God's message or falling as martyrs in the continuing battle between the truth and falsehood, Islam and *jāhiliyyah*, God's law and tyranny, divine guidance and error.

Life is not all play, or all enjoyment and eating as animals eat. Nor is it cheap, humble safety and comfort. True living means doing what is necessary in support of the truth, striving for the cause of goodness, the achievement of victory for God's cause or sacrificing one's life for that, and then earning God's pleasure and admittance into heaven. This is the true life which the believers are called upon to seek: *"Believers, respond to the call of God and the Messenger when he calls you to that which will give you life."* (8: 24)

An Example to Follow

The believers whose lives and property God has bought in return for His promise to admit them to paradise are a unique community, because faith is their only bond which unites them and makes of them a well-knit community. This *sūrah* which outlines the relationship between the Muslim community and others who do not belong to it also makes a final judgement in respect of relationships not based on this bond, particularly after the rapid expansion of the Muslim community following the conquest of Makkah, when large numbers of people embraced Islam without being fundamentally affected by its way of life. They continued to attach great importance to blood relations. The verses that follow sever the ties that existed in the past between the believers who have made this deal and those who have not taken part in it, even though they may be related to them by blood. This is because they have two different courses to follow and two widely different ends in the hereafter.

It is not for the Prophet and the believers to pray for the forgiveness of those who associate partners with God, even though they may be their close relatives, after it has become clear that they are destined for the blazing fire. Abraham prayed for the forgiveness of his father only because of a promise he had made to him. But when it became clear to him that he was God's enemy, he disowned him; Abraham was most tender-hearted, most clement. Never will God let people go astray after He has given them guidance until He has made plain to them all that they should avoid. God has perfect knowledge of all things. To God belongs the kingdom of the heavens and the earth; He alone gives life and causes death. Besides God, you have none to protect or support you. (Verses 113–116)

It appears that some Muslims used to pray to God to forgive their parents who were unbelievers, and to request the Prophet to pray for their forgiveness. These verses were then revealed to state that such prayer was evidence of their continued attachment to blood relations which was unacceptable from true believers. It was not right or up to them to do so. But the question arises here: how can the believers be certain that those relatives were destined for hell-fire? Most probably that ensues once those relatives die without having accepted the divine faith, when they can no longer believe.

Faith is the great bond that regulates all human bonds and relationships. If it is severed then all other bonds are uprooted. There can be no more value for bonds of blood or marriage relationships, or bonds of race and nationality. It is either that faith unites people and maintains their bonds, or there are no relationships when faith does not exist: "*Abraham prayed for the forgiveness of his father only because of a promise he had made to him. But when it became clear to him that he was God's enemy, he disowned him; Abraham was most tender-hearted, most clement.*" (Verse 114)

Abraham's example in this regard should not be followed, because he was only fulfilling a promise which he made to his father to pray for his forgiveness in the hope that he would follow God's guidance. At the time Abraham said to his father: "*Peace be on you. I shall pray to my Lord to forgive you; for He has always been very kind to me. But I shall withdraw from you all and from whatever you invoke instead of*

God, and I shall pray to my Lord alone. Perhaps, by my prayer to my Lord I shall not be unblest." (19: 47–48) When his father died an unbeliever and Abraham realized that he was an enemy of God, he disowned him and severed all relations with him.

"Abraham was most tender-hearted, most clement." (Verse 114) He used to pray to God very often and with great sincerity. He was also clement and he would forgive those who treated him badly. His father ill-treated him but he was forbearing. Yet only when he realized that there was no hope that he would ever believe in God, did he give up on him.

It has been reported that when these verses were revealed those believers who were in the habit of praying for the forgiveness of their relatives feared that they might have gone far astray because their action was against God's law. The following verse was then revealed to reassure them that no punishment could be incurred prior to a clear definition of error: *"Never will God let people go astray after He has given them guidance until He has made plain to them all that they should avoid. God has perfect knowledge of all things."* (Verse 115)

God does not hold against people anything He has not made clear that they should avoid. He does not let them go astray because of certain actions unless these are of a type which He has clearly forbidden them in advance. Human knowledge is limited and it is God alone who has perfect knowledge of all things. God has made this religion easy to follow, explaining what should be done and what should be avoided with all clarity. He has left certain things without giving a clear verdict on them. This is done on purpose to make things easier for people. He has made it clear that we need not ask about those matters where a clear verdict has not been given, lest such questioning should lead to more restrictions. Hence no one may forbid what God has not clearly forbidden.

At the end of this passage, in an atmosphere which calls for abandoning blood ties and being ready to sacrifice one's life and property, the *sūrah* makes a clear statement that it is God alone who protects and supports the believers. He is the One who has sovereignty over the heavens and the earth and it is He who controls life and death: *"To God belongs the kingdom of the heavens and the earth; He alone gives life and causes death. Besides God, you have none to protect or support you.*" (Verse 116) All property, all human beings and all creation, the heavens and the earth, life and death, support and protection are all in God's hands. To maintain a strong tie with Him is sufficient for anyone.

These categorical statements concerning blood relations indicate the hesitation that some people might have shown and their leaning at one time to such ties and at another to their bond of faith. It is fitting that this final definition is made in this *sūrah* which outlines the final shape of the relationship between the Muslim community and other communities. It was not permissible to pray to God to forgive those who died unbelievers. This is meant to purge the hearts of believers from any lingering bonds. The only tie to unite the advocates of Islam is that of faith. It is an aspect of their conceptual beliefs and also of their method of action. This is made abundantly clear in this *sūrah*.

Acceptance of Repentance

With the nature of the deal between God and the believers being such, to refrain from joining a *jihād* campaign by people who are able to do so is a very serious matter indeed. Hence it was necessary to examine why some people were reluctant to join such an expedition. The passage we are looking at explains how much grace God bestows on the believers, overlooking their hesitation and their slips, serious as these may be. It also speaks of the three people whose cases were deferred for judgement.

> *God has assuredly turned in His mercy to the Prophet, the* Muhājirīn *and the* Anṣār, *who followed him in the hour of hardship, when the hearts of a group of them had almost faltered. Then again He turned to them in mercy; for He is compassionate towards them, merciful. And [so too] to the three who were left behind: when the earth, vast as it is, seemed to close in upon them, and their own souls had become too constricted, they realized that there was no refuge from God except by returning to Him. He then turned to them in mercy, so that they might repent. God is indeed the One who accepts repentance, the merciful.* (Verses 117–118)

278

That God turned in His mercy to the Prophet should be understood with reference to the events of this expedition as a whole. It seems to be in line with what God said earlier to the Prophet: "*May God forgive you [Prophet]! Why did you grant them permission [to stay behind] before you had come to know who were speaking the truth and who were the liars?*" (Verse 43) That was when some of them who were really able to join the expedition came to him with fabricated excuses and he allowed them to stay behind. God pardoned him for his attitude which was based on his own discretion. He is told that it would have been better to wait until he had learnt who really had valid reasons for staying behind.

As for turning in mercy to the *Muhājirīn* and the *Anṣār*, the verse outlines its causes. They are the ones "*who followed him in the hour of hardship, when the hearts of a group of them had almost faltered.*" (Verse 117) Some of them were slow to join the Muslim army, but they joined as it marched, as will be given in detail. These were among the most sincere of believers. Others listened to the hypocrites as they tried to dissuade the believers from going out to confront the Byzantines whom they described as fearsome fighters. Those, however, joined the army after their initial reluctance.

We will review briefly some of the events of this expedition in order to capture a sense of the prevailing atmosphere which God describes as 'the hour of hardship.' This may give us an insight into the feelings and actions that shaped the different attitudes.[1]

An earlier verse in the *sūrah* gives the following instructions: "*Fight against those who – despite having been given Scriptures – do not truly believe in God and the Last Day, and do not treat as forbidden that which God and His Messenger have forbidden, and do not follow the religion of truth, till they [agree to] pay the submission tax with a willing hand, after they have been humbled.*" (Verse 29) Upon receiving this revelation the Prophet instructed his Companions to get ready to fight the Byzantines. [It should be noted here that the first engagement against the Byzantines was at the Battle of Mu'tah which preceded the revelation

---

1.   This account is a consolidated summary of the detailed reports of the Tabūk Expedition given in *Al-Sīrah al-Nabawiyyah* by Ibn Hishām, *Imtāʿ al-Asmāʿ* by al-Maqrīzī, as well as *Al-Bidāyah wa'l-Nihāyah* and *Tafsīr al-Qur'ān al-ʿAẓīm*, both by Ibn Kathīr.

of these verses. Hence, these orders simply outline a permanent course of action which the Muslim community should always follow.]

This call to arms occurred at the height of the summer, when resources were scarce, the weather was extremely hot, and when fruits had ripened. At such a time people would prefer to stay at home and do very little work; travelling in the desert was almost unbearable. It was the Prophet's habit, whenever he intended to attack any people that he would not specify the particular place he was going to, or the particular people he wanted to attack, hoping to take his enemies by surprise. This time, the difficulties presented by the journey made him inform the Muslims exactly where they were going, so that they could prepare themselves as best as they could for the difficult task ahead.

Some hypocrites went to the Prophet seeking leave to stay behind, giving the absurd excuse that they might be infatuated with Byzantine girls when they saw them, and he let them stay. It is in connection with this that God remonstrated with the Prophet, but this remonstration opens with the statement that God has pardoned the Prophet and turned to him in mercy: *"May God forgive you [Prophet]! Why did you grant them permission [to stay behind] before you had come to know who were speaking the truth and who were the liars?"* (Verse 43) In their reluctance to join the campaign of *jihād*, and the doubts they raised about the truth of the Islamic message and their hostility to the Prophet, the hypocrites advised one another not to join the army because the hot summer was not a suitable time for war. Commenting on this, the following verse was revealed: *"They said [to one another]: 'Do not go to war in this heat.' Say: 'The fire of hell is far hotter.' Would that they understood. They shall laugh but a little, and they will weep much, in return for what they have earned."* (Verses 81–82)

The Prophet was informed that a group of hypocrites were meeting in the house of a Jew called Suwaylim to discourage people and dissuade them from joining the expedition. He sent Ṭalḥah ibn 'Ubaydullāh with a group of his Companions giving them instructions to burn the house down. Ṭalḥah carried out the Prophet's instructions. One of the people inside called al-Ḍaḥḥāk tried to run away from the back of the house and he fell and broke his leg, but later repented. The others also jumped to safety.

The Prophet then gave orders to his Companions to speed up their preparations and urged those with money and property to spend generously, and to provide camels and horses for those who had none. Many of those who were rich came forward with generous donations. The one who gave the greatest donation was 'Uthmān ibn 'Affān. One report suggests that 'Uthmān's donation was 1,000 dinars (which was the gold currency). The Prophet said: "My Lord, be pleased with 'Uthmān, for I am pleased with him."

Another report transmitted by Aḥmad ibn Ḥanbal says: "When the Prophet made his speech encouraging his Companions to donate generously, 'Uthmān said: 'My commitment is to provide 100 camels with all their equipment.' As the Prophet descended one step from the pulpit, 'Uthmān made a further equal commitment. The Prophet came one step further down and 'Uthmān increased his commitment to 300 camels, fully equipped. The Prophet was so deeply touched by the donation made by 'Uthmān that he waved with his hand to express his admiration. He also said: ' 'Uthmān will not suffer in consequence of anything he does in future.'

Other reports mention the donations given by various people, each according to his means. 'Abd al-Raḥmān ibn 'Awf brought a donation of 4,000 dirhams (the silver currency at the time). He said to the Prophet: "All I own is 8,000 dirhams. I brought one half and kept the other half." The Prophet said to him: "May God bless you for what you have kept and what you have donated." Abū 'Aqīl brought a quantity of dates and said: "Messenger of God, I have only some dates and I brought half of what I have, retaining the other for my family." The hypocrites spoke ill of him, saying he only did this to remind the Prophet of his poverty. They further asked: would God and His Messenger be in need of this amount of dates?

A Turn of Mercy

Some Muslims were so poor that they could not find transport for themselves to join the army. There were seven people, mostly from the *Anṣār*, who could obtain neither a camel nor a horse. They, therefore, went to the Prophet to explain their situation and requested him to provide them with some transport. The Prophet explained that he had nothing available. All the horses and camels were allotted to other people and he had none left. The seven men went back to their homes with tears in their eyes. They were made entirely helpless by their poverty.

Two of the seven men, 'Abd al-Raḥmān ibn Ka'b and 'Abdullāh ibn Mughaffil, were still in tears when they met a man called Yāmīn ibn 'Umayr. He asked them why they were crying and they told them that they were prevented from joining the army by their poverty and the fact that the Prophet did not have any spare camels to give them. He offered them a camel of his own to share between them and also gave them some dates to eat on their journey. Thus they were able to join.

Another report speaks of another man among the seven, 'Ilbah ibn Zayd. That night, knowing he could not join the army, he prayed for a long while. He reflected on the situation and tears sprang to his eyes. Then he addressed God with this emotional prayer: "My Lord, You have commanded us to go on *jihād* and You have encouraged us not to abandon this duty. Yet You have not given me what I need in order to be able to go on this campaign. Your Messenger cannot give me any means of transport. I, therefore, give in charity to every Muslim any right which I hold against him for a wrong he has done to me, whether in matters of money or self or honour."

The following morning, the man joined the dawn prayers as he always did. The Prophet asked, "Where is the man who was charitable last night?" Nobody replied. The Prophet repeated the question and said, "Let this man stand up." 'Ilbah stood up and explained to the Prophet what he had done. The Prophet said, "By Him Who holds my soul in His hand, this has been credited to you as *zakāt* accepted by God."

The Prophet then ordered the Muslims who joined him to march. There were about 30,000 in the army, made up of the people of Madinah and the bedouin tribes in the surrounding area. A few individuals among the Muslims did not join the army, although they did not entertain any doubt about the truth of Islam, or their duty to be in the army. Among these were Ka'b ibn Mālik, Murārah ibn al-Rabī' and Hilāl ibn Umayyah, [these were the three whose cases will be discussed in detail shortly] and also Abū Khaythamah and 'Umayr ibn Wahb al-Jumaḥī. The Prophet ordered his forces to encamp at a place called Thanīyat al-Wadā', just outside Madinah, while 'Abdullāh ibn Ubayy, known as the chief of the hypocrites, encamped with his followers separately a short distance apart. One report by Ibn Isḥāq suggests that his group was claimed to be of similar strength, but this was highly unlikely. Other reports confirm that those who actually stayed behind were less than one hundred. When the Prophet moved on, 'Abdullāh ibn Ubayy stayed behind along with other hypocrites.

The Prophet and his army then started their march. The going was very tough indeed. It was only natural that among the 30,000 who were in the army, there would be some who might not be able to keep pace with the rest. Every time a man fell behind, his case was reported to the Prophet. Every time the Prophet gave the same answer: "Leave him alone. If he is good, God will see to it that he will catch up with you. If he is otherwise, good riddance."

At one stage of the journey, a man of no lesser standing in the Muslim community than Abū Dharr, one of the *Muhājirīn* and also among the earliest of them to accept Islam, was falling behind. His camel was no longer able to keep pace with the army. Some people went to the Prophet to report the fact, but he gave them the same answer: "Leave him alone. If he is good, God will see to it that he will catch up with you. If he is otherwise, good riddance."

Abū Dharr gave his camel every chance to pick up strength. He then realized that it was useless: the camel was absolutely exhausted. Feeling that there was no alternative, Abū Dharr dismounted, took his belongings off his camel and walked at a fast pace, hoping to catch up with the Prophet.

Soon, the Prophet stopped for a short while to allow the army a little rest. This stop gave Abū Dharr the chance to catch up. Someone standing near the Prophet pointed to the direction from which Abū Dharr was coming and said, "Messenger of God, there is a man walking alone in our trail." The Prophet said, "Let it be Abū Dharr." When the man drew nearer, they said: "Messenger of God, it is indeed Abū Dharr." The Prophet said, "May God have mercy on Abū Dharr: he walks alone, dies alone and will be resurrected alone."

One of the few believers who stayed behind in Madinah was Abū Khaythamah. A few days after the army had moved out, he went back home to rest on a day when it was extremely hot. He had two wives.

At home, there were all the comforts one needed on such a hot day. Each of his two wives had prepared her sitting place in a well-shaded area of the yard. Each had prepared food and cold water for her husband. When he came in, he looked at his two wives and what they had prepared for him. He reflected a little, then he said to his wives: "God's Messenger (peace be upon him) is suffering the burning sun and the stormy wind, while I, Abū Khaythamah, enjoy the cool shade and delicious food in the company of two pretty women in my own home? This is unfair. By God, I will not enter either of your two places until I have caught up with God's Messenger. Prepare some food for me to keep me going on my journey." When the food was prepared, he mounted his camel and went as fast as he could. He did not manage to catch up with the army until it arrived at Tabūk.

On his way, Abū Khaythamah met 'Umayr ibn Wahb al-Jumaḥī, who was also travelling fast to catch up with the army. Apparently, 'Umayr had some good reason for his delay. The two travelled together until they were close to Tabūk. Abū Khaythamah then said to 'Umayr: "I have perpetrated something bad. It may be advisable for you to slow down a little until I catch up with the Prophet (peace be upon him)."

'Umayr slowed down and Abū Khaythamah continued to travel at speed. When his figure was visible to the army encamping at Tabūk, some of the Prophet's Companions drew his attention to the person travelling alone. The Prophet said: "Let it be Abū Khaythamah." When the man drew nearer, they said: "Messenger of God, it is indeed Abū Khaythamah."

When he reached the place where the Prophet was, he dismounted and greeted the Prophet. The Prophet spoke to him a phrase which implied warning. Interpreters suggest that it meant that he, Abū Khaythamah, had brought himself very close to destruction. Abū Khaythamah related his story, and the Prophet prayed to God to forgive him.

The Hour of Difficulty

One factor that contributed to the difficulty facing the Muslims was the attitude of the hypocrites who not only tried to seek excuses for themselves to stay behind, but also tried to show the decision to fight the Byzantines as lacking careful planning and consideration.

A report mentions that a group of hypocrites, including Wadī'ah ibn Thābit, as well as a man called Makhshī ibn Ḥimyar, an ally of the tribe of Salamah, were with the Muslim army when the Prophet headed for Tabūk. Some of them tried to frighten the believers and spread doubt in their ranks. They said: "Do you think fighting the Byzantines the same as internal warfare between Arabian tribes? We can even now see how you will all be taken captive tomorrow and will be put in chains." Makhshī said: "I wish we could escape with only 100 lashes each, without having verses of the Qur'ān revealed to expose us as a result of what you have said."

The Prophet was informed of this and he said to 'Ammār ibn Yāsir: "Rush to those people for they are burnt. Ask them about what they have said and if they deny it, tell them that they have said these very words." 'Ammār went to them and told them exactly what the Prophet said. They came to the Prophet to apologize. Wadī'ah ibn Thābit said to the Prophet as he mounted his camel, and Wadī'ah holding its reins: "Messenger of God, we were only talking idly and jesting." Makhshī said: "Messenger of God, my name and my father's name prevented me from leaving these people." (This is a reference to the fact that he was only an ally occupying a weak position.) He was the one among those to whom this verse refers who was pardoned. He changed his name to 'Abd al-Raḥmān and appealed to God to grant him martyrdom where his body would not be found. He was killed when he was fighting with the Muslim army at Yamāmah against the apostates. His body was lost without trace.

Another report suggests that when the Prophet and the Muslim army were on the way back from Tabūk, a group of hypocrites tried to assassinate him by throwing him from the top of a high peak along the road. He was informed of their design. He ordered the bulk of the army to travel through the valley, while he went up the mountain trail, instructing two of his trusted Companions, 'Ammār ibn Yāsir and Ḥudhayfah ibn al-Yamān, to go with him. 'Ammār held the rein of his she-camel while Ḥudhayfah drove it. They were followed by that group of hypocrites trying to catch up with them, having drawn their headcovers over their faces to hide their identities. When the

Prophet heard the sound of their camels travelling close behind, he was angry. Ḥudhayfah recognized how angry he was, and he went back towards them. He held out his shield to stop their camels. When they saw him, they thought that their scheming was discovered. So they made haste to join the bulk of the army and mix among them. Ḥudhayfah went back to the Prophet who instructed him and 'Ammār to make haste until they passed the peak of the trail, and rejoined the road. They stopped for the army to catch up with them.

The Prophet asked Ḥudhayfah whether he recognized those people? He said: "I could only see their camels as it was dark when I met them." The Prophet asked both his Companions: "Do you know what those people were after?" When they answered in the negative, he told them of their conspiracy, and named them asking his two Companions to keep that information to themselves. They wondered: "Messenger of God, should you not order their execution?" He said: "I hate that people should say that Muḥammad is killing his Companions." Another report suggests that the Prophet told only Ḥudhayfah of their names.

As for the hardship encountered by the Muslims in this expedition, a number of reports give us a clear picture of it. Some of these emphasize that the expedition took place at a time of scarcity, in the height of a very hot summer, when provisions and water were in extremely short supply. Qatādah, an early scholar, says: "They set out to Tabūk when it was burning hot, and they encountered great difficulty. It is reported that two men would share a single date. Indeed a few men would all share one date, with one of them sucking it a little and drinking some water, then he would give it to another to do the same, and so on. God then turned to them in mercy and brought them back safely."

Al-Ṭabarī, a leading historian and scholar, mentions a report that 'Umar was asked about the difficulty. He answered: "We marched with the Prophet to Tabūk. We encamped at a place where we were so thirsty that we felt our throats were cracking with thirst. Any one of us might go out looking for water, and by the time he came back he would have felt his throat cut. Any of us might slaughter his camel and take out its inside, extracting all the fluid to drink. He would place the rest over his belly."

In his commentary on the Qur'ān, al-Ṭabarī mentions the following comments on this verse: "*God has assuredly turned in His mercy to the Prophet, the* Muhājirīn *and the* Anṣār, *who followed him in the hour of hardship.*" (Verse 117) This refers to the scarcity of funds, transport, equipment, provisions and water. "*When the hearts of a group of them had almost faltered.*" (Verse 117) They almost deviated from the truth. With all the difficulties they encountered, doubts might have crept in about the Prophet's message. "*Then again He turned to them in mercy.*" (Verse 117) He guided them to revert to the truth and to show real steadfastness. "*He is compassionate towards them, Merciful.*" (Verse 117)

These reports depict for us a picture of the reality of the Muslim community at the time. We see a whole spectrum of different standards of faith. We see those who had unshakeable faith, and those who were seriously shaken as a result of the hardship, as well as those who stayed behind, although they had no doubt about the truth of Islam or their duty to join the expedition. We also see a whole range of hypocrisy, with some hypocrites adopting a soft attitude and others speaking out bluntly, and still others conspiring to kill the Prophet. This gives us an impression of the overall structure of society at the time. It also shows us how hard this expedition was, not only in respect of a fearsome enemy but also in terms of the hardship faced by the Muslim community. It was a test to the core so that people could prove their metal. Perhaps it was intended by God to serve as such.

The Case of One Honest Man

Such was the hardship which some people tried to evade. The majority of these were hypocrites, and their case has already been discussed. Some, however, were believers who entertained no doubt about Islam or the Prophet's message. They were simply people who preferred the comforts of home when the going got tough. These include two groups, one of whom received their judgement earlier. They had added some bad deeds to their good ones and acknowledged their mistake. The case of the second group was deferred for judgement: "*God would either punish them or turn to them in His mercy.*" (Verse 106) This group included three people whose case now comes in for detailed treatment.

Before we say anything about the statement describing their case, and before we speak about the artistically miraculous picture the *sūrah* paints in describing it, let us look at the account given by one of them, Ka'b ibn Mālik:

> I have never stayed behind when the Prophet went on any expedition, except that of Badr. Neither God nor the Prophet blamed anyone for staying behind at the time of Badr, because the Prophet set out from Madinah to intercept a trade caravan which belonged to the Quraysh. The battle took place without any preparation or prior planning. On the other hand, I had attended the pledge of the *Anṣār* to the Prophet at 'Aqabah when we made our commitment to Islam absolutely clear. I would not exchange my attendance there with taking part in the Battle of Badr, although Badr is the more famous occasion.

> Nevertheless, I failed to join the army of the expedition of Tabūk. I was never in better circumstances or more physically able than I was then. At no time did I have two means of transport except on that occasion. It was the habit of the Prophet to keep his destination secret. This time, however, setting his destination so far away, and moving in an exceptionally hot climate, he made it clear to the people that he intended to attack the Byzantines. Those who joined the Prophet were in such large numbers that no register of them could have been kept.

> In the circumstances, anyone who wished to stay behind might have thought that he would not be noticed, unless God chose to inform the Prophet about him by revelation. The Prophet decided to launch that attack at a time when fruits were abundant and people preferred to stay in the shade. The Prophet and the Muslims, however, were busy getting ready for their impending task. I went out day after day to the marketplace in order to get my equipment, but I always came back having done nothing. I always thought that I was able to get whatever I needed in no time. Nevertheless, I continued in that condition until it was time to move. The Prophet and the army with him started their march and I had not got my preparations under way. I thought to myself: 'I can still get myself ready in a day or two and should be able to

catch up with them.' When they had covered quite a distance, I went out to the market and came back having done nothing. This continued day after day. By this time, the army must have covered quite a long distance. I thought I must make a move now and catch up with them. I wish I had done that, but I did not. Every time I went out after the Prophet and the army had left, I was troubled by the fact that I saw only people who were known to be hypocrites or people who were physically unable to join the army. My place was not with either group. I was told that the Prophet did not mention me until he had arrived at Tabūk. He remarked once to those who were present at Tabūk: 'What has happened to Kaʿb ibn Mālik?' A man from the tribe of Salamah said to him: 'Messenger of God, his wealth and arrogance made him stay behind.' Muʿādh ibn Jabal said to him: 'What a foul remark! Messenger of God, we have known nothing bad of the man.' The Prophet made no comment.

I soon heard that the Prophet and his Companions had started on their journey back from Tabūk. I felt very sad. To tell a lie was paramount in my mind. I started thinking about what to say to the Prophet tomorrow, after his arrival, in order to spare myself his anger. I sought the help of everyone in my household. When it was mentioned that the Prophet was soon to arrive, all thoughts of seeking a false excuse disappeared from my mind. I realized that the only way to spare myself the Prophet's anger was to tell the truth. I was determined, therefore, to say exactly what happened.

The Prophet then arrived in Madinah. It was his habit when he came back from travelling to go first to the mosque and pray two *rakʿahs* before sitting to meet the people. When he did that, those who had stayed behind went to him and stated their excuses, swearing to their truth. They were over 80 people. The Prophet accepted their statements and oaths and prayed to God to forgive them, leaving it to God to judge them by His knowledge. I then followed and greeted the Prophet. He met my greeting with an angry smile. He then told me to come forward. I went to him and sat down facing him. He said, 'What caused you to stay behind? Have you not bought your transport?'

I said to him, 'Messenger of God, had I been speaking to anyone on the face of the earth other than you, I would have been able to avoid his anger by giving some sort of an excuse. I can make a case for myself. But I know for certain that if I were to tell you lies in order to win your pleasure, God would soon make the truth known to you and I would incur your displeasure. If, on the other hand, I tell you the truth and you are not happy with me because of it, I would hope for a better result from God. By God, I have no excuse whatsoever. I have never been more physically able or in better circumstances than I was when I stayed behind.' The Prophet said to me: 'You have certainly said the truth. You await God's judgement.'

After I left, some men from the clan of Salamah followed me and said: 'We have never known you to commit a sin before this. You could certainly have given the Prophet an excuse like all those who stayed behind. You would have been spared this trouble had the Prophet prayed to God to forgive you, as he would surely have done.' They continued pressing me on this to the extent that I wished to go back to the Prophet and tell him that I was lying. Before I did that, however, I asked whether anyone else said the same thing as I did. They replied that two more people said the same and were given the same answer. When I asked their names, they mentioned Murārah ibn al-Rabīʿ and Hilāl ibn Umayyah. I knew these two to be men of faith and sincere devotion. I realized that the proper attitude for me was to be in their company. I therefore made no further move.

The Prophet ordered all his Companions not to speak to us three. He made no similar instruction concerning anybody else of those who stayed behind. All people were now evading us. Their attitude was changed. It was very hard for me that I did not even know myself or the place I was in. This was no longer the town I lived in. My world had changed. We continued in this condition for 50 days.

My two Companions, Murārah ibn al-Rabīʿ and Hilāl ibn Umayyah, stayed at home. I was the youngest of the three. I continued to go out and attend the congregational prayers with other Muslims. I frequented all the markets, but nobody would speak to me. I would also go to the Prophet and greet him as he sat down after prayers. I would always think to myself: 'Have I detected any movement on his lips suggesting that he has answered my greeting?' I would pray close to him and look at him stealthily. When I was preoccupied with my prayers, he would look at me, but when I looked towards him, he would turn his face the other way.

When this boycott by all the Muslim community seemed to have lasted too long, I climbed the wall of an orchard which belonged to a cousin of mine named Abū Qatādah, who was very close to me. I greeted him, but he did not answer. I said to him: 'Abū Qatādah, I beseech you by God to answer me: do you know that I love God and His Messenger?' He did not answer. I repeated my question three times, but he still did not answer.

I then beseeched him once again, and his answer came: 'God and His Messenger know better.' Tears sprang to my eyes and I came down. I went to the market and as I was walking I saw a man, apparently a stranger from Syria, enquiring about me. People pointed me out to him. He came to me and handed me a letter from the King of Ghassān, the Arab tribe in Syria. The letter was written on a piece of silk and read: 'We have learnt that your friend has imposed a boycott on you. God has not placed you in a position of humiliation. If you join us, we will endeavour to alleviate all your troubles.' When I read it, I thought it to be yet another test of my sincerity. I have reached so low that an unbeliever hopes that I would willingly join him. I put the letter in an oven and burnt it.

When we had spent 40 nights in that situation, a messenger from the Prophet came to me and said: 'God's Messenger (peace be upon him) commands you to stay away from your wife.' I asked whether that meant that I should divorce her and he answered in the negative. He told me only to stay away from her. My two Companions also received the same instruction. I told my wife to go to her people's home and stay there until God had given His judgement in this matter.

Hilāl ibn Umayyah was an old man. His wife went to the Prophet and said, 'Messenger of God, Hilāl ibn Umayyah is very old and has no servant. Do you mind if I continue to look after him?' He said, 'That is all right, but do not let him come near you.' She said, 'By God, these things are far from his mind. He has not stopped crying ever since this has happened to him. I indeed fear for his eyesight.' Some people in my family suggested that I should seek the Prophet's permission to let my wife look after me. I said, 'I am not going to ask him that. I do not know what his answer would be, considering that I am a young man.'

Another ten nights passed, to complete 50 nights since the Prophet instructed the Muslims not to talk to us. At dawn after the 50th night I prayed at the top of one of our houses. I was still in that condition which I have described: the world seemed to me suffocatingly small and I did not recognize myself any more. As I sat down after the dawn prayers, however, I heard a voice from the direction of Mount Sal' saying: 'Ka'b ibn Mālik! Rejoice!' I realized that my hardship was over, and I prostrated myself in gratitude to God.

What happened was that the Prophet informed the congregation after finishing the dawn prayer that God has pardoned us. People moved fast to give us that happy news. A man came at speed on horseback to bring me the news, while another from the tribe of Aslam went on top of the mountain to shout it to me. His voice was quicker than the horse. When I heard that man's voice giving me the happiest piece of news I ever received, I gave him my two garments as a gesture of gratitude. By God, they were the only clothes I had at the time. I borrowed two garments and went quickly to the Prophet. People were meeting me in groups, saying, 'Congratulations on being forgiven by God.' I entered the mosque and saw the Prophet sitting with a group of people around him. Ṭalḥah ibn 'Ubaydullāh came quickly towards me, shook my hand and congratulated me. He was the only one from the *Muhājirīn* to do that. I will never forget Ṭalḥah's kindness.

When I greeted the Prophet, he said to me, with his face beaming with pleasure, 'Rejoice, for this is your happiest day since you were born!' I asked him: 'Is my pardon from you, Messenger of God, or is it from God?' He said, 'It is from God.' When the Prophet was pleased at something, his face would light up and look like the moon. We always recognized that."

When I sat down facing him, I said to him, 'Messenger of God, I will make my repentance complete by giving away all my property in charity.' The Prophet said, 'Keep some of your property, for that is better for you.' I answered that I would keep my share in Khaybar. I then added that I was forgiven only because I told the truth, and I would make my repentance complete by never telling a lie at any time in my life.

I feel that the greatest grace God has bestowed on me ever since He guided me to accept Islam is my telling the truth to the Prophet on that day. Had I invented some false excuse, I would have perished like all those who told him lies. God has described those people in the worst description ever. He says in the Qur'ān: *'When you return to them they will swear to you by God so that you may let them be. Let them be, then: they are unclean. Hell shall be their abode in recompense for what they used to do. They swear to you trying to make you pleased with them. Should you be pleased with them, God shall never be pleased with such transgressing folk.'* (Verses 95–96) I have never knowingly or deliberately told a lie ever since I said that to the Prophet. I pray to God to help me keep my word for the rest of my life.[2]

Vacillating between Extremes

This is then the story of the three people whose cases were deferred, as related by one of them, Ka 'b ibn Mālik. There is a lesson in it at every juncture. It gives us a very distinct picture of the solid base of the Muslim community, how closely knit it is, the purity of its people, the clarity of their vision with respect to their community and their

---

2. This account is related in detail in all early biographies of the Prophet Muḥammad (peace be upon him) but we have retained its English account as given by Adil Salahi, *Muhammad: Man and Prophet*, The Islamic Foundation, Leicester, 2002, pp. 711–717. – Editor's note.

duties towards their faith, the importance of the commands issued to them and their need to obey these commands.

Those three people stayed behind at a time of hardship. Human weakness got the better of them when they preferred the shade and comfort of their own homes. That seemed much more preferable than enduring the summer heat and a long traverse. Yet when the Prophet and his Companions had left Madinah, Ka'b felt that he was committing a terrible error. Everything around him pointed to it: "Every time I went out after the Prophet and the army had left, I was troubled by the fact that I saw only people who were known to be hypocrites or people who were physically unable to join the army." Those in the latter group were people who were either sick or weakened by old age, or those who could not find any means of transport. This means that the hardship did not cause the Muslims to give a cold shoulder to the Prophet's command to get ready for a very tough expedition. The only ones who stayed behind were those suspected of hypocrisy, or those who had genuine excuses. The solid base of the Muslim community was strong enough to overcome the hardship and to give the right response.

The second point is that of fearing God. When a sinner is truly God-fearing, he will certainly acknowledge his error, and leave judgement in his case to God. In his account Ka'b states why he did not try to give the Prophet a false excuse: "Had I been speaking to anyone on the face of the earth other than you, I would have been able to avoid his anger by giving some sort of an excuse. I can make a case for myself. But I know for certain that if I were to tell you lies in order to win your pleasure, God would soon make the truth known to you and I would incur your displeasure. If, on the other hand, I tell you the truth and you are not happy with me because of it, I would hope for a better result from God. By God, I have no excuse whatsoever. I have never been more physically able or in better circumstance than I was when I stayed behind."

This shows how an errant believer was keen to watch God and seek not to incur His anger. He was certainly keen to win the Prophet's pleasure, which in those days could lift a person to the highest standard or allow him to fall into an abyss, and make a Muslim enjoy high esteem or leave him in total oblivion. Nevertheless, fearing God was a stronger motivation, and the hope to win His forgiveness was more deeply entertained.

Let us look at another aspect of the story: "The Prophet ordered all his Companions not to speak to us three. He made no similar instruction concerning anybody else of those who stayed behind. All people were now evading us. Their attitude was changed. It was very hard for me that I did not even know myself or the place I was in. This was no longer the town I lived in. My world had changed. We continued in this condition for 50 days.

"My two Companions, Murārah ibn al-Rabī' and Hilāl ibn Umayyah, stayed at home. I was the youngest of the three. I continued to go out and attend the congregational prayers with other Muslims. I frequented all the markets, but nobody would speak to me. I would also go to the Prophet and greet him as he sat down after prayers. I would always think to myself: 'Have I detected any movement on his lips suggesting that he has answered my greeting?' I would pray close to him and look at him stealthily. When I was preoccupied with my prayers he would look at me, but when I looked towards him he would turn his face away.

"When this boycott by all the Muslim community seemed to have lasted too long, I climbed the wall of an orchard which belonged to a cousin of mine named Abū Qatādah, who was very close to me. I greeted him, but he did not answer. I said to him: 'Abū Qatādah, I beseech you by God to answer me: do you know that I love God and His Messenger?' He did not answer. I repeated my question three times, but he still did not answer. I then beseeched him once again, and his answer came: 'God and His Messenger know better.' Tears sprang to my eyes and I came down."

These details give us a clear impression of the level of discipline and obedience in the Muslim community, despite all the looseness that crept in after the fall of Makkah to the Muslims, and the confusion that accompanied the preparations for the expedition to Tabūk. The Prophet gave his instructions that nobody should speak to those three, and hence no one uttered a word to them. None would even meet Ka'b with a smiling face, and none would give or take anything from him. Even his closest cousin and friend would not return his greeting or answer his question, after Ka'b had climbed the fence to enter his garden. When he answered after much beseeching, his answer was far from reassuring. He only said: "God and His Messenger know better."

In his eagerness to know his position, after his whole world had changed, Ka'b would try to detect a faint movement on the lips of the Prophet to know whether he had answered his greetings. He would look sideways to find out whether the Prophet had looked at him in a way which would renew his hopes, and tell him that his situation was not totally desperate.

Left all alone, with no one saying a word to him even as a gesture of charity, he receives a letter from the King of Ghassān offering him a position of honour and influence. He turns his back on all this in a single movement. His only reaction is to throw the letter into the fire, considering this tempting offer as part of his trial.

Yet the boycott is extended and he is ordered not to go near to his wife, so that he is totally alone, isolated, hanging in the air. He feels too shy to request the Prophet to let his wife look after him, because he was unsure what the answer would be like.

The Whole World Seems Too Narrow

This should be contrasted with the piece of really happy news subsequently given to the three offenders. It is the news of rehabilitation, acceptance of the three men's repentance and their return to the fold and to life. Let us remind ourselves of Ka'b's own account of that happy moment:

> I was still in that condition which I have described: the world seemed to me suffocatingly small and I did not recognize myself any more. As I sat down after the dawn prayers, however, I heard a voice from the direction of Mount Sal' saying: 'Ka'b ibn Mālik! Rejoice!' I realized that my hardship was over, and I prostrated myself in gratitude to God.

> What happened was that the Prophet informed the congregation after finishing the dawn prayer that God had pardoned us. People moved fast to give us that happy news. A man came at speed on horseback to bring me the news, while another from the tribe of Aslam went on top of the mountain to shout it to me. His voice

was quicker than the horse. When I heard that man's voice giving me the happiest piece of news I ever received, I gave him my two garments as a gesture of gratitude. By God, they were the only clothes I had at the time. I borrowed two garments and went quickly to the Prophet. People were meeting me in groups, saying, 'Congratulations on being forgiven by God.' I entered the mosque and saw the Prophet sitting with a group of people around him. Talhah ibn 'Ubaydullāh came quickly towards me, shook my hand and congratulated me. He was the only one from the *Muhājirīn* to do that. I will never forget Talhah's kindness.

Such was the true value of events in that community. An accepted repentance was given such importance that a man would ride on horseback to deliver the news to its recipient, and another would go to the top of a mountain to shout it over so that he could be faster than the herald on horse. Joy felt by a brother and genuine congratulations are felt as a kindness that will never be forgotten by yesterday's outcast who has just been rehabilitated. His is a day that is fittingly described by the Prophet: "Rejoice, for this is your happiest day since you were born!" As Ka'b says, the Prophet's face was shining with delight. How kind and compassionate the Prophet was that his face beamed with pleasure because three of his Companions had been returned to the fold.

This, then, was the story of the three people who were left behind until God accepted their repentance. We have highlighted some of the impressions it gives us of the life of the early Muslim community and its values. As related by one of the three people who went through its experience, the story brings clear before our minds the meaning of the verse which states: "*when the earth, vast as it is, seemed to close in upon them, and their own souls had become too constricted, they realized that there was no refuge from God except by returning to Him.*" (Verse 118)

"*When the earth, vast as it is, seemed to close in upon them.*" (Verse 118) What is the earth? Its world is that of its inhabitants and the values that are upheld by them. Its expanse is as vast as the relationships between its people make it to be. Hence the description here is very truthful in its practical significance, as much as it is truthful in its artistic beauty. It shows the whole expanse of the earth becoming too narrow for those three. Its outer limits are brought too near to make it extremely tight, closing in on them. *"And their own souls had become too constricted."* (Verse 118) It is as if their souls are a sort of a container that has become too small and tight. They can hardly breathe as it tightens over them. What happened then was that *"they realized that there was no refuge from God except by returning to Him."* (Verse 118) That applies to all creation. None can have any refuge from God except in Him, because He has power over the whole universe. Yet stating this fact at this point, in an atmosphere of sadness imparts an air of stress and despair that can only be cleared by God Himself.

Then hope is restored and release is granted: *"He then turned to them in mercy, so that they might repent. God is indeed the One who accepts repentance, the Merciful."* (Verse 118) He has turned to them in mercy with regard to this particular error, so that they might make a general repentance which covers all their past sins. This means that they would watch God eagerly to guard against any future error. This is explained by Ka 'b:

> When I sat down facing him, I said to him, 'Messenger of God, I will make my repentance complete by giving away all my property in charity.' The Prophet said, 'Keep some of your property, for that is better for you.' I answered that I would keep my share in Khaybar. I then added that I was forgiven only because I told the truth, and I would make my repentance complete by never telling a lie at any time in my life. I feel that the greatest grace God has bestowed on me ever since He guided me to accept Islam is my telling the truth to the Prophet on that day... I have never knowingly or deliberately told a lie ever since I said that to the Prophet. I pray to God to help me keep my word for the rest of my life.

That is all that we can say in comment on this highly inspiring story and the unique style in which it is reported in the Qur'ān. We praise God for what He has guided us to write about it here, and we hope to make a longer discussion of it in future.[3]

---

3. The author apparently intended to write a whole book discussing the events that took place at the time of the Prophet and his Companions and highlighting the lessons that could be learnt from them and how Muslims today can benefit by them in shaping their lives in accordance with Islamic guidance. He did not live to see that project implemented. – Editor's note.

A Reward for Every Little Thing

The element of truth is highly significant in the story of those three Companions of the Prophet. To give this element its due importance, all believers are advised to fear God and to align themselves with those truthful people of the early believers. On the other hand those people in Madinah and the surrounding desert who stayed behind are strongly criticized. This is followed by a promise of generous reward to those who strive for God's cause: "*Believers, have fear of God and be among those who are truthful. It does not behove the people of Madinah and the bedouins who live around them to hold back from following God's Messenger, or to care for themselves more than for him; for, whenever they endure thirst, stress, or hunger for the sake of God, or take any step which would irritate the unbelievers, or inflict any loss on the enemy, a good deed is recorded in their favour. God does not suffer the reward of those who do good to be lost. And whenever they spend anything for the sake of God, be it little or much, or traverse a valley [in support of God's cause], it is recorded for them, so that God will give them the best reward for what they do.*" (Verses 119–121)

The people of Madinah were the ones who rushed to support the Islamic message, which meant that they were truly its basic core of supporters. They had given shelter to God's Messenger, pledged their total loyalty to him and constituted the hard nucleus of the Islamic faith in the Arabian Peninsula. The bedouin Arabs in the surrounding area, having also adopted Islam as a faith and a way of life, formed the outer belt of defence. Hence those two groups could not refrain from joining the Prophet or spare themselves from any risk to which they might be exposed. When God's Messenger set out to attend to a certain task that served Islamic interests, then the people of Madinah, the vanguard of the Islamic message, and those of the surrounding area could not but join him. Whether this happened to be in the burning summer heat or the extreme winter cold, in times of strict hardship or easy affluence, it does not behove them, being so close to the Prophet, to try to spare themselves a difficulty that God's Messenger is undertaking. They could not excuse themselves by protesting ignorance or lack of awareness of the real task in hand.

The *sūrah* appeals to them to fear God and to join the truthful believers who have never entertained any thoughts of staying behind and who have maintained their strong commitment to their faith at times of hardship. Those were the cream among the early believers and those who followed in their footsteps: *"Believers, have fear of God and be among those who are truthful."* (Verse 119)

The *sūrah* follows this appeal by a strong censure of the very thought of staying behind when God's Messenger is setting out: *"It does not behove the people of Madinah and the bedouins who live around them to hold back from following God's Messenger, or to care for themselves more than for him."* (Verse 120) The statement implies a strong reproach. No Companion of God's Messenger can be reproached in a stronger way than by saying that he puts his own safety ahead of the Prophet's. How could he when he is the Prophet's Companion and follower? The same applies to the advocates of Islam in all generations and periods. It does not behove a believer to try to spare himself a risk that the Prophet himself was willing to undertake for the cause of Islam. How could he when he claims that he is an advocate of the cause of Islam, and a follower of the Prophet Muḥammad (peace be upon him)?

Taking up such a responsibility is a duty imposed by God's order and emphasized by our love of the Prophet that makes any believer too ashamed to put himself ahead of him. At the same time it earns a very generous reward indeed: *"Whenever they endure thirst, stress, or hunger for the sake of God, or take any step which would irritate the unbelievers, or inflict any loss on the enemy, a good deed is recorded in their favour. God does not suffer the reward of those who do good to be lost. And whenever they spend anything for the sake of God, be it little or much, or traverse a valley [in support of God's cause], it is recorded for them, so that God will give them the best reward for what they do."* (Verses 120–121)

Every feeling is rewarded, be it thirst, hunger or mere stress and tiredness. Taking up a position which irritates the unbelievers and inflicting any loss or damage on them is credited as a good deed. When a believer goes out on a *jihād* campaign, he is included among those who do good. God will not suffer the reward of such servants of His to be lost. Furthermore, any financial contribution, be it little or much, and the mere walking across a valley are also rewarded as God rewards the best of His servants. By God, this is a rich reward indeed. It is a reward by God whose generosity is beyond any limit. How embarrassing to us all that such a great reward is given for something that is much less than the hardship suffered by the Prophet himself for the cause of Islam. It is the advocacy of this cause that we should now assume. Most certainly, we must be true to our trust.

A Task Akin to Fighting

As we have seen in this *sūrah*, the Qur'ān repeatedly denounces, in very clear terms, those who stay behind at the time when a *jihād* campaign is announced, particularly those from Madinah and the bedouins in the surrounding area. This denunciation made people come to Madinah in large numbers, particularly from the tribes living nearby, so that they would be ready to join the Prophet at any moment. Hence it was necessary to spell out the limits of all-out mobilization at the appropriate time.

The Muslim area had expanded. With the whole of Arabia practically adopting Islam, large numbers were ready to fight. At Tabūk, there were about 30,000 of them, which was a much larger number than at any earlier battle the Muslims had fought. It was time that different people should attend to different tasks, so that no area, such as agriculture or trade or social concerns, was neglected. All these are necessary for an emerging nation, whose needs are far more sophisticated than those of a tribal community. Hence the present verse was revealed to set out certain limits: "*It is not desirable that all the believers should go out to fight. From every section of them some should go forth, so that they may acquire a deeper knowledge of the faith and warn their people when they return to them, so that they may take heed.*" (Verse 122)

Several reports have been mentioned in explaining the meaning of this verse, giving different views on which group is to acquire deeper knowledge in faith so as to warn their people when they return. The view which we find to be soundest suggests that a section from each group in the Muslim community should go out to fight, with a system that allows alternation between the fighters and those who stay behind to attend to other tasks. The group of fighters acquires a more profound understanding of this faith as they take practical action seeking to consolidate its base. Hence these fighters are the ones who, on their return, warn their people against any complacency in attending to their duties.

This interpretation is based on views expressed by such leading commentators as Ibn 'Abbās, al-Ḥasan al-Baṣrī and Ibn Kathīr. It is also the view of Ibn Jarīr al-Ṭabarī. Its central point is that this faith has its own method of action, and it cannot be properly understood except by those who actively implement it. Hence those who go out to fight for its cause are the ones most likely to understand it best. Its underlying meanings, its implications, its practical implementation and its main features unfold to them as they move under its banner. Those who stay behind are the ones who need to be informed by those who take practical action, because the latter are the ones who witness and learn all these aspects. They are the ones who probe its secrets. This is particularly so, if the campaign they join is one led by the Prophet himself. However, every *jihād* campaign is a means to acquire a better understanding of this faith.

This is perhaps the reverse of what may appear at first sight, with those who are not on a *jihād* campaign being the ones who devote time to studying and understanding this faith. But this is a delusion that does not fit with the nature of this faith, which makes action one of its basic requirements. Hence it is understood more profoundly by those who take action and strive to establish it as a code of living in spite of the opposition they encounter from the forces of *jāhiliyyah*. Experience confirms that those who are not involved in the method of action to serve this faith do not understand it properly, no matter how much time they spend in studying it from books. That is a cold study, while real insight is acquired only by those who join the efforts aiming to establish it as a practical code of living. It is never acquired by those who only look at books and papers.

Proper understanding of this faith does not evolve except where action is taken to serve its cause. It cannot be taken from a scholar who stays idle when action is needed. Those who occupy their time with studying books to deduce rulings and 'renew' or 'develop' Islamic law, as the Orientalists say, do not really understand the nature of this faith. They take no part in the movement which aims to liberate humanity from different tyrannical authorities, and from submission to others, so that they may submit to God alone. With such lack of action, they cannot put its laws and concepts into their proper form.

Islamic law came about after Islamic action had moved ahead. First, submission to God was properly established when a community had determined to submit itself to God alone and to abandon the laws, customs and traditions of *jāhiliyyah*. That community also decided that no aspect of its life could be governed by human law. The community then started to shape its life on the basis of the main Islamic laws, without neglecting the details outlined in the sources of this law. As the community continued to do so, new issues came up in its practical life that needed to be sorted out on the basis of Islamic law. At this point new rulings were deduced and *Fiqh*, or the formal study of Islamic law, started to develop. It is then the action itself which allowed *Fiqh* to develop and flourish. It did not develop as a cold academic study that had no bearing on active and practical life. Thus scholars were able to develop a profound insight into this faith based on interaction with a real community shaping its life on the basis of this religion and striving to make its cause triumphant.

What do we find today in place of that? No one can claim that a proper Islamic community, determined to submit to God alone and to live by His law, rejecting any laws and regulations that are not based on His guidance exists anywhere. Hence no true Muslim who has an insight into this religion of Islam, its method of action and its history would try to 'develop' or 'renew' Islamic law in communities that are unwilling to declare that they recognize no other law. Serious Islamic action should start by making submission to God alone the first step, followed by acknowledging that sovereignty belongs only to Him. Hence no legislation is acceptable unless it is based on His law. To do otherwise is no more than a silly joke. Moreover, to imagine that one can have a proper understanding of this faith looking only at books and papers, without being involved in real action to serve the Islamic cause betrays deep ignorance of this religion.

Submission to God alone gives rise to an Islamic community, which in turn helps Islamic scholarship to flourish. This is the proper order. There can be no situation where specially tailored Islamic laws are prepared in advance for an Islamic community that is expected to be established. The fact is that every ruling seeks to implement the Islamic law, and its basic principles, in a practical case that has its own clear shape, dimensions and circumstances. Such cases arise from practical life within the Islamic community which gives it its particular shape, dimensions and circumstances. Hence a ruling that addresses each particular case is deduced. The rulings that we find today in books of *Fiqh* addressed similar practical cases in the past, when Islamic law was implemented by an Islamic community. They were not ready made in advance. Today we need to have similar rulings that address our own issues, provided that the community decides first of all to submit to God alone and to accept no ruling unless based on God's law.

When this happens, then our efforts will yield proper fruits. Striving for God's cause, or *jihād*, will open people's eyes and give them real knowledge and understanding of the faith. Unless we do this, then we are evading our real duty of *jihād*, seeking flimsy excuses of 'developing' or 'renewing' the study of Islamic *Fiqh*. It is far better to acknowledge our weakness and lack of effort, seeking God's forgiveness, than to resort to such evasiveness.

Uncompromising Fight

We then have a verse outlining the plan and extent of *jihād*, which was implemented by the Prophet Muḥammad (peace be upon him) and his successors generally. The only exceptions were limited cases dictated by special circumstances: "*Believers, fight those of the unbelievers who are near you, and let them find you tough; and know that God is with those who are God-fearing.*" (Verse 123)

The *jihād* movement marched on, confronting those who were near to the land of Islam, one stage after another. When practically the whole of Arabia had adopted Islam, after Makkah itself fell to Islam, leaving only scattered individuals and groups who did not form any threat to the land of Islam, the Tabūk Expedition took place, threatening the outer areas of the Byzantine Empire which were closest to the Muslim state. This was followed by open warfare, with the Muslim armies moving far into the lands of both the Byzantine and Persian Empires, leaving no pockets behind them. The areas that were now under Islam were united, having continuous borders. It was a vast land area with solid loyalty to one authority.

Weakness only crept in after its division into different units, with artificial borders to allow the governments of certain ruling families or certain races and nationalities. This was the outcome of plans that the enemies of Islam tried hard to bring to fruition, as they still do today. The different ethnic communities which Islam united in a single nation or community in the land of Islam, superseding the divisions of race, language and colour, will continue to suffer from inherent weaknesses until they return to their faith. Only when they once again follow the guidance of God's Messenger, the Prophet Muḥammad (peace be upon him), and allow only a single banner to unite them shall they recognize the implications of divine leadership which will once again bring them power and victory. When that happens, it will ensure that they are held in awe by other nations and powers.

Let us now reflect on this verse: *"Believers, fight those of the unbelievers who are near you, and let them find you tough; and know that God is with those who are God-fearing."* (Verse 123) What we find here is an order to fight those unbelievers who are near to the Muslim state, without specifying whether these have launched any aggression on the Muslims or their land. We understand that this is the final situation which makes the need to carry Islam forward the basis of the principle of *jihād*. This will ensure that Islam is available to mankind. It does not have a defensive outlook, as was the case with the provisional orders in the early days after the establishment of the Muslim state in Madinah.

Some of those who speak about the Islamic view of international relations or about the rulings that govern *jihād*, as well as those who write essays interpreting the Qur'ānic verses speaking about *jihād*, try to show this verse, which is the final one, limited by the earlier provisional rules. Hence they impose on it a restriction, limiting its application to cases of aggression being launched or expected against the Muslim community. But this statement is general and has no restriction attached to it. Besides, it is the final one. What we have learnt is that when the Qur'ān lays down legal provisions, it states them in a clear and precise way, without referring one situation to another. It resorts to precise expression, adding at the same point any exceptions, limitations or restrictions it wants the Muslim community to observe.

We have already commented in detail, in the Prologue and Chapters 1 and 2, on the meanings of the verses and the final rulings they provide, shedding light on the nature of the Islamic method of action.

However, those speakers and writers find it incomprehensible that Islam lays down such an order commanding the believers to fight those unbelievers who are near to them, and to continue to do so as long as there remain unbelievers in their vicinity. Hence they try to find limits restricting this general statement, but they can only find these in the earlier statements which were, by nature, provisional.

We understand why they find it so incomprehensible. They simply forget that *jihād* is meant to serve God's cause. It aims to establish God's authority and to remove tyranny. It liberates mankind from submission to any authority other than that of God. "*Fight them until there is no more oppression, and all submission is made to God alone.*" (8: 39) *Jihād* does not aim to achieve the hegemony of one philosophy or system or nation over another. It wants the system laid down by God to replace the systems established by His creatures. It does not wish to establish a kingdom for any one of God's servants, but to establish God's own kingdom. Hence it has to move forward throughout the earth in order to liberate the whole of mankind, without discrimination between those who are within the land of Islam and those who are outside it. The whole earth is populated by human beings who are being subjected to different types of tyrannical authority wielded by fellow human beings.

When they lose sight of this fact they find it odd that one system and one nation should move forward to remove all systems and dominate all communities. If things were such, that would be odd indeed. But the systems that exist today are all man-made. None of them has any right to say that it alone should dominate the others. The same does not apply to the divine system which sets out to overthrow all man-made systems in order to liberate all mankind from the humiliation of submission to other human beings, so that they can submit to God alone and worship Him only without any partners. Moreover, they find it odd because they face a concentrated and wicked crusade which tells them that the Islamic faith managed to spread only because it used the sword. *Jihād*, it claims, wanted to force other people to accept Islam, depriving them of the freedom of belief.

Had things been so, they would have been odd indeed. But the truth is totally different. Islam lays down a rule stating that "*There shall be no compulsion in religion. The right way is henceforth distinct from error.*" (2: 256) Why does Islam, then, move forward to fight, and why has God bought the believers' souls and property, so that "*they fight for the cause of God, kill and be killed*"? (Verse 111) The answer is that *jihād* has a reason which is totally different from compelling other people to accept Islam. Indeed *jihād* seeks to guarantee the freedom of belief.

As we have stated on several occasions, Islam is a declaration which liberates mankind throughout the earth from submission to human beings. As such, Islam always faces tyrannical forces and systems which seek to subjugate people and dominate their lives. These systems are backed by regimes and powers of different sorts, which deprive people of the chance to listen to the Islamic message and to adopt it if they are convinced of its truth. Or they may force people, in one way or another, to turn away from the Islamic message. That is an ugly violation of the freedom of belief. For these reasons, Islam moves forward, equipped with suitable power, to overthrow these systems and destroy their forces.

What happens then? It leaves people entirely free to adopt the faith they like. If they wish to be Muslims, they will have all the rights and duties that apply to all Muslims. They will have a bond of real brotherhood with those who have been Muslims long before them. On the other hand, if they wish to maintain their religions, they may do so. They only have to pay a tribute, i.e. *jizyah*, which has a clear purpose: to acknowledge the freedom of movement for Islam among them, to contribute to the treasury of the Muslim state which is required to protect them against any outside aggression, and to look after those of them who are ill, disabled and elderly in the same way as Muslims are looked after.

Never in its history did Islam compel a single human being to change his faith. That is alien to Islamic beliefs and practice. On the other hand, crusades were launched to kill, slaughter and eliminate entire communities, such as the people of Andalusia in the past and the people of Zanzibar in recent history, in order to compel them to convert to Christianity. Sometimes, even conversion was not accepted. They were killed only because they were Muslims, or because they followed a brand of Christianity which was different from that of the dominating

Church. For example, 12,000 Egyptian Christians were burnt alive only because they differed with the Byzantine Church over matters of detail, such as whether the soul originated with the Father alone, or with the Father and the Son together, or whether Jesus had a single divine nature or a united one in which both the divine and the human combine. These are basically the causes which make some writers about Islam find the general statement in this verse rather odd, and they try to explain it away by limiting the *jihād* movement to a defensive strategy only.

Moreover, the thought of moving forward to confront the unbelievers who are near to the Muslim state sounds too awesome to those defeatists who look at the world around them today and find this requirement totally impractical. Are those who have Muslim names in communities that are weak, or subject to foreign domination, to move forth in the land, challenging all nations in open warfare, until there is no more oppression and all submission is declared to God alone? That is totally unrealistic. It cannot be imagined that God would give such an order.

All such people forget the timing and the circumstances leading to this order. It was given after Islam had established its state, and the whole of Arabia adopted the Islamic faith and started to organize its life on its basis. Prior to that a community was established which dedicated itself totally to its cause, with everyone in that community ready to sacrifice his life and property in order for Islam to triumph. This community was given victory in one battle after another, stage after stage. Today we are in a situation which is highly similar to that which prevailed at the time when Prophet Muḥammad was sent to call on mankind to believe in God's oneness and to declare that *"There is no deity other than God, and Muḥammad is His Messenger."* Together with the small band who believed in him, the Prophet strove hard until he managed to establish the first Muslim state in Madinah. The orders to fight the unbelievers were modified stage after stage, facing the prevailing situation at each stage, until it reached its final version.

The gulf that separates people today from that final version is wide indeed. Hence, they have to start again at the beginning, with the declaration that *"There is no deity other than God, and Muḥammad is His Messenger."* They will have to move forward on the basis of this declaration until they reach, in their own good time and with God's help, the final stage. At that time they will not be the sort of powerless multitude divided by a variety of creeds and desires, and declaring their affiliation to different races and nationalities, as they are today. They will be a united Muslim community that accepts no banner, or man-made creed or system. They will only move with God's blessings to serve His cause.

Encumbered with their pathetic weakness, people will not understand the rules of this religion. It is only those who strive in a movement dedicated to the establishment of God's sovereignty on earth, and the removal of false deities, that fully understand its rules. Understanding this religion in its true nature cannot be taken from those who deal only with books and papers. Academic study is insufficient on its own to formulate any real understanding of Islam, unless it is coupled with striving in a movement.

Finally, this verse, giving such a clear order, was revealed in circumstances that suggest that the first to be meant by it were the Byzantines, who belonged to an earlier religion, or, to use the Islamic term, People of the Book. The *sūrah*, however, has already made it clear that they had distorted their faith and obeyed man-made laws and systems, so they were truly unbelievers. We should reflect here on the line of action Islam takes towards communities of the People of the Book who have turned away from their faith and adopted man-made laws. This line of action applies to all such communities everywhere. God has commanded the believers to fight those unbelievers who are near to them, and to be tough on them, but then concluded the verse making this order by saying: *"Know that God is with those who are God-fearing."* (Verse 123) This is a significant comment on the order preceding it. The type of fearing God that He appreciates and gives His support to those who have it is the same that emboldens believers to show toughness in fighting the unbelievers. This means that there is no compromise *"until there is no more oppression and all submission is made to God alone."* (8: 39)

Nevertheless, everyone should know that this toughness is directed against only those who fight, and it remains controlled by Islamic ethics. Before Muslims fight, they give a warning and offer the other party a choice between three alternatives: to adopt Islam, or to pay the tribute, i.e. *jizyah*, or to fight. If there is a treaty between the Muslim state and another community and the Muslim state fears that there may be treachery on the latter's part, then a notice terminating the treaty should be served on them. It is useful to mention here that treaties may be given only to communities that are ready to be bound by a peace agreement and to pay the *jizyah*. The only other situation where a treaty may be signed is that when the Muslim community is lacking in power. In this situation, some provisional rules are applicable to it.

The Prophet himself set out the ethics of war which must be observed by the Muslim community in any battle it may fight.

Islamic War Ethics

Buraydah, a Companion of the Prophet, reports:

> When the Prophet appointed someone to command an army or an expedition, he would recommend him to be God-fearing in his public and private affairs, and to take good care of those who were under his command. Then he would tell them: 'March by God's name and to serve His cause. Fight those who deny God. March on; but do not be unfair, and do not commit any treachery. Do not disfigure the bodies of any enemy soldiers killed in battle. Never kill any children. When you meet your enemies, call upon them to choose one of three alternatives. If they choose one of them, accept it from them and do not fight them. Call on them first to accept Islam. If they agree, accept their pledges and do not fight them. Then ask them to move over to the land of the *Muhājirīn*, and tell them that they would then have the same duties and privileges of the *Muhājirīn*. If they do not wish to move from their quarters, tell them that they would then be in the same position as the bedouin Muslims. They will be subject to God's orders that are applicable to all believers, but they will have no share of any booty that is gained through war or peaceful campaigns, unless they fight with the Muslims. If they refuse to accept Islam, then offer them the alternative of paying *jizyah* [or tribute]. If they agree, accept it from them and do not fight them. If they refuse, then seek God's help and fight them.

'Abdullāh ibn 'Umar, a Companion of the Prophet reports: "A woman was found killed in one of the Prophet's expeditions. He immediately issued an order that no women or children may be killed." [Related by al-Bukhārī and Muslim.]

The Prophet sent his Companion Mu'ādh ibn Jabal to the Yemen to teach the people there. As he departed the Prophet said to him: "You will be among people who follow earlier revelations. Call on them to believe that there is no deity other than God and that I am God's Messenger. Should they accept that from you, then tell them that God has commanded them to pray five times every day. If they accept that from you, then tell them that God has imposed on them the payment of zakāt, i.e. a charity which is to be levied from the rich and given to the poor among them. If they accept that, then do not touch their good earnings. Guard against an appeal to God by a person who suffers injustice, for such an appeal goes straight to God, without any hindrances."

Abū Dāwūd relates that the Prophet said: "You may fight some people and overcome them. They may then try to protect themselves and their children from you by their money, and they may make an agreement with you. Do not take anything from them over that, for it is not lawful to you."

Al-Irbāḍ ibn Ṣāriyah reports: "We arrived at Khaybar Castle with the Prophet when he had a large number of Muslims with him. The chief of Khaybar, an arrogant gigantic man, came to the Prophet and said, 'Muhammad! Do you permit yourselves to slaughter our cattle, devour our produce, and force our women?' The Prophet was very angry. He said, 'Ibn 'Awf! Mount your horse and announce: Only believers are admitted into heaven. Then, gather around for prayers.' They were all gathered and the Prophet led the prayers. When he finished, he stood up and said, 'Does any of you think as he reclines over his couch that God has not forbidden anything other than what is stated in the Qur'ān? I have certainly admonished you, given certain orders and forbidden certain things. These are as much prohibited as those in the Qur'ān or even more so. God has not permitted you to go into the homes of the people of the earlier revelations without first having permission, nor has He allowed you to force their women or devour their produce when they have paid what is due from them."

After a certain battle, it was reported to the Prophet that a few boys were killed during the fighting. He was very sad. Some of his Companions said, "Why are you so sad when they are only the sons of unbelievers?" The Prophet was angry and said words to this effect: "These were better than you, because they still had uncorrupted natures. Are you not the children of unbelievers. Never kill boys. Never kill boys."

These instructions by the Prophet were strictly followed by his successors. Abū Bakr is reported to have said: "You will find people who claim that they have dedicated themselves to God. Leave them to their dedication. Never kill a woman, a child or an elderly man." Zayd ibn Wahb reports that the army he had joined received written instructions from the Caliph, 'Umar, in which he said: "Do not be unjust; or commit treachery; or kill a young person. Fear God in your treatment of peasants." His instructions to his commanders always included the following: "Do not kill an elderly person, a woman or a child. Guard against accidentally killing them when you engage your enemy in battle and when you launch any attack."

Reports are numerous which make clear the general method Islam adopts in fighting its enemies, as well as its commitment to a high standard of ethics in war, giving high respect to human dignity. Fighting is targetted only against real forces which prevent people's liberation from subjugation by other creatures, so that they submit to God alone. Kind treatment is extended even to enemies. As for toughness, this applies only to fighting when Muslims are expected to fight hard. It has nothing of the barbarism against children, women and elderly people who do not fight in the first place, or the disfigurement of dead bodies. These practices are often committed by the barbaric armies of countries which these days claim to be highly civilized. Islam has given more than adequate orders to ensure the safety of those who do not fight, and to respect the humanity of the fighters. The toughness required is that sort of attitude which ensures that the confrontation does not fizzle away. As Muslims have been ordered time and again to show mercy and kindness, an exception needs to be made in the state of war, in as much as that state requires, without allowing any extreme practices of torture or disfigurement of bodies.

Hypocritical Attitudes

Since the *sūrah* has spoken extensively about the hypocrites, we have here some verses showing how those hypocrites used to receive any new revelation outlining certain duties imposed by the faith they falsely claimed to accept. This is contrasted with the way believers used to receive the revelation of new verses of the Qur'ān: "*Whenever a sūrah is revealed, some of them say: 'Which of you has this strengthened in faith?' It certainly strengthens the believers in their faith, and so they rejoice. But as for those whose hearts are diseased, it only adds wickedness to their wickedness, and so they die unbelievers. Do they not see that they are tested once or twice every year? Yet they do not repent, and they do not take warning. Whenever a sūrah is revealed, they look at one another [as if to say]: 'Is anyone watching?' Then they turn away. God has turned their hearts away, for they are people devoid of understanding.*" (Verses 124–127)

It is a strange and suspicious question the first verse quotes: *'Which of you has this strengthened in faith?'* It is asked only by one who has not felt the impact of the new *sūrah* as it is revealed. Otherwise he would have spoken about its effect on him instead of wondering how it has affected other people. At the same time, it betrays a sense of belittling the importance of the new revelation and its effect on people's hearts and minds. Hence a decisive reply is given by the One who has the ultimate knowledge: "*It certainly strengthens the believers in their faith, and so they rejoice. But as for those whose hearts are diseased, it only adds wickedness to their wickedness, and so they die unbelievers.*" (Verses 124–125)

The believers receive with every new *sūrah* and new revelation a new pointer to the truth of the faith. They also remember their Lord when they listen to His revelations, and they appreciate the care He takes of them by sending down these revelations. All this adds to the strength of their faith. On the other hand, those who have sickness in their hearts, the hypocrites, will have their wickedness increased. They will die unbelievers. This is a true piece of information given by God who knows everything.

Before the *sūrah* portrays the opposite picture, it wonders at those hypocrites who never take an admonition, and never reflect on an event to gather the lesson that may be learnt from it: *"Do they not see that they are tested once or twice every year? Yet they do not repent, and they do not take warning."* (Verse 126) The test may have taken the form of exposing their reality, or that the believers achieve victory without those hypocrites taking any part. There could be many other forms of test, which were all too frequent at the time of the Prophet. Still hypocrites today are tested and they pay no heed.

The next verse portrays a vivid scene, full of details, showing their behaviour: *"Whenever a sūrah is revealed, they look at one another [as if to say]: 'Is anyone watching?' Then they turn away. God has turned their hearts away, for they are people devoid of understanding."* (Verse 127)

When we read this verse, the scene of these hypocrites is large in front of us. We see them at the moment when a new *sūrah* is revealed, with some of them looking at each other winking and wondering: *"Is anyone watching?"* (Verse 127) Then they feel that the believers are preoccupied with their own business, so they go out stealthily, hoping not to be noticed: *"Then they turn away."* (Verse 127) But the eye which never loses sight of anything follows them with a curse that suits their suspicious deed: *"God has turned their hearts away."* (Verse 127) Their hearts are turned away from the right guidance. They deserve to remain deep in error, *"for they are people devoid of understanding."* (Verse 127) This is because they have kept their hearts and minds idle, unable to function properly. All of this scene is portrayed so skilfully and vividly using only a few words.

The Prophet's Relationship with the Believers

The *sūrah* concludes with two verses which different reports suggest were revealed in Makkah or Madinah. We are inclined to support the latter view, as these verses fit with various aspects of the last passage in the *sūrah* and with its general message. The first of these two verses explains the bond between God's Messenger and his people, and how compassionate and full of concern he was for them. This is perfectly fitting with the tasks assigned to the Muslim community who are required to support the Messenger, convey his message, fight his enemies and endure whatever trouble or hardship they may face in doing so. The final verse directs the Messenger to rely only on his Lord when people turn away from him. It is sufficient for him to have God's help and support.

"*Indeed there has come to you a Messenger from among yourselves: one who grieves much that you should suffer; one who is full of concern for you; and who is tender and full of compassion towards the believers. Should they turn away, then say to them: "God is enough for me! There is no deity other than Him. In Him have I placed my trust. He is the Lord of the Mighty Throne."*" (Verses 128–129) The statement here does not say 'a Messenger from among you' has come to you. Instead it describes the Messenger as being one 'from among yourselves' to add connotations of closer contact and firmer ties. It shows the type of bond that exists between them and their Messenger. He is one of them, with very close contact between them, and he feels for them.

Another characteristic of this Messenger is that he is "*one who grieves much that you should suffer.*" (Verse 128) He is keen that you should come to no hardship. He is also "*full of concern for you... tender and full of compassion towards the believers.*" (Verse 128) He would never lead you to ruin. If he calls on you to strive for God's cause, and to endure any difficulty in doing so, then you should know that he does not take this lightly, and that there is no cruelty in his heart. His call is a manifestation of compassion. He simply does not like to see you humiliated. He is too concerned that you should not suffer the ignominy of sin. He is keen that you should have the honour of conveying this message, earn God's pleasure and admittance into heaven.

The *sūrah* then addresses the Prophet, showing him what attitude to take when people turn away from him and his message. It points to the source of power which gives him all the protection he needs: "*Should they turn away, then say to them: 'God is enough for me! There is no deity other than Him. In Him have I placed my trust. He is the Lord of the Mighty Throne.'*" (Verse 129) To Him belong all power, dominion, greatness and honour. His support is sufficient for everyone who seeks His patronage.

The *sūrah* which concentrates mainly on fighting and striving for God's cause is thus concluded with the directive to rely on God alone, trust Him and seek His powerful support. After all "*He is the Lord of the Mighty Throne.*" (Verse 129)

Conclusion

This *sūrah* outlines the final rulings on the permanent relations between the Muslim community and the outside world, as explained in our commentary on its various passages. Hence we have to refer to its latest statements since these represent the final say on these relations. These statements must not be restricted or narrowed down in their applicability on the basis of earlier statements and rulings, which we described as provisional. In doing so, we have relied on the chronological order of the revelation of these verses and statements, and on the progress of the Islamic movement at the time of the Prophet, as well as the events marking that progress.

We have also been guided by our understanding of the nature of the Islamic message and its method of action which we have explained in our presentation of the *sūrah* and our commentary on its verses. This method of action is only understood by those who deal with this faith of Islam as a movement striving to establish itself in human life. As we have explained, the goal of that striving is to liberate mankind from submission to others so that they submit to God alone.

There is a wide gap between an understanding based on active striving and one based on academic study which is bound to ignore action. The first type of understanding looks at Islam as it conducts its direct confrontation with the system of *jāhiliyyah*, taking one step after another and moving from one stage to the next. It also looks at it as it proclaims its legislation to deal with the changing situation in its confrontation.

Moreover, these final laws and verdicts outlined in this last *sūrah* were actually revealed when the general situation of the Muslim community and the world around it required such legislation. Prior to that, when the situation required different rulings, these were given in earlier *sūrahs* to serve as provisional rulings.

When a new Muslim community emerges again and starts to strive for the establishment of this faith in human life, it may be appropriate for this community to apply the provisional rulings, provided that it remains well aware that these are only provisional. It should also be aware that it must strive to reach the stage when only the final rulings govern its relations with the world around it. God will certainly help that community and guide it on its way.

Index